THE MOUNTAINEERS, founded in 1906, is a non-profit outdoor activity and conservation club, whose mission is "to explore, study, preserve and enjoy the natural beauty of the outdoors. . . ." Based in Seattle, Washington, the club is now the third largest such organization in the United States, with 12,000 members and four branches throughout Washington State.

The Mountaineers sponsors both classes and year-round outdoor activities in the Pacific Northwest, which include hiking, mountain climbing, ski-touring, snowshoeing, bicycling, camping, kayaking and canoeing, nature study, sailing, and adventure travel. The club's conservation division supports environmental causes through educational activities, sponsoring legislation, and presenting informational programs. All club activities are led by skilled, experienced volunteers, who are dedicated to promoting safe and responsible enjoyment and preservation of the outdoors.

The Mountaineers Books, an active, non-profit publishing program of the club, produces guidebooks, instructional texts, historical works, natural history guides, and works on environmental conservation. All books produced by The Mountaineers are aimed at fulfilling the club's mission.

If you would like to participate in these organized outdoor activities or the club's programs, consider a membership in The Mountaineers. For information and an application, write or call The Mountaineers, Club Headquarters, 300 Third Avenue West, Seattle, Washington 98119; (206) 284-6310.

D0596910

Other books from The Mountaineers you may enjoy:

Trekking in Nepal, 6th Edition, by Stephen Bezruchka
Extensively detailed, best-selling guide covers the most rewarding trekking routes, permits, maps, health care, language, natural and cultural history, trip preparations. $16.95

Nepali for Trekkers: Language Tape and Phrasebook, by Stephen Bezruchka
Comprehensive phrase book covers common words and phrases, pronunciation, practice sessions, and grammar. Easy-to-use 90-minute tape covers the above and additional Nepali terms and place names. Spoken by a native Nepali to ensure accuracy, authenticity. $16.95

Himalayan Passage: Seven Months in the High Country of Tibet, Nepal, China, India, and Pakistan, by Jeremy Schmidt, with photographs by Patrick Morrow
Winner of the first Barbara Savage Memorial Award. Two couples who circumnavigated the base of the Himalaya by bike, foot, taxi, and donkey cart share their adventures and experiences of a vast, varied region. $22.95

South America's National Parks: A Visitor's Guide, by Bill Leitch
Unique guide to 32 parks and their varied climates, recreational opportunities, and amenities, with information on trails, flora and fauna, and geology. Color photos, maps. $16.95

The Galapagos Islands, by Marylee Stephenson
Complete, practical guide to touring isolated archipelago off Ecuador. History, necessary travel information, and descriptions of plants' and animals' unique adaptations to environment. $12.95

Mount Everest National Park: Sagarmatha, Mother of the Universe, by Margaret Jeffries
Reference and guide to the Khumbu, a World Heritage site. Covers the region's human history, biology, geography and geology, plus access and visitor facilities. Color photos. $18.95

Royal Chitwan National Park: Wildlife Sanctuary of Nepal, by Himanta R. Mishra and Margaret Jeffries
Reference and guide to this World Heritage site, the last refuge for much of Asia's rarest wildlife. Covers park's human history, biology, geography and geology, region's people and conservation efforts, plus access and visitor facilities. Color photos. $18.95

Available from your local book or outdoor store, or from The Mountaineers Books, 1011 SW Klickitat Way, Seattle, WA 98134. 1-800-553-4453.

Trekking in
Tibet

The Mountaineers/Seattle

Trekking in Tibet

Tibet

Gary McCue

In memory of Joseph F. McCue, Jr.
1928–1988

© 1991 by Gary McCue

4 3 2 1
5 4 3 2 1

Published by The Mountaineers
1011 SW Klickitat Way, Seattle, Washington 98134

Published simultaneously in Canada by Douglas & McIntyre, Ltd., 1615 Venables Street, Vancouver, B.C. V5L 2H1

Published simultaneously in Great Britain by Cordee, 3a DeMontfort Street, Leicester, England, LE1 7HD

Manufactured in the United States of America

Edited by Miriam Bulmer
Maps and art by Kathy Butler
Cover photograph: 55 km circumambulation of Mount Kailas, holy mountain for Buddhists and Hindus. Photo by Patrick Morrow.
Frontispiece: Chiu *gompa* and Mount Kailas
All photographs by the author
Cover design by Betty Watson
Book layout by Constance Bollen

Library of Congress Cataloging in Publication Data

McCue, Gary, 1953-
 Trekking in Tibet / Gary McCue.
  p. cm.
 Includes bibliographical references (p.) and index.
 ISBN 0-89886-239-6
 1. Mountaineering—China—Tibet—Guide-books. 2. Hiking—China—Tibet—Guide-books. 3. Tibet (China)—Description and travel—Guide-books. I. Title.
GV199.44.C552T536 1991
796.5'22'09515—dc20   91-24874
                          CIP

Contents

PREFACE 11
ACKNOWLEDGMENTS 12

SECTION I. ABOUT TREKKING 15

1. INTRODUCTION TO TREKKING IN TIBET 17 • A History of
    Trekking and Exploration in Tibet 18 • Trekking in a Private Group 19
    • Trekking with a Commercial Company 21 • Trekking as an Indi-
    vidual 21 • Hints for Women Trekkers 22 • When to go Trekking 24
2. PREPARING FOR YOUR TREK 25 • Physical Conditioning 25
    • Learning about Tibet 25 • Visa Regulations and Alien's Travel
    Permits 26 • Getting to Tibet 26 • Maps 28 • Equipment and
    Clothing 29 • Photography in Tibet 32 • Mountaineering in Tibet 34
3. STAYING HEALTHY 37 • Pre-trek Preparations 37 • Immuniza-
    tions 37 • First-Aid Kit 38 • Health and Medical Problems 40
    • Hospitals and Other Health Facilities 51
4. TRAVELING IN TIBET 53 • Accommodations 53 • Transpor-
    tation 54 • Money 54 • Cultural Considerations 55 • Environmental
    Awareness 58 • Dealing with Dogs 60 • Shopping for Food in Tibet 60
5. TIBETAN FOR TREKKERS 63 • Learning to Speak Tibetan 63
    • Pronunciation 65 • Grammar 67 • Useful Phrases and Conversa-
    tion 73 • English–Tibetan Vocabulary List 82

SECTION II. THE TREKS AND TRAILS 91

6. USING THE TREK DESCRIPTIONS 93 • Key to Maps 95 • Highway
    Kilometer Markers 95
7. THE LHASA REGION 101
    Dayhikes near Lhasa 101
        Within Lhasa 101 • *Sera Monastery Region 104* • *Drepung
        Monastery Region 112* • *Bumpa Ri 117*
    Ganden and Samye 118
        The Ganden to Samye Trek 125 • *The Samye to Dechen Dzong
        Trek 135* • *The Gyama Valley to Samye Trek 136*
    Dayhikes near Tsethang 140
    Tshurphu and the Yangpachan Valley 147
        Tshurphu to the Yangpachan Valley Trek 152
    The Nyanchhan Thanglha–Nam Tsho Trek 159
8. THE SHIGATSE REGION 173
    Shigatse 173
        Dayhikes in and near Shigatse 174
    Shalu, Ngor, and Narthang 177
        Dayhikes near Shalu 179 • *The Shalu–Ngor–Narthang Trek 181*

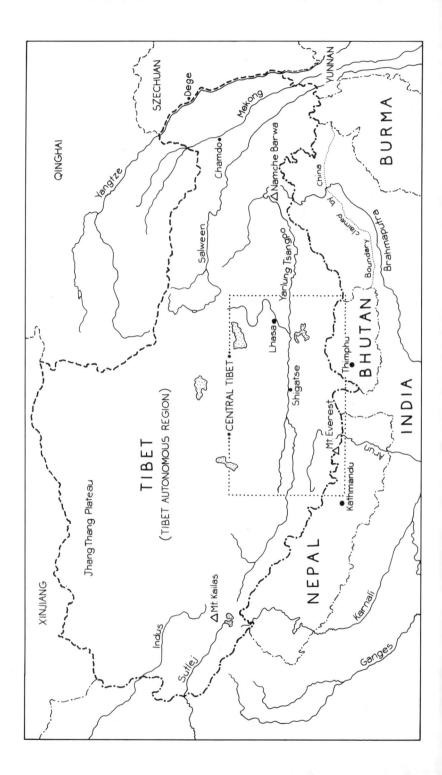

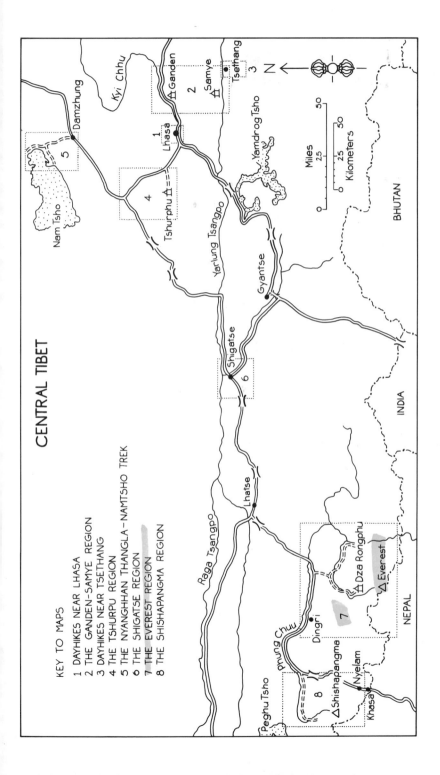

CENTRAL TIBET

KEY TO MAPS

1 DAYHIKES NEAR LHASA
2 THE GANDEN-SAMYE REGION
3 DAYHIKES NEAR TSETHANG
4 THE TSHURPU REGION
5 THE NYANGHHAN THANGLA–NAMTSHO TREK
6 THE SHIGATSE REGION
7 THE EVEREST REGION
8 THE SHISHAPANGMA REGION

Miles
0   25   50
Kilometers
0   25   50

N

9. THE EVEREST REGION 187
    Introduction to the Everest Region 187
    The Trek to Everest Base Camp via Pang La 192
        From Dza Rongphu to Everest Base Camp 201 • *Leaving Dza Rongphu 202*
    The Dingri to Dza Rongphu Monastery Loop 204
        Dingri 205 • *Dingri to Cho Oyu Base Camp 206* • *Dingri to Dza Rongphu via Lamna La 207* • *Phadhruchi to Dingri via Dingri Lama La 211*
    Beyond Everest Base Camp 213
    The Kangshung Valley to East Everest Base Camp Trek 219
10. THE SHISHAPANGMA REGION 229
    Dayhikes near Nyelam 230
    Dayhikes from the North Shishapangma Base Camp 233
    The South Shishapangma Base Camp Trek 234
11. THE MOUNT KAILAS REGION 241
    Dayhikes near Mount Kailas 244
    The Mount Kailas Circuit Trek 246
12. BICYCLING IN TIBET 255
    Preparations 256
        Bicycle Equipment 256 • *Other Supplies 256* • *Weather and Clothing 257* • *Physical Preparation 257*
    Classic Bicycle Routes 257
        Lhasa to Kathmandu 257 • *Mount Everest Base Camp 258* • *The Lhasa Valley 259* • *Other Options 259*

SECTION III. THE COUNTRY AND ITS PEOPLE 261

13. THE NATURAL HISTORY OF TIBET 263 • Physical Geography 263 • Geology 264 • Mammals 266 • Fish 270 • Birds 271
14. THE PEOPLE AND THEIR CULTURE 277 • The People of Tibet 277 • History and Religion 283 • Festivals 287

APPENDICES 291

A. Trekking and Mountaineering Agencies 291
B. Suggested Reading 293
C. Glossary of Tibetan and Foreign Words 296
D. Mountaineering Peaks in Tibet 298

Index 299

Preface

Many changes have occurred in Tibet since I first visited in the summer of 1985. It was an exciting time, for the land border between Nepal and Tibet had just opened. It seemed as if half the people I met were journalists, guidebook writers, or photographers, and almost everybody was bent on adventure: seeking out hidden temples, hitchhiking to the forests along the southern border, trying to be the first to visit an "oracle lake" or a remote cave hermitage. During my six weeks in Tibet I went with several friends on a short trek that had already become popular, from Samye monastery to the town of Dechen Dzong, near Lhasa. It was only a two-and-a-half-day walk, but I remember thinking how amazing it would be to research a trekking book, to have the opportunity to hike throughout a country as unusual as Tibet.

I went back in 1986 for the Tibetan New Year celebrations and the revival of the Monlam Chenmo, the Great Prayer Festival. Once again I went on a short trek, this time from Tshurphu monastery to the Yangpachan Valley, northwest of Lhasa. By 1987 I had definitely decided to compile a trekking guide, and returned to Tibet for nearly four months to research routes. Tibet's trekking and travel scene had become a free-for-all by then, with tens of thousands of tourists moving through the country. I left in September that year, only weeks before the first big political demonstrations rocked Lhasa.

Restrictions were placed on individual travelers, but in 1988 I managed to spend another five months trekking in Tibet. I had grand hopes of completing my trek research in 1989, but only two weeks after I had secured a six-month visa for China, fresh demonstrations erupted and Lhasa was placed under martial law. My visa melted into the page of my passport, unused.

As a result, people who are well versed in the treks of Tibet may notice a few gaps that otherwise would have been filled in. My dream of trekking to the four great river sources near Mount Kailas never materialized—I hope I can include it in a future edition. Also, I purposely omitted several of Central Tibet's most sacred pilgrimage destinations, which I feel should not be broadcast in a book like this; these are for you to discover.

I have walked each of the treks described; none of the route information is second-hand. Many of the place names used in the descriptions were derived from my conversations with local people. Undoubtedly changes will need to be made, names respelled, and so on. Any corrections or suggestions regarding the text will be greatly appreciated and should be sent to me care of the publisher.

I hope this book will allow you to enjoy Tibet as much as I have. Treat Tibet kindly, and ask others to do the same. The trekking industry in Tibet is still young and impressionable, but not incapable of learning how to care for the countryside and the culture, especially where trekking and tourism are most popular. This 1200-year-old civilization is rich with unique religions, music, literature, and art. True, many of the important historical sites and monasteries have been knocked down, but like a rare book with the cover torn off, much has remained intact . . . especially in the hearts of the Tibetan people.

GARY McCUE
Kathmandu, Nepal

Acknowledgments

Many people helped me during the more than three years that I was involved with this project. First and foremost I want to thank Kathy Butler; she not only created the fine maps in this book, but also accompanied me on many of the treks and has shared my life for the past five years. I also want to extend hearty thanks to Wendy Fleming, for her valuable comments regarding the text, for sending food parcels to Lhasa, and for watching our house; Ravi Chandra and Chris Lachman at Ama Dablam Trekking, for all their help in so many ways; Pam Steele, for making us feel at home during our long stays in Tibet; Mr. G. T. Sonam with Chinese Workers Travel Service (CWTS) in Lhasa, who spent hours answering my questions and helped me finish my field research; Tony Huber, for providing endless sources of information and for reviewing the "Tibetan for Trekkers" chapter; wildlife biologist George B. Schaller, for his kind assistance with the "Mammals" section; ornithologists H. S. Nepali and Robert Fleming Jr., for their help with the "Birds" section; geologist Peter Molnar at Massachusetts Institute of Technology, for his valuable comments regarding the "Geology" section; Tsetan Chonjore in Kathmandu and Ugen Gompo in New York, for helping me develop the "Tibetan for Trekkers" chapter; anthropologist Charles Ramble, who wrote "The People and Their Culture" section; Charles Houston, M.D., for his assistance and comments regarding the "Staying Healthy" chapter; Tim Young, who contributed the chapter on "Bicycling in Tibet"; John Frederick, for his suggestions on the trek descriptions; A. Bradley Rowe/Stone Routes and Keith Dowman, for all their useful information over the years; Tsering from CWTS in Lhasa, who helped me translate the Tibetan history murals at the Norbulingka; Jungly John, for trading a piece of cheese for a book I really needed; Phu Dorje at Bodhnath, for all his help and information in Dingri and in Nepal; Susan Perry, and Althea from the exiled Travellers Co-op, for their suggestions regarding women trekkers; Becky Kinsey, Phil Schack, Marta Wagner, Sara White, and Arthur Grollman, for sharing their homes while I researched the text; Chris Nielsen, for his help and friendship; Alec Le Sueur at the Holiday Inn, Lhasa; Salik Ram at J. S. Photo, Kathmandu; Bidur at Mandala Book Point, Kathmandu; Ashok the Magician; Dza Rongphu *lama* Thrulzhig Rimpoche; Austin Canty in Wollongong, Australia; Donna DeShazo, Margaret Foster-Finan, and the entire Mountaineers Books staff, for being fantastic to work with since the day I first called on the phone; all the monks, villagers, and pack animal guides in Tibet who shared their homes and patiently (at least for the first few hours) answered my unending questions; and of course my mother, Gail McCue, for her support and for handling my mail, finances, photographs, phone calls, and much more since I've been based in Asia.

A Note About Safety

Safety is an important concern in all outdoor activities. No guidebook can alert you to every hazard or anticipate the limitations of every reader. Therefore, the descriptions of roads, trails, routes, and natural features in this book are not representations that a particular place or excursion will be safe for your party. When you follow any of the routes described in this book, you assume responsibility for your own safety. Under normal conditions, such excursions require the usual attention to traffic, road and trail conditions, weather, terrain, the capabilities of your party, and other factors. Keeping informed on current conditions and exercising common sense are the keys to a safe, enjoyable outing.

Political conditions may add to the risks of travel in Tibet in ways that this book cannot predict. When you travel, you assume this risk, and should keep informed of political developments that may make safe travel difficult or impossible.

The Mountaineers

SECTION I

ABOUT TREKKING

Pilgrims circumambulating Mount Kailas, the most sacred peak in Asia

1   Introduction to Trekking in Tibet

Tibet, the largest and highest plateau on the earth, is surrounded by the most extensive jumble of mountains found on any continent. Stretching for almost 1900 miles (3000 km) and forming its entire southern boundary is the Himalaya, and along its western extremity is the equally rugged Karakoram; between these two ranges are all fourteen of the world's 8000-meter peaks (greater than 26,250 feet in elevation), including the soaring heights of Mount Everest. In Northern Tibet the plateau is a high, arid expanse known as the Jhang Thang, the "Northern Plains," where no trees grow and summer temperatures can fall far below freezing. Eastern Tibet is bounded by a succession of mountains, the Hengduan Shan, where three of Asia's largest rivers cut deep, parallel gorges on their journey from the plateau to the sea.

Many people in the West think Tibet is like the Jhang Thang—a desolate, cold, windswept desert on the roof of the world—but an unusually diverse and strikingly beautiful landscape of snowcapped summits, lush rhododendron and conifer forests, and fertile agricultural valleys also lies beyond the Himalaya.

Tibet is presently known as the Tibet Autonomous Region (TAR), a political entity created by the Chinese government in the 1960s that encompasses an area a little larger than three times the size of California (470,000 sq m, 1.2 million sq km) to the north of the Indian and Nepal Himalaya. Within the jurisdiction of the TAR are the traditional Tibetan provinces of Ü and Tsang (Lhasa and Shigatse were their capitals, respectively), which are collectively known as Central Tibet; most of the province of Ngari, which formerly included all of Western Tibet and extended into Ladakh; the southern third of the Jhang Thang; Lhodrag, the southern province that borders Sikkim and Bhutan; Kongpo, the region to the east of Ü province; part of Amdo, the land of nomadic herders to the north of Ü; and a long sliver of Kham, the easternmost of Tibet's traditional provinces. In general, the term "Tibet" is used in this book when referring to these provinces, which are now included within the TAR.

Geographic Tibet, which includes the entire Tibetan plateau, is nearly twice as big as the TAR. The outlying regions of the plateau that are not included in the TAR—including large areas of the Jhang Thang and the former provinces of Amdo and Kham—are now, from west to east, within the Xinjiang, Qinghai, Gansu, Szechuan, and Yunnan provinces of China. The ethnographic distribution of the Tibetan people, which includes Tibetans south of the Himalaya as well as those in Ladakh, Spiti, and Lahaul in northern India, is nearly twice as big again, covering an area about half the size of the continental United States.

A History of Trekking and Exploration in Tibet

Until the early eighteenth century only a handful of Europeans had ever traveled in Tibet. By the dawn of the twentieth century fewer than two dozen Westerners, most of them missionaries, had managed to visit the Holy City of Lhasa. Natural barriers (the Himalaya and the vast alpine desert along Tibet's northern frontier) and political barriers (erected to check the colonial expansion of Russia and Britain) were equally formidable, sealing off Tibet from most of the world and giving it an aura of mystery fueled by romantic authors in the West.

Europeans first learned of a distant land called "Tubbat" from the ninth- and tenth-century Arab traders who plied the silk routes. In the thirteenth century several Franciscan friars passed to the north of Tibet when they were sent by the Pope on peace-keeping missions to the royal court in Mongolia. One friar, William de Rubruquis, returned home with tales of visiting a Buddhist temple, which he mistakenly believed was part of a wayward branch of Christianity. Marco Polo also traveled near Tibet on his journey to Emperor Kublai Khan's capital in central China. After the Mongols were driven from China by the Ming dynasty in the fourteenth century, the subsequent rise of powerful Moslem empires in Central Asia closed off the silk routes to any further Western exploration.

Two centuries later the Portuguese Jesuits arrived in India, establishing a religious mission in Goa. Over the years they repeatedly heard stories about a religion with Christian-like rituals in a land far to the north called "Bhottan." Hoping to locate a "lost" Christian sect, two Jesuit priests, Father Andrade and Father Marques, set off in 1624 disguised as Hindu pilgrims. They hiked along the Ganges River to its source, then crossed the Himalaya to become the first Europeans to enter Tibet. Their warm welcome at Tsaparang, the capital of the Guge kingdom in Western Tibet, encouraged them to return the following year to establish a Catholic mission. Within a few years this form of "religious" trekking became rather popular with the Jesuits. They penetrated elsewhere into Tibet, walking overland from Sikkim to Shigatse, and in 1661 Johann Gruber and Albert d'Orville became the first Europeans to reach Lhasa. Capuchin monks also joined in the efforts to convert the Tibetans, but pressure from the Chinese political officers in Lhasa and the Buddhist *lamas* forced the last of the missions to close in 1745. Over the next hundred years the only Europeans to reach Lhasa were an unusual British chap named Thomas Manning and two French Lazarist priests, E. R. Huc and Joseph Gabet, who arrived via the northern caravan route from China.

A border war between Nepal and Tibet in 1791 prompted a large Chinese army to advance on Kathmandu, but after withdrawing from Nepal the army remained in Tibet, officially isolating the country for many years. The British Indian government's support of this closure (if the British couldn't go in, they didn't want anyone else in there) eventually set the stage for a new generation of "unofficial" trekkers: adventurous European travelers, sans Bibles, who came dressed in disguise and armed with pens and journals. Encouraged by the success of Huc and Gabet's route from the north, an unprecedented number of these adventurers attempted to cross the Jhang Thang. Their goal was the Forbidden City of Lhasa. British, Americans, French, Russians, and Swedes all tried their luck, but only Ekai Kawaguchi, a Japanese intelligence agent and devout Buddhist, was successful because he could pass for Chinese.

With the collapse of the Manchu dynasty in 1911, the thirteenth Dalai Lama expelled the Chinese and assumed complete control of the Tibetan government. Under his leadership the strict closed-door policy toward foreigners was eventually relaxed and climbing expeditions were permitted to attempt Mount Everest from Tibet.

The British conducted two reconnaissances and six expeditions to Mount Everest, some of huge proportion, between 1921 and 1938. After Mao Zedong's Communist Chinese army entered Lhasa in 1950, Tibet was closed to most foreigners and climbing expeditions, so the British as well as the Swiss tried routes from the newly opened kingdom of Nepal. In 1953 the British successfully placed Sir Edmund Hillary and Sherpa Tenzing Norgay on the summit. The same year a large Russian expedition is rumored to have attempted Everest from Tibet, and the Chinese launched a momumental summit bid in 1960.

As the constraints of the Cultural Revolution relaxed in the late 1970s the Chinese government allowed an Iranian expedition to Mount Everest. Soon afterwards the first commercial tour groups arrived in Lhasa. In the spring of 1981 the first commercial trekkers walked to Dza Rongphu monastery and Everest base camp with photographer Galen Rowell as their group leader. In a style Rowell describes as "truck trekking," the group hiked to the base camp along a dirt road that had been built for the 1960 Chinese Everest expedition while a truck hauled their gear to each successive campsite. Government-organized tours were the only way to trek in Tibet until September 1984, when Lhasa was officially opened to individual travelers. Suddenly several hundred years of barriers to foreign travel crumbled and the Tibetan countryside was open to anyone keen enough to load a backpack or duffel bag with gear and set off into the mountains. The number of tourists visiting Tibet quickly mushroomed, peaking at about 43,000 visitors in 1987.

The political disturbances in Tibet between 1987 and 1989 led government officials to close the country to foreigners for nearly three months in 1989. When Tibet reopened, tourists and trekkers were again welcomed, but the freedom to travel as an individual without a fixed itinerary was no longer permitted. Currently, foreigners have the choice of either arranging a private group with an itinerary of their own design or joining a commercially organized trek. Both styles of trekking are explained in the following sections.

Trekking in a Private Group

Although the days of trekking independently in Tibet are presently just a memory, the next closest alternative is to organize your own private group. The TAR government now requires that all tourists coming to Tibet be part of a group with a minimum of two people, although "groups" of one have been allowed. This policy is presently enforced by requiring all foreigners in Tibet to carry an Alien's Travel Permit (ATP), a small folded card with your name, passport number, and official itinerary, all written in Chinese.

A private group has two options for obtaining ATPs for Tibet. The first is to organize the trek through a commercial travel or trekking agency based in the United States, Nepal, Hong Kong, or Chengdu (the capital of Szechuan province and gateway for Lhasa flights from the Chinese mainland). If time is limited and you want to have all the details of your trek arranged before you leave home, consider using one of the large, well-known trekking agencies in the United States (or your home country). Although these companies mostly sell pre-arranged trekking packages, they also specialize in arranging private "free independent traveler" (FIT) groups. They can handle your international air reservations and help plan your itinerary.

The other option is to have a local travel agent arrange your air tickets while you deal directly with one of the trekking companies now operating within Lhasa (see "Trekking and Mountaineering Agencies," Appendix A). Queries should be made by telex or by phone; the Asian mail system is often slow and unreliable. The price per person per day can be almost half the rate of having a trekking agency based in the United States handle your plans, but it means you will be doing all the secretarial work and financial transactions. Usually trek rates are scheduled according to group sizes: the larger the group, the lower the price per person. The "leader" usually goes for free if there are more than ten people, though some companies require a minimum group size of fifteen for this discount.

Before a price can be fixed for your trek, you must advise the company of the proposed itinerary, the total number of days the group will be in Tibet, the total number of days to be spent trekking, the number of people in the group, and how many nights you plan to stay in Lhasa. You must also specify whether you want:
1. Budget accommodation or the Lhasa Holiday Inn (presently the finest Lhasa has to offer).
2. Full board (meals) at hotels or breakfast only.
3. Full board on trek (a good idea; you can bring extra food to supplement their menu).
4. Box lunches while driving overland (expensive and not very exciting; you're better off putting together your own picnic-type lunch).
5. Sightseeing with a guide and vehicle each day you're in Lhasa.
6. Special sightseeing excursions, such as visiting sites outside the Lhasa Valley.
7. Personal tents for the trekkers, dining tent, kitchen tent, toilet tent, and tents for the trekking staff (be sure to check on this; some companies have chronic tent shortages).
8. Cooking pots and other kitchen equipment.
9. Pack animals pre-arranged before the start of your trek.
10. Single-room and single-tent requests (this usually costs extra and is called a single supplement).

Once the trekking company has this information, its quoted price will also include a local English-speaking trekking guide, a cook, transport to and from the airport if you fly, transport before and after the trek, a supply truck, fuel, drivers, trekking staff, cooking stoves and other camp necessities, and pack animals or porters during the trek. The trekking company will also make arrangements for processing the group's visas, though each member must pay for his or her own visa, and the local trekking guide will have your ATPs when you arrive in Tibet. You will need to bring your own sleeping bag, sleeping pad, daypack or backpack, water bottles, down jacket, and other warm clothing. This may seem like a lot of work, but it can be fun becoming personally involved with organizing a trekking expedition—and it can save you money.

Arranging a private trekking group for Tibet can also be handled by many of the trekking agencies in Kathmandu, Nepal. Travel agents in Hong Kong or Chengdu can organize treks as well, but remember that their expertise is oriented to overland tour groups.

Trekking with a Commercial Company

The beauty of using a commercial company is that it takes care of all the day-to-day details, and typically in a very professional manner. If your holiday time is limited, if money is not a problem (in 1990 commercial treks in Tibet rarely cost less than $180 (U.S.) per person per day, not including international airfare), and you don't want to plan your own itinerary, then a commercial trek is definitely the way to go.

The major trekking companies all produce beautiful color brochures (I call them "wish books") that list the various trips they offer to Tibet, the departure dates, plus information about other destinations all over the world. The services offered by these companies are generally of a very high standard, though companies that don't have a fancy brochure can provide fine service as well. A Western group leader will usually accompany the group in addition to a local leader, one or more Sherpa guides are often brought from Nepal to assist with the trek, high-quality tents are provided, and all meals are included once you're in Tibet. Recommendations from friends are the best way to learn about a good trekking company, and most companies have a list of former clients you can contact to ask candid questions about their experience. Adventure travel directories and advertisements in outdoor-oriented magazines are another way to get the names of companies specializing in trekking.

If you want to go on a trek but haven't found anyone to go with, don't let that stop you. Often half the people who sign up for a trek are on their own. It's a great way to meet new friends, both your fellow trekkers as well as the local guides and trekking staff. Group dynamics are one of the hidden bonuses that help to make a trek memorable. Perhaps the biggest drawback to being with a commercial trek is the inflexible nature of the itinerary: once the trip starts, you're on a fixed schedule that can rarely be altered. If you are a person who enjoys the spontaneity of travel, arranging your own private group may be the preferred alternative to signing on with a commercial company.

Trekking as an Individual

Alas, the days of setting off on a trek in Tibet with just a few friends or by yourself, unburdened by a trekking staff and pre-arranged itineraries are currently something of the past. But if these regulations happen to change, the main options available to individual trekkers are carrying your own pack (backpacking) or hiring a local guide with pack animals. Due to the high elevations in Tibet, however, backpacking should not be attempted unless you are physically fit and well acclimatized to the altitude; many people become breathless after climbing their hotel stairs in Lhasa. The best way to arrange for a guide and pack animals is to inquire at the village or settlement nearest to where your trek begins. The standard procedure is to hire one or more pack animals (10 to 30 *yaun* per animal per day) and the person who will tend the animal(s) (typically 10 to 15 *yaun* per day). Usually one animal can carry the gear necessary for two or three trekkers on a two-week walk; the regional daily rate for a pack animal is the same, whether you hire a yak, burro, or horse. Be warned, however, that most yaks in Tibet do not have nose rings; they cannot be led by a rope nor will they remain on a trail unless they're following another yak. So, if you have a small group, and yaks are the only animals available, you may have to hire two even though you only need one. Remember bargaining is all part of the game. Another consideration is to negotiate a price for the guide's journey home if the trek does not finish where you started. Paying half wages for each day of his return is fair, though in some regions they insist on full wages. Let's hope that the near future will make all this information relevant again.

Hints for Women Trekkers

Tibet is probably one of the safest travel destinations in Asia for female travelers and trekkers. Sexual harassment is almost nonexistent and the towns and cities are particularly safe, even at night. Westerners are generally well accepted by the Tibetans and the culture has few taboos that might inadvertently be broken. Nonetheless there are some do's and don'ts for women that will help bridge the differences between the Tibetan way of life and ours.

Your clothes are one of the first things people will notice. Modesty should be a prerequisite. Do not wear shorts or other revealing clothes; long, loose trousers and calf-length skirts or dresses are best. Tibetan women typically wear an ankle-length dress, called a *chhupa,* with a blouse and, often, some type of coat.

A long skirt or dress can be handy for a little privacy while urinating. Tibet has few toilets (most of them you wouldn't want to use) and there seems to be a chronic shortage of handy rocks or bushes to duck behind. Tibetan women simply hike up their dress and squat, with little concern toward who's nearby. If you're wearing a long dress you can do the same, though wearing underwear makes it a bit more difficult. Trying to find somewhere private to change your clothes and have a good wash can be difficult once you are out of the cities and away from the luxury of hotels. On a commercial trek you can bathe with a wash basin in the privacy of your tent. If you want to bathe near a stream, wearing a bathing suit or washing in your underwear is not appropriate. Instead, wrap a piece of material around you sarong-style. Tibetan women usually don't wash their bodies except during a yearly bathing festival, so there really isn't a local example to follow. Try sponge bathing; it's easier to be modest washing small areas of your body at a time. Packaged, pre-moistened towelettes are also handy for a quick clean-up. Bring plenty of facial lotion, moisturizer, and hand cream—the combination of cold water and dry winds can cause chapping and cracked skin.

Women can freely enter the Buddhist temples and shrines, but occasionally

The bhung-ghu *(burro), Tibet's most loveable pack animal*

a protector's chapel (*gön-khang*) in a monastery will have a sign requesting that they not enter. Women having their period are sometimes discouraged from entering monasteries, and I have heard stories of women being asked to leave someone's home when it's been learned that they were menstruating. Tampons and sanitary napkins are generally not available in Tibet; bring enough and then some. Also note, it is not that unusual for women to skip their period while on a trek.

When to go Trekking

In general the best season for trekking is from May through October. The weather during these months is surprisingly mild with warm days and cool to chilly nights in the mountains: not very different from summer conditions in the Rockies or the Cascades. July and August can be very rainy, receiving over half of Tibet's annual precipitation. India's monsoon manages to push over the Himalaya into much of Central Tibet, bringing rain most nights and occasional showers during the day. This time of year is also prime wildflower season, when even the most barren hills don a fuzzy green coating of grass. Higher up in the alpine areas the valleys become lush and speckled with innumerable types of flowers and blooming shrubs.

By September autumn is knocking on the door. The days are cooler and the willow and poplar leaves acquire a yellowish cast. Indian summers are not uncommon and may last into late October or early November, bringing sunny days and clear, crisp nights with temperatures often dropping below freezing. But September and October can also bring surprise snowstorms to the mountains.

The coldest time of the year is from December through February, but that doesn't rule out the potential for trekking. A big high-pressure system often hovers over Tibet in the winter, bringing extended periods of clear, sunny weather to the plateau. Of course, in some regions—including Nam Tsho, the Nyanchhan Thanglha range, the Kangshung Valley near Mount Everest, and the south side of Shishapangma—the snowfall is too great to consider winter treks. The regions around Lhasa, Shigatse, and Dingri, however, receive relatively little snow, and though cold the trekking can be enjoyable.

In March the large lower valleys start to warm considerably and show signs of spring. A jacket is no longer needed on sunny afternoons and the winds lose their chill. May and June are usually the hottest and windiest months. Wind is common throughout the year in Tibet, but during these months it is particularly bad. Billowing afternoon dust storms occasionally engulf the larger river valleys such as Lhasa and Shigatse. A cotton surgical-type mask is highly recommended for dusty road conditions.

As in any mountainous region, the weather can change quickly and snow is a possibility *any* month of the year. Even in summer it is advisable to carry winter-oriented clothing, particularly if you plan to ascend above 16,000 feet (4880 m). But more often than not the weather is fine and wonderfully clear.

2   Preparing for Your Trek

Getting ready to travel internationally and trek in a remote region such as Tibet can be surprisingly time-consuming. The whole process of booking air tickets, obtaining a passport (if you don't have one or if it has expired), applying for visas, and putting together clothes and trekking gear is almost like taking on a second job. Start working on these details at least three months in advance—even then you'll be surprised at how much you haven't done by the last week before you head off. And no matter how busy you are, don't neglect getting those legs and lungs in shape.

Physical Conditioning

Start your physical fitness program several months before you arrive in Tibet. Walking, hiking, and backpacking over rugged terrain are the best ways to prepare for a trek. Any regular regime of strenuous aerobic exercise is also beneficial, especially running, cross-country skiing, swimming, and bicycling. Be creative. Regular sessions of running up and down multiple flights of stairs in an office or apartment building can improve fitness. Interestingly, people who frequently practice a more passive type of exercise such as yoga are often in excellent shape for trekking. Don't tell yourself you'll get in shape after a few days of walking. When you climb toward a high pass on your second or third day of trekking, you'll be a lot happier if you exercised regularly before coming to Tibet.

Learning about Tibet

Your trek and travels will be enhanced tremendously if you make the effort to learn about Tibet's unique culture and people. "Suggested Reading" (Appendix B) lists works on various subjects concerning Tibet. If your local library doesn't have some of the books, ask the librarian if they can be ordered through an interlibrary loan system. Other resources include university libraries, particularly if the school has an Asian Studies program, mountaineering club libraries, and specialty bookstores. A "dream" catalogue of titles on the Himalaya, Tibet, and mountaineering is available through Chessler Books, P.O. Box 4267, Evergreen, Colorado 80439; (800) 654-8502, (303) 670-0093.

In addition, *The Reader's Guide to Periodical Literature,* a voluminous series of catalogues, indexes articles from hundreds of magazines according to subject.

Visa Regulations and Alien's Travel Permits

United States citizens traveling abroad are required to carry a valid U.S. passport. If you do not have a passport or if it has expired, you will need to apply for a new one at least a month before your departure. Larger cities have government passport agencies, and your local post office should have the proper application forms. It takes about four weeks after submitting your application to receive the new passport by mail. You also will need a Chinese visa, which is required for everyone visiting Tibet. These visas can be obtained from the Embassy of the People's Republic of China, 2300 Connecticut Avenue, Washington, D.C. 20008; (202) 328-2500; or at the Chinese consulates in Chicago, New York, and San Francisco. In addition, all tourists are required to possess an Alien's Travel Permit (ATP), which lists each of your travel destinations in Tibet. This card can be obtained only by organizing your trek through a commercial trekking company (see "Trekking with a Private Group" and "Trekking with a Commercial Company" in "Introduction to Trekking in Tibet"). If you try to enter Tibet without an ATP you may be able to reach Lhasa, but your ability to go beyond the city limits will be restricted.

On your journey to Tibet you may pass through Hong Kong, Thailand, or Nepal. Each of these places will issue a visa good for fifteen days upon your arrival. Only the Thai visa is difficult to extend beyond the initial entry period; if you plan to stay in Tibet more than fifteen days you must apply for a proper tourist visa ahead of time or at the airport when you arrive. India does not allow travelers to enter without a valid Indian visa. You will be sent back on the next plane if you try! Even transit passengers are advised to have a visa to prevent being locked in the transit lounge if their plane is delayed. The Indian Embassy is located at 2107 Massachusetts Avenue Northwest, Washington, D.C. 20008 (202) 362-4764; with consulates in Chicago, New York, and San Francisco.

Most commercial trekking companies now use expensive but efficient visa processing agencies to handle clients' visa applications. The alternative is go to the embassy yourself or call to request application forms, then submit them by mail along with your passport (not a copy) and the appropriate visa fee. To be safe, use only registered or express mail. If you ask ahead of time the embassy will tell you the return express mail charge, which can be included with the visa fee. Money orders or bank drafts are the preferred form of payment, for personal checks must clear before a visa will be issued.

Getting to Tibet

The only flights to Lhasa (as of 1990) are the daily service from Chengdu, in Szechuan province of mainland China, and once- or twice-a-week flights from Kathmandu, Nepal, in the summer. The service from Chengdu has been the more reliable, and there are connecting flights to and from Beijing, Guangzhou (Canton), and Hong Kong. All incoming flights to Lhasa land at Gongkar Airport in the Yarlung Tsangpo Valley. The 56-mile (90 km) drive to the city takes about two hours in a minibus, three hours on the local CAAC (China National Airline Corporation, the airline of the People's Republic of China) bus. Due to the current

Mount Everest from the Kathmandu–Lhasa flight

restrictions on individual travel in Tibet, CAAC offices have been instructed not to sell air tickets for Lhasa to anyone who is not part of a bona fide group.

The principle overland route into Tibet is from Nepal along the Lhasa–Kathmandu Highway. The 600-mile (1000 km) journey between these capital cities is a rugged but beautiful drive, requiring four days and crossing the Himalaya over 17,060-foot (5200 m) Thang La. The restrictions on individual travelers in Tibet also apply to entry by land: you must be part of an officially recognized group in order to enter from Nepal, even if you have a Chinese visa. Groups are met at the Tibetan border town of Khasa (Zhangmu) by their local tour guide, who then presents the ATPs to the Chinese immigration officials.

Two other major land routes into Tibet are the northern road from Golmud in Qinghai province, which crosses the eastern corner of the Jhang Thang plateau, and the long, mountainous road from Chengdu, in the east. The road to Lhasa from Chengdu is one of the most spectacular journeys anywhere, climbing over perhaps a dozen mountain ranges and crossing the Yangtze, Mekong, and Salween rivers in Eastern Tibet. Unfortunately, it is currently off-limits to foreigners, though rumors keep circulating that it may re-open. The fourth major overland gateway to Tibet is the road from Kashgar, an oasis market town in far western China. Several travel agencies operate tours that originate in Pakistan, drive over the Karakoram Highway's Khunjerab Pass to Kashgar, then go on to Mount Kailas in Western Tibet before continuing to Lhasa. Between Kashgar and Mount Kailas the road passes through Aksai Chin, an area controlled by China since a 1962 border war with India, and crosses four major passes over 17,000 feet (5200 m) in elevation.

The overland routes are considerably more time-consuming than flying, but the experience of gradually being introduced to the Tibetan landscape and life-style as you travel is far superior to being plunked down on the pavement at Gongkar Airport in the middle of Tibet. For an outline of destinations along the Lhasa–Kathmandu Highway and the two overland routes between Mount Kailas and Lhasa, refer to "Highway Kilometer Markers" in "Using the Trek Descriptions."

Maps

While road maps of Tibet are readily available, good topographical maps for trekking there are almost impossible to find. The best maps are the Joint Operations Graphic (JOG) maps, Series 1501, with 100-meter (320 ft) contours, published by the Defense Mapping Agency Topographic Center in Washington, D.C., and the similarly scaled L500 Series (China) printed by the Army Map Service (AMS), Corps of Engineers, Washington, D.C. These have been produced using fair to poor information; their accuracy is generally good but cannot be taken for granted. (On a few occasions I have found myself in a valley or on a ridge, with my map spread out, unable to determine my exact location.) Nonetheless they are a useful complement to the trekking maps in this book, particularly for their topographical data. Because the scale is so big (1 inch:4 miles, roughly the distance of a day's trek), try tracing the major ridge lines with a felt pen to help you visualize the drainage patterns.

One reason for the absence of accurate topographical maps of Tibet is the Chinese government's request to control their distribution. The map libraries of the Library of Congress in Washington, D.C., and the National Archives in Alexandria, Virginia, have most of the 1501 and L500 series maps that were produced (not all of Tibet was mapped in these series), but they do not sell photocopies as they do for less sensitive areas such as Nepal. If you are allowed to see these maps, you may be able to trace them. The best alternative is to visit a university map library, particularly if the university has a large Asian Studies or Geography department. Most libraries have do-it-yourself photocopying services, but some will meticulously mask a border around the area to be copied. If the copier cannot make a full-size reproduction, copy the map onto several pages and then tape the different sections together.

The following 1:250,000 topographical maps exist for Tibet. Seven of these maps (marked with an asterisk) seem to have been approved for distribution, for they are often in large map libraries; the others are more difficult to locate. Note that several small corners of Tibet occur in yet another set of 1:250,000 maps covering India and Nepal, the AMS Series U502 maps.

Joint Operations Graphic (JOG), Series 1501 Maps: La-tzu-Tsung (west of Shigatse), NH 45-11; Zih-k'a-tse (Shigatse), NH 45-12; Tamshun (Damzhung, north of Lhasa), NH 46-5; Shunta (north of Tsethang), NH 46-6; *Lhasa, NH 46-9; Tsethang, NH 46-10; *Namche Barwa, NH 46-12.

Army Map Service (AMS), Series L500 Maps: Kang-ti-ssu Shan-mo (Mount Kailas, west Tibet), NH 44-3; *Manasarowar, NH 44-7; *Mustang, NH 44-12; *Tingri

Dzong (Shishapangma/western Everest region), NH 45-14; *Gyantse, NH 45-16;
*Yamdrog Tsho, NH 46-13.
Army Map Service (AMS), Series U501 Maps (1:253,440): Khampa Dzong (west
of Gyantse), H-45 W.

———————

A more readily available but far less accurate set of maps covering Tibet
and Asia is the Operational Navigational Chart maps, Series ONC (1:1,000,000).
Sheets ONC H-9 and ONC H-10 include the entire southern half of Tibet. Another
set of maps, the Tactical Pilot Charts, Series TPC (1:500,000), also is now available. Sheets H-9-B and H-10-A cover most of Central Tibet. They are meant for
aeronautic navigational use, and can be ordered from the Defense Mapping
Agency, DMA CSC, Attention: PMSR, Washington, D.C., 20315-0020; (800)
826-0342.

Equipment and Clothing

If you trek in Tibet with a commercial company, it will supply all the necessary camping equipment. Some outfits provide sleeping bags and parkas for use
during the trek, a bonus that can save you hundreds of dollars if you have little use
for such gear after the trek. If you are organizing a private group, ask whether
the necessary tents and kitchen equipment are included in the price quote. Read
through the trek description introductions to determine whether a tent or stove is
necessary for a particular walk. In regard to clothing and equipment, you must
constantly compare an item's effectiveness against its weight: a thick rubberized
raincoat will keep you very dry in a rainstorm, but do you want to carry it everywhere in your daypack? Price is another consideration. Good outdoor gear and
clothes are not cheap: a decent three-season sleeping bag is rarely less than
$200; lightweight hiking boots easily go for $100. Even if you're not buying
top-of-the-line equipment, starting from scratch is an expensive venture if you buy
everything new. One alternative is to rent gear. If you plan to enter Tibet from Nepal
and return there, it is possible to hire camping equipment and winter clothing such
as parkas from trekking shops in Kathmandu, particularly in the tourist area
of Thamel. (Trekking gear is not presently available for rent or sale in Lhasa.)
Another way to save money is to purchase used gear or buy "seconds" from factory outlets. Local newspapers and bulletin boards at grocery stores or outdoor
stores are good places to advertise or find ads for used equipment.

When planning your clothing needs for a trek, think in terms of layers.
Layers of clothing will keep you warm, but can be removed to gradually prevent
overheating. During spring and autumn the night temperatures in the mountains
often dip below freezing, making warm gear essential. In the summer the days
can be hot, requiring light cotton clothing. Adequate wet-weather gear is also a
priority during the summer. Remember that the mountainous regions of Tibet can
receive snow any month of the year, and always be prepared for cold weather if
you will be trekking at elevations much above 16,000 feet (4880 m). Make sure
that the clothing you will wear most often can be washed in cold stream water
and dries quickly. Below are lists of equipment, clothing, and accessories you
will need in Tibet.

EQUIPMENT

Footwear: Your hiking boots should have thick soles and be high enough to provide adequate ankle support. The newer lightweight boots are more comfortable but less durable than all-leather hiking boots. Consider Goretex-lined hiking boots for the varying weather conditions in the Himalaya. Optional: A pair of thongs or sneakers to wear in camp.

Packs: If you plan to carry your own gear, you will want a backpack that comfortably supports the weight. A wide, cushioned waist belt and thick shoulder straps are essential. If you are trekking with a commercial company, you will need a daypack to carry your daily essentials. Choose one with padded shoulder straps, a wide, cushioned waist belt, and about 1500- to 2000-cubic-inch volume.

Duffel bag: Long (36 inches or so), heavy-duty canvas or nylon bag that can be secured with a padlock. Waterproof it by lining with a thick plastic bag.

Sleeping bag: A three-season (spring-summer-autumn), mummy-style down or fiber-filled bag rated to about 15°F.

Inner sleeping sheet: Silk or cotton, to minimize the need to wash your sleeping bag.

Sleeping pad: A full-length, self-inflating pad or the standard closed-cell foam pad.

Rain gear: Your raincoat should be roomy, be mid-thigh in length, and have a waterproof hood. Rain pants can double as wind pants. Goretex, Japara, or high-quality coated nylon materials are best.

Tent: A sturdy, lightweight, waterproof nylon tent with collapsible aluminum poles is best. Dome tents are heavy but well liked for their high ceilings.

Fuel stove: Choose an efficient lightweight camping stove that can burn kerosene, the most readily available fuel in Tibet.

Water bottle: A plastic or metal leakproof quart/liter bottle. The plastic-lined aluminum foil bladders from bulk wine casks make durable, lightweight water containers good for hauling water when you're camping.

CLOTHING

Thermal underwear: Long-sleeve tops and bottoms made from wool, silk, polypropylene, or a similar synthetic fiber. Bring one or two pairs. Short-sleeve thermal tops are good on cool days while trekking. Avoid cotton long underwear, which is virtually useless if it becomes wet from perspiration.

Cotton underwear: Four or five pairs.

Socks: At least three pairs of wool/cotton-mix socks, and three pairs or more of cotton socks for warmer temperatures. Hand-knit wool socks can be purchased in Lhasa and Kathmandu.

Shirts: A long-sleeve shirt made of wool, flannel, or chamois, or a track-suit top. A long-sleeve stay-press cotton shirt for warmer temperatures. Bring two or three cotton T-shirts as well.

Pants: For men, one pair of loose-fitting wool pants, wool knickers, or fiber-pile pants, and one pair of lighter-weight cotton pants. Women should wear a mid-calf dress or skirt, though pants and knee-length knickers with socks are also acceptable. Shorts are not appropriate at any time in Tibet for men or women.

Sweater: Wool or wool mix with a high neck for extra warmth.

Jacket: A fiber-pile jacket is ideal for trekking and evenings in camp.

Insulated coat or parka, with hood: A heavy-duty down or fiber-filled coat is usually not necessary between mid-May and mid-September. During other months you'll want to wear one most evenings. It should be big enough to fit over bulky clothing, with fourteen to sixteen ounces of down or eighteen to twenty ounces of a fiber-fill material.

Headwear: Wool or fiber-pile ski-style cap or balaclava for warmth. A lightweight brimmed hat is good for sun protection. Inexpensive broad-brimmed straw and felt hats are sold in Tibet's city markets.

Scarf: Wool or silk is best.

Mittens or gloves: Wool, pile, or polypropylene are best.

Bandanna or handkerchief: Bring several.

ACCESSORIES AND EXTRAS

Many of the following items are optional. Don't try to bring everything—you would need a herd of yak to carry it all! If you are on a commercial trek, the weight limit for personal duffel bags is usually thirty-three pounds (fifteen kg).

Pocket knife: Swiss army-style is best.

Sewing kit: One small kit. A leather sewing awl is ideal for big repairs.

Duct tape: One small roll for repairs.

Compass: For use with trail descriptions and orientation with maps.

Altimeter: Measures altitude as a function of the barometric pressure.

Maps: I wouldn't go trekking without them. See "Maps" in this chapter.

Gaiters: Good for winter treks or wet trail conditions during monsoon.

Insulated booties: Down or fiber-filled, for the colder months.

Umbrella: The lightweight collapsible kind for rain and hot sunshine.

Waterproof ground sheet or poncho: Handy for laying out gear on wet ground.

Cooking pots: Necessary only if you are trekking as an individual.

Utensils: Supplied on commercial treks. Have your own pair of chopsticks if you plan to eat in local restaurants.

Drinking cup: For the ubiquitous cups of butter tea that will be served if you visit a monastery or Tibetan home. Carry it in your daypack.

Nylon cord: Fifteen to twenty feet for a clothesline.

Toilet paper: Stock up before the trek starts. Always burn it after using.

Tampons or sanitary napkins: Not available in Tibet.

Butane cigarette lighter: Superior to matches when burning used toilet paper in windy conditions.

Toiletries: Use a small stuff sack to hold your toothbrush, toothpaste, comb, soapdish, dental floss, skin moisturizer, and perhaps a mirror.

Towel: Two small, thin towels are preferable to one thick towel; theoretically one will be clean while you wash the other.

Flashlight: A headlamp is ideal for camping. AA and D batteries are the most common in Tibet and China, but of poor quality. Bring extra alkalines from home.

Plastic bags: A few of each size, from sandwich style to strong trash bags.

Sunglasses: Necessary for Tibet's bright, high-altitude sunlight. Darker glacier-type glasses with side hoods are necessary in the mountains and after fresh snowfalls.

Sun creams and lip balm: Sun block with a 15 SPF rating or higher is recommended. Zinc oxide is the best total blockout. Lip balms prevent burning and chapping.

Journal, reading book, writing materials: For quiet moments.

Camera: You'll regret not bringing one.

Binoculars: Good for observing birds, wildlife, and distant scenery.

Shortwave radio: With an earphone, so you don't disturb others.

Portable tape recorder: A great way to bring home the music and sounds of Tibet.

Money pouch or belt: Safer than a wallet for keeping your passport, money, and valuable papers.

Frisbee: Great entertainment.

Pictures from home: Personal photographs of your children, pets, city, house, and so on are a great way to communicate with local people.

Snack foods: Nuts, chocolate bars, granola bars, dried fruit, hard candies, beef jerky, and flavored drink mixes are much-appreciated trail treats.

Watch: Useful for pacing yourself with the trek descriptions in this book.

Photography in Tibet

One key to taking good photographs in Tibet is being prepared to deal with difficult environmental conditions. Your camera equipment and accessories should be reliable and in good working order, and you must take extra care to protect your gear.

Contrary to what many people believe, a fancy camera is not necessary to take excellent photographs: the person who stands behind the camera is responsible for that. A 35mm single-lens reflex (SLR) camera with interchangeable lenses is the most versatile for creative travel photography. Zoom lenses are great for framing pictures quickly and capturing candid photos of people. With a 35–70mm zoom and a 70–210mm zoom you can cover a wide range of photographic possibilities. The main drawbacks are their weight and the difficulty of getting sharp pictures due to camera shake. Zooms require very slow shutter speeds in limited light situations compared to faster, fixed focal-length lenses. Faster film speeds such as 200 ASA slide or print film help remedy this. Buy the best lens you can afford, and don't be tempted to save money by purchasing a lens made by an unknown manufacturer. Most of the broken or jammed lenses I've seen during treks have not been major brand names. Before you set off on your trek, test any new camera gear by shooting a roll of film at home and having it processed.

I typically bring four fixed-aperture lenses—24mm and 28mm wide angles, a 50mm normal lens, and a 135mm telephoto, all with relatively fast apertures ranging from f 1.2 to f 2.8; two camera bodies, one for color slides and one for black-and-white; plus a flash and a small collapsible tripod. If I'm traveling light I carry just one camera body, a normal lens, and either a wide-angle or a telephoto lens. Remember that you must carry your own camera gear while trekking.

Don't overload yourself.

Dust is a big concern in Tibet's arid climate. Always keep your camera in its protective case or in a padded carrying bag. When changing film or lenses, stay out of the wind to prevent grit from getting inside. A lens-cleaning kit with a camel-hair brush is a must. Avoid packing any camera equipment in your duffel bag, for it may be nonoperational after being banged about all day in the back of a vehicle or tied onto a yak.

Temperature extremes can also cause problems. In cold weather, cover your gear at night or put it inside your sleeping bag to prevent mechanical parts from freezing. Bring several extra sets of camera batteries, for they are not available in Tibet. If you are shopping for one of the new electronic cameras, consider one that will operate on a manual setting without batteries. The light meter won't work, but at least the shutter will continue functioning.

The light in Tibet can be tricky to capture properly on film. Early mornings and late afternoons are typically the best times for dramatic pictures. The midday light in Tibet is harsh, often causing washed-out colors. Sometimes the only remedy is to wait until the sun is lower in the sky. Try using a polarizing filter to enhance colors and the sky, especially on hazy days. Don't dial the polarizer to the darkest setting. Back it off about one-third of a turn from dark for the best results. If you're shooting pictures on snow-covered ground, open the aperture by one or two f-stops over the meter reading to prevent underexposed pictures. Color slide film with an ASA of 25, 50, 64, or 100 is best for sharp, vivid outdoor photography, but can be used only in strong light conditions unless you have a tripod. Bring enough film to last your entire stay in Tibet; ten or fifteen rolls for a three-week trip should be sufficient. If you need to buy film in Lhasa, good-quality print film is available in several camera shops on the street running south from the main post office, near the entrance to a park.

The Tibetan people are as tough to capture on film as the high-altitude light. They are rather adverse to being photographed, or may demand money. No matter how interesting a person may look, *never* pay for a photograph. Always ask permission to take someone's picture, and respect a refusal. The typical Tibetan reaction is to wave you away and say no, so try to break the ice by encouraging them to look through the view finder (a wide-angle or telephoto lens is good for this), or point to the shutter and have them take a picture of you. Most Tibetans are convinced every camera will produce instant pictures. To be fair, be sure to explain that you have only film inside your camera. Phrases such as *"Nga khyayrang-ghi paa gyebna drig ghi repay?"* ("May I take your picture?") and *"Paachay nangla pingshuo duu. Dhanda paa minduu,"* ("Inside my camera is only film; no pictures now") are worth learning.

Always ask permission before taking any photographs at a monastery. Monks at the larger monasteries are required to collect photography fees from tourists, usually a flat rate ranging from five to twenty *yuan* ($1 to $5 U.S.). Sometimes an entire group will be allowed to take pictures once one person has paid. However, certain monasteries and temples, such as those around the Mount Kailas circuit, do not allow any photography. To avoid an unpleasant scene, don't try to sneak photographs. If you decide to pay the photo fee, wide-angle lenses are good for capturing the feeling of temple interiors. If enough

Fox-skin hat

natural light filters in, use a tripod for time exposures rather than the harsh light from a flash. When photographing wall frescoes, try to bounce your flash off a reflective surface to prevent flash flaring on the shiny murals.

Mountaineering in Tibet

Since the late 1970s the Chinese and Tibetan mountaineering associations have been issuing permits to foreign climbers for Mount Everest and twenty other summits. The majority of these mountains are part of the high Himalaya between Everest and Shishapangma, though several interesting 7000-meter and 6000-meter peaks have opened in other regions of Tibet. Prior to arriving in Tibet all expeditions must have their climbing permits authorized by either the Tibet Mountaineering Association (TMA) in Lhasa or the Chinese Mountaineering Association (CMA) in Beijing (see "Trekking and Mountaineering Agencies," Appendix A). These two organizations usually work together, though it may be more efficient to work directly with the TMA. Applications for expedition permits should be submitted at least eight months in advance in order to secure the preferred season and route on a peak. The spring pre-monsoon climbing season is from March to June and the autumn post-monsoon season is from August to October. May and

September are considered the best months.

Initial enquiries should be made by telex to expedite the application process. Include your name or your organization's name, a mailing address, and a telex reply number. Request a list of the open peaks and an "Application for Mountaineering in Tibet." Let them know if you already have a mountain and a date in mind. The application form includes a fee schedule for climbing permits. In 1990 the highest fee listed was $2703 (U.S.) for Mount Everest. Unlisted was Namche Barwa (25,446 ft, 7756 m), the world's highest unclimbed mountain. Located in Eastern Tibet at the far end of the Himalayan chain, this grand prize of modern mountaineering will probably fetch a permit fee of $100,000 (U.S.) or more if it is ever offered to foreign climbers.

Once the completed application has been received by one of the mountaineering organizations, they will confirm whether the mountain is available and send notification that the permit has been approved. They will then request that the registration fee be paid by bank transfer to reserve the mountain and specified route for your team.

The next process is working out the expedition budget. The mountaineering associations require that you use them (and pay them) to organize all ground transportation, all food and lodging to and from base camp, as well as the hiring of porters and yaks during the expedition. Let them know if your team has special vehicle requests or if you want a four-wheel-drive vehicle kept at base camp for emergencies. Climbing teams typically bring their own expedition food. Meals for the Chinese and Tibetan staff (translator, drivers, guide, and liaison officer) are provided by the mountaineering association, but billed to the expedition.

About three months before the expedition date the association will need to know the passport details for each expedition member and any Sherpas accompanying the climb. Also specify which Chinese embassy (Washington, D.C.; Kathmandu; and so on) is the preferred location(s) for issuing the team's Chinese visas. Payment for the expedition services provided by the mountaineering association must be sent by bank transfer about two months in advance. Upon receipt of the money a formal notice authorizing the climb will be sent stating the name of the mountain, the dates for the expedition, and the approved number of climbers. The association then sends a telex confirmation to the requested Chinese embassy to issue the visas.

See "Mountaineering Peaks in Tibet" (Appendix D) for the 1990 list of mountains in Tibet open to foreign climbing expeditions. It is grouped according to geographical regions and in descending order of height. Most of the peak names used by the TMA and CMA are the new Chinese names, which in many cases are not well known to foreign climbers nor used on maps. To minimize confusion, I haved listed the more common name of a mountain first, with the new Chinese name(s) in parentheses. Seven of the open peaks do not have Western names; a color pamphlet produced by the TMA has a map showing their approximate locations.

Nomadic herder tent near Nyanchhan Thanglha mountains

3   Staying Healthy

Trekking in Tibet is relatively safe despite the remoteness of trekking areas. The trails generally are not precipitous, and the chance of intestinal disorders and illnesses typically experienced by travelers in other Asian countries is greatly reduced by Tibet's higher elevations; the colder temperatures are not conducive to bacterial growth. With a bit of common sense, preparation, and some basic medical knowledge, most illnesses or injuries can be safely treated with an adequately stocked personal first-aid kit.

In the event of a real emergency it is important to know that hospitals and clinics in Central Tibet are primarily located in the larger cities of Lhasa, Shigatse, and Tsethang. *There is no emergency helicopter service in Tibet.* If anybody in your party becomes sick or injured and requires evacuation, he or she will have to be carried or ride a pack animal to the nearest roadhead.

This chapter outlines some of the more important health concerns for travelers and trekkers in Tibet. Due to the unusually high elevations in Tibet, it is particularly important to be well versed in recognizing and treating the symptoms of altitude-related problems, such as mountain sickness. Respiratory ailments are common due to dusty road conditions and the dry air of the Tibetan plateau. Diarrhea plagues travelers the world over. A must for all trekking group first-aid kits is James Wilkerson's *Medicine for Mountaineering.* A pocket-sized alternative is *First Aid: Quick Information for Mountaineering and Backcountry Use.* (See "Suggested Reading," Appendix B.)

Pre-trek Preparations

Prior to departure, visit your physician. Most treks in Tibet are rather strenuous and occur at elevations between 12,000 and 17,000 feet (3660 to 5200 m). People with diabetes, asthma, or high blood pressure can successfully trek in Tibet, but should check with a doctor about potential problems and precautions. Most commercial companies require all clients to submit a medical examination report signed by a physician as a pre-condition for acceptance.

It is also advisable to have a dental checkup before you set off. Except for street "dentists" in the markets, with foot-treadle drills, the only dental facility in Central Tibet is in Lhasa.

Immunizations

Obtain information about immunizations several months before your departure. Your local public health center, a university medical center, or the Centers for Disease Control (CDC), Atlanta, GA (404-639-3311) can provide the most up-to-date information. Some areas of the United States have specialized travelers' health clinics that provide inoculations and advise people about health situations around the world. Update your diphtheria, measles, polio, and rubella immunizations, even though China and Tibet require no specific inoculations for entry. Visitors should also consider the following:

Recommended Immunizations: Gamma globulin (Immune Serum Globulin, or ISG for protection from Hepatitis A); tetanus; and typhoid.

Immunizations or Protection Worth Considering: Malaria (not a concern in Tibet, though it may be necessary to take a prophylactic course if travel plans include countries with known malarial areas); meningitis (not necessary for Tibet— however doctors at the Canadian International Water and Electricity Commission (CIWEC) Clinic in Kathmandu recommend the vaccine for anyone spending more than a week in Nepal, where an epidemic occurred in 1983–84); rabies (the existence of rabies in Tibet has not been officially confirmed, though the fact that it is widespread in Nepal and India increases the likelihood. Some people have allergic reactions to this vaccine).

Not Recommended: Cholera.

Record all immunizations on a yellow International Certificates of Vaccination card, available at most passport and public health offices.

First-Aid Kit

It is important to carry a basic first-aid kit with you, even if you are trekking with a commercial company. Few drugs familiar in the West are available in China and Tibet. The following medications and supplies will prepare you to meet most medical situations. (If you are trekking independently or in a private group, your first-aid kit should be more complete than if you are with a commercial company.) Be familiar with the proper use and potential side effects of the drugs. Some of these medications can only be purchased with a prescription, which most doctors will provide if they know you are going trekking. If you plan to travel through Nepal, you can purchase many of the antibiotics and pain killers cheaply in Kathmandu without a prescription.

Medications and supplies that are useful but not essential are labeled as optional. The suggested quantities of medicines and materials are based on the needs of one person during a three- to four-week visit in Tibet. Check with your doctor on appropriate dosage.

MEDICATIONS

Analgesics/Antiinflammatories

Aspirin or Acetominophen. Ten to twenty tablets (5 grains/325 to 500 mg) for pain, colds, and reducing fever. Aspirin is better as an anti-inflammatory.

Acetominophen with codeine. Ten tablets (325 mg plus 30 mg codeine), or twenty (15 mg) codeine phosphate or codeine sulfate tablets and ten aspirin or acetominophen tablets. Good for moderately severe pain and to suppress coughs.

Ibruprofen. Ten tablets (400 mg). An all-purpose pain reliever and anti-inflammatory for muscles and joints.

Antibiotics

Cephalexin. Fifteen to thirty tablets (250 mg), a penicillin-based drug used to treat skin infections and abscesses, and chest, urinary, inner ear, and sinus infections. Erythromycin (250 mg) is an appropriate substitute for people allergic to penicillin.

Trimethoprim/sulfamethoxazole. Ten tablets of "double-strength" (160 mg/800 mg) for urinary and chest infections, sinusitis, and intestinal infections such as bacterial diarrhea.

Tinidazole. Four to eight tablets (500 mg) for intestinal parasites such as *Giardia* and amoebas, or substitute fifteen to thirty tablets of metronidazole (200 mg).

Naladixic acid. Twenty-four tablets (500 mg) for treating bacterial diarrhea and dysentery.

Opthalmic Antibiotic Cream or Drops. Will help relieve conjuctivitis and other eye infections. *Optional:* A small tube of skin antibiotic cream.

Anti-diarrhea/Gastro-intestinal Medications

Loperamide or Lomotil. Ten tablets to stop diarrhea and associated abdominal cramps. While these medications are especially helpful for controlling diarrhea when traveling on buses or planes, they might prolong the cause of the illness and are dangerous for children.

Anti-acid tablets. Twenty-four to treat upset or acid stomachs.

Anti-worm Medication/Antihelminth. *Optional:* Six tablets (100 mg).

Laxative. *Optional:* Five tablets or suppositories.

Oral Rehydration Salts. *Optional:* Two packets.

Anti-vomiting Medication. *Optional:* Five tablets (25 mg) or suppositories.

Antihistamine

Diphenhydramine (50 mg) **or chlorpheniramine** (4 mg). *Optional:* Five tablets for severe itching, rashes or swelling from allergic reactions or insect bites, hay fever, cold symptoms, and motion sickness.

Decongestants/Respiratory Medications

Nasal decongestant. *Optional:* Ten tablets for relief of cold symptoms, and sinus and inner ear infection; reduces decompression discomfort while flying.

Nose spray or drops. One plastic squeeze bottle (0.25 to 0.50 percent solution).

Throat lozenges. Ten pieces or more (hard candies are a good substitute).

Eucalyptus oil. *Optional:* Five to seven drops of oil in a small basin or large mug of steaming hot water makes a good inhalant.

Aromatic balms. *Optional:* Used as an inhalant or a chest rub; several brands are also excellent topical anti-inflammatories for muscle pain.

High Altitude Medication

Acetazolamide. Ten tablets (250 mg) to prevent symptoms of acute mountain sickness.

BANDAGES AND DRESSINGS

Ten adhesive strips; one roll of 1-inch or 2-inch cloth adhesive tape or micropore tape; one 3-inch-wide elastic bandage; two packets of 4-inch by 4-inch sterile gauze pads; two 2-inch or 3-inch gauze rolls; five butterfly bandages; one triangular bandage or a large handkerchief; two 3-inch by 5-inch sheets of moleskin (cotton felt sheets with an adhesive backing) to place over "hot spots" and blisters. *Optional:* One packet of pre-moistened gelatinous pads for preventing or covering blisters.

BURN TREATMENTS

One or two 5-inch by 9-inch sheets of petroleum dressing (sterile, fine-mesh gauze pads impregnated with a petroleum base, for use on burn wounds). Aloe vera lotion, excellent for healing burns.

DISINFECTANTS

Merbromine solution, highly effective as a drying agent for small cuts, scrapes, and blisters. *Optional:* Povidone-iodine, a topical disinfectant for washing cuts and abrasions, and preventing skin infections; alcohol pads.

MISCELLANEOUS SUPPLIES

Safety pins, sewing needles, scissors, tweezers, thermometer (low-reading, if possible). *Optional:* Cotton swabs; three to five cotton surgical masks (for dusty road conditions); tincture of benzoin, which can help adhesive bandages stick to skin, toughen skin to prevent blisters, and stop bleeding of facial and scalp cuts; it also acts as an inhalant when mixed with hot water.

WATER PURIFICATION

See "Water Purification" under "Health and Medical Problems."

Health and Medical Problems

DIARRHEA AND DYSENTERY

The most common health problems facing travelers in Asia are diarrhea and dysentery. Often given graphic names like "Delhi belly" and the "Kathmandu Quick-step," these chronic intestinal disorders are usually caused by ingesting food or water contaminated by certain pathogenic microorganisms originating from human or animal feces. Because sewage disposal and food preparation conditions in Asia are not always up to Western standards, a few precautions regarding personal hygiene and what you eat or drink can help reduce the chances of getting diarrhea.

Wash your hands often with soap, especially before meals, and don't lick your fingers or use them as a toothpick. Drink only water that has been boiled properly or purified with a form of iodine (see "Water Purification"); this includes the tap water in Lhasa. The Tibetans and Chinese rarely drink water that hasn't been boiled first; their example is a good one to follow. Fresh fruits and vegetables should be peeled or washed in sanitary conditions before they are eaten.

Avoid food in restaurants that obviously has been sitting out for a long time or has been exposed to flies.

Most Chinese and Tibetan hotels and guest houses provide a thermos in every room containing safe, boiled water. *Chhang,* the popular homemade Tibetan beer, is made by mixing fermented barley berries with water, but the water may not have been boiled first. Butter tea and *araa,* a distilled clear alcohol, are safe because they have been boiled, but the cup or bowl it's served in could be your downfall.

The intestinal infections that cause diarrhea in travelers are usually self-limiting and often go away on their own within two days to a week. For most people, this is too long to wait. The best course is to identify the intruding microorganism by means of a laboratory stool test, then take an appropriate antibiotic, but if you are on a trek the only choice is to weigh the evidence of your symptoms and make an educated guess regarding the proper treatment. Most cases of diarrhea fall into one of three categories: simple diarrhea, dysentery, or persistent diarrhea.

Simple Diarrhea

Diarrhea is defined as an abnormally frequent number of unformed stools. The symptoms can vary from mild discomfort and inconvenience to frequent watery stools accompanied by nausea, cramping, vomiting, or fever. Most cases of simple diarrhea are caused by a bacterial infection, particularly from certain pathogenic strains of *E. coli.* Once these bacteria enter the digestive system, they release a toxin that prevents the bowel from absorbing liquids, causing the feces to be expelled as a watery stool. This type of diarrhea usually begins with a sudden onset of symptoms. A person who suddenly has to run to the toilet in the middle of the night, or accidentally has a "liquid fart," most likely has a bacterial intestinal infection. Sulfur-smelling burps and gas will sometimes be present, though these are also common with diarrhea caused by *giardia.*

At present, the drug of preference for bacterial diarrhea is naladixic acid (500 mg). An inexpensive, slightly less effective alternative is the combination antibiotic trimethoprim/sulfamethoxazole, double strength (160 mg/800 mg). Pepto-Bismol has also been found effective for stopping some cases of diarrhea.

Many travelers make the mistake of instantly popping a few Lomotil or loperamide tablets once they have a loose bowel movement. While these two medications are very effective bowel paralyzers and stop diarrhea by constricting the gut, they do not kill the microorganisms causing the problem.

Using antibiotics prophylactically can decrease the likelihood of contracting diarrhea, though there are some drawbacks. Antibiotics can have side effects, such as increased photosensitivity of the skin, which is already a problem in the thin air of Tibet. Extra care must be taken to prevent sunburning, particularly on the back of the hands and the top of the ears. Certain antibiotics can increase the chance of vaginal yeast infections in women.

Some people prefer not to use drugs and attempt to control diarrhea by altering their diet. Eating only simple boiled foods such as plain white rice, boiled noodles, boiled potatoes, plain *daal* (a popular Nepali lentil dish), and weak black tea seems to help ease the stomach back to normal. Greasy or spicy foods, dairy products (except yogurt), meats, nuts, chocolate, coffee, and alcohol should be avoided. Some people feel that yogurt (*zho*) can help reestablish the natural bacterial flora in the intestines. Plain yogurt is sold in jars in most of Tibet's city markets and is usually available where nomadic herders are camped.

Dehydration from diarrhea can cause dizziness and weakness. Ample fluid intake should be encouraged, and a packet of rehydration salts added to a quart (liter) of purified water will help restore the body's depleted electrolytic salts.

Dysentery

Dysentery, a more serious intestinal infection than simple diarrhea, is most easily recognized by the presence of bloody diarrhea or diarrhea with pus, and may be accompanied by stomach cramping and fever. The most common cause of dysentery is the bacteria *shigella,* though in long-term travelers amoebas may be the offending organism. Infection from *shigella* bacteria is spread by contaminated food and water. Like simple diarrhea, the onset of bacterial dysentery is often abrupt, but the symptoms are generally more severe and may persist longer. The treatment for bacterial dysentery is naladixic acid or trimethoprim/sulfamcthoxazole.

Most people who have been in Asia less than a month don't contract amoebas. Amoebic dysentery is caused by the protozoa *Endamoeba histolytica,* a large, single-celled waterborne microorganism. Initial symptoms may be vague or nonexistent, with only mild diarrhea. Eventually chronic diarrhea may occur, with frequent bowel movements producing only small amounts of feces. Blood and pus may be present.

Diagnosing an amoebic infection is not easy, even for a laboratory. The treatment is initially a course of tinidazole, followed by a second drug, diloxanide furoate.

Infection by salmonella bacteria can also cause diarrhea with blood or pus (see "Food Poisoning").

Persistent Diarrhea

Travelers who spend a month or longer in Asia are more prone to persistent types of intestinal infections than short-term travelers. Although these infections are sometimes bacterial, cases of nondysentery diarrhea (with no blood or pus present) that last more than a week are often caused by the protozoa *Giardia lamblia.* Animal feces are a common source of this waterborne parasite, which is found throughout the world.

The symptoms of *giardia* are usually less severe than a bacterial infection and may take a week or two to manifest. Typically the onset is not sudden and may be preceded by stomach rumbles or mild cramping. The diarrhea is usually not watery but moderately frequent, occurring three to five times a day. A bloated stomach, intestinal gas, and sulfurous, rotten egg-smelling burps or gas are common complaints. Fever rarely accompanies *giardia* and vomiting is uncommon. Unlike bacterial infections, this type of diarrhea can linger for weeks if left untreated.

The standard medication for *giardia* is tinidazole, which is available in most Asian countries but not in the United States. A substitute is metronidazole. Avoid alcohol while using either of these drugs.

WATER PURIFICATION

Even high in the mountains of Asia and Tibet, water is often contaminated by herders or livestock and should be treated before drinking, either by boiling or purifying with iodine. Filtering has the advantage of removing sediments, but does not remove certain microorganisms. Most types of chemical purifiers are un-available in Tibet.

Boiling

Water must come to a rolling boil to kill most pathogenic organisms. Al-though water boils at a lower temperature at higher elevations, the boiling point at 20,000 feet (6100 m) is still high enough (176°F, 80°C) to kill all the micro-organisms that cause intestinal infections.

Chemical Disinfectants

Any one of several forms of iodine purification can be used to treat con-taminated water. Chlorine can also be used, though it is less effective at killing amoebas. Iodine is hampered by cold water and sediments. Allow murky water to sit for an hour or two, then decant the clear top layer into another container before purifying. For extremely cold water, double either the time needed for purifica-tion or the dosage. If a sweetener or flavoring is used to mask the iodine taste, add it after the iodine has had time to purify the water. Dissolving a vitamin C tablet in your water can also remove the iodine taste.

Iodine tablets (tetraglycine hydroperiodide) are the most convenient chemical disinfectant for purifying water. Dissolve a tablet in a quart (liter) of water, shake the container, then wait twenty minutes before drinking. Unfortunately, they are relatively expensive and tend to decompose with time after the bottle is opened.

Iodine crystals are the cheapest of all the chemical purifiers and will last for years. Some people find them extremely inconvenient to use. The standard method is to place five to seven grams of iodine crystals in a one-ounce (30 ml) brown glass bottle, fill it with clean water, then let the mixture sit for one hour. A half ounce (15 ml; about four capfuls) of the saturated iodine solution from the storage bottle is then added to a quart (liter) of water. Purification takes twenty minutes. As long as crystals are visible in the storage bottle, even a small amount will con-tinue to disinfect water. Try not to let any of the crystals enter the water bottle, for they are poisonous.

Iodine liquids are inexpensive and easy to use, though they can give water a strong iodine taste. They also have a tendency to leak from Asian-made storage containers. Lugol's solution is an iodine disinfectant available in most Nepali and Indian pharmacies; use five drops per quart (liter) of water and wait twenty minutes before drinking. Tincture of iodine, a 2 percent iodine solution in an alco-hol base, can be found throughout most of Asia, including some pharmacies in Lhasa. Add eight drops per quart (liter) of water and wait twenty minutes before drinking.

State-of-the-art, portable hand-operated water filters that filter out sediments and unpleasant tastes as well as bacteria, *giardia,* and amoebas are now available. They do not, however, filter out hepatitis A or other viruses. Other disadvantages are their weight and the need to frequently change the filter papers or canisters if the water is very dirty.

FOOD POISONING

Food poisoning is the general term for intestinal illnesses caused by eating food contaminated with salmonella or staph bacteria. These microorganisms thrive in warm foods that have been left sitting for several hours without proper refrigeration. Poultry, eggs, mayonnaise, raw meat, and casserole-type dishes are particularly susceptible. As the colonies of bacteria grow, they release very strong toxins into the food. To avoid food poisoning do not eat these foods if they have not been stored properly. The onset of food poisoning is typically abrupt and violent, often within hours after ingesting these toxins. Severe vomiting and frequent diarrhea, sometimes with blood and pus, are the primary symptoms. Nausea, abdominal cramps, and fever with chills can also be present. The recovery time is usually quick, with symptoms lasting twelve to twenty-four hours or until the toxins are eliminated. Usually medication is not necessary.

WORMS

Intestinal worms are the largest of the parasites that can inhabit the intestinal tract. Studies in Kathmandu indicate the incidence in travelers is very low, though roundworms, pinworms, and hookworms are the more common types that can be picked up in Asia. They are contracted by consuming food or water contaminated by feces that contain the eggs of these worms. Rarely are there symptoms other than vague abdominal pains, unexplained weakness, or the presence of worms in the stool. For treatment take an anti-worm medication (antihelminth) such as mebendazole.

ALTITUDE SICKNESS

Acute mountain sickness is better prevented than treated.
Peter Hackett, M.D.

Altitude sickness is an environment-related condition that can affect anyone who ascends too rapidly to high elevations without acclimatizing properly. High elevations are usually considered to be above 10,000 feet (3000 m). In rare cases serious complications, including death, have occurred as low as 8000 feet (2500 m). The most common problem at altitude is acute mountain sickness (AMS). Headache, lack of energy, and shortness of breath while exercising are typical of the symptoms experienced, though the severity and onset vary with each individual. They do not necessarily occur together, nor do they appear at any specific elevation. In extreme situations, the symptoms of AMS may be the preliminary stages of the most serious and potentially deadly altitude-related illnesses, high altitude pulmonary edema (HAPE) and high altitude cerebral edema (HACE). Making a correct diagnosis, and making correct decisions to prevent further complications, are often a matter of following your instincts and using common sense.

The most effective way to prevent altitude-related problems is to give your body sufficient time to adjust to your new environment. Gradual acclimatization is important because the amount of atmospheric oxygen available for breathing at high elevations is considerably less than it is at sea level. At 10,000 feet (3000 m) the partial pressure of oxygen is 30 percent lower than at sea level, at 18,000 feet (5,500 m) it's 50 percent lower. With less oxygen in the air, the ability to perform tasks, even easy chores such as getting dressed, may be exhausting until the body adjusts. The lack of oxygen might also be responsible for triggering the symptoms of AMS.

In popular Himalayan trekking regions such as Nepal, trekkers are encouraged to ascend to high elevations at a slow rate that allows everyone in the party to acclimatize properly. In Tibet, gradual acclimatization is difficult due to the extreme elevation of the entire country: flying into Lhasa means landing at an elevation of around 12,000 feet (3660 m), while driving to Tibet from Nepal involves crossing Thang La (17,060 ft, 5200 m), followed by a night in Dingri or Shegar at about 14,000 feet (4270 m).

For most people the physical adjustment to higher elevations can happen rather quickly, requiring as little as a night of rest at the new elevation. If you fly into Tibet, the ideal situation is to spend three or four days in Lhasa before setting off on a trek. The first day should be treated as a rest day, though a half day of sightseeing at the Jokhang or strolling the Barkor market is fine. During the next few days be more active and try to spend at least a few hours every day going for walks, preferably into the hills. Dayhikes will help you warm up for your trek and the exercise seems to help the body adapt to the altitude. If your time is limited, a minimum of two nights should be spent in Lhasa before starting a trek that ascends above 14,000 feet (4270 m) on the first day.

If you are driving into Tibet from Nepal, consider spending a night acclimatizing in Nyelam before crossing Thang La. The stopover can make a big difference as to how you adapt to the higher elevations over the next few days.

Once a trek begins, the rule of thumb is not to ascend at a rate of over 1300 feet (400 m) per day. For every 3000 feet (1000 m) of ascent, plan on taking one entire rest/acclimatization day. If you're feeling well, use these days to explore nearby valleys or climb onto a ridge for panoramic views; it's better to stay active than laze around camp.

Some people just don't acclimatize well at high elevations, regardless of the precautions taken and how slowly they ascend. One medication that has been found useful for preventing the symptoms of AMS is acetazolamide, a sulfa drug and a mild diuretic. Anyone ascending rapidly to high elevations (which is the case with all tourists coming to Tibet) or having a history of altitude-related problems should consider taking acetazolamide a few hours before the flight to Lhasa, or the morning of departure from the Nepal–Tibet border. The usual dosage is one 250 mg tablet, two times a day, though some people prefer to take only half a tablet each time. (The smaller dosage is still effective but helps reduce the need to urinate frequently.) Do not take acetazolamide if you are allergic to sulfa drugs. It has no known harmful side effects and can be taken for several days, even weeks, though some people experience an unpleasant tingling feeling in the fingers, toes, or lips. Be sure to drink plenty of fluids to prevent dehydration while using this drug.

Maintaining an adequate fluid intake at high elevations may also be helpful in preventing altitude sickness. Most people need between two to five quarts (liters) of liquid per day to remain properly hydrated in Tibet's dry mountain climate. The color and volume of your urine is generally a good clue: drink enough to keep it clear and abundant.

Acute Mountain Sickness (AMS)

AMS is the general term for a number of high altitude–related symptoms. The severity of these symptoms and the rate of their onset depend on factors such as how fast a person ascends at high elevations, the maximum elevation reached, and the susceptibility of each individual. Most people who ascend to elevations between 11,000 to 20,000 feet (3,350 to 6100 m) will experience one or more of the following mild symptoms of typical AMS: headache, lack of energy, lack of appetite, nausea, vomiting, shortness of breath while exercising, difficulty sleeping at night, light-headedness, peripheral edema (swelling of the hands, feet or face), Cheyne-Stokes breathing (a condition of unusual respiration patterns), or feelings similar to those accompanying a case of the flu.

Any of these symptoms can appear on its own and be unrelated to an increase in elevation. If more than one symptom is present, the likelihood of having AMS is increased. A headache is one of the most common symptoms of AMS, though other factors such as overexertion, dehydration, and prolonged exposure to the intense mountain sunlight may also be the cause. Headaches of this type will usually go away after resting, having a cup of hot soup or tea, or taking aspirin or acetaminophen. An AMS headache does not go away so easily and may linger on despite medication. Waking in the morning with a headache is also a sign of not acclimatizing properly, especially if the headache does not go away after you have moved about or taken aspirin. A severe or progressively worsening headache, particularly if accompanied by vomiting, lassitude, or ataxia (loss of balance), could well be the first sign of HACE.

In general, the best approach is to consider any symptom observed at high elevations to be altitude-related until it can be proven otherwise. Mild to moderate AMS symptoms are typically self-limiting and improve on their own after a day, or can be treated by stopping an ascent. Acetazolamide may be helpful for relieving AMS symptoms, though it is important to realize that it is not a cure for AMS. Acetazolamide can also be useful for stopping altitude-related insomnia and irregular breathing. Aspirin or acetaminophen can be taken along with acetazolamide to relieve altitude headaches. Pain medications with codeine should be avoided because they can suppress the respiratory system, depressing the body's blood oxygen levels. The same is true for sleeping pills, barbituates, sedatives, and alcoholic drinks. Administering oxygen (some rooms at the Lhasa Holiday Inn have oxygen outlets near the beds) is sometimes helpful at a flow of two liters per minute, though oxygen is not necessarily curative and the problems could return once it is discontinued.

If symptoms do not improve or become worse despite treatment, a more severe stage of AMS is indicated and further action is necessary to prevent deadly complications such as HAPE or HACE. Although several drugs are known to temporarily relieve these symptoms, the most guaranteed means for alleviating AMS is to DESCEND TO A LOWER ELEVATION.

Often a descent of 1000 to 3000 feet (600 to 900 m), or to the elevation where the person last felt well, is all that is needed for rapid improvement. After a few days of rest, it may be possible to resume the trek and continue beyond the highest elevation previously gained if care is taken to acclimatize during the re-ascent.

Descending to a lower elevation is not always practical in Tibet; with serious cases of AMS the only choice may be evacuation by plane to the lower elevations of Kathmandu or to Chengdu in China's Szechuan province. Vehicle evacuation to Nepal may be the quickest alternative from the Everest region, though this involves crossing Thang La to reach the border.

Some people refuse to accept that they could have an altitude-related problem, or refuse to admit it to others in their group for fear of upsetting everyone's trekking plans. This is especially true with people who have had previous experience at high altitudes, but ascending to high elevations without complications in the past does not mean altitude problems cannot occur the next time. Something —perhaps diarrhea or a cold—can tip the balance, causing symptoms of AMS to manifest. There are cases of mountaineers who successfully climbed Mount Everest, yet died later of severe mountain sickness while climbing a lower mountain. The majority of AMS deaths seem to occur when people deny their situation.

High Altitude Pulmonary Edema (HAPE)

HAPE and HACE are considered the most dangerous forms of altitude sickness. Anyone suspected of suffering from their symptoms should be watched carefully; both illnesses can worsen overnight, becoming life-threatening in as little as eight to twelve hours after being recognized. In many cases HAPE and HACE occur together.

HAPE occurs when the alveoli, or air spaces, that comprise most of the lung tissue become flooded with fluids. One of the first symptoms is a dry, persistent cough that is present during exercise as well as at rest. Coughs caused by the dry air are common in Tibet, but a persistent cough that is not associated with a cold or a chest infection is a warning sign of HAPE. Other important symptoms are excessive shortness of breath and a long recovery time after exercise. Most people will experience some shortness of breath after being active at high elevations, but unusually labored breathing compared to others in the group could be due to HAPE. In HAPE's more advanced stages breathlessness occurs even after resting fifteen to twenty minutes. The cough becomes wet and eventually produces frothy sputum (phlegm) that may have a pinkish color or be streaked with blood. Sometimes a gurgling sound can be heard in the chest. At this point death could be only hours away.

Once HAPE has been diagnosed or is highly suspected, it is imperative that the affected person *descend immediately* to a lower elevation, even if it's late at night. If the person cannot walk unassisted, he or she should be carried in a litter or ride on a horse or yak. If oxygen is available, an initial flow of four to six liters per minutes should be used for fifteen minutes, followed by two liters per minute. Oxygen is sometimes helpful for mild cases of pulmonary edema, but it is usually not curative without descending to a lower elevation. Recovery after descent can be rapid. There is no completely effective drug regime for treating HAPE once the symptoms are present.

High Altitude Cerebral Edema (HACE)

HACE occurs when the brain cells fill with abnormal quantities of fluid, preventing the brain from functioning normally. The symptoms of HACE are basically the same as a moderate case of AMS, but are much more severe and unresponsive to treatment. It is important to differentiate between the two; the condition of someone with HACE can deteriorate rapidly, causing him or her to go into a coma or possibly resulting in death. Important signals to watch for are ataxia (lack of muscular coordination or balance), a severe headache, and vomiting. A headache caused by AMS can be difficult to differentiate from one due to HACE, but a crushing headache accompanied by vomiting and/or ataxia is not a good sign and must be treated as a preliminary stage of HACE. Lassitude (unusually intense, persistent weariness or marked indifference to everyday events such as eating or personal hygiene), mental confusion, and unusual behavior may also be present.

Ataxia is probably the best indication that a person has HACE. If someone staggers into camp at the end of the day looking quite ill, an easy test for ataxia is to have him or her walk slowly for ten to fifteen feet (3 to 5 m), heel to toe, along a line drawn on the ground (heavy hiking or climbing boots should first be removed). A normal person should not have any difficulty passing this test; someone with mild ataxia will sway and be off-balance but can complete the test. Suspect HACE if the person steps off the line, staggers, or falls down. However, if a person has no other signs of AMS the lack of coordination or balance might be due to hypothermia or exhaustion. If the ataxia has not improved after he or she has warmed up with a hot drink and had a rest, preparations should be made to go immediately to a lower elevation. Ataxia may worsen quickly, forcing the victim to be carried in a litter. Oxygen should be administered at a flow of four to six liters per minute if available. Dexamethasone—a 10 mg injection initially, then 6 mg every six hours for no more than three or four days—is helpful when descent is impossible, or can be used in conjunction with descent to allow the victim to assist with the rescue efforts. *This powerful anti-inflammatory steroid should only be administered by a doctor.*

RESPIRATORY AILMENTS

Coughs and colds caused by the dry air in Tibet are a common problem with trekkers. Throat lozenges and hard candies are good for soothing irritated throats. Aspirin or acetaminophen with codeine will help control coughs, though codeine has a tendency to suppress the respiratory system, making its use at high elevations questionable. If a person is coughing up phlegm, use a cough expectorant rather than a cough suppressant. Yellow or green phlegm is probably a sign of a chest infection.

The common cold is a viral infection. Runny nose, stuffy head, and a low-grade fever are the usual symptoms. Aspirin or acetaminophen can offer some relief, as can nasal sprays, cold tablets, or antihistamines.

Sinusitis is a bacterial infection of the sinus passages, which are located beside the nose and the eyebrows. Headache and localized pain at the sinuses help differentiate it from a common cold. Treatment with an antibiotic such as cephalexin is sometimes necessary.

A chest cold that produces thick yellow or green phlegm accompanied by a fever is probably bronchitis, a bacterial respiratory infection. Steam inhalants, especially with eucalyptus oil added, can help break up congestion in the lungs. Using antibiotics is not necessarily recommended, but they can help prevent more serious complications such as pneumonia. Ampicillin, trimethoprim/sulfamethoxazole, or erythromycin are usually prescribed.

Pneumonia, a more advanced chest infection than bronchitis, occurs when the alveoli in the lung tissues fill with infected fluid. Persistent coughing, chest pain, difficulty breathing, and a fever of more than 102°F (39°C) are usually present. Sputum will be yellow or green, but streaked with blood and often containing pus. Ampicillin, penicillin, or cephalexin are recommended antibiotics for pneumonia.

HYPOTHERMIA

Also referred to as exposure, hypothermia occurs when the body's internal temperature drops to a dangerously low level. The combination of being wet, cold, and physically exhausted often leads to hypothermia. If it is not treated properly, it can quickly lead to death, even at temperatures well above freezing.

The symptoms of hypothermia are often subtle and difficult to detect. When a body becomes cold, its natural reaction is to shiver, sometimes uncontrollably. Muscular coordination decreases and simple tasks, especially those using the hands, become difficult. If body temperature continues to fall the body's mechanism for shivering can actually stop; this is a classic sign that someone is suffering from hypothermia. In some cases, a severely chilled person may no longer realize he or she is very cold. Mental confusion, unusual behavior, slurred speech, and ataxia can also occur with hypothermia. If no attempt is made to raise the body temperature, unconsciousness or even death will follow.

Anyone showing the first signs of hypothermia should seek shelter from the conditions causing the problem, particularly the wind. Wet clothes should be removed and the person should drink hot, sweetened liquids; a quick calorie boost is important. If the person cannot be warmed by conventional means, he or she should be stripped to the skin or a layer of underwear and put into a sleeping bag with another person dressed similarly.

Diagnosing hypothermia is easier if you have a low-reading thermometer. Body temperatures a degree or two below normal (98.6°F, 37°C) are not unusual; temperatures below 96°F (35.6°C) are probably due to hypothermia.

Effective waterproof raingear and protection from the wind are essential for preventing hypothermia. Avoid wearing cotton clothing against the skin; when cotton gets wet it loses 90 percent of its ability to retain heat. Instead, wear wool, silk, or synthetics such as polypropylene next to your skin; they remain warm even when wet.

FROSTBITE

Frostbite, the freezing of body tissues, most commonly affects the fingers, toes, and face. It can occur due to internal heat loss in the extremities or through direct exposure to cold temperatures and windy conditions. Hypothermia and the constriction of the blood vessels caused by high elevations can also be contributing factors. Initially the affected areas feel cold, painful, and may be pale. As the tissues freeze, the pain subsides to numbness.

Prevention is the best remedy, for many cases can be avoided by wearing adequate protection from the cold. Good footwear is essential in snowy conditions, particularly for winter treks. Wear warm gloves and use a scarf or balaclava to protect the face from wind and cold.

If you think you have frostbite, try to rewarm that part of the body by placing it under your armpit, between your legs, or even on someone else's stomach. If the frostbite is minor, the color and feeling will eventually return. In more serious cases the frozen tissue will feel hard, cold, and be unresponsive to warming. Do not rub the affected area with snow or try to restore circulation by rubbing it vigorously with your hands; do not immerse it in water to encourage thawing. Less damage will be done to a frozen foot by walking out on it than by thawing it too soon. A frozen foot or hand should be left alone until a medical facility can be reached.

SUN-RELATED PROBLEMS

Tibet's high altitude and thin atmosphere allow the sun's solar radiation to strike the earth with unusual intensity. Very little of the ultraviolet light is filtered out, causing skin to burn much more rapidly than at lower elevations. A sunscreen with a sun protection factor (SPF) of 15 or more is recommended to guarantee protection of exposed skin. Sunscreens with para-aminobenzoic acid (PABA) in an alcohol base are considered the most effective and longest lasting, but they do tend to stain light-colored clothes. Lip creams and balms are also sold with SPF ratings; zinc oxide creams provide 100 percent blockout. In a pinch use toothpaste as a substitute. Sun hats are essential; broad-brimmed Tibetan felt hats cost only $5 to $7 (U.S.) and can be purchased in the Lhasa and Shigatse markets. Inexpensive woven straw hats are also available.

Treat sunburn as you would any other burn. For skin that is red and painful, use a soothing cream such as aloe vera. If blisters have formed try not to break them. For particularly bad burns, bathe the area gently with cold clean water and cover with a bandage that won't stick to the burn.

Snowblindness occurs when bright sunlight reflected off snow, ice, or water burns the cornea of the eye. It can happen after only a few hours of exposure, but is easily prevented with adequate eye protection. Sunglasses with polarized lenses are fine around cities and on the trail, but for winter treks or visits to the mountaineering camps near Mount Everest or other mountains, darker glasses are needed that will filter out all ultraviolet light. These glasses typically have hoods on the stems and are known as glacier glasses.

Snowblindness is hard to detect because initially there is no pain nor other sensations to warn that the eyes are being burned. Symptoms usually develop in the evening after exposure. The eyes become painfully irritated, feeling as if there is sand in them. They usually appear watery and bloodshot, and the eyelids may swell shut. Cold compresses will temporarily ease the discomfort; aspirin or another analgesic can be taken for pain. An antibiotic ophthalmic ointment or drops can help soothe the eyes and shorten the recovery time, which is usually two to three days.

ANIMAL BITES

Animal bites should be taken seriously, for the chances are high that an infection will occur. Unfortunately for trekkers, the dogs in Tibet do not seem to like the smell of foreigners and bites are not uncommon. If you are bitten, immediately wash the wound site with soap and water, then rinse it for at least twenty minutes, preferably with an iodine disinfectant or with water purified with a double dose of iodine. It is especially important to wash out any saliva that might have entered the wound. Cover the bite with a sterile bandage and watch for signs of infection.

The presence of rabies in Tibet must be assumed. Because it is transmitted by the saliva of an infected animal, the bite must break the skin to spread the infection. It is easy to determine if an animal has rabies: observe the animal for ten days, if possible, and if it is still alive and healthy at the end of that time it was not infected. If the animal is unavailable or if it dies, the bitten person should begin the series of rabies immunization shots as soon as possible. A delay of a week to ten days is usually not a problem, but the sooner the series begins the better. The rabies vaccine is available at the Renmin, or People's Hospital, in Lhasa and at a number of clinics in Kathmandu.

Hospitals and Other Health Facilities

Hospitals and health clinics in Central Tibet are primarily located in Lhasa, Shigatse, and Tsethang. The language barrier can be a problem, so it is a good idea to bring along a Chinese interpreter.

HOSPITALS

In Lhasa, the main hospital recommended for foreigners is the Renmin, or People's Hospital, on Dzugtrun Lam, the east–west street north of the Potala. It has an emergency room as well as an aliens' (foreigners) clinic with a doctor generally on duty from 9 A.M. to 5 P.M.

The Lhasa People's Hospital (the City Hospital) is located at the east end of Lhasa on Dekyi Bhar Lam, just past the Banok Shol hotel. Although the recommended hours for visitation are 9 A.M. to 5 P.M., the doctor who sees foreigners is generally available in the evenings from 7 P.M. to 9 P.M.

The Holiday Inn in Lhasa has a doctor's clinic for their guests, with a medical staff provided by the People's Hospital. Consultations are arranged through the assistant manager in the hotel lobby. Visitation fees are in addition to the costs of any medicines provided.

The Tibetan Medicine Hospital, called the Menzi Khang, is located across from the Barkor Square. Hours are from 9:30 A.M. to 1:30 P.M. and 3:30 P.M. to 6 P.M.; the hospital is closed on Sunday. Diagnosis of an illness is done by traditional Tibetan medicinal techniques, such as feeling the pulse and examining the urine, and the medicines prescribed are mostly traditional Tibetan herbal preparations. Foreigners should report to the outpatient section. If you have a chance, ask permission to see the beautiful collection of medical-oriented *thangka* paintings displayed on the hospital's top floor.

In Shigatse, a modern, multistory hospital is located about a ten-minute walk north of the Shigatse Hotel. If the main central entrance is locked, try the emergency room entrance to the right.

In Tsethang, the hospital is located on the north side of the main road to Gongkar Airport, near the T intersection with the road leading south toward the main part of the city. There is also a hospital in Chonggye.

The hospital closest to the Everest region is in Shegar (turnoff at km marker 482/3). It has several inpatient wards and a few doctors, though the Shigatse hospital is better equipped for serious injuries or illnesses.

DENTISTS

The only proper dental facility (by Western standards) in Central Tibet is in Lhasa at the Military Hospital Dental Clinic on Xingfu Xi Lu Street, near the Holiday Inn. It has modern equipment and will accept foreigners. The only alternative is to use one of the streetside dentists displaying sets of false teeth in the city markets.

PHARMACIES

Most of the pharmacies in Lhasa are located along the main street, Dekyi Shar Lam, either below the Potala or closer to the Barkor near the Yak and Kirey hotels. Some of these shops have signs with a red cross or the word *"Pharmacy."* They typically sell Chinese and Tibetan medicines, but also some Western antibiotics, analgesics, and vitamins. Many pharmacies double as outpatient clinics. If you need a specific drug, bring a sample if you have one.

The best pharmacies in Shigatse and Tsethang are located in the city hospitals. The usual procedure is to meet with a doctor, who will then prescribe the medicine. If a doctor is not available, you might be able to convince a nurse to sell you medicine if you can mime your complaint or if you have a drug sample.

CLINICS IN NEPAL

Sometimes it is best to see a Western doctor in a private, Western-style clinic, either out of necessity or simply for peace of mind. If someone is injured or becomes seriously ill during a trek in the Everest or Shishapangma regions, you should seriously consider going to one of the clinics in Kathmandu. They are closer than the hospital in Shigatse and the facilities are superior. The best-known (and most expensive) clinic with Western doctors is the CIWEC clinic in Baluwatar (phone 410983) across from the Russian Embassy. Another reliable clinic with a highly qualified Western-trained doctor is the Nepal International Clinic (phone 412842), located across from the Royal Palace on a side street near the cinema. The Tribuwan University Teaching Hospital on Maharaj Ganj Street has a good emergency room–outpatient service.

4   Traveling in Tibet

Accommodations

In the days before restrictions were placed upon individual travel, it was possible to stay in any of Tibet's hotels or guest houses. In Lhasa, most overland travelers stayed in budget-oriented accommodations such as the Yak, Banok Shol, Kirey, and Snowlands hotels at the eastern end of the city. Since martial law was lifted in May 1990, all official tour and trekking groups coming to Lhasa, including private FITs, are required to stay at the larger, more expensive hotels such as the Holiday Inn, the Tibet Guesthouse, the Sunlight Hotel, or the new Himalaya Hotel near the river. The few individuals who manage to sneak into Lhasa are once again staying in the smaller, Tibetan-run hotels, though the Public Service Bureau has threatened to stop these establishments from accepting foreign guests.

Accommodation restrictions have not been enforced outside of Lhasa. In Gyantse and Shigatse, tour groups typically stay at the expensive but poorly managed Gyantse Hotel and Shigatse Hotel. If you are arranging a private group and want to keep the budget low, consider staying at one of the local Tibetan or Chinese hotels. The last time I was in Gyantse I found two truck stops with dormitory rooms located across from each other just before the main part of town. In Shigatse, the Tenzin Hotel across from the covered Tibetan market is a homey-feeling guest house with nicely decorated rooms on the top floor. There may not be hot showers or running water here, but the atmosphere more than makes up for the lack of modern facilities. Two Chinese-run hotels are located near the Shigatse bus station.

Beyond the cities the quality of accommodation is rather similar from one town to another: basic. Large towns and some villages along the main roads will have a truck stop with dormitory rooms; you can also camp or possibly find a family to take you in. If you stay in a private home, your guide can help arrange the price for sleeping and any meals provided.

Truck-stop dormitories are notorious for having sheets and quilts that haven't been washed in weeks. Just give them a good shake to knock off the dust and sleep in your inner sheet beneath the quilt. The pillows can be real classics—my favorites are the ones filled with sand. For privacy you may want to pay for all the beds in one room to avoid new roommates stumbling in late at night; truck-stop managers try to keep everyone in as few rooms as possible. Boiled hot drinking water is provided in a thermos, usually once in the morning and again at night. Metal wash basins should be under the beds or with the manager. If there are no restaurants nearby or you arrive late, it may be possible to have the manager prepare tea or even a meal. The manager also handles the keys for your room; every time you go out the manager must be found to get back in.

Rooms are paid for in the evening, not in the morning. If you plan to return after your trek, it should be possible to have gear stored until you get back.

Transportation

The current rules governing tourism in Tibet require that all groups be accompanied by a local tour guide and a driver. Whether you are with a commercial trek or have organized a private group, transport will be prearranged as part of your trek and tour package. Japanese minibuses and four-wheel-drive vehicles are the standard form of transportation. The handful of individuals who have found their way into Lhasa since martial law ended have not been allowed to purchase tickets on local buses, though this restriction could be lifted if Tibet's tourism policies change in the future. Ironically, they *have* been able to hire four-wheel-drive vehicles and drivers from local travel companies and go almost anywhere in Central Tibet anyway.

Local buses are often tumble-down affairs that typically set off in the cold, predawn hours. The large "new" bus station in Lhasa is a twenty-minute walk to the south of the Holiday Inn, near the river. Buses depart from here for Shigatse, the Nepal border (Khasa), Golmud, Chengdu, and places in between. Previously, individuals could also purchase tickets from the sidewalk booths and tables set up near the old bus station, just east of the post office by the Potala. Seats are sold several days in advance to Shigatse, Nagchhu, Tsethang, Madhrogongkar, and Golmud. Pilgrim trucks and buses gather passengers for Ganden almost every morning before dawn on the Barkor, and there may be trucks heading to other pilgrimage sites on special festival days. In Shigatse the bus station is a few minutes' walk west of the Shigatse Hotel, across from the truck stop.

The only CAAC (China National Airline Corporation) airline offices are in Lhasa. The main ticketing office is tucked into a compound near the Potala, behind the post office. The Holiday Inn has a CAAC branch office on the ground floor.

Money

The Tibetan monetary system was dismantled in the 1950s and replaced with the Communist Chinese currency, *renminbi* ("Peoples' Money"), which is based on the *yuan*. One *yuan* is treated much like a dollar in our currency, being divided into 100 cents, called *fen*. Coins of one, two, and five *fen* are in circulation. The paper money starts with one-, two-, and five-*fen* notes, which are tough to identify because they lack numerals. Instead they have pictures of trucks, planes, and ships, respectively. All notes are color- and size-coded. The lowest paper note with a numeral is worth one *jiao*, or ten *fen*, much like a dime equals ten cents. The people in Tibet and western China often call this denomination by another name, one *mao*. Two other small notes are worth two *jiao* (twenty *fen*) and five *jiao* (fifty *fen*). The one-*yuan* note is most commonly called one *kwai* by locals. Larger denominations include the two-, five-, ten-, fifty-, and 100-*yuan* notes. As of 1990, 4.7 *yuan* equal $1 (U.S.).

There's more. Tourists are given an entirely different currency, called Foreign Exchange Certificates (FEC), when exchanging cash or traveler's checks at a bank. The proletariat images on the *renminbi* are replaced by waterfalls, the Great Wall, and other scenic settings, yet FECs are worth exactly the same as an equivalent-denomination *renminbi* note. Theoretically, foreigners must conduct all financial transactions in FEC. In practice, half the people in Tibet have never seen these notes and refuse to accept them, especially out in the country. If you go trekking, you are forced to use the black market to acquire *renminbi.* Because the Chinese *renminbi* is not a recognized international currency, a premium is placed on FECs since they are only issued against hard currency. To the city folk of China they are as good as dollars, and can be used to purchase imported foreign goods that otherwise would not be available to them. The street rate in 1990 was about 120 *renminbi* for 100 FEC. Remember, the black market is illegal.

When you leave Tibet or China, leftover FEC can be exchanged back to hard currency if you have your bank encashment receipts. The banks refuse to exchange any *renminbi,* even if you didn't use the black market but received it as change.

Cultural Considerations

Tourism is often viewed as a two-headed monster, providing a major source of hard currency for many developing countries while eroding the very culture and environment that attracted the tourists in the first place. Tibet opened to tour groups in 1979, but travel restrictions kept the annual tourist numbers below 2000 for the first five years. When you visit Tibet, you are still, in a sense, a pioneer of tourism. Your actions and the actions of others in your group, especially while you are trekking in remote areas, will have a bearing upon the way people will react toward other trekkers who visit in later years.

One of the first priorities is to wear proper attire in Tibet. As I mentioned in "Hints for Women Trekkers," shorts should never be worn by women, or men, even during a trek. The Tibetan people never show their legs; you should do the same. Men should wear long pants, though knickers are fine for trekking. Women should wear loose-fitting long pants or a calf-length skirt or dress. Women's shirts should be loose-fitting and not revealing, and a bra should be worn. This may seem trivial or an inconvenience, but remember that you are a visitor in their country.

BEGGARS

Religious beggars are an accepted part of society in Tibet and most of Asia. Both lay people and monks may set off across the length of Tibet to Mount Kailas, often on foot, requesting alms to finance pilgrimages that could last months or years. Giving money or food to a pilgrim is considered an act of merit. During important religious festivals, particularly Monlam Chenmo and Saga Dawa, thousands of beggars line the Lingkor and Barkor circuits in Lhasa.

The local Tibetans go from beggar to beggar handing each of them a small coin, for an act of merit is said to be multiplied ten million times on these special occasions. Even when there isn't a festival, religious pilgrims often sit along the Barkor beating drums and chanting prayers, asking for offerings toward their journey. Donations of five *fen* to two *jiao* are appropriate. Have a pocketful of coins ready when visiting the Barkor.

While eating in local restaurants, beggars may approach your table asking for food or money. One standard method of asking is not to extend a hand but to give you the thumbs-up sign and say "guchi guchi," which means "please." In the past few years beggars from mainland China have been turning up in Lhasa. Old men and women dress in shredded, bulky clothing, while the younger ones may have a monkey on a chain, a spectacle of great interest to the Tibetans. These beggars are professionals, having less meritorious intentions than religious pilgrims. Just wave them off as the locals do if you don't want to give anything.

Children have become a nuisance in a few villages of the Everest region, begging for *jhiri,* or sweets. Whatever you do, never give in to their demands. Complying just makes it more difficult for the next trekkers who come along; besides, sugar is bad for those beautiful teeth.

DALAI LAMA PHOTOGRAPHS

When Tibet first opened to tourists, word spread quickly that Dalai Lama photos were a wonderful gift to hand out to the locals. As much as this was appreciated, it had the sad effect of encouraging many Tibetans to endlessly hassle foreigners for pictures of their exiled leader. They may have five photographs of him on their altar at home, yet they will still try to secure one more. Although his photos are available in the markets, you could actually cause a small riot in the Barkor if you started handing out pictures; the pure and un-questioned devotion to this man is unparalleled in our society.

It is not illegal (at this time) to bring "plain" Dalai Lama photos across the borders into Tibet. Any picture portraying him with the Tibetan national flag (a series of blue and red stripes radiating from a sun above two snow lions) or bearing his signature will be confiscated. Although every Tibetan who receives a picture will be thankful from the bottom of his or her heart, use discretion in handing them out. Save them for only the most special recipients and occasions: the friendly monk who brings you to his room for a cup of butter tea; the kind-faced old woman who clasps your hand in hers and leads you around the Barkor; or as a special thank-you for someone who has done you a favor.

The basic rule I use is (almost) never give a Dalai Lama photograph to someone who asks; it will only encourage that person to bother other travelers for more. Also, don't make a big scene in public as you give a photo away. Though nothing would probably happen to you, Big Brother may be watching and the person who receives the picture could be harassed by plainclothes policemen. Tashilhumpo monastery in Shigatse is one place to especially watch your actions. Don't give Dalai Lama photos to any of the monks, for word seems to travel surprisingly fast to the Public Security Bureau.

VISITING MONASTERIES

Tibetan Buddhist monasteries welcome foreign visitors, though a few unwritten rules of conduct should be observed. Women may go into the monasteries and shrines, although several of the larger monasteries, particularly Ganden, have a protector's shrine (*gön-khang*) with a sign requesting that women not enter. Wearing shorts or revealing clothing is not appropriate. Most monasteries in Tibet do not require that you remove your shoes, which is contrary to the rules in Nepal and India (probably due to the colder climate), but if you do notice a pile of shoes at the entrance to a temple, take yours off as well. Always remove your hat (Tibetan women loosen their braids), and never smoke in or near a monastery.

As you enter a temple or shrine, angle to the left so that you will walk around the room in the respectful, clockwise manner. Always keep prayer walls and offering cairns to your right, and walk clockwise around pilgrimage circuits. If the monks are chanting or obviously involved with a religious service, lower your voice and try not to disturb them. If they ask you to join them on the rows of cushions where they are performing the ceremony, go right ahead. Take your shoes off first, then sit cross-legged. Get into the habit of carrying a cup in your daypack, for you'll undoubtedly be offered butter tea. If you don't like butter tea or have had enough, politely say *may,* which means no, and put your hand over the cup. They will still try hard to serve you more.

Don't take photographs in a monastery without first asking permission. Besides potentially angering the monks, you might have to pay a stiff photography fee. The monasteries along the main tourist routes tend to be the worst, for the government requires the monks to collect money for photographs, usually a flat fee of five to twenty *yuan.* Sakya monastery, between Shigatse and the Nepal border, is particularly expensive, charging fifty FEC—about $12 (U.S.)—or more per photo! The Potala Palace also demands high photo fees. The more remote monasteries rarely ask for money; nevertheless, always enquire before snapping pictures. Regardless of whether you take photographs, the smaller temples appreciate donations of one to ten *yuan* to help finance their reconstruction or pay for butter in the lamps. After placing the money on the altar you can ask to have a butter lamp lit, a Tibetan Buddhist practice for offering a blessing to someone.

If you spend the night in a monastery the monks usually won't ask for money, though a donation of ten *yuan* is appropriate, especially if they provide you with butter tea and *thugpa* stew. Don't, however, treat monasteries as hotels; consider it a privilege to be staying there. If the room where you stay has an altar or a picture of the Dalai Lama, sleep so your feet aren't pointing toward any holy images.

VISITING A TIBETAN HOME

Just as in the West, you will be treated with great respect if you are invited into a Tibetan family's home (or tent). Once you are ushered into the darkened room, you will be directed to a raised platform along the wall padded with carpets or yak-hair blankets. As your eyes adjust, many curious, wind-burned little faces will probably be peering at you. The children are shy but brave, and may cautiously poke at your clothes or pull the hairs on your arm. The mother or daughter will stoke the fire, then pour hot tea from a kettle into a large churn. She'll add a few chunks of yak butter, whoosh the mixture up and down with precise motions, and serve it. Get your cup ready! A worn goatskin bag containing *tsampa* will be passed your way. If you like, add a few spoonfuls to your tea, or mix in a few handfuls as the Tibetans do, kneading it to create a ball of dough. "Eat up," they'll imply, and perhaps a leg of dried goat meat and a hefty knife will be offered so you can carve off a slice, then pass them on to the next person.

If you stay the night, they will show you where to sleep. In general, your belongings will be left alone, but keep valuables in a safe place and don't leave your pack open. The children are sometimes prone to pinching little, easy-to-hide objects. In the Everest region, the old grandmothers are the ones to watch. One octogenarian decided my water bottle was just the container she'd been looking for; it took me half a night of polite negotiation to get it back.

Tibetan homes do not have toilets inside and many don't even have one outside; you just wander off and find a private spot—a difficult task in the daytime. To the west of Shigatse many villages have toilets consisting of an elevated, mud-brick platform with a stairway leading up. Around the squat spot is a low wall about one to two feet high, exposing you to the chilly winds and allowing the entire village to watch the foreigner, as if you were onstage. Never drop anything valuable down the hole.

An invitation to stay in a Tibetan home does not always mean you must pay, but you should at least offer. Five *yuan* per person per night is the standard fee for lodging and meals, but this will undoubtedly go up. Establish the price before you sleep to avoid misunderstandings in the morning. As in a monastery, if there is an altar or a holy image in the room where you are staying, sleep with your feet pointing in the opposite direction.

Environmental Awareness

The Sierra Club adage "Take only pictures, leave only footprints" is an appropriate philosophy for preserving Tibet's wilderness. The vast herds of rangeland animals have been greatly reduced over the last several decades and logging interests continue to pressure the virgin southern forests, yet Tibet is probably the least spoiled region along the Himalaya. The low population has much to do with this, but so has the delayed introduction of tourism. The trails in Tibet are surprisingly litter-free, even along the popular routes near Samye monastery and Mount Everest, with the main exception being the Dza Rongphu/Everest base camp area.

It should go without saying that you are not to litter or leave garbage at your campsites. If you smoke cigarettes, the butts look as bad as other types of litter once they are on the ground—put them in your pocket. When you have a bowel movement, dig a hole or scrape away fallen leaves and vegetation, then be like a cat and cover up what you deposit. Always burn your toilet paper, don't just bury or hide it. Use a cigarette lighter (superior to matches if it's windy) and unfold the paper first before burning. Light it from the bottom, allowing the flame to burn upwards. If the paper is wadded into a ball it won't burn very well.

When the flame is out, step on the ashes to knock them apart. If you're with a commercial trekking company it may provide a toilet tent for use in camp, erected over a narrow pit dug into the ground. Be sure to ask your trek staff if a shovel or ice ax is provided for digging toilet holes, for the ground tends to be very hard. The toilet tents should be 150 feet (46 m) or more from any streams, and don't let the staff dig the toilet hole in the middle of a beautiful meadow; the scar could last for decades. Burn toilet paper in the toilet tent as well (animals and curious herders sometimes dig up these holes, scattering the used paper), and kick a bit of dirt over your business before you exit the tent. Each morning after breaking camp, someone in your group should check to see if the toilet hole has been properly filled in, not just partially covered with a big rock. Trekking staffs throughout the Himalaya are very slack about covering the toilet holes; it's a job they prefer to avoid.

Another way you can help Tibet's environment is to watch how your staff disposes of garbage. Hiding cans and bottles in the bushes or under rocks is not acceptable, and burying is difficult due to the hard ground. If the yaks can bring them in, they can haul them back out again. Some trek staffs may resist this idea, saying the yak men won't agree, but they're mostly trying to avoid the inconvenience of handling garbage. Organic wastes can be buried or fed to the yaks, and paper waste should be burned. All other trash should be packed out for disposal, preferably in a plastic-lined sack or duffel bag. Because small towns have no landfill system nor garbage collection service, the best place to dispose of the refuse from a trek is usually at the next large hotel you stay in.

Discarded rubbish left by mountaineering expeditions, Everest base camp (photo by Wendy Brewer-Lama)

Children will sometimes come to your camp begging for empty cans. While bottles with tops can be used as storage containers, pop-top soft drink or beer cans will merely be used as playtoys until the novelty wears off, and then will be discarded. Crush all cans after use to prevent this indirect form of littering.

Wherever you camp, try to leave the site in better condition than when you arrived. If paper or trash is around, pack it out with the garbage from your trek. If you are camped in an area where bushes or trees grow, encourage your staff to use their kerosene stoves instead of the local wood. If other members of your group are not properly disposing of their toilet paper or personal trash, perhaps you could initiate a discussion after dinner one night, asking if everyone is burning their toilet paper. Some people have no idea that burning is preferred to burying or hiding it.

Washing your clothes or body will inevitably introduce soap into the streams, but you can reduce the amount by using a wash basin fifteen feet or more from the water's edge. Toss the soapy water away from the stream, then refill the basin with more water. Encourage your trek staff to do the same. Never wash pots and pans directly in a stream or lake. (Bring biodegradable soap from home, for it is difficult to find in Asia.)

Dealing with Dogs

The Tibetan mastiff guard dogs are very aggressive, for they are trained to protect the sheep and goats from wolf attacks and rustlers. Whenever you approach a herders' camp or a village, always keep in mind that a guard dog may be off its chain. Foreigners especially seem to spook the Tibetan dogs, perhaps because we smell different. In the cities the dogs are somewhat calmer in our presence, though in the countryside they're ferocious. I always carry a handful of golfball-size stones as I enter a new settlement or encampment. The dogs are wary of being hit and often keep their distance if you just pretend to throw a stone. A sturdy walking stick is also handy for fending off dogs, and loose long trousers can prevent them from biting your leg if they get close enough to try. If you are bitten, wash the wound with plenty of soap and water for at least twenty minutes; infection is a common problem with any animal bite. The presence of rabies has not been confirmed in Tibet, but you must assume it exists. For more information on treating animal bites, see "Staying Healthy."

Shopping for Food in Tibet

The trekking company handles all the food purchasing and preparation on a commercial trek; the kitchen staff even does the dishes. On private treks you have the choice of organizing your own food or paying the trekking agent to arrange it. The latter choice is probably the best: all you will need to do is spend a few hours in the market before your trek buying fresh vegetables and any special food preferences to supplement what the company provides.

If you have trekked in Nepal, you may be spoiled by the incredible selection of tasty Western-type foods available there. The range of food items in Tibet has improved much since 1985, but the variety pales compared to Nepal. Nonetheless, it is possible to find sufficient types of food to outfit your trek, though a few items brought in from elsewhere can help brighten up the meal selections. One of the big surprises in Tibet is the wide variety of vegetables, most of which are flown or driven in from China's Szechuan province.

Breakfast is the most difficult to prepare on a trek with locally available foods. Rice porridge, flat breads, steamed breads, pancakes, and different egg preparations are some possibilities. If you like a hearty breakfast you'll want to bring oat or wheat porridge, muesli, or granola from home or Nepal. For other meals, stock up on peanut butter, jam, honey, and other spreadables to have with the various types of bread in Tibet. Packets of soup mix from home bolstered with extra spices and chopped vegetables can be used to make sauces for noodle or rice dishes. Desserts are a problem if you enjoy something sweet after the evening meal; consider bringing packets of custard powder, fruit-flavored gelatin, and instant mixes such as pudding, mousse, and cheesecakes.

The following foods are available in the city markets, particularly in Lhasa; remember that little is available once you are off the main roads. The standard measurement for weighing goods is the Chinese *jin,* which equals 1.1 pounds (0.5 kg).

Rice: Difficult to find in the markets because it is rationed. Purchase from a local Chinese restaurant.

Noodles: Delicious wheat noodles made locally are sold in bundled packets. Instant noodle soups from China and Nepal are also available.

Tea: Chinese green tea (jasmine) and Tibetan brick tea are the standard. Bring black tea from home or Nepal. Most Tibetans drink salted tea churned with butter, though sweet milky tea is served in Tibetan tea houses.

Coffee: Indian-made Nescafé is now available, but can't compare to Western instant brands.

Hot chocolate mix: Sold in six-inch-tall beige- and gray-colored cans with Chinese characters, but difficult to recognize that it is chocolate.

Milk powder: So sweet you should consider bringing powdered milk from home or Nepal.

Sugar: Large crystals but widely available.

Butter: Yak butter is the standard. Try it before buying, for it tends to be a bit rancid.

Cooking oil: Low-quality, strong-tasting mustard oil is usually the only choice in the markets.

Bread: Baked flat breads are sold every morning in the larger cities, as are twisted fried breads. Some Chinese restaurants make steamed bread, called *mon-tou,* each morning, and Tibetan families sometimes make a flat brown bread called *bhalay.*

Flour: *Tsampa,* roasted barley flour, is the staple food of Tibet and available everywhere. It can be used to make a slightly nutty-tasting porridge. Wheat flour is also available.

Eggs: Plenty around, but rarely are there chickens in the villages.

Yogurt: Each morning women come to the city markets to sell jars of fresh yogurt. It is safe and delicious; only the *droqpa,* the nomadic herders of Tibet, have a yummier version. Mix the yogurt with fresh or bottled fruit, have it with muesli, or put it through a strainer to make cream cheese. Three of the thin Chinese-style nylon socks (washed, of course), one put inside another, provide the proper thickness for straining. For a savory treat stir in chopped garlic and a few spices (basil or oregano). Hang the sock strainer above a pan for about half a day to drain off excess liquid, then spoon out the resulting cream cheese into a storage container.

Jam: Very sweet fruit jams can be found in some shops.

Walnuts: Unshelled nuts are abundant during autumn.

Raisins: From Xinjiang province, they're delicious but tend to be filthy. Wash raisins several times before eating.

Cheese: Hard, dried types of cheese are widely available. Some of the finer grades taste something like Parmesan. Nepal has large wheels of aged cheeses if you're passing through en route to Tibet.

Tinned meats: Pork, a staple in the Chinese diet, comes in many forms, including tinned pig's feet. Canned sardines in tomato sauce may be more appetizing. Tuna is not available.

Salt: Rock salt is most common.

Spices: Chile peppers are widely available, along with lemon pepper and Aji-no-moto, a common brand name for monosodium glutamate (MSG). Bring curry-type spices, black pepper, cinnamon, basil, oregano, and other standard spices from home.

Meat: Yak meat is most common in the markets, though beef, goat meat, and mutton are also available.

Vegetables: Many kinds of vegetables are sold in the markets, particularly in Lhasa's covered Chinese vegetable market behind the post office, near the Potala Palace. Bargain hard for the correct price. If someone is being difficult, move on to another seller. Most of the following vegetables can be found during the summer months: bean sprouts, cabbage, carrots, cauliflower, Chinese cabbage, Chinese parsley, cucumber, eggplant, garlic, ginger, green beans, lettuce, onions, peas, potatoes, radishes, spinach, tomatoes, turnips, and zucchini and other squashes.

Fruit: Apples and pears fill the markets during autumn. In summer bananas and mandarin oranges are brought in from Nepal and India.

Preserved fruit: Many different kinds of fruits are bottled or tinned in syrup. Canned peaches prepared for export are some of the nicest. Other good export-quality foods include fruit juices, tomato paste, and tomato puree.

5 Tibetan for Trekkers

Every district its own dialect; every lama his own doctrine.
Tibetan proverb quoted in the
1920 edition of Charles Bell's
*English Tibetan Colloquial
Dictionary*

Learning to Speak Tibetan

As this old saying suggests, the spoken word of Tibet is not a single standardized language, but a wide-ranging group of related local dialects that are scattered across the Tibetan Plateau and the northern Himalaya. Scholars classify Tibetan as a Tibeto-Burmese language, a small linguistic subfamily that includes Burmese and the languages of a number of hill tribes that range from Southeast Asia across to the indigenous Newari people of the Kathmandu Valley.

The written form of the Tibetan language may have its origins in the ancient scripts of India and perhaps in the Buddhist kingdoms that once flourished along the Central Asian silk routes. According to traditional accounts, Tibetan **u-chaen** (literally, script with a head, or brushstroke over each character; sometimes called **u-chhen**) was the creation of Tonmi Sambhota, a renowned minister under Tibet's seventh-century king Songtsen Gampo. This script, said to be modeled after the Gupta alphabet used in northern India at that time, consists of thirty consonants (including the vowel *a*), four vowel signs, and a unique array of prefixes, suffixes, post-suffixes, superscripts, and subjoined letters. Of the half-dozen or more scripts currently utilized in Tibet, **u-chaen** is the printed script of block prints and typewriters used in documents, manuscripts, newspapers, and on signboards. The other scripts, which include **u-may** (without a head) and **kyug,** are more fluid, handwritten forms of **u-chaen** used on an everyday basis in schools, for letter writing, and so forth. **Ü-kay,** the "central" dialect of Lhasa (some scholars prefer to call it Lhasa-**kay**), is the most practical form of the language to use while traveling in Central Tibet. The transliterations in this chapter are based upon the pronunciations of this dialect. Although some of the treks and dayhikes in this book are not in the Lhasa/Ü province area, such as those near Mount Everest or in Western Tibet, the people in these areas usually understand at least the basics of **Ü-kay.** It is the language of the capital city and therefore the most widely understood dialect of the Tibetan countryside. Keep in mind that there will be different pronunciations and vocabularies used not only in these outer regions, but also in areas that may be very close to the Lhasa Valley.

Although an outline of Tibetan grammar is included in this chapter, study-ing the rules of grammar is probably the most difficult way to begin learning this language. Instead, first look carefully through the section on pronunciation. Note how the vowels and the consonants are pronounced, and become familiar with those that vary from standard English usage. Next try learning a few key phrases, especially those that are useful in everyday situations. Although your initial attempts to speak Tibetan may be clumsy, the Tibetans are friendly people who respond receptively when foreigners make the effort to learn their language.

As soon as you arrive in Tibet, start practicing with the Tibetan staff at your hotel or at a nearby restaurant. **Tashiy delay,** which is the closest equivalent to our "hello," and **ghale zhuu,** one of several ways to say "good-bye," should be quickly understood even if the pronunciation is not perfect. Memorize the numbers from one to ten. This will enable you to use the question most commonly asked by travelers: **Day ghong ghatshay ray?**—"How much does this cost?" Often the first thing a Tibetan will ask you is **Khyayrang ghane yin?**—"Where are you from?" (There are many other ways of asking this.) The reply to learn is **Nga . . . Amerika . . . nay yin** meaning "I am from . . . America." (Sentences in this chapter that have words separated by three dots [. . .] indicate where other words can be substituted according to your needs.) Other helpful sentences are included in the section "Useful Phrases and Conversation."

Before your trek starts, practice each new phrase until nearly everyone can understand. Visit the markets and the temples, asking what everything is and how much it costs, querying the vendors and monks about their families, anything to make conversation. The people you meet make up one of the best classrooms available.

Listen carefully when you are being spoken to and encourage people to repeat what you have just said. Try to have them repeat words slowly at first to help learn how to shape your mouth for the different sounds. Then have these words pronounced quickly, for this is the best way to hear the true sounds as they are spoken in conversation. Being a good listener is essential to being a good speaker.

If you have problems with the pronunciation of certain words or phrases, jot down a few notes using your own system of phonetics. If several attempts at a new phrase fail to get the point across, remember that a bit of pantomime is always helpful. Certain types of body language are universal, such as laying your head in your hands to indicate sleep. One trick that works quite well is to point at an object, or mime an activity, and then ask:

In the Tibetan language, what is this called?

day	**Bhökay la,**	**ghare**	**zi ghi ray?**
For this	Tibetan language in,	what	is called?

Or add just "*Bhökay la* . . ." at the beginning of any phrase. Many times people are not listening for their own language when a foreigner approaches them. If you still can't get your point across, then it's time to move on to someone else who might understand. Once you have some success with the sample phrases, experiment by inserting different words from the "English–Tibetan Vocabulary List" at the end of this chapter.

To further improve your vocabulary, consult Charles Bell's *English Tibetan Colloquial Dictionary*. The English and Tibetan words in it are somewhat outdated (it was originally published in 1905), but it is still the most detailed of the English–Tibetan dictionaries presently available in a size practical for carrying. Unfortunately, it does not include alphabetized Tibetan–English translations. See "Suggested Reading" (Appendix B) for other useful Tibetan language books as well as Chinese phrase books.

If you want to go beyond this introductory chapter and study Tibetan more seriously, locating Tibetan language instructors or classes may be difficult in the West unless you live near a university with an Asian Studies or Religious Studies department, or near a Tibetan Buddhist religious center. At present, no language institutes or study centers have been established in Lhasa for foreigners. If you have a few weeks or more to spend in Kathmandu before going to Tibet, several organizations there offer classes and/or private tutoring in Tibetan:

NEPAL ADDRESS:

Experiment in International Living
Kamala Joshee, Director
P.O. Box 1373
Kathmandu, Nepal
Phone: 414516

UNITED STATES ADDRESS:

Experiment in International Living
School for International Training
Kipling Road
P.O. Box 676
Brattleboro, Vermont 05301
Phone: (802) 257-7751

(Language classes are not open to the public, though private tutors are available)

NEPAL ADDRESS:

University of Wisconsin
College Year in Nepal Program
P.O. Box 3059
Kathmandu, Nepal
Phone: 415560

UNITED STATES ADDRESS:

International Studies and Programs
University of Wisconsin
1410 Van Hise
1220 Linden Drive
Madison, Wisconsin 53706
Phone: (608) 262-2851

(Language classes are not open to the public, though private tutors are available)

Tsetan Chonjore, Director
Tribuwan University, Campus of International Languages
Exhibition Road, Kathmandu, Nepal; Phone: 226713

Pronunciation

The script that Tonmi Sambhota designed thirteen centuries ago bears no resemblence to the Western alphabet. To help you gain an understanding of the Tibetan language without memorizing these unique symbols, the Tibetan vowel and consonant sounds are presented in a more readable form using combinations of letters from our Western alphabet. Like many Asian languages, Tibetan is spoken with tonal inflections. In Thailand and China the people practically sing their words, using combinations of rising and falling pitches or tones. The Tibetans, however, utilize a variety of high, deep, and falling sounds, as well as long and short vowel sounds, instead of varying the pitch. Although these tones greatly affect the meanings of words and word combinations, many of the correct sounds can be learned just by mimicking the songlike beat of Tibetan speech patterns. If you mispronounce a word, the meaning can often be conveyed by the context of your sentence. The italicized words in parentheses following the vowel and consonant descriptions are Tibetan words exemplifying each sound, accompanied by their English translation.

VOWELS

The five basic Tibetan vowel sounds resemble the five main English vowels: *a, e, i, o,* and *u.* They are pronounced with an exhale and in a more clipped, staccatolike manner than their English equivalents. Because Tibetan is a tonal language, many variations of these five basic sounds occur, including two vowels sounds found in French and German but not in English.

a   short, like the *a* in *father* (**gompa;** monastery).

aa   short, like the *a* in *father,* but the vowel sound is held longer (**yaa;** yak).

aen like the nasalized *a* in *can* or *ant,* but the vowel sound is held longer; the *n* is from the literary form of the language, but in the colloquial language it is not pronounced (**sipaen;** chile pepper).

aw   like the *o* in *ox* (**yaw-ray;** there is).

ay   like the *ay* in *pay,* but the vowel sound is held longer (**ray;** is).

e   short, like the *a* in *ate* (**me;** fire).

i   short, like the *ee* in *feet* (**ri;** mountain).

iy   like the *ea* in *eagle,* but the vowel sound is held longer (**miy;** eye).

o   short, like the *o* in *orange* (**momo;** dumpling).

oe   like the *oe* in *hoe,* but the vowel sound is held longer (**choe;** yak dung).

ö   no equivalent in English; something like the *e* in *met,* but pronounced with closely rounded lips; closest to the *eu* sound in French, e.g., *fleur* (**Bhö;** Tibet).

u   short, like the *oo* in *boot* (**thugpa;** Tibetan noodle soup).

uu   like the *oo* in *fool,* but the vowel sound is held longer (**luu;** sheep).

Ü   no equivalent in English; something like the *ew* in *new,* but almost nasalized and pronounced with a high tone that falls, then rises slightly at the end; closest to the *u* in German, e.g., *füllen* (**ngü;** silver).

CONSONANTS

All Tibetan consonants contain an inherent **a** sound (like the *a* in *father*), so that **k, kh, gh,** and **ng** are pronounced **ka, kha, gha, nga.** While many of these consonants can be pronounced using English phonetic equivalents, a few sounds are not so familiar and require further explanation. The **d** and **t** sounds are somewhat different in Tibetan, with the tongue being placed farther back in the throat than in English, but the subtleties of these pronounciations are not crucial to speaking and understanding the language. Other exceptions include:

ch   much like the *ch* in *cheek,* but short, sharp and unaspirated (**semchaen;** animal).

dr   pronounced with the tongue farther back in the throat than an English *d,* with only a slight *r* sound (**dro-;** to go).

dz   like the *ds* sound in *fads* (**dzong;** fortress).

g   always hard, like the *g* in *goat* (**gompa;** monastery).

ng   pronounced like the nasalized *ng* in *sing-a-long* (**Nga;** I).

tr   pronounced with the tongue farther back in the throat than an English *t,* with only a slight *r* sound (**trimpa;** cloud).

ts   like the almost *z* sound in *tsar* (**tsampa;** barley flour).

Some Tibetan consonants are aspirated, which means that they are pronounced with a slightly exaggerated puff of air. To differentiate between aspirated and nonaspirated sounds, the aspirated consonants are followed by an **h** in this text, with the exception of **ch.** These are designated by using **kh, gh, chh, jh, th, thr, dh, dhr, ph, bh, tsh, sh, zh,** and **lh.**

chh   like the *ch* in *chair* (**chhu;** water).

dhr   pronounced with the tongue farther back in the throat than an English *d,* with only a slight *r* sound (**dhrapa;** monk).

thr   pronounced with the tongue farther back in the throat than an English *t,* with only a slight *r* sound (**dünthraa;** week).

zh   like the *s* in *leisure* (**zhimpo;** delicious).

Remember,

ph   never like the *f* sound in *photograph* (**pha;** father).

th   never like the *th* in *think* (**theb-ri;** fresco).

Also note that in areas to the west of Shigatse, especially in the Everest region, people often pronounce the suffixes at the end of words that would usually be silent in the Lhasa colloquial dialect.

luu (sheep) may be pronounced **lug**
may (medicine) may be pronounced **men**
paa (photograph) may be pronounced **par**
saapa (new) may be pronounced **sarpa**

Grammar

Grammar is usually the most boggling aspect of any language. If it makes you nervous, just skip this section or have a quick look through it, then go on to "Useful Phrases and Conversation." Once you feel comfortable using these sentences, come back to the grammar section to get a better idea of how the language works.

Tibetan is an inflected language, much like Russian or Latin. This means that in addition to the verb endings changing to indicate a sense of time, the pronouns and sometimes the nouns also change, or inflect, according to the pronoun's relationship with the object of the sentence. These inflected pronouns, like the tonal aspect of Tibetan, can generally be ignored without seriously affecting how well you are understood.

PRONOUNS AND POSSESSIVE PRONOUNS

An unusual feature of the Tibetan language is the use of a specialized system of honorific words to address elders, government officials, nobility, and high *lamas*. Honorific pronouns are the most respectful way to address anyone you meet. Use informal pronouns only when speaking to close friends, children, or animals.

PERSON	PRONOUNS		POSSESSIVE PRONOUNS	
First	I	**nga**	my	**ngay,** or **ngarang-ghi**
	we	**ngan-tshö**	our	**ngan-tshö**
Second	you	**khyö**	your	**khyörang**
	you (hon.)	**khyayrang**	your (hon.)	**khyayrang-ghi**
	you, plural	**khyörang-tsho**	your, plural	**khyörang-tshö**
	you, plural (hon.)	**khyayrang-tsho**	your, plural (hon.)	**khyayrang-tshö**
Third	he	**kho**	his	**khö**
	he/she (hon.)	**khong**	his/hers (hon.)	**khong-ghi**
	she	**mo**	her	**mö**
	they	**kho-tsho**	their	**kho-tshö**
	they (hon.)	**khong-tsho**	their (hon.)	**khong-tshö**

SENTENCE STRUCTURE

The correct structure for a simple Tibetan sentence is subject-object-verb. German and the Indian/Nepali languages construct sentences in much the same way, placing the verb at the end:

SUBJECT	OBJECT	VERB
Nga	**Lhasa la**	**dro ghi yö**
I	Lhasa to	am going
Nga	**America nay**	**yin**
I	America from	am

VERBS

Tibetan verbs consist of a verb stem and an ending that conjugates according to a specific time reference. Tibetan also has special conjugations for events in the past depending on whether the speaker has first-hand knowledge of an event (attested statement), whether someone informed the speaker (reportative statement), or whether the speaker is making a general statement. Other verb endings indicate if an action is habitually repeated. The proper usage of these verb endings can be confusing, though most Tibetans will understand if you conjugate a verb incorrectly or switch the various ways of expressing the verb *to be*. The following is a list of verb conjugations for the past, present, and future according to the person (pronoun) and the knowledge of the speaker. The verb **dhriy-** (*to write*) is used as an example.

PERSON	PAST	PRESENT	FUTURE
First			
(singular and plural)	**dhriy pa yin**	**dhriy ghi yö**	**dhriy ghi yin**
Second and Third			
(attested statements)	**dhriy song**	**dhriy ghi duu**	**dhriy ghi ray**
(reportative statements)	**dhriy duu**	**dhriy ghi duu**	**dhriy ghi ray**
(general statements)	**dhriy pa ray**	**dhriy ghi duu**	**dhriy ghi ray**

Several common verbs, known as time verbs, also have their verb stem change when they are conjugated to imply the past.

dro- (*to go*) changes to **chhin-** (Note: Use **chhim-** before the endings **pa yin** and **pa ray**)

They went to Shigatse (reportative statement)

khong-tsho	**Shigatse**	**la**	**chhin duu**
they	Shigatse	to	went

They went to Shigatse (general statement)

khong-tsho	**Shigatse**	**la**	**chhim pa ray**
They	Shigatse	to	went

za- (*to eat*) changes to **zay-**

You ate **momos** (attested statement)

khyayrang	**momo**	**zay song**
You	momos	ate

(Plurals in Tibetan are not usually indicated by the noun changing, but by the sentence context. Sometimes **-tsho** is added to a noun to emphasize that there is more than one object, and **-tsho** is the suffix used to indicate plural pronouns, e.g., **khong-tsho**: they [literally, "he/she-plural"].)

ta- (*to look*) changes to **tay-**

She looked at a book (reportative statement)

khong	**dheb**	**tay duu**
She	book	looked

nyo- (*to buy*) changes to **nyö-**

Sonam bought **chhang** (attested statement)

Sonam	**chhang**	**nyö song**
Sonam	chhang	bought

The easiest way to conjugate verbs to indicate that you (first person) have felt or done something in the past is to add **pa yin** to the verb stem. For the second and third persons the verb ending is **song** when the speaker has first-hand knowledge of a previous event:

dhriy- (*to write*)

I wrote a letter

Nga	**yi-ge**	**dhriy pa yin**
I	letter	wrote

He wrote a letter (attested statement)

khong	**yi-ge**	**dhriy song**
he	letter	wrote

When the speaker has been told that an event occured in the past, but did not witness it, the reportative verb ending for the second and third person is **duu**. If the speaker is making a general statement about a previous event, the verb ending for the second and third persons is **pa ray**:

She wrote a letter (reportative statement)

khong	**yi-ge**	**dhriy duu**
she	letter	wrote

The students wrote letters (general statement)

labdhraa	**yi-ge**	**dhriy pa ray**
students	letters	wrote

To conjugate verbs to indicate that you (first person) are feeling or doing something at that moment, **ghi yö** is added to the verb stem. For the second and third persons, **ghi duu** is the ending added to the verb stem regardless of the speaker's knowledge:

I am writing a letter

Nga	**yi-ge**	**dhriy ghi yö**
I	letter	am writing

You are writing a letter

khyayrang	**yi-ge**	**dhriy ghi duu**
you	letter	are writing

To conjugate verbs to indicate that you (first person) will do something in the future, add **ghi yin** to the verb stem. For the second and third persons, add **ghi ray** to the verb stem regardless of the speaker's knowledge:

I will write a letter

Nga	**yi-ge**	**dhriy ghi yin**
I	letter	will write

He will write a letter

khong	**yi-ge**	**dhriy ghi ray**
he	letter	will write

THE VERB TO BE

The English language utilizes just one form of the verb *to be* (is, am, are, was, were, and so on) in order to identify, qualify, locate, indicate existence, or convey possession, regardless of the subject or pronoun in a sentence. Past, present, and future tenses are also specified by these verbs. In Tibetan, five different words express the various uses of *to be*. Time references are indicated not by these verbs, but by the sentence context. Like other Tibetan verbs, correct usage sometimes depends on whether the speaker has first-hand or general knowledge of the subject.

The form of *to be* used to identify something in the first person is **yin** (the negative is **maen**). For the second and third persons the verb used is **ray** (the negative is **maray**):

I am from America

Nga	Amerika	nay	yin
I	America	from	am

My name is not Bill

ngay	ming	Bill	maen
my	name	Bill	is not

The yak is black

yaa	nagpo	ray
yak	black	is

To indicate existence, quality, possession, or to express location, the form of the verb *to be* for the first person is **yö** (the negative is **may**). For the second and third person, the verb **duu** (the negative is **minduu**) is used when the speaker has first-hand knowledge of the matter being discussed. **Yaw-ray** (the negative is **yaw maray**) is the verb used when making a general statement. Note that the preposition **la** needs to be inserted into all sentences expressing possession or location, and it always follows the subject or object being discussed.

I have a camera (possession)

	Ngaa	paachhay	yö
	(to) I	camera	is
or,	I	camera	have

Note: When **la** is placed after certain words ending with the open vowel sound **a**, **i**, or **o**, the **l** is dropped and the sound of that word's final syllable becomes modified: **Ngaa** is the colloquial way to pronounce **Nga la**; **day** is the colloquial way to pronounce **di la**; **khong-tshaw** is the colloquial way to pronounce **khong-tsho la**.

Tsering has a book (possession)

Tsering	la	dheb	duu
Tsering	to	book	has

The restaurant is here (location)

day	zakhang	duu
in here	restaurant	is

There are many yaks in Tibet (attested statement)

Bhö	la	yaa	mangpo	duu
Tibet	in	yaks	many	are

There are many yaks in Tibet (a general statement)

Bhö	la	yaa	mangpo	yaw-ray
Tibet	in	yaks	many	are

ASKING QUESTIONS

There are two main ways to formulate a question. One is to use an interrogative:

How	**ghawndray**
How much	**ghatshay ray**
What	**ghare**
When	**ghadhü**
Where	**ghapa**
Where from	**ghane** (the contraction for **ghapa nay**)
Which	**ghaghi**
Who	**su**
Whose	**sö**
Why	**ghare jhaynay**

The other way is to add the ending **-gay** to the verb **duu,** or the ending **-pay** to the verbs **yin, yö, ray,** and **yaw-ray** (note that the pronunciation of the verb stems **duu, ray,** and **yaw-ray** becomes shortened to **du-, re-** and **yaw-re-,** respectively):

There are hotels in Lhasa

Lhasa	**la**	**drön-khang**	**duu**
Lhasa	in	hotels	there are

To create a question,
Are there hotels in Lhasa?

Lhasa	**la**	**drön-khang**	**dugay?**
Lhasa	in	hotels	are there?

This is a hotel

di	**drön-khang**	**ray**
this	hotel	is

To create a question,
Is this a hotel?

di	**drön-khang**	**repay?**
this	hotel	is it?

IMPERATIVES

The Tibetan language has several ways to create a command. Polite imperatives can be constructed by adding the ending **rawnang** to the verb stem:

for **nang-** (*to give*)

Please give me tea

Ngaa	**jha**	**nang**	**rawnang**
(to) I	tea	give	please

For informal imperatives, add the ending **da** to the verb stem:

Give me tea

Ngaa	**jha**	**nang da**
(to) I	tea	give

ADJECTIVES

Adjectives always follow the noun they are describing:

big monastery

gompa	**chhempo**
monastery	big

When a statement is made with the subject being described by an adjective, the **duu** form (negative is **minduu**) of the verb *to be* is used when the speaker has first-hand knowledge. If the speaker is making a general statement, the **ray** form (negative is **maray**) of the verb *to be* is used. When a color describes the subject, the **ray** form of *to be* is usually used:

These **momos** are delicious (attested statement)

momo	**dintsho**	**zhimpo**	**duu**
momos	these	delicious	are

Momos are delicious (general statement)

momo	**zhimpo**	**ray**
momos	delicious	are

The lake is blue

tsho	**ngompo**	**ray**
lake	blue	is

To make an adjective become a superlative, add the suffix **-shö** to the first syllable or the stem of the adjective:

good	best
yagpo	**yagshö**

many	most
mangpo	**mangshö**

One exception is when big becomes biggest, for the **m** is dropped from the stem of the adjective:

big	biggest
chhempo	**chheshö**

Useful Phrases and Conversation

In the following sections, some English words are translated into both Tibetan (Tib.) and Chinese (Chi.).

English nouns are designated by (n.), adjectives by (adj.), and adverbs by (adv.). For verbs (v.), only the stem is given for the Tibetan equivalent (e.g., **dro-** *to go*).

In some cases the honorific form (hon.) of a word is given as well as the informal (inf.).

USEFUL PHRASES

Hello! Good day!	**tashiy delay!**
	(Literally, good luck!)

Where are you going?	**ghapa**	**paygay?**
(typical greeting)	where	going (hon.)?

Good-bye (if you are leaving)	**ghale zhuu** slowly stay (Literally, take care)
Good-bye (if you are staying)	**ghale phay** slowly go (Literally, take care)
Yes	**yin, yö, duu, ray,** or **yaw-ray** yes
No	**maen, may, minduu, maray,** or **yaw-maray** no
Thank you (hon.)	**tho je chhe** thank you
You're welcome	**ghaye jhay ghi maray** nothing to do it isn't (Literally, it's my pleasure)
You're welcome (hon.)	**gha ghaye nang ghi maray** nothing to do (hon.) it isn't
No thank you	**lamaen, tho je chhe** oh no, thank you
OK (don't substitute for thank you)	**drig ghi ray** all right it is
OK?	**drig ghi repay?** all right is it?
This is good	**di yagpo duu** this good is
This is not good	**di yagpo minduu** this good is not
I understand	**hagho song** (I) understand
I don't understand	**hagho masong** (I) understand don't
I know	**shing ghi yö** (I) know it is
I don't know	**shing ghi may** (I) know it is not
What is this?	**di ghare ray?** this what is?
What to do?	**ghare jhay go ray?** what to do?

What do you want?	**ghare gaw?**
	what want?
Come in	**ya phay**
	come
Sit!	**zhuu!**
	sit!
Drink tea! (inf.)	**jha thung!**
	tea drink!
Excuse me! Pardon me!	**gongdha!**
	sorry!
Goodnight	**sim jaa nang-gho**
	sleep please do (hon.)
Go slowly!	**ghale ghale phay!**
	slowly slowly!
Be careful!	**sabsaa nang!**
	careful be (hon.)
Move back!	**pha gyuu!**
	back!
Just a minute	**day-tsha guu-a**
	little wait
I know a little Tibetan	**Ngay Bhökay day-tsha shing ghi yö**
	My Tibetan little knowing
Say it again, please	**yangkyaa sung rawnang**
	again say please
No thank you.	**lamaen, tho je chhe.**
I don't smoke cigarettes	No thank you.
	Nga thama thin ghi may
	I cigarette smoke do not

CONVERSATIONS AND TYPICAL SITUATIONS

| What is your name? | **khyayrang-ghi ming la ghare yin/ray?** |
| | your name what is? |

(Note: **yin** is the correct form of the verb *to be* if the emphasis in this sentence is placed on **khyayrang-ghi** [your]; **ray** is the correct usage if the emphasis in this sentence is placed on the object **ming** [name].)

My name is ... Tashi	**ngay ming ... Tashi ... yin/ray**
	my name Tashi is
Pleased to meet you	**khyayrang jaaba gapo chhung**
	you meet pleased to

How are you?	**khyayrang**	**kuzuu**	**depo**	**yinpay?**
(How is your health?)	your	body	healthy	is it?

Yes, I am fine	**la yin,**	**depo**	**yin**
	yes	healthy	it is

Where are you from?	**khyayrang**	**ghane**	**yin?**
	you	where from	is?

I am from . . . America	**Nga**	**. . .**	**Amerika**	**. . .**	**nay**	**yin**
	I	. . .	America	. . .	from	am

Where are you going?	**khyayrang**	**ghapa**	**dro ghi yin?**
	you	where	going?

I am going to . . .	**Nga**	**. . . Dza Rongphu**	**. . .**	**la**	**dro ghi yin**
Dza Rongphu	I	Dza Rongphu		to	going

How old are you?	**khyayrang**	**lo**	**ghatshay**	**yin/ray?**
	you	years	how many	is?

I am . . . twenty-five	**Nga**	**lo**	**. . .**	**nyi-shu tsay-nga**	**. . .**	**yin/ray**
. . . years old	I	years		twenty-five		am

Are you married?	**khyayrang**	**chhangsa**	**tsaa pay?**
	you	marriage	occurred?

Yes, I am married	**La yin.**	**Ngay**	**chhangsa**	**tsaa pa yin**
	Yes.	My	marriage	has occurred

Do you have children?	**khyayrang la**	**bhughu**	**yöpay?**
	you	children	have?

Yes, I have . . . one . . .	**La yö.**	**Ngaa bhu**	**. . .**	**chig**	**. . .**
daughter and . . .	Yes.	(to) I son		one	
one . . . son	**dhang bhumo**	**. . .**	**chig**	**. . .**	**yö**
	and daughter		one		have

What is your occupation?	**khyayrang-ghi**	**layka**	**jhay ghi yö?**
	your	work	are you doing?

I am a . . . student	**Nga**	**. . .**	**labdhraa**	**. . .**	**yin**
	I	. . .	student	. . .	am

Addressing Others

When Tibetans call out to someone, they do not just yell "Hey you!" or "Pardon me!" Instead they use a system of names that depend on the age and the sex of the person being called. If you're not sure whether a person is younger or older than yourself, use the honorific pronoun **khong** (he/she). When addressing a person by his or her given name, it is polite to add the word **laa** after the name:

Excuse me, is this the	**khong,**	**di**	**Lhasa**	**ghi**	**lamka**	**repay?**
road to Lhasa?	Mister/Miss,	this	Lhasa	to	road	is it?

Sonam, how are you?	**Sonam laa,**	**kuzuu**	**depo**	**yinpay?**
	Sonam,	body	healthy	is it?

Numbers

The counting system in Tibet is very similar to ours. However, the word for "and" that connects the units of ten with the units of one, starting with the twenties, is somewhat unpredictable. Don't worry about trying to learn every one of these. At first, just leave out these connectors or use the translation for "and," **dhang,** to join numbers (e.g., use **nyi-shu chiy** or **nyi-shu dhang chiy** instead of trying to memorize **nyi-shu tsa-chiy,** then **nyi-shu tsang-nyi,** and so on). You'll still be understood.

1	**chiy, chig**	30	**sum-chu**
2	**nyi**	31	**sum-chu saw-chiy**
3	**sum**	35	**sum-chu saw-nga**
4	**zhi**	40	**zhibchu**
5	**nga**	41	**zhibchu shaa-chiy**
6	**dhruu**	45	**zhibchu shay-nya**
7	**dün**	50	**ngabchu**
8	**gyay**	51	**ngabchu ngaa-chiy**
9	**gu**	55	**ngabchu ngay-nga**
10	**chu**	60	**dhrugchu**
11	**chug-chiy**	65	**dhrugchu raa-nga**
12	**chung-ngi**	70	**dün-chu**
13	**chug-sum**	75	**dün-chu dhün-nga**
14	**chub-zhi**	80	**gya-chu**
15	**chö-nga**	85	**gya-chu gyhaa-nga**
16	**chu-dhruu**	90	**gub-chu**
17	**chup-dün**	95	**gub-chu ghaw-nga**
18	**chub-gyay**	100	**gya**
19	**chu-gu**	200	**nyi gya**
20	**nyi-shu**	1000	**chig tong**
21	**nyi-shu tsa-chiy**	2000	**nyi tong**
22	**nyi-shu tsang-nyi**		
23	**nyi-shu tsag-sum**	$^1/_4$	**zhichha chiy**
24	**nyi-shu tsab-zhi**	$^1/_2$	**chhayka**
25	**nyi-shu tsay-nga**	$^3/_4$	**zhichha sum**
26	**nyi-shu tsu-dhruu**	first	**dangpo**
27	**nyi-shu tsup-dün**	second	**nyipa**
28	**nyi-shu tsub-gyay**	third	**sumpa**
29	**nyi-shu tsu-gu**	zero	**layko**

Time

What time is it now?	**dhanda**	**chhu-tshö**	**ghatshay**	**ray?**
	now	hours	how much	is?

Now it is . . . one o'clock	**dhanda**	**chhu-tshö**	**. . . dhangpo**	**. . . ray**
	now	hours	. . . first	. . . is

| . . . two o'clock | | **. . . nyipa . . .** | | |

... 2:30	...	**nyi**	**dhang**	**chhayka**	...
	...	two	and	a half	...

... 2:40	...	**nyi**	**dhang**	**kama**	**zhibchu**	...
	...	two	and	minutes	forty	...

What time will this monastery ... open?	**gompa** **di** **chhu-tshö** **ghatshay la**
	monastery this hours what
	... go chhay ghi yaw-ray?
	... door will open?

... close?	**... go gyeb ghi yaw-ray?**

It will open at 8:00 in the morning	**zhokay** **chhu-tshö** **gyaypa** **la** **go**
	morning hour eight at door
	chhay ghi ray
	will open

Getting Around/Directions

Where is ... the hotel?	**drön-khang** **...** **ghapa** **yaw-ray?**
	hotel ... where is?

I want to go to ... Shigatse	**Nga** **...** **Shigatse** **...** **la** **dron duu yö**
	I ... Shigatse ... to going (desire)

How many hours is it to ... Lhasa?	**Lhasa** **...** **bhardhu** **chhu-tshö**
	Lhasa ... up to hours
	ghatshay **ghoe ghi ray?**
	how many taking?

Please stop at ... Gyantse	**Gyantse** **...** **la** **kaa** **rawnang**
	Gyantse ... at stop please

What time will this ... bus ... leave?	**motra** **...** **di** **chhu-tshö**
	bus ... this time
	ghatshay la **dro ghi ray?**
	what will be going?

Is this the road to ... Sera?	**di** **...** **Sera** **...** **ghi** **lamka** **repay?**
	this ... Sera ... to road is it?

Shopping

Although the prices for goods in the shops and department stores are usually fixed, be sure to bargain for all souvenirs, carpets, vegetables, fruit, truck rides, pack animals, and porters.

How much does this cost?	**day** **ghong** **ghatshay** **ray?**
	this cost how much is?

| Two yuan (Chinese dollars) | **gomo** (or **pyau**) | **nyi** | **ray** |
| | dollars | two | it is |

This is too expensive!

day ghong pay chhempo duu!
this cost too big is!

Is there bargaining?

ghong drigya yaw ray pay?
price adjusting is there?

How much is a pound (¹/₂ kg) of apples?

kushu ghi jin chig ghong
apples for pound one cost
ghatshay ray?
how much is?

I'll buy . . . two
. . . pounds

jin . . . nyi . . . nyo ghi yin
pounds . . . two . . . I will buy

Do you have any
. . . matches?

tshagdra . . . yöpay?
matches . . . do you have?

I don't want . . . these

dintsho . . . Ngaa mogaw
these . . . (to) I don't want

Are there others?

shaendha yaw-repay?
others are there?

Now I am just looking

dhanda Nga miy ta ghi yö
now I am looking

I will return tomorrow

sang-nyiy Nga yong ghi yin
tomorrow I will come

Food, Eating, and Restaurants

I am hungry

Nga dhrokhaw taw ghi
I stomach has hunger

I am full

Nga dhrokhaw gya song
I stomach has been filled

Enough! (thank you)

drig song (tho je chhe)
enough (thank you)

This food is delicious

khala di zhimpo duu
food this delicious is

I don't eat meat

Nga sha za ghi may
I meat eat do not

Is there any . . .
   noodle soup?

thugpa . . . **yaw-repay?**
noodle soup . . . is there?

Please give me . . .
   a glass of tea

jha   chig . . . **nang   rawnang**
tea   one . . . give   please

How much is . . .
   the total cost?

köndhom . . . **ghong   ghatshay ray?**
total   . . . how   much is it?

Accommodations

I need . . . a place to sleep

Ngaa . . . **nyaysa** . . . **gaw**
(to) I . . . sleeping place . . . need

How much is . . .
   a room . . . per day?

nyima   chig la . . . **khangmi   chig la**
day   each . . . room   one
. . . ghatshay   ray?
. . . how much   is?

. . . each bed . . .

. . . nyaythri chig la . . .

There are two of us

ngan-tshö   mi   nyi   yö
we   people   two   are

How much will food and
   a place to sleep cost?

khala   dhang   nyaysa la   ghatshay   ray?
food   and   sleep place   how much   is?

Is there . . . a toilet
   . . . here?

day . . . **sangchö** . . . **yaw-repay?**
here . . . toilet . . . is there?

Where is . . . the key?

demiy . . . **ghapa yö?**
key . . . where is?

Does this dog bite?

khyi   di   so gyeb ghi   repay?
dog   this   bite   does it?

Trekking

Tomorrow we are
   going to . . . Dingri

sang-nyin . . . **Dingri** . . . **la   dro ghi yin**
tomorrow . . . Dingri . . . to   are going

We want to hire a
   . . . burro

ngan-tshö . . . **bhung-ghu   chig** . . . **lay**
we . . . burro   one . . . hire
gaw   yö
want   to

How much is . . . a yak
   . . . per day?

nyima   chig la . . . **yaa   chig la** . . .
day   one . . . yak   one . . .
ghong   ghatshay   ray?
cost   how much   is?

| Where can we buy ...food? | **khala** | **...** | **nyosa** | | **ghapa** | **yaw-ray?** |
| | food | ... | buying place | | where | is? |

Where can we put our ...tent?	**ngan-tshö**	**...**	**ghur**	**...**	**ghapa**	**gyebna**
	our	...	tent	...	where	make
	drig ghi	**ray?**				
	OK	is it?				

What is the name of that ... mountain?	**ghangri**	**...**	**phaghiy**	**ming la**
	mountain	...	over there	name
	gharay	**ray?**		
	what	is?		

Visiting a Monastery

How many monks are in this monastery now?	**dhanda**	**gompa**	**day**	**dhrapa**
	now	monastery	this in	monks
	ghatshay	**yaw-ray?**		
	how many	is?		

Thirty years ago how many monks were there?	**lo**	**sum-chu**	**kongla**	**dhrapa**
	years	thirty	before	monks
	ghatshay	**yaw-ray?**		
	how many	were?		

| I don't have any Dalai Lama photos | **Dalai Lama ghi** | **kupaa** | | **may** |
| | Dalai lama | religious picture | | no |

| Which deity is this? | **lha** | **di** | **ghaghi** | **ray?** |
| | deity | this | which | is? |

| How old is this ...monastery? | **gompa** | **di** | **nying** | **lo** | **ray?** |
| | monastery | this | old | years | is it? |

| What school of Buddhism is this monastery? | **gompa** | **di** | **chhöluu** | **gharay** | **ray?** |
| | monastery | this | order | what | is? |

Photography

| May I take ...a photograph? | **Nga ...** | **paa** | | **gyebna** | **drig ghi** | **repay?** |
| | I ... | photo | ... | take | all right | is it? |

| ...your picture? | **...** | **khyayrang-ghi** | **paa** | **...** |
| | ... | your | photo | ... |

Inside my camera is only film. No pictures now.	**paachhay**	**nangla**	**pingshuo**	**duu.**	**dhanda**
	camera	inside	film	is.	now
	paa	**minduu**			
	photo	there isn't			

Sickness/Emergency

I am sick	**Nga**	**na ghi**	**duu**	
	I	sick	am	

I have . . . diarrhea	**Ngay**	**. . .**	**dhrokhaw shay**	**. . .**	**ghi duu**
	I		diarrhea		have

It hurts here	**day**	**na ghi duu**
	here	hurts

Please call . . . a doctor	**amchhi**	**. . .**	**kay tang**	**rawnang**
	doctor	. . .	call	please

Where is . . . a hospital?	**mengkhang**	**. . .**	**ghapa**	**yaw-ray?**
	hospital	. . .	where	is?

Please help me	**Ngaa**	**rogpa**	**nang**	**rawnang**
	(to) I	help	give	please

English–Tibetan Vocabulary List

a (indefinite article)	**zhig, zhiy**	Australia	**Astraliya**
after	**jayla, jayma**	backpack	**töpay**
afternoon	**nyin-gung**	barley (toasted flour)	**tsampa**
	gyabla	barley (uncooked)	**dru**
again	**yangkyaa**	be able (v.)	**tub-**
ago	**kongla, nyayla,**	beautiful	**nying-jaypo**
	nyöma	because	**ghare ray**
airplane	**namdhru**		**seyna**
airport	**namdhru**	bed	**nyaythri**
	bhabthang,	beer, brewed (Chi.)	**pijyu, payjyu**
	namthang	beer (Tib.)	**chhang**
all	**tshangma**	before	**kongla,**
alone	**chigpo**		**nyayma,**
always	**tagpa, tagpa**		**nyöma**
	resh	behind	**gyabla**
America	**Amerika**	bicycle	**kang gari**
and	**dhang**	big	**chhempo**
and then	**ani, dhang**	bird	**jha**
animal	**semchaen**	bite (v.)	**so gyeb-**
apple	**kushu**	black	**nagpo**
arm	**lagpa**	blanket	**kampaliy,**
arrive (v.)	**leb-**		**nyayzaen**
ask (v.)	**dri-**	blue	**ngompo**
assembly hall	**dukhang**	boat (ferry)	**dhru**
at	**la**	book	**dheb**

English	Tibetan	English	Tibetan
bolo (sling)	**wordo**	China	**Gyana**
bowl	**phopa**	Chinese (people)	**Gyami**
boy	**bhu**	chopsticks	**khotsay**
boy friend	**togpo**	cigarette	**thama**
bread (Tib.)	**bhalay**	circumambulate (v.)	**kora gyeb-**
bread, steamed (Chi.)	**mon-tou**	city	**dhrong-khyay**
bread, steamed (Tib.)	**tin-momo**	clean	**tsangma**
break (v.)	**chhaa-**	close (v.)	**go gyeb-**
bridge	**zampa**	cloud	**trimpa**
brother	**bhu pün**	cold, to feel (v.)	**khyaa-**
brother, elder (title)	**jholaa**	cold (adj.)	**dhrangmo**
brother, younger	**bhu pün woma**	come (v.)	**yong-**
Buddhist (lit. insider)	**nangpa**	companion	**rogpa**
building	**khangpa**	cook (n.)	**machhaen**
burro	**bhung-ghu**	cook (v.)	**khala zo-/zö-**
bus	**motra, bus**	coral	**jhiru**
bus (Chi.)	**gunggung**	cost	**ghong**
	chiche	cotton	**tringbay**
bus station	**motra tisen**	country (birthplace)	**kyesa, lungpa**
businessman	**tsongpa**	crops	**tönthaw,**
but	**yinay**		**zhingkha**
butter	**maa, mar**	cup	**phopa**
butter lamp	**chhö-me**	daughter	**bhumo**
butter tea	**Bhöjha**	day	**nyima**
buy (v.)	**nyo-**	day after tomorrow	**nang-nyiy,**
call (v.)	**zi-**		**nang**
camera	**paachhay,**	day before yesterday	**khay-nyima**
	parchhay	deity	**lha**
Canada	**Janada**	delicious	**zhimpo**
candle	**yangla**	destroy (v.)	**dor-**
candy	**jhiri**	Dharamsala	**Daram**
car	**motra**	diarrhea,to have (v.)	**dhrokhaw**
carpet	**daen**		**shay-**
cart (for horses)	**da gari**	die (v.)	**shi-**
cat	**shimi**	different (other)	**zhempa**
cave	**phuu,**	different than	**khawkhaw**
	dhraaphuu,	difficult	**khagpo, kalay**
	drubphuu		**khagpo**
cent (Tib.,		dirty	**tsogpa**
1/100 dollar)	**ping**	do (v.)	**jhay-**
cent (Chi.)	**fen**	doctor	**amchhi**
cheap	**ghong**	dog	**khyi**
	chhungchhung	door	**go**
cheese, dried	**chhokom,**	down	**maa**
	chhura	down there	**maghay**
child/children	**bhughu**	dress (Tib.)	**chhupa**
chili pepper	**sipaen**	drink (v.)	**thung-**

drive (v.)	**tang-**	fox	**wa, wamo**
drunk, to get (v.)	**zi-**	France	**Pharansi**
dumpling	**momo**	Friday	**zaa pasang**
dust	**thala**	friend	**rogpa**
each	**re-re**	from	**nay**
early	**ngapo**	front, in	**dünla, ngayla**
earthquake	**sa-yö, sa-yum**	fuel (oil)	**num**
east	**shar, shaa**	gazelle	**gaa, gowa**
easy	**lay-lapo**	Germany	**Germani**
eat (v.)	**za-**	girl	**bhumo**
egg	**go-nga**	girl friend	**tongmo**
empty	**dongpa**	give (v., hon.)	**nang-**
England	**Inchi-lungpa**	glacier (ice)	**kyagpa**
enough	**drig song**	go (v.)	**dro-/chhin-**
evening	**gondhaa**		**/chhim-**
every day	**nyintaa, nyima**	goat	**ra**
	tagpa	good	**yagpo**
eye	**miy**	good-bye	
family	**khim-tsang**	(if you're going)	**ghale zhuu**
famous	**kedhra**	good-bye	
	chhempo	(if you're staying)	**ghale phay**
far	**thag-ringpo**	grandfather	**polaa**
farmer	**zhingpa**	grandmother	**molaa**
farmer/herder	**sa-ma-drog**	guide	**lamka**
father	**pha**		**taenkhaen**
ferry boat	**dhru**	hail (v.)	**sera gyeb-**
festival	**düchhan**	half	**chhayka**
fever, to have a (v.)	**tshawa na-**	hand	**lagpa**
few	**nyung-nyung**	happy	**kyipo**
field	**zhingkha**	hat	**zhamo**
film, photographic		have (v., first person)	**yö**
(Chi.)	**pingshuo**	have (second and	
fire	**me**	third person)	**duu, yawray**
firewood	**me-shing**	he (inf.)	**kho**
first	**dhangpo**	he (hon.)	**khong**
fish	**nya**	head	**go**
fix (v.)	**zo-/zö-**	headache,	
flower	**me-taw**	to have a (v.)	**go na-**
fog	**mugpa**	hear (v.)	**gho-**
food	**khala, zama**	heavy	**jipo**
footprint (in stone)	**zhabjay**	hello	**tashiy delay**
foot road (trail)	**kang-lam,**	here	**day**
	lamka	hermit	**gomchhaen,**
for	**la**		**tsampa**
forest	**shing-na**	hermitage	**rithrö,**
forget (v.)	**jay-**		**tsamkhang**
fortress	**dzong**	hire (v.)	**la-/lay-**

home	**nang**	letter	**yi-ge**
horse	**ta**	light (weight)	**yangpo**
hospital	**mengkhang**	like (v.)	**gapo-**
hot (water, etc.)	**tshapo**	little (quantity)	**day-tsha**
hot (temperature)	**tshawa**	little (size)	**chhungchhung**
hot springs	**chhutsaen**	live (reside, v.)	**day-**
hotel	**drön-khang**	lock	**gochaa**
hour	**chhu-tshö**	look (v.)	**ta-, miy ta-/tay-**
house	**khangpa, nang**	lose (v.)	**laa-**
how	**ghawndray**	Ma'am (respectful)	**gaenlaa**
how long, to take (v.)	**ghoe-**	Ma'am	
how many/how much	**ghatshay,**	(elder sister, title)	**achhalaa**
	ghatshö	Ma'am	
hundred	**gya,**	(lit. grandmother)	**molaa**
	gya-thampa	make (v.)	**zo-/zö-**
hunger, to have (v.)	**dhrokhaw taw-**	man	**kyoga**
hurt (v.)	**na-**	many	**mangpo**
husband	**kyoga**	many times	**theng mangpo**
husband/spouse (hon.)	**kunda**	map	**sabtra**
I	**Nga**	market	**throm**
ice	**kyagpa**	marmot	**jhibi, jhiba**
if	**na**	marriage	**chhangsa**
immediately	**lamsong**	matches	**tshagdra, musi**
in	**la**	maybe	**chig-jhayna**
incense	**pö**	meadow	**pang**
incense bush	**sang-shing**	meat	**sha**
India	**Gyaghaa**	medicine	**maen**
inside	**nangla**	meditate (v.)	**gom-**
Japan	**Ribiy**	meditation cave	**dhraaphuu,**
juniper	**shugpa**		**drubphuu**
kerosene	**sanum**	meet (v., inf.)	**thug-**
key	**demiy**	meet (v., hon.)	**jaa-**
kilometer (Chi.)	**gung-li**	midnight	**tshenmo**
knife	**dhri**	milk	**oma**
know (v.)	**shing-/shaen-**	minute	**kama**
lake	**tsho**	Miss	**khong**
lamp, kerosene	**zhuma**	Mister	**khong**
lantern, tilly	**sazhu**	monastery	**gompa**
last night	**dang-gong**	Monday	**zaa dawa**
last week	**dünthraa**	money	**ngü**
	nyayma	monk	**dhrapa**
last year	**danyi**	monk, highly educated	**lama**
late	**chhipo**	monk, incarnate	**truku**
later	**jayla, jayma**	month	**dawa**
learn (v.)	**jhang-**	morning	**zhokay**
left (direction)	**yön**	(this) morning	**dharang**
leg	**kangpa**		**zhokay**

mother	ama	other	shaendha
motor vehicle	motra	outside	chhila
mountain	ri, tse	over there	phaghay
mountain, snowy	ghang-ri	painting (fresco)	theb-ri
mountain pass	la	painting	
mountain sheep	na, naya	(wall hanging)	thangka
mountaineer	ghang-ri	paper	shughu
	dzaakhaen	pay (v.)	tay-
mouse	tsi-tsi	peak	tse
mud	dam	peas	tayma, kung-ü
my	ngay	pen	nyu-ghu
nauseous, to be (v.)	dhrokhaw na-	people	mi
near	nyepo	petrol (Chi.)	chiyo
need (v.)	gö-	photograph	paa, par
Nepal	Bhay-yü	photograph (v.)	paa gyeb-
nettles	za, zapho	photograph (religious)	kupaa, kupar
new	saapa	pika	abra, dzabra,
next (later)	jayma		pu-se
next (immediately)	jayla	pilgrim	naykorwa
night	gongmo	pill	riybhu
(last) night	dang-gong	place	sachha
no	maen, may,	police (Chi.)	gong-an
	mindu, maray,	police station (Chi.)	gong-an ju
	yaw-maray	potato	zhogho
nomad	drogpa	pound (½ kg, Chi.)	jin
noodles/soup, Tibetan	thugpa	prayer beads	tra-nga
noodles/soup, Chinese	Gyathug	prayer ceremony	chho-gha
noodles (Chi.)	mien	prayer flags	lungdaa,
noon	nyin-gung		daa-chhoe
north	jhang	prayer stones	mani do
now	dhanda	prayer wheel	mani
nowadays	dhering sang,	price	ghong
	dheng sang	protector's temple	gön-khang
nun	ani	quarter (one)	zhichha (chig)
occupation	layka	quickly	gyogpo
often	yangsay	quilt	pokhay,
OK	drig ghi ray		kampaliy
old (objects)	nyingpa	rabbit (hare)	righong
old (people)	lo chhempo	rain	chhapa
one	chig, chiy	rain (v.)	chhapa gyeb-
one hundred	gya,	read (v.)	law-
	gya-thampa	red	maapo, maamo
onion	tsong	religion	chhö
only	chigpo	religious sect	chhöluu
open a door (v.)	go chhay-	restaurant	zakhang
open an object (v.)	kha chhay-	return (v.)	law-
or	yang-na	rhododendron	bhalu

rice	**dray**	snow	**ghang**
rice (Chi.)	**mi, mifan**	snow (v.)	**ghang gyeb-**
ridge	**ritse**	snow leopard	**saa**
right (correct)	**duu, ray**	snow lion	**seng-ge**
right (direction)	**yay**	snow mountain	**ghang-ri**
river (major)	**tsangpo,**	sometimes	**tshamtsham-la**
	tsangchhu	son	**bhu**
river/stream	**chhu**	song	**lu, zhay**
road (path)	**lamka**	soon	**gyogpo**
road (vehicle)	**motra lamka**	soup (noodle, Tib.)	**thugpa**
rock	**dhra**	south	**lho**
room	**khangmiy**	speak (v.)	**kaychha lab-**
ruins	**ghogpo**	spinach	**pay-tshay**
rupee	**gomo**	spouse (hon.)	**kunda**
salt	**tsha**	statue	**ku**
same	**chigpa, chha**	stay (v.)	**dhay-**
Saturday	**zaa pempa**	steep	**zaapo**
say (v., inf.)	**lab-**	stomach	**dhrokhaw**
say (v., hon.)	**sung-**	stomach ache,	
school	**labdhra**	to have (v.)	**dhrokhaw na-**
second	**nyipa**	stone	**do**
see (v.)	**thong-,**	stop (v.)	**kaa-**
	miy-thong-	store	**tshong-khang**
sell (v.)	**tshong**	stove, fuel	**me-thab**
she	**mo**	stove, wood	**chag-thab**
she (hon.)	**khong**	strong	**shug-chhempo**
sheep	**luu, lug**	student	**labdhraa**
shop	**tshongkhang**	stupa	**chötaen**
sick, to be (v.)	**na-**	sugar	**jhema-kara,**
silver	**ngü**		**chini**
sing (v.)	**zhaydang-**	sun	**nyima**
Sir (respectful)	**gaenlaa**	Sunday	**zaa nyima**
Sir (elder brother,		take (v.)	**laen-**
title)	**jholaa**	take (a photo)	**paa gyeb-**
Sir (grandfather)	**polaa**	talk (v.)	**kaychha lab-**
sister	**bhumo pün**	tea	**jha, söjha**
sister, elder (title)	**achhalaa**	tea, sweet	**jha-ngamo**
sister, younger	**bhumo pün**	tea, with butter	**Bhöjha**
	woma	teahouse	**jhakhang**
sit (v.)	**dhay-**	teach (v.)	**lab-**
sleep (v.)	**nyi-nyay-,**	teacher	**gegen**
	nyay-	telephone	**khapaa khapaa**
sleeping bag	**nyay-chhay**	temple	**lhakhang**
sleeping place	**nyaysa**	tent	**ghur**
slowly	**ghale ghale**	tent (nomad)	**ba**
small	**chhungchhung**	thank you	**tho je chhe**
smoke	**dhuko**	that (distant)	**phaghi**

that (nearby)	**dhe**	until (up to)	**bhar, bhardhu**
there	**phaghay**	up	**yaa**
therefore	**jhaytsang**	up there	**yaghay**
thermos	**jhadam**	up to	**bhar, bhardhu**
these	**dintsho**	urinate (v.)	**chimpa dang-**
they	**kho-tsho**	valley	**lungpa**
they (hon.)	**khongtsho**	vegetables	**tshay**
thirsty, to be (v.)	**khakom-**	Venerable (hon. title	
this	**di**	for high **lama**)	**rimpoche**
those (distant)	**phantsho**	very	**shedhra**
those (nearby)	**dintsho**	village	**dhrongsay,**
Thursday	**zaa phurbu**		**dhrongtsho**
Tibet	**Bhö**	wait (v.)	**guu-**
Tibetan language	**Bhökay**	walk (v.)	**ghompa gyeb-**
Tibetan people	**Bhöpa**	want (v.)	**gö-**
Tibetan writing		wash (v.)	**thrü-**
(printed)	**u-chaen**	wash basin	**dhungbaen**
Tibetan writing		watch (n.)	**chhu-tshö**
(handwriting)	**u-may, kyug**	water	**chhu**
ticket	**pass-se**	water, boiled	**chhu kö**
ticket office	**pass-se nyosa**	we	**ngantsho**
time	**chhu-tshö**	weather	**namshi**
times (one, two . . .)	**theng**	Wednesday	**zaa lhagpa**
	(dhangpo,	week	**dünthraa**
	nyipa . . .)	west	**nub**
tired, to be (v.)	**thang chhay-**	what	**ghare**
to	**la**	what places	**ghapa ghapa**
today	**dhering**	wheat	**dhro**
toilet	**sangchö**	when	**ghadhü**
tomorrow	**sang-nyiy**	where	**ghapa**
tonight	**dhogong**	where from	**ghane**
total	**köndhom**		**(ghapa nay)**
tractor (Chi.)	**thola**	which	**ghaghi**
trail/path	**lamka,**	white	**kaapo**
	kang-lam	who	**su**
train	**rili**	whose	**sö**
tree	**shingdong**	why	**ghare jhaynay**
trek (v.)	**rilam ghompa**	wife	**kyimaen**
	gyeb-	wife (spouse, hon.)	**kunda**
trek leader	**rilam**	wind	**lung**
	taenkhaen	wine (distilled)	**araa**
trekker/traveler	**takorwa**	with	**nyamdhoe**
truck	**motra**	wolf	**changku,**
Tuesday	**zaa migmaa**		**changki**
turnip	**tuluu, lawuu**	woman	**kyimaen**
turquoise	**yu**	wood	**shing**
understand (v.)	**hagho-**	wool	**bhay**

word	**tshig**	year	**lo**
work	**layka**	yes	**yin, yö, duu,**
work (v.)	**layka jhay-**		**ray, yaw-ray**
write (v.)	**dhriy-**	yesterday	**khaysa**
wrong	**minduu,**	yogurt	**zho**
	maray	you	**khyö**
yak (female)	**dri**	you (pl.)	**khyörang**
yak (male)	**yaa, kama**	you (hon.)	**khyayrang**
yak (cattle hybrid, f.)	**dzomo**	you (pl., hon.)	**khyayrang-**
yak (cattle hybrid, m.)	**dzo**		**tsho**
yak dung (fuel)	**choe**	zero	**layko**

"Om Mani Padme Hum," the mantra of Tibet's patron saint Chenrezig, is the most common of the Buddhist prayers carved into mani *stones.*

The yak is an important source of dairy products and meat. Its hair is woven into tents and blankets.

SECTION II

THE TREKS
AND TRAILS

When in doubt, don't ask a drogpa.

Advice overheard in a Lhasa
restaurant from a trekker who
had recently returned from the
Everest region

Road sign atop Lagpa La, the highest pass on the Lhasa–Kathmandu Highway

6   Using the Trek Descriptions

The following trek descriptions, when combined with the relevant maps, should get you to your intended destination with as few difficulties as possible. In the introduction to each description a time frame is suggested and noted in bold type (e.g., **3¹/₂ to 5 days**), giving a range broad enough to accommodate both fast-paced trekkers and leisurely walkers. I have intentionally avoided the use of day-by-day itineraries; instead, each trek is explained in terms of the time it takes to travel from one landmark, geographical feature, or campsite to the next. The suggested walking times, which are also set in bold type, are based upon the pace set by a pack animal or my own walking pace while carrying a moderately heavy backpack (forty to fifty pounds, eighteen to twenty-three kilograms). These figures *do not include any rest stops* unless the text states otherwise. Members of commercial treks who are well acclimatized and carrying only daypacks may find the times a bit slow, while private groups carrying their own packs may find them somewhat fast.

In general, four to six hours of actual walking time per day (not including breaks) is a comfortable trekking pace, depending on the terrain and altitude. Due to the extreme elevations in Tibet, it is a good idea to allow at least half an hour of rest stops for every hour of walking detailed in the trek descriptions (i.e., six hours of actual walking time will usually take most people about nine hours, including rest stops and the time required for a lunch break). Even more time should be allowed if you enjoy visiting monasteries and villages or have interests such as photography, wildflowers, or bird-watching. For pass crossings allow onwards of an hour of rest for every hour of actual walking time outlined in the trek descriptions. These times are meant only as helpful recommenda-tions. Pace yourself according to your abilities. Don't be discouraged if these times seem too quick (or too slow). If you find that it takes three hours to walk a section of trail that is described as taking two hours, the chances are you will continue to take an extra hour for every two hours described in the text. This difference should be taken into consideration for the remainder of the trek description.

In addition to suggested walking times from landmark to landmark, the routes are described as heading to the right or to the left, with the corresponding compass direction following in parentheses. When a trail or route follows a valley, a drainage, or any flowing water, the standard directional terminology from rafting and kayaking is used: right means the right shore or bank of running water as you face downstream, and is symbolized by a capital R in parentheses and usually preceded by a compass direction, "south (R)"; left means the left shore or bank as you face downstream, and is symbolized by a capital L in parentheses and usually preceded by a compass direction, "north (L)."

If you are not part of an organized group or in the company of a guide with a pack animal, the chances of becoming temporarily "geographically embarrassed" (i.e., lost) are greatly increased. Even if you are using this book, I strongly advise bringing along a compass to assist with directions. Good land marks are often few and far between in Tibet, and finding someone to ask about directions can be difficult, especially in remote areas. I have had herders run away when they saw me approaching, and as I climbed toward their hiding spot they bolted farther up the ridge, refusing to answer any of my questions.

Another problem, suggested by the quote at the beginning of this section, is when the local people purposefully give false directions to trekkers. Luckily this doesn't happen often, but the fact that such situations occur emphasizes the importance of learning a few Tibetan phrases, such as "Where is . . .?", "What is the name of that . . .?", "Is this the road to . . .?", and so on. If you feel lost, ask questions at each settlement and herding camp to verify where you're going and how much farther it is to the next landmark. Ask several different people the same question to help confirm the accuracy of the information, but avoid questions that encourage simple yes or no answers. People throughout the world have a tendency to give answers that will please rather than a correct but disappointing reply. The chapter "Tibetan for Trekkers" has been designed to ease the problem of communicating with Tibetans, and the sections "Getting Around/ Directions" and "Trekking" have phrases that are particularly useful on the trail.

A number of common Tibetan words have been used throughout the text. Except for proper names, Tibetan words are printed in italics (e.g., *gompa*). If the meaning does not accompany the italicized word, refer to the "Glossary of Tibetan and Foreign Words" (Appendix C).

Some towns and settlements have a Chinese name as well as a Tibetan name, especially if a town is an administrative post. A few places also have other traditional or local names. The town of Phadhruchi in the Everest region is a good example; it is also known as Phadhru, older Tibetans refer to it as Tashiy Dzum, and the Chinese call it Paru. Variations can also occur with the common names of important passes, rivers, mountains, and valleys. When I first encountered discrepancies, I tried to standardize the place names by asking locals to write down the Tibetan characters in order to record the correct pronunciation. Unfortunately, all I ever managed was to embarrass myself and the fellow I asked to write the name. Much to their disappointment, many Tibetans living in the country have not learned how to read or write. I now resort to using my own phonetic spelling for place names if I cannot find a standardized spelling.

Most of the maps throughout this book are based upon the 1:250,000 Joint Operations Graphic (JOG) maps, Series 1501, which are produced by the Defense Mapping Agency Topographic Center in Washington, D.C. The map illustrations have been enlarged and simplified to detail trekking routes and other necessary geographical information for each area. The scale differs from map to map, and a key for all the maps follows this section.

The elevations used in the route descriptions were determined by readings taken with an altimeter, a hand-sized instrument that translates the barometric pressure for a location into an elevation reading. The theory is that once the altimeter is set to a known elevation, it should then measure with reasonable accuracy any changes in elevation from that point. An altimeter's readings, however, can vary as much as 300 feet (90 m) from one day to the next in the same location due to natural fluctuations in the atmospheric pressure and temperature. Another problem is the lack of locations with known elevations in Tibet where one can reset an altimeter. I have found no fewer than four different but commonly used elevations for Lhasa, varying from 11,830 feet to 12,087 feet (3607 m to 3684 m). For the sake of simplicity I always set my altimeter in Lhasa at 12,000 feet (3658 m) before departing on a trek, then reset it if I crossed Lagpa La (also called Jia Tsuo La, kilometer marker 5082 on the Lhasa–Kathmandu Highway), which has a known elevation of 17,126 feet (5220 m). Except for the heights of mountains, which were taken from recent topographical maps, all of the elevation readings have been rounded off to the nearest 100 feet (31 m), but if a reading was exactly on the fifty-foot increment I recorded it as such. The equivalent measurements in meters have been rounded off to the nearest ten meters.

Tibet has no road signs, though all of the main highways radiating from Lhasa have small kilometer marking stones beside the road. They are a reliable means of determining where you are and useful for locating obscure junctions. The kilometer marker readings for important towns and turnoffs in the trek descriptions are usually noted in parentheses (e.g. km marker 494), and a detailed list of these is included in the "Highway Kilometer Marker" section of this chapter. Note that the odometers in some vehicles may not synchronize with these markers.

Key to Maps

LEGEND

════════	Main road	●	Towns and villages
═ ═ ═ ═ ═	Secondary road	☖	Monastery
------------	Trail	♔	Fort
·—·—·—·—	International boundary	▲	Cave
– – – – – –	National boundary	⋈	Bridge
━)(━	Ridges and passes	BC	Base camp
△	Peak	ABC	Advance base camp
⬭⬭⬭⬭⬭⬭	Glacier	IC	Interim camp
	Rivers	C1	Camp 1
	Lakes	C2	Camp 2
	Marsh	C3	Camp 3

Highway Kilometer Markers

Every major highway in Tibet has a series of stone kilometer markers set into the road shoulder. Because there are no road signs, these markers are useful for locating turnoffs and obscure sites. The counting systems, however, are not synchronized and have different points of origin; four separate systems are currently in use along the road from Lhasa to the Nepal border via Gyantse. In 1989 a new marker system with red numerals on the kilometer stones was introduced along the Chengdu–Lhasa–Kathmandu Highway and the Lhasa–Golmud Highway; all of the older systems have black numerals. In some areas the two types of markers overlap.

The following tables list the kilometer marker systems presently in use in Central and Western Tibet, and give elevations for pass crossings. When a location falls halfway between two markers, both readings are listed, e.g. 54/5 or 89/90. Readings have been approximated where marker stones are missing.

Southern Road to Shigatse from Lhasa

Km marker	Location
4638 (marker missing)	Lhasa (new bus station)
4646 (marker missing)	Golmud/Qinghai highway turnoff
4662	Drolma *lhakhang*/Netang monastery
4703	Yarlung Tsangpo/Chogsam bridge
59/60 (old system resumes)	Yarlung Tsangpo/Chogsam bridge
94/5	Kampa La; 15,728 ft, 4794 m

View of Yamdrog Tsho along the Lhasa–Kathmandu Highway

152	Nakartse/Samding monastery turnoff
180	Karo La; 16,437 ft, 5010 m
251	Gyantse turnoff
90 (start of different system)	Gyantse turnoff
88	Yadong Valley turnoff
19	Shalu monastery turnoff
0	Shigatse

New Yarlung Tsangpo Road to Shigatse from Lhasa

4638 (marker missing)	Lhasa (new bus station)
4646 (marker missing)	Golmud/Qinghai highway turnoff
4703	Chogsam bridge/Shigatse turnoff
4779 (marker missing)	Yarlung Tsangpo bridge crossing
4904 (marker missing)	Shigatse (Tashilumpo monastery front gate)

Northern Road to Shigatse from Lhasa

4638 (marker missing)	Lhasa (new bus station)
3879 (new system begins; marker missing)	Golmud/Qinghai highway turnoff
3853	Tshurphu monastery turnoff
3804/5	Yangpachan
3803	Shigatse Northern Road turnoff
0 (different system begins)	Northern Road turnoff
19 (marker missing)	Yangpachan monastery turnoff
20 (marker missing)	Dorjeling monastery turnoff
56	Shuga La; 17,400 ft, 5300 m
105	Dunggu La; 15,900 ft, 4840 m
158/9	Tagdhrukha ferry crossing
4821 (new system begins)	Tagdhrukha ferry crossing
4853	Shigatse airport
4904 (marker missing)	Shigatse (Tashilhumpo monastery front gate)

Shigatse to Nepal Border/Kathmandu

4904 (marker missing)	Shigatse (Tashilhumpo front gate)
4917	Narthang monastery
5014	Tsho La; 14,763 ft, 4500 m
5028/9	Sakya monastery turnoff
5040 (marker missing)	Zhiychhen hot springs turnoff
5051/2	Lhatse
5057/8	Mount Kailas turnoff
5082	Lagpa La (Jia Tsuo); 17,126 ft, 5220 m)
432/3 (old system resumes)	Lagpa La
482/3	Shegar (New Tingri) turnoff
488/9	Chinese checkpost
494	Dza Rongphu/Everest base camp turnoff
542	Ra Chhu village turnoff
544	Dingri

554	Tsamda village/Langkor monastery turnoff
555	Tsamda hot springs
581	Gutsuo army camp/lodging
614	Kyirong/Shishapangma North base camp turnoff
637	Thang La; 17,060 ft, 5200 m
667	Ngora village turnoff
683	Pelgyeling monastery/Milarepa cave
694	Nyelam
731 (marker missing)	Khasa/Zhangmu/immigration post
737 (marker missing)	Friendship Bridge/Nepal border
116 (new system begins)	Friendship Bridge
0	Kathmandu

Lhasa to Gongkar Airport/Tsethang

4638 (marker missing)	Lhasa (new bus station)
4703	Yarlung Tsangpo bridge
59/60 (old system resumes)	Yarlung Tsangpo bridge
84/5	Gongkar airport turnoff
47 (different system begins)	Dorje Drag monastery ferry crossing
81	Mindroling monastery turnoff
89/90	Old Samye ferry crossing
112	New Samye tourist ferry crossing
123/4	Tsethang traffic circle
135/6	Yumbu Lagang

Lhasa to Madhrogongkar via Chengdu Highway

4632 (new system)	Lhasa bridge
4612	Dechen Dzong
4591	Ganden monastery turnoff
4573	Gyama valley turnoff
4564	Madhrogongkar

Lhasa to Damzhung via Golmud Highway

4638 (marker missing)	Lhasa (new bus station)
3879 (new system begins; marker missing)	Golmud/Qinghai highway turnoff
3803	Shigatse Northern Road turnoff
3727/8	Damzhung
1774/3 (old system)	Damzhung

Northern Road to Mount Kailas from Lhasa

4638 (marker missing)	Lhasa (new bus station)
4904 (marker missing)	Shigatse (Tashilhumpo front gate)
5057/8	Mount Kailas turnoff
2137 (new system begins)	Mount Kailas turnoff
2135	Yarlung Tsangpo ferry crossing
1906 (marker missing)	Ragaa Junction/Sagaa turnoff

*No markers beyond this point; the following kilometer readings to Darchhan/
Mount Kailas start from zero at Ragaa Junction*

0	Ragaa Junction
20	Tahejia geyser
102	Lagan La; 18,000 ft, 5490 m
228	Tshochhan Dzong (Coqen)
396	Amdo turnoff/Tung Tsho
476	Gertse (Gerze or Gerje)
641	Tshakaa Chhu (Qagcaka)
948	Ali/Shiquanhe
1021	Tsaparang turnoff
1079	Toling/Dawa Dzong turnoff
1134	Mon-tsher/Tirthapuri turnoff
1189	Darchhan turnoff
1195	Darchhan/start of Mount Kailas pilgrimage

Southern Road from Mount Kailas to Lhasa–Kathmandu Highway

*No markers for first part of route; the following kilometer readings start from
zero at Darchhan/Mount Kailas*

0	Darchhan
22	Bharka/turnoff to Purang
137	Mayum (Marium) La; 17,000 ft, 5180 m
161	Paayang Qu
255	Drongpa Xian
1703 (new system begins)	Drongpa Xian
1846	Sagaa
1906 (marker missing)	Ragaa Junction
2137	Lhasa–Kathmandu highway junction

7   The Lhasa Region

Although the snowy peaks of the Himalaya range are far to the south and west, the mountainous areas near Lhasa offer some of the finest trekking in Central Tibet. The monsoon from India bathes this region with summer showers, encouraging wildflowers, tall stands of brush, and scattered groves of trees along the streams and lower slopes of the valleys. Families of nomadic herders establish summer camps throughout these drainages, which they share with a wide variety of wildlife. Although few glaciers lie in these intermediate ranges, the countryside here is as rugged and "Tibetan" as anyplace near the 26,000-foot (8000-m) peaks of the Himalaya.

Dayhikes near Lhasa
(Map 1, page 102)

Before starting off on a trek in Tibet, plan to spend a minimum of 2 to 3 days in Lhasa (or in a similar destination such as Shigatse, Tsethang, or Dingri) acclimatizing to the unusually high altitude. One of the best ways to get into shape and reduce the risk of serious elevation-related problems is to base yourself in one location and go on dayhikes as often as your time and energy will allow. I need a week or more to feel my best while exercising at these elevations, though commercial groups typically allow a maximum of three full days. Whatever your plans, the more time you spend preparing, the more you will be able to enjoy everything around you once the trek begins.

A great way to limber up upon arrival in Lhasa is to walk around the Barkor, the main Tibetan market area and the popular pilgrimage walk encircling the seventh-century Jokhang temple. Situated in the heart of the old Tibetan part of Lhasa, this circuit around the holiest shrine in Tibet takes **about 20 minutes** to complete, not including the inevitable stops for souvenir hunting.

WITHIN LHASA

The Lingkor

Many of the monasteries in Tibet, especially the larger, more famous complexes, have a well-traveled *kora* (a pilgrimage circuit, walked clockwise) around their premises. If care is taken to observe the religious significance of these circuits, they are an excellent source of warm-up walks throughout Central Tibet.

The Lingkor, which literally means "outer pilgrimage circuit," is the traditional walk around the Holy City of Lhasa, and can be walked in **about 1½ hours.**

Pilgrim praying before the Blue Buddha on the Lingkor circuit, Lhasa (photo by Kathy Butler)

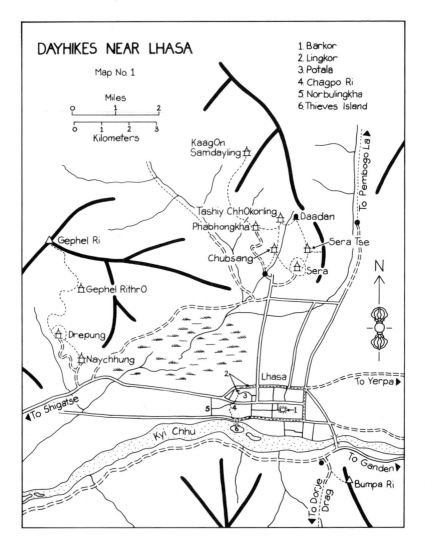

DAYHIKES NEAR LHASA

Map No. 1

1. Barkor
2. Lingkor
3. Potala
4. Chagpo Ri
5. Norbulingkha
6. Thieves Island

Early each morning steady streams of worshippers can be seen completing their rounds with prayer wheels in hand. On certain Tibetan holidays, especially the Saga Dawa festival in the fourth Tibetan month, an almost endless procession of pilgrims follows this route around the city, mumbling prayers and adding incense offerings to the smoking hearths.

The large exit gate at the west corner of the Potala Palace is a convenient though arbitrary place to start the Lingkor. From this gate, walk north beside the Potala's boundary wall. The Lingkor circles behind the palace and around a small lake with a Chinese-looking temple in the center. This is the Lu *lhakhang,* or Serpent temple, said to have been a late-night haunt for the sixth Dalai Lama and his secret paramours. Follow the large piles of offering stones to the right (east) around the trees and the lake to a wide city street called Dzugtrun Lam. Although it doesn't look like part of a pilgrimage circuit, continue straight ahead (east) on this road for **30 minutes** to a large traffic circle intersection, passing the Renmin People's Hospital along the way. The Plateau Hotel and the Telecommunications Building with the clock tower are at this intersection.

The Lingkor now turns right (south) for **20 minutes** onto Dode Lam; in this section, most pilgrims walk on the left side of the street. The next intersection is Dekyi Shar Lam, the main road through the city. The Banok Shol Hotel is a short walk to the right (west), and the first entrances to the Barkor are several minutes farther. Continue south on Dode Lam to the next major intersection with a traffic light, where the Lingkor turns right onto a tree-lined street, Tsanggyu Shar Lam. The scenery is obscured by high-walled compounds for the first **20 minutes,** then the walls suddenly open out and the mountains come into full view. The pilgrims' circuit now becomes a path along the banks of the Kyi Chhu.

A few minutes beyond the last walls a bridge smothered with prayer flags spans the river to Thieves Island, a favorite picnic spot for Tibetans. This island is somewhat like a wilderness park, with trails through willow groves and alongside the river. Facilities here include a small shop, a *momo* restaurant, and even a swimming pool filled with chilly river water.

The Lingkor continues past the bridge for **a few more minutes,** then crosses to the right (north) side of the road toward a huge offering cairn. Do as the pilgrims do when they walk around this circuit and toss three stones onto the mound to acknowledge the local spirits, then enter the stone-walled corridor leading to the north. Reach the base of Chagpo Ri in **less than 5 minutes.** The side of this hill is covered with a grand display of rock paintings and carvings, including the well-known "Blue Buddha" image. The *kora* climbs briefly above this Buddhist art gallery, then descends to another walled corridor, meeting the road between the Potala and the Norbulingka entrance gate in **5 minutes.** The exit gate of the Potala is **less than 10 minutes** to the right (east) along this street.

Chagpo Ri

The "Iron Hill" of Lhasa, with its tall communications tower rising across from the Potala Palace, was formerly the site of the Tibetan Medical College. This famous school of traditional Tibetan medicine was built in the late seventeenth century by Sangye Gyatsho, the regent of Tibet who completed the construction of the Potala while concealing the death of the fifth Dalai Lama for fifteen years. An entrance *chötaen* known as the Western Gate once connected this rocky ridge with the base of the Potala, but that structure and the medical college were destroyed about 1959. Most of Chagpo Ri has now gone back to nature, though a water storage tank and a derelict observation deck accompany the communication tower on the ridge line. Along the cliffs at the eastern end of the hill is the recently rebuilt Serpent cave of Dhraglha Lu-phuu, plus several nearby buildings used as Chinese army barracks.

One of the more direct trails to the top of Chagpo Ri is a **20-minute** ascent that begins at the eastern corner of the hill, directly across from the Potala Palace's exit gate. While photographers prefer the morning and late-afternoon light to

The Potala Palace of the Dalai Lamas, from Chagpo Ri, Lhasa

capture the soaring walls of the enormous castle, the Tibetans come throughout the day to sit for hours, drinking *chhang* and shouting prayers into the wind.

SERA MONASTERY REGION

Sera monastery is one of the four great Gelugpa monasteries in Tibet. This fifteenth-century sprawl of golden roofs and whitewashed walls is just a few miles north of Lhasa at the base of a long, dry ridge called Phurbu Chog. Above the monastery and scattered across the face of this ridge are several old hermitages and temples connected by a series of trails that are some of the nicest, most accessible dayhikes in the Lhasa area.

Sera Monastery *Kora*

A walk around the *kora* is an appropriate way to complete a visit to Sera. Although the actual walking time is **less than 1 hour,** extra time should be allowed for the inevitable encounters with monks and pilgrims making their rounds. Above this circuit is a short side trip to Chhöding *drubphuu,* a famous meditation cave used by Tsong Khapa, founder of the Gelugpa sect.

The ridge behind Sera monastery is very exposed to Tibet's high-altitude sun; all of the walks in this region are in the open along this backdrop of reflective white granite. During the summer, consider starting the *kora* early in the morning or later toward evening. When the weather turns colder, take advantage of these warm rocks by walking in the afternoon.

Sera is connected to Lhasa by Ngangra Lam, a wide arterial road that leads north from near the Potala. The long but gradual uphill climb takes **about 20 minutes** by bicycle. To travel the way many pilgrims do, wave down one of the tractor taxis (they resemble souped-up rototillers pulling a cart) that frequently ply this route seeking riders bound for the monastery. Some taxis stop at a tea shop junction just before the gates of a walled hospital compound where this road ends. Sera is only a few hundred yards farther to the right (east) on a dirt road. To the left of this same junction is the road up to Phabhongkha temple.

The *kora* begins in front of Sera's main entrance (12,150 ft, 3700 m), where the narrow, tree-lined access road opens into a parking area for tourist buses and tractor taxis. Monks are stationed here to collect an entrance fee from foreigners. Tour groups are usually led through here up the shady main service road that bisects the monastery grounds. Most pilgrims who come to see the temples or walk the *kora* bypass this main gate for another entrance 150 feet (45 m) farther to the left (west), where a section of the whitewashed wall enclosing Sera has been pulled down. From here a wide path enters the network of corridors and buildings on a prescribed inner pilgrimage circuit that leads to each of the main temples and monastic colleges, starting with the Sera May tantric college.

The pilgrimage path that circles the entire monastery does not enter the building complex. Instead, continue straight ahead (west) for **a few minutes** along the walled-in dirt trail, then turn to the right around the tall boundary wall toward the base of Phurbu Chog. A short switchback trail leads up the granite slopes to a large offering mound of white stones and strings of prayer flags. To the left (west) across an alluvial outwash is a trail from Sera to Chubsang *ani gompa.*

Continue past more cairns to a gap in a ruined wall. The pilgrim trail now circles behind the golden-roofed colleges of Ngagpa Dhra-tshang, a center for tantric studies, and then behind Jhaypa Dhra-tshang, a large school established for wandering monks from Eastern Tibet. Beyond the Jhaypa college the trail wanders into a beautifully shaded setting. The large willow trees here are nourished by a spring in the ridge. This refreshing little creek is also a laundry area for Sera's monks; purify the water before drinking.

The service road bisecting the monastery grounds ends near this grove of willows, between Jhaypa Dhra-tshang and a large residence hall for monks, Hamdo *khangtsaen.* Due to this area's popularity with the resident monks and picnicking Tibetans, a series of trails has developed that seems to lead everywhere except around the monastery. Ask anyone where the *kora lam,* or pilgrimage trail, continues. You will be enthusiastically guided to the right (east) away from the creek and the trees toward a stone-walled corridor behind Hamdo *khangtsaen.* This passage leads to a granite outcrop rising behind the Tsogchhan, a grand assembly hall for hundreds of monks. One of the routes to Chhöding *drubphuu* (12,500 ft, 3810 m) ascends the ridge from this point toward the prayer flags on the cliffs, reaching this seldom visited temple in **15 minutes.** This is also the turnoff for the trail leading up to Sera Tse hermitage. Another way to Chhöding temple follows the line of electricity poles ascending the ridge.

The *kora* route now descends behind the Tsogchhan along a stone wall. In **a few minutes** a diversion from the main trail climbs up to the left to a large blue image of Jigjhe, the pig-faced protecting deity of the Gelugpa sect, painted onto

The ruins of Tashiy Chhökorling gompa, *Lhasa Valley*

a rock. This upper route is the most active section of the *kora* for pilgrims, with special rocks that are to be touched or circumambulated, many brightly colored rock paintings, and plenty of puppies and dogs who rely upon food offerings from the pilgrims. Some Tibetans believe that these dogs are fallen monks who have been reduced to begging for scraps near monasteries due to misbehavior in their previous lives. If you happen to have a ball of *tsampa* in your pocket, feel free to share it with these fellows.

Sera's more desolate eastern flanks are completely exposed from this upper path. The monastery was hit hard by the Chinese due to its active participation in the 1959 uprising. Although Sera looks impressive from the south, the number of buildings in use is considerably less now than several decades ago, when more than 6000 monks were in residence. The buildings and temples near the entrance gate have been repaired and most of the rubble has been cleared away, though many of the structures to the east have yet to be restored. A few of

the vacated temples still contain piles of discarded statues and building orna-
mentation damaged during the Cultural Revolution.

This upper route continues through the boulders for **5 minutes** before rejoining the main pilgrimage circuit. Descend steeply to the edge of Sera's eastern
boundary wall. Although a larger trail continues straight ahead (south), most
pilgrims turn right through a break in the wall. The path from this gap winds
through the buildings and ruins for **a few minutes** to the tree-lined service road.
The main entrance gate is 100 feet (30 m) to the left. A *thugpa* and tea shop is
in the courtyard of the last building on the right.

If you don't have transport waiting for you, you can catch one of the tractor
taxis that usually sit near the entrance gate until late afternoon. These taxis continue operating on the road to the Potala until dark.

The Phabhongkha Area

Although its white walls glow like a beacon against the hills of Phurbu Chog,
Phabhongkha temple (12,700 ft, 3870 m) is a relatively unknown historical site
very close to the center of Lhasa. Rivaling the Jokhang in antiquity, this chapel
was founded in the seventh century by King Songtsen Gampo. According to
traditional Tibetan history, the land near Phabhongkha was once owned by a
divine golden tortoise. Wanting to honor this holy sage, Songtsen Gampo ordered
a nine-story temple to be built at this site upon a huge tortoise-shaped boulder.
Four great chains radiating in the four cardinal directions were used to anchor
the tower, which was called Phabhongkha ("On Top of the Big Rock"). After the
temple was completed, the king and his parents meditated here for three years.
During this time they were visited by Tibet's three most revered *bodhisattva,*
collectively known as Riysum Gompo, or "the Protectors of the Three Mystic
Families." Songtsen Gampo then formulated the first laws and the famous Moral
Code of Tibet, based upon his Buddhist-oriented list of Ten Good Deeds and
Ten Sinful Deeds.

Some 200 years after Songtsen Gampo's era the first Buddhist monks in
Tibet, seven in all, established their residence at Phabhongkha. But their per-
secution during the reign of King Langdarma in the ninth century led to the
temple's destruction. Phabhongkha has been rebuilt and destroyed several times
since. The most recently restored temple is still on the tortoise boulder, but is
now only two stories high. Phabhongkha is also an important pilgrimage destination for followers and practitioners of Chakrasamvara tantricism, a highly developed form of Tibetan Buddhism involving worship of the tantric deity Demchog.

Phabhongkha is the focal point for several dayhikes to nearby temples and
hermitages. These walks are an ideal way to get the legs moving and prepare for
treks to higher elevations. The 600-foot (180 m) climb to this temple follows a
well-graded road; most people can manage the elevation gain within a few days
of arriving in Lhasa. Tashiy Chhökorling monastery (13,250 ft, 4040 m) is nearby on a ridge spur to the east, and farther up on the cliffs is the cave hermitage of
Daadan *drubphuu* (13,800 ft, 4210 m). Each of these sites is on a tier where you
can rest from the well-spaced succession of climbs. By descending from Tashiy
Chhökorling to Chubsang *ani gompa* (12,400 ft, 3780 m) and returning to the tea
shops at the Sera turnoff, the hike up from Phabhongkha to Daadan *drubphuu*

can be made into a **half-day** loop walk.

The walk to Phabhongkha takes **1 hour** and starts on the opposite side of the main road from the turnoff for Sera monastery. One hundred feet (30 m) beyond the tea shops, turn left (west) onto a dirt road entering a cluster of Tibetan homes. In **5 minutes** the road turns to the right around a stone wall. Continue for **a few minutes,** then turn into a thick grove of willow trees on the first road to the left. Pass more houses, some with junk collections much like homes in rural America, then turn right at a T junction. The white exterior of Phabhongkha is almost straight ahead (north) on the side of the ridge. The road winds beyond the houses along terraced fields. During the months between May and September, the valley is alive with farmers plowing, planting, or harvesting the barley crop.

Once the road leaves the fringes of agriculture and irrigation the terrain quickly returns to desert. Among the cluster of buildings up on the hillside are three main *lhakhangs;* Phabhongkha is in the middle, perched on the boulder. It takes **40 minutes** to reach the first *lhakhang* beyond the last houses. This is an interesting little temple, though it is often locked. The centerpiece of this shrine is a *rangjön,* or self-manifested image of Riysum Gompo.

Just above this shrine are the rounded walls of Phabhongkha temple. If your timing is right, the monks may be chanting upstairs within this *lhakhang.* Walk clockwise around the large "tortoise" boulder to approach the entrance on the far, uphill side. At the base of this boulder is an encased shrine with the characters *Om mani padme hum* carved and painted onto a rock. This is the prayer of Chenrezig, Tibet's god of compassion, and means "Hail to the jewel in the lotus," a reference to the Buddhist philosophy that everyone inherently possesses the wisdom and insight necessary to achieve spiritual enlightenment. According to tradition, this particular inscription was the first example of Tibetan writing presented to Songtsen Gampo after his minister Tonmi Sambhota returned from a lengthy period of studies in India. On the left side and set under the base of the boulder is the meditation cave of Songtsen Gampo. According to the caretaker, the raised stone platform in the center of this retreat is where the king would sit while meditating.

The monks usually gather to chant in the morning and early evening in a small assembly hall on the *lhakhang*'s second floor. If a prayer ceremony is in progress, take off your shoes, have a seat, and be prepared for a bowl of Tibetan butter tea. The main image above the altar is Songtsen Gampo, with his Nepali and Chinese wives to either side. A darkened *gön-khang* is tucked into a narrow room behind the alter.

The grounds around Phabhongkha have a peaceful desert garden atmosphere, shaded in places by gnarled old willow trees surviving on the trickles of a spring from the mountain. Adjacent to the main *gompa* is the kitchen, the source of the butter tea. Farther up the hillside is the third temple, a *lhakhang* for Je Rimpoche, the revered Tsong Khapa.

A stunning but difficult walk climbs steeply to the left (northwest) from Phabhongkha, in the opposite direction from Tashiy Chhökorling, to Kaagön Samdayling *ani gompa* (13,850 ft, 4220 m). This is one of the oldest remaining monasteries near Lhasa, founded 900 years ago by Padampa Sangye, an Indian ascetic who resided in the Dingri area near Mount Everest. One hundred twenty *ani* are presently at this nunnery. The ill-defined route is a surprisingly tough walk over rugged terrain. Somehow the *ani* have managed to walk back and forth across this ridge for hundreds of years without creating a well-marked track. Allow **at least 6 hours** for the round trip from Phabhongkha.

Reaching Tashiy Chhökorling monastery is a much easier prospect, though connecting with the wide, obvious trail leading up to this *gompa* can be a little confusing. A few hundred feet to the right (northeast) from Phabhongkha's main temple is a large granite boulder that rivals the size of the tortoise boulder. Climb toward this big rock using the trail that ascends behind the kitchen building. About 30 feet (10 m) below the boulder a narrow path drops to the bottom of a dry gully, then ascends the east (L) bank to join the wide trail. Tashiy Chhökorling is a climb of **20 minutes** to the east from the edge of this drainage.

The trail forks near the base of an overgrown stone wall below the monastery: both forks lead around to the *gompa*'s stone courtyard. Although the large building above the entrance foyer has been repaired, all of the other structures on the ridge remain in ruins. Several monks live in the rebuilt residence hall. One small temple, a simple *gön-khang,* has been established in a room along the entrance passage. Some of the old *thangka* in here are fine examples of traditional Tibetan artistry.

Daadan *drubphuu* is **40 minutes** above this monastery, set into the limestone cliffs on the east (L) side of the deep creek gorge. This walk ascends from the stone courtyard up through the crumbling ruins onto the ridge overlooking the monastery. Continue up the ridge along a series of dusty switchbacks to a stone monument. Cross the ridge spur, then traverse on a well defined trail into the gorge. The *drubphuu* is **less than 10 minutes** up from the creek crossing on the east (L) ridge side.

The caves of Daadan are situated on a natural platform under sweeping waves of limestone. Water flows from several springs, sunshine warms the towering, overhanging cliffs, and tangles of shrubs thrive in the protection and moisture of the gully. The views stretch across the valley, from the small mound occupied by the Potala to the rounded shoulders of Gephel Ri, the holy mountain behind Drepung monastery and one of the highest peaks (17,200 ft, 5240 m) around Lhasa.

The *drubphuu* is the smallest of the three caves, located up to the left above the stone abode of a *gom-chhaen,* or hermit monk, from northern Kham who has lived here since the early 1980s. This cave shrine contains a self-manifested image of the protector Demchog's third eye etched into the rock. Next to the altar is a small opening at the back of the cave where a spring issues forth water said to be a manifestation of the protectress Dorje Phagmo. (This female deity has a human incarnation whose earthly residence is Samding monastery near Yamdrog Tsho.) When Tibetan pilgrims visit the caves, the *gom-chhaen* pours them a handful of this spiritual fluid from a narrow-necked pitcher. The proper way to receive this blessing is to cup your right hand, slurp down about two thirds of the water, then run the rest of it back through your hair with the same hand. May the powers of Dorje Phagmo, the "Adamantine Sow," be with you.

By the way, the hermit here isn't as reclusive as the term implies. When he's gone on a tea run to the lower temples, the stairway to the *drubphuu* is closed off by a wooden door.

The larger caves at the other end of the platform are too wet to be occupied. Below is another stone hut, which the local herders use, and a few steps down the ridge—beyond some healthy stinging nettles—is the neighborhood latrine, situated to provide the ultimate in geographic contemplation.

From the hermitage there are several ways to return to the road junction near Sera monastery. The trail up to Daadan can be retraced back toward Phabhongkha, though a more direct route descends from Tashiy Chhökorling for **30 minutes** to Chubsang *ani gompa* (12,400 ft, 3780 m). The locals claim this *gompa* has seventy nuns and six monks, though the monastery has little more than a quaint *lhakhang,* a kitchen, and a few sleeping rooms. At the end of 1988, a residence hall was under construction on an adjacent piece of property. The hillside down from Chubsang is covered with trails. The dirt access road to Phabhongkha is **15 minutes** below this monastery, and the tea shops at the Sera turnoff are **another 15 minutes** through the Tibetan settlements.

Another alternative is to continue up the ridge from the Daadan caves, then traverse to the east across Phurbu Chog on to Sera Tse hermitage and Sera monastery. This walk is described below in reverse, starting from Sera.

Sera Tse to Phabhongkha Loop Walk

The brown, windowed walls of Sera Tse cling to the rocky face of Phurbu Chog directly above Sera monastery. Believed to predate Sera in origin, this hermitage is now mostly in ruins, but two small temples have been rebuilt and several monks have returned to this lofty retreat.

The climb up and back from Sera Tse is a strenuous **half-day** outing. With an early start, keen hikers can combine this walk with the panoramic traverse across Phurbu Chog's western flanks and finish on the trail from Daadan *drubphuu* to Phabhongkha temple. This **full-day** loop walk is one of the finest dayhikes in Tibet.

The most direct approach to Sera Tse starts from the pilgrimage *kora* behind Sera monastery, then climbs up to the temples at Chhöding *drubphuu* (12,400 ft, 3780 m). Before setting off, take a minute at Sera's entrance gate to locate the hermitage on the ridge. Chhöding is much lower and farther to the right, set in a grove of trees not far above the monastery.

The most direct route to Chhöding bypasses the first half of the *kora* by following the willow-lined service road through the center of the monastery. This road jogs left at a boulder with painted rock carvings, then ends at the base of the ridge between two large buildings: Jhaypa Dhra-tshang on the left and Hamdo *khangtsaen* on the right. The pilgrim *kora* is only 20 feet (6 m) up this ridge under a canopy of large willow trees. Several routes lead up to Sera Tse from this point; the best one follows the pilgrimage walk to the right (east) through a stone-walled corridor behind Hamdo *khangtsaen*. Where the *kora* emerges onto a smoothed outcrop of granite rock, look high to the left for clusters of prayer

Wall fresco of a guardian king, Chhöding lhakhang, *Sera monastery (photo by Kathy Butler)*

flags decorating the cliffs. These are good landmarks for finding the way to Chhöding, a **10-minute** climb from this point. Sera Tse is **another hour** beyond Chhöding.

The trail up the ridge is rather faint, though the occasional footprints, rock cairns, and scraps of prayer flags in the bushes help verify a correct choice. A relatively flat, well-marked trail follows the cliff top to the left (southeast) around the curve of the ridge to a huge tree and to Chhöding *khang,* a retreat house for monks. The building had been defunct since the 1960s, the temple gutted, and the frescoes obliterated with coats of white paint. With the recent return of six monks, the temple is being renovated and the figures of the *yab-se-sum,* Tsong Khapa and his two main disciples, will again grace the central altar.

Directly above this *khang* is Chhöding *drubphuu,* a small shrine over a meditation cave used more than five centuries ago by Tsong Khapa. This great reformer of Tibetan Buddhism composed two of his most famous treatises on Buddhist scriptures and philosophy during the several years he is said to have spent here.

The monks reach Sera Tse via a shortcut that climbs straight up the ridge behind the cave temple. An easier approach begins at the doorstep of Chhöding *khang.* Using the trail leading to the left (south) from the temple entrance, pass a grove of trees and a freshwater spring, the last water until Sera Tse. Keep contouring across the ridge to reach an outcrop of rock with prayer flags in **less**

than 5 minutes from the *khang.*

Though there isn't much of a trail, you can climb up the ridge from these prayer flags along a hump of smoothed granite. In **less than 10 minutes** join a well-defined trail angling to the left (north) across Phurbu Chog from the base of the ridge. Desert conditions prevail: lizards laze on hot rocks and monstrous Himalayan griffin vultures sweep along on the heated currents rising from these south-facing slopes. The trail enters some switchbacks, then climbs steadily to the ruins at the base of Sera Tse within **another 40 minutes.**

Zigzag up through the broken walls to a small paved courtyard and a re-built *lhakhang* (13,500 ft, 4110 m) with commanding views of the Lhasa Valley. This shrine is another Tsong Khapa meditation cave. Farther up the hill is a *gön-khang* with images of the protecting deities Pehar, who possesses the State Oracle during his trances, and the horse riding championess of the Gelugpa sect, Pelden Lhamo. Simple stone quarters have been rebuilt from the rubble by the two *dhrapa* who have returned to this retreat.

Although the quickest way back to Sera is to return on the same trail, the loop walk to Phabhongkha is a scenic alternative. The terrain is less desertlike and most of the climbing for this walk has already been accomplished while coming up to Sera Tse.

A high trail leads in both directions from Sera Tse. **Less than 10 minutes** to the east is a saddle in the ridge offering fine views of the upper Kyi Chhu Valley. To the west beyond the hermitage's water source is the traverse across Phurbu Chog and the loop walk to the Daadan caves and Phabhongkha temple. Although Phabhongkha can be reached in 1^1/$_2$ **hours** of steady walking, allow considerably more time to visit the temples en route, plus **another hour** for the return walk to Sera monastery.

From Sera Tse, descend beyond the water source to the crest of a ridge spur, then reach a second spur in **25 minutes** from the hermitage. The ruined walls of Tashiy Chhökorling can be seen up ahead (west) on a distant ridge. The hills here don't face the intense sun, allowing grasses, wild iris, and other wild-flowers to spring up during the wet summer months. Continue the traverse, then climb steeply to a high ridge spur (13,800 ft, 4210 m), reaching the crest in **another 15 minutes.** The point on this spur a little below the trail is a great spot for taking a break. It's hard to believe that such a remote mountain walk can be so close to Lhasa.

Tashiy Chhökorling is on the opposite ridge, across a deep creek gorge. Follow the trail into this drainage for **10 minutes,** then climb a short distance to Daadan *drubphuu* (13,800 ft, 4210 m). These caves and the trails leading down to Phabhongkha and Chubsang *ani gompa* are described in the section on Phabhongkha.

DREPUNG MONASTERY REGION

Drepung Monastery *Kora*

Five miles (8 km) to the west of the Lhasa Holiday Inn is Drepung monas-tery, once the largest and most powerful of the four great Gelugpa religious centers in Tibet. This huge monastic university lies hidden from most of Lhasa, cradled within the rocky ridges just beyond the city limits.

The *kora* at Drepung is a·panoramic **1-hour** walk that climbs into the foothills around this fifteenth-century network of stone temples and colleges. The views of the Lhasa Valley and the monastery grounds from these hills are outstanding.

The first half of the journey to Drepung is a pleasant **20-minute** bicycle ride west from the Holiday Inn along the far end of Dekyi Nub Lam. Even though it is an extension of the main east-west road through the city, this wide avenue quickly becomes a country lane surrounded by grassy meadows and lined with poplars and willows. The road is flat for most of the ride, then ascends a small hill. Once the road levels again, a walled compound with a Chinese mural at the entrance gate will be on the right. Spread across the nearby hills is the monastic city of Drepung. The huge ridge dominating the skyline is the holy mountain of Gephel Ri (also known as Gambay Utse), and Gephel *rithrö* is the small white building about halfway up its flanks.

The dirt access road to Drepung is the next turn to the right (north) beyond this walled enclosure. Because this road climbs steeply to reach the main parking area and the entrance gate (12,450 ft, 3790 m), most people leave their bicycles at the base of this rise. Bikes can be parked all day for a nominal fee at a house a few minutes up the access road. Tractor taxis heading toward Drepung can be flagged down along Dekyi Nub Lam near the Lhasa Holiday Inn. They usually don't go up the access road, but drop passengers off at the base of the hill. The walk up to the monastery's main parking area takes **about 30 minutes.**

The road to Drepung forks near some tea shops just beyond the house where you can leave your bicycle. Naychhung monastery, the former residence of Tibet's State Oracle, is **a few minutes** up the right fork. A wide pilgrimage path continues up the hill, connecting this abode of demons and ghoulish deities with Drepung. You can also take the left fork, which winds toward Drepung in long switchbacks, or follow any of the pilgrims who often shortcut through the orchard to reach the parking area.

Monks are stationed in a small building beside the parking area to collect entrance fees from foreigners. The nearby flight of stone stairs leads through the main entrance gate and into the monastery. This is the start of the traditional inner circuit used by pilgrims to visit each of the important temples and shrines, beginning with the Ganden Phodhrang, the sixteenth-century quarters used by Tibet's spiritual leaders for 150 years, until the fifth Dalai Lama initiated the construction of the Potala Palace. If you want to visit the temples first, the *kora* around the outer walls can be joined by walking **a few minutes** west from the stone courtyard of the Tsogchhan, Drepung's main assembly hall.

To begin the pilgrimage *kora* from the main parking area, look for a wide path lined with gnarled willow trees leading up from the far left (northwest) corner of this lot. Climb to a small entrance gate and enter a stone lane between the tightly packed residence buildings. At the first junction follow the cobbled route to the left (west). The white-painted walls soon end and open onto a long two-storied residence hall. Veer to the right past a small water channel and two shrub-encrusted stone shrines, then climb among the rocks, carvings, and ruined walls between Drepung's western boundary wall and a rocky creek bed. The

Above: Monks enjoying view of the Lhasa Valley from the Drepung pilgrims'
kora. *Below: Views of Drepung from the monastery's pilgrimage circuit*

Ganden Phodhrang is nearby but hidden from view by this stone rampart.

A stairway of paved stones ascends beside the creek. The bulbous outcrops of white granite are decorated with colorful paintings, the largest being an image of Tsong Khapa. A little farther up and across the creek is a cleared area on the hillside where Drepung displays its giant *thangka* at the onset of the annual Opera Festival, usually held in August. Continue climbing beside the tall boundary wall to a trail junction near several large boulders with carvings and painted *mantra* (12,800 ft, 3900 m). The *kora* now turns to the right (east), away from the creek bed and into a corridor of stone walls overgrown with wild rosebushes. Within the walls to the right is the Sankhang, a former meditational retreat of the Dalai Lamas and the highest of Drepung's buildings.

An opening in the upper left wall at this junction leads into a clearing dotted with shade trees. The wide path winding north up this meadow toward the large cleft in the ridge is the pilgrimage route to Gephel *rithrö* and the summit of Gephel Ri. This trail wanders into the creek gorge for **about 20 minutes** before climbing up the mountain. During the summer this area is verdant with blooming bushes, wildflowers, and patches of grass between the rocks near the creek. Bring a book or a picnic lunch and relax in the company of brown dippers diving underwater as they hunt for aquatic insects.

The pilgrim's route around the monastery continues east from the overgrown walls on a fairly level path. Immediately below are the devastated buildings of Drepung's eastern limits, as well as the golden roofs of the four colleges and the assembly hall that somehow survived Tibet's recent past. (This once vast religious university was founded in 1416 by a disciple of Tsong Khapa. Until the 1950s, Drepung was the heart of the Gelugpa sect's political power, housing more than 8000 monks (from all over Tibet) who had come to study the Tantras and Buddhist philosophy.)

The *kora* weaves through more rocks and paintings, then descends in a dusty series of switchbacks to an elevated iron water pipe. Above this pipe is a dirt road that continues down the hill to Naychhung monastery. To return to the parking area at Drepung's main entrance, follow this road for less than 300 feet (90 m) to where the water pipe ends, then turn right (west) onto a trail that runs beside an earthen wall. Keep heading west for **several minutes,** then join a crooked stone lane below a row of tall buildings. The main entrance gate will be on the left.

Gephel Ri

Rising above Drepung monastery is Gephel Ri (17,200 ft, 5240 m), the most sacred summit in the Lhasa area and one of the highest. Every year, hours before daybreak on the morning of Saga Dawa, hundreds of pilgrims begin their devotional climb from Drepung to the top of Gephel Ri to celebrate the birth, enlightenment, and death of Buddha. Giant bundles of incense bush are hauled to the top to be ceremonially lit, sending billowing plumes of fragrant smoke toward the heavens. Traditionally, the Dalai Lama would also go up Gephel Ri, riding a horse in a grand procession on a wide, well-graded trail that ascends nearly 5000 feet (1520 m). Only two other points around the Lhasa Valley are taller, but none are as accessible.

The hike up Gephel Ri is very strenuous, requiring **at least 12 hours** (in-cluding breaks, lunch, and so on) for the round trip from Drepung, plus the travel time from Lhasa to the monastery and back. As the monastery does not have overnight accommodations, hiring a Landcruiser from one of the travel companies is probably the best means of assuring a predawn start.

A climb of this magnitude flirts with your body's ability to cope with elevation-related problems: pay attention to all members in your party. Only hikers who are well acclimatized should consider this walk. Because this summit can become mighty blustery during the summer thunderstorm season, bring a hat, gloves, adequate sun protection, and reliable rain gear.

The trail to Gephel Ri follows the pilgrimage *kora* clockwise up the stairs from the far left (northwest) corner of the Drepung monastery parking area, described in the "Drepung Monastery *Kora*" section. Climb for **10 minutes** beside the boundary wall until the *kora* turns to the right (east) from the creek bed. The trail to Gephel Ri continues straight ahead (north) from here, entering a large clearing through the opening in the upper left wall. Ascend for **20 minutes** beyond the meadows and willow trees into the rocky gully, weaving in and out of boulders above the east (L) bank of the creek. The canyon soon forks and the trail splinters here into a braid of choices climbing up the east (L) ridge. Eventually these small paths merge into a wide, graded trail with rein-forced embankments. Climb steadily for **1 hour** through a desert of weathered granite to a flat ridge spur (13,900 ft, 4240 m) decorated with prayer flags. Gephel *rithrö* (14,700 ft, 4480 m) is **another hour** across the ridge face to the east.

This 600-year-old hermitage was in a sad state in 1988: goats, not monks, were occupying the buildings, and an unsightly communication relay station had been installed nearby. A small work crew of monks and laborers was begin-ning to restore Naychhung *lhakhang,* the larger of the two main buildings. There are also plans to restore the Simju, a sleeping house used during ceremonial visits by the Dalai Lama. The views of the Kyi Chhu Valley from here are breathtaking and the seldom-visited monks enjoy an opportunity to socialize and share revitalizing cups of butter tea with visitors. The spring for this hermitage is usu-ally the last chance to get water before the summit.

The trail to Gephel Ri climbs north from Naychhung *lhakhang* for **75 min-utes** in a series of long switchbacks, passing cushion plants and sprinklings of wildflowers en route to the crest of the main ridge (16,150 ft, 4920 m). If the weather is agreeable, this tundra-covered ridge is an excellent spot to have lunch. The Sera Valley falls away to the north, allowing views of the remote Kaagön Samdayling *ani gompa;* the dip in the ridge line farther to the right is Pembogo La, the first pass on the old northern caravan route from Lhasa to central China. On clear days the peaks of Bhutan show their snowy faces far to the south beyond the Kyi Chhu Valley.

The final **hour**'s walk to Gephel Ri looks deceptively easy and resem-bles a path in the land of Oz: hundreds of cairns piled by Buddhist pilgrims line the sides of this regal route to the domed crest (17,200 ft, 5240 m); even the trig marker at the lower end of this slope is blessed with thick clutters of prayer flags. Not far from the top the trail enters a stunning labyrinth of devotional monuments. Thousands of narrow, columnar rock piles compete for space on this rolling summit, complicating attempts to reach the whorl of colorful prayer flags radiating from the main summit cairn.

There is a peculiar tradition at certain holy sites, including Mount Kailas in Western Tibet, whereby pilgrims leave behind a piece of clothing, usually the hat they are wearing. Straw hats, felt hats, fur hats, visors, and baseball caps, as well as shoes, jackets, and gloves, are scattered everywhere among the cairns and prayer flags as special personal offerings to the mountain spirits. One of the real treats of this climb, besides the panoramas and the satisfaction of success, is the exhilaration and awe that is generated from being in the presence of such a grand display of devotion and faith.

Although several very steep shortcut trails lead down some of the ridges below Gephel *rithrö,* the route used to ascend to the summit is also the most practical way back down. Allow **at least 3 to 4 hours** for the long return to the parking area. When rejoining the Drepung *kora,* remember to descend clockwise around the monastery.

BUMPA RI

The ascent of Bumpa Ri (14,250 ft, 4340 m) is a tough but rewarding dayhike to a pair of rocky crags towering more than 2000 feet (610 m) above the south (L) banks of the Kyi Chhu. Shaped like a pair of offering vases, or *bumpa,* this ridge is another lofty site near Lhasa where incense bushes are burned to celebrate special occasions such as Losar, the Tibetan New Year. On the second day of this festival, when deep horns rumble during the predawn hours from within the Jokhang and people bundled in sheepskin coats throng around the Barkor spinning their prayer wheels, Bumpa Ri glows red with fires that send plumes of smoke skyward throughout the morning. A keen eye can spot the streams of prayer flags hung between these rocky points to the south of Lhasa on the ridge directly above the Lhasa bridge.

The number of pilgrims climbing this promontory is far fewer than the crowds ascending Gephel Ri for the Saga Dawa festival. The route up Bumpa Ri is a steep climb on a faint but negotiable trail that should be attempted only by people who are accustomed to scrambling over rugged terrain. The total walking time required to reach the summit and return, starting from the turnoff at the Lhasa bridge, is **5 hours.** If you are walking from the center of Lhasa (the Barkor), add **another 1½ hours.**

Starting from the end of the Lhasa bridge, turn right (west) along the south (L) bank of the Kyi Chhu. The highway to Ganden monastery and eastern Tibet turns left from this bridge. Follow the dirt road to the right for **15 minutes,** passing several houses and a small mud brick factory on the right. **A few minutes** farther is a forked intersection by a walled compound. Take the smaller road on the left that heads away from the river onto a broad plain. The twin summits of Bumpa Ri, which are part of the long ridge to the left that borders this plain, are a useful bearing; the route beyond here is obscure in places.

Ten minutes beyond this intersection turn left (southeast) onto a rutted cart track that angles across several low hills toward a broad alluvial fan. Follow this cart track up the barren hillside to the right of a gravel wash. Although the track quickly narrows to a path and then disappears altogether, continue climbing cross-country for **30 minutes** to where the alluvial fan spills from the mouth of two converging drainage gullies. The terrain is so dry along here that only wisps of grass and spherical clusters of white and pink blooming daphne (*Stellera chamaejasme*) manage to survive. In these gullies, though, enough water drains from the hills to nourish thick clumps of tall grasses, wildflowers, and, surprisingly, jack-in-the-pulpits (*Arisaema*), a plant more commonly found in rain forests along the Himalaya's southern slopes.

A small rock enclosure has been built at the base of the spur separating these two drainages. Bumpa Ri is the ridge directly above. Prayer flags hang across the dip between its rock towers. The summit is a steep 1500-foot (460 m) climb along hot, dry slopes, and takes **about 2^1/$_2$ hours** including breaks. Even during the July and August wet season little water flows in these creek beds, so bring enough water to last the entire day; it's easy to be caught short here.

The most obvious route to the summit is a well-defined trail leading into a gully up to the left (east) from the rock enclosure. Though it is possible to reach the top this way, the trail fizzles out and quickly becomes a difficult but scenic scramble. An easier, cairned route actually begins up the right-hand (south) gully. This trail is quite faint for the first few minutes until it starts ascending the south side of the central ridge separating these two drainages. The trail is very steep in places, with sections of loose talus and a continuous series of switchbacks crossing slabs of bare rock. Many false turns lead away from the correct trail; follow the small rock cairns.

Eventually the path climbs onto the nose of the ridge, presenting the first good views of the Lhasa Valley. Ascend through a series of rock outcrops, then cross into the drainage gully on the left, below the gap near the summit. Each of these rocky spires has a route leading to the top, though the more southern (right) of the two is slightly higher.

The ashes of burnt incense bushes rest silently in small offering hearths, thick strands of *lungdaa* flutter their prayers aloft, and the Lhasa Valley falls away at your feet. Across the broad river plain is Gephel Ri, rising behind Drepung monastery. Farther to the right (north) are the golden roofs of Sera monastery, and above these buildings is a dip in the ridge where the old trade route from Lhasa crosses Pembogo La into the Phenyul Valley. The highest peak around Lhasa, Maendrub Tsari ("meditation medicine grass" mountain; 18,160 ft, 5535 m), rises nearby from the ridge continuing south behind Bumpa Ri.

The return to the Lhasa bridge is a descent of **2 hours** along the same route.

Ganden and Samye
(Map 2, page 119)

In early 1985 the trek from Ganden monastery to Samye monastery was little more than a rumored alternative to the shorter, more established walk from the town of Dechen Dzong to Samye over the Gokar La trade route. By that summer, the first summer that Tibet was open to individual travelers, news of the everchanging landscape of mountain passes and alpine lakes between these two historical monasteries quickly changed this walk from an unknown route to the

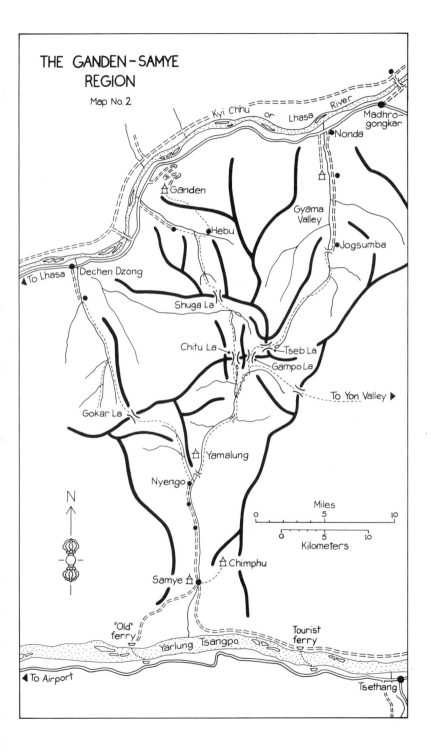

THE GANDEN – SAMYE
REGION

Map No. 2

Kyi Chhu or Lhasa River

Madhro-gongkar

Nonda

Ganden

Gyama Valley

Hebu

Jogsumba

To Lhasa

Dechen Dzong

Shuga La

Chitu La

Tseb La

Gampo La

To Yon Valley ▶

Gokar La

Yamalung

Nyengo

N

Miles
0   5   10

0   5   10
Kilometers

Chimphu

Samye

"Old" ferry

Tourist ferry

Yarlung Tsangpo

◀ To Airport

Tsethang

premier trek of the Lhasa region. With minimal backtracking, the shorter trek from Samye to Dechen Dzong can be used as the second half of a beautiful loop walk of **8 to 10 days** that originates in Ganden (or in the Gyama Valley, a route described in "The Gyama Valley to Samye Trek"), visits Samye, and finishes at Dechen Dzong, 14 miles (23 km) to the east of Lhasa.

Despite its popularity, the Ganden to Samye trek is a tough walk that crosses two high passes through a remote region. The easiest starting point is Ganden (13,900 ft, 4240 m), for it is considerably higher in elevation than Samye (11,800 ft, 3600 m). The average walking time in this direction is **4 to 5 days;** strong parties can complete it in **3¹/₂ days.** The best time for trekking in this region is from late April until late October, though the intermediate valleys between these monasteries receive a healthy share of the summer monsoon from the middle of June until early September—a deterrent for some but prime wildflower season for others. Snow is a possibility any time of year, making knitted gloves, a wool cap, and good rain gear recommended equipment even in the summer. Winter crossings are possible but should be attempted only by strong, well-equipped parties.

All food must be brought from Lhasa and a tent and fuel stove are highly recommended. Beyond Ganden there is only one small village and the occasional *drogpa* camp before reaching the settlements in the Yamalung and upper Samye valleys. Although it is sometimes possible to stay with these herders, their woven yak-hair tents are notorious for leaking. Even the "caves" that some trekkers use along this route are nothing more than rock overhangs offering little protection in bad weather.

If individual trekking is again allowed in Tibet, note that pack animals are not usually available at Ganden, for there are no villages nor settlements near the monastery. It may be possible to hire a burro or a horse at one of the villages below the monastery closer to the Kyi Chhu, or in Hebu, the small village **4 hours** past Ganden on the trail to Samye.

The nature of the terrain on the Ganden to Samye trek can create serious difficulties for anyone who suffers from acute mountain sickness (AMS) while crossing Shuga La (17,200 ft, 5240 m) from Ganden, or Chitu La (16,700 ft, 5090 m) from Samye, for the valley between these passes is quite high in elevation (16,200 ft, 4940 m) and very remote. The only way to descend to lower ground or to seek medical assistance is to retrace your route back over the previous pass to the nearest roadhead, so don't risk the dilemma of an evacuation from this high valley. If someone in your party shows preliminary signs of mountain sickness while ascending to these passes, turn around and camp at a safer, lower elevation rather than pushing on with hopes of completing the crossing that day.

One of the best ways to acclimatize for this trek is to spend at least two nights in Ganden before setting off. The extra day and night at this elevation will make a big difference in how your body responds to the altitude during the trek. In addition to exploring Ganden's ruins and visiting the rebuilt temples, stretch your legs with a dayhike in the surrounding hills. A good pre-trek warm-up hike with panoramic views of the ruins and the distant valleys is the high pilgrimage *kora* along the Angker Ri ridge top, the southern wall of the basin cradling Ganden. From the west end of this ridge the trail drops down to connect with the main pilgrim circuit around the monastery. Remember to approach either of these walks in the proper, clockwise manner that the pilgrims follow. A longer, more challenging dayhike is the walk out to the unnamed peak resembling a shark's fin on the ridge beyond Angker Ri.

Ganden Monastery

The Ganden monastery complex was formerly one of the three great religious centers for the Gelugpa sect of Tibetan Buddhism. Even with the majority of its buildings in ruins, Ganden remains a stunning sight. It is situated high in a natural amphitheater above the Kyi Chhu, or Lhasa River, about 32 miles (52 km) by road from Lhasa. Pilgrim buses to Ganden leave Lhasa almost every morning about 6:30 A.M. from the southwest corner of the Jokhang temple on the Barkor. The trip usually takes two hours or more. The buses remain at the monastery for the day, returning to Lhasa later in the afternoon. If you miss the bus look for the pilgrim trucks that often gather passengers on the Barkor as well. Private transport can be arranged through the various tourist and transport agencies in Lhasa or through your hotel.

Overnight accommodation at Ganden is dormitory style, located in the first large building to the north of the monastery parking area, across from the shop. It's a good idea to bring enough food from Lhasa for your stay in Ganden as well as for the trek, though simple meals of *thugpa* and *momo* can be purchased at the small restaurant beside the parking area. The shop sells few food items other than sweets, brick tea, and yak butter. A number of potential campsites can be

The sprawling ruins of Ganden, one of the three major monasteries in the Lhasa region

found around the ruins, but check first with the monks before setting up your tent.

The monastery was founded as a cave hermitage in 1409 by Tsong Khapa (known to the Tibetans as Je Rimpoche), one of the most revered figures in the religious history of Tibet. It was through his teachings and reform efforts that one of the first organized schools of Tibetan Buddhism, the Kadampa sect, was transformed into the largest and most influential religious body established in Tibet, the Gelugpa sect.

Nearly every rebuilt temple at Ganden has Tsong Khapa's likeness behind the altar, usually flanked by images of his two disciples, Gyaltshab and Khaydhrub. This trio is known as the *yab-say-sum,* "the father and his two sons." One of the most important shrines formerly at Ganden was the Ser Dung, the gold-covered tomb of Tsong Khapa. This monument, along with the monastery, was destroyed in 1966 during the Cultural Revolution. A new *chötaen,* said to contain fragments of Tsong Khapa's skull, is now housed upstairs in the rebuilt Ser Dung, the large, maroon-walled temple in the center of Ganden's ruins.

While most of the rubble from the Cultural Revolution has been cleared away from Sera and Drepung and many of their remaining temples restored with financial aid from the Chinese government, Ganden has had only minimal assistance. As of 1988 about 400 monks and several *rimpoche* had returned to Ganden, but the rebuilding efforts were still dwarfed by the ruins of the former monastery.

Nevertheless, a number of reconstructed temples and residence halls have appeared across the hillside over the past few years. Above and to the east of the Ser Dung is a smaller temple, also painted maroon, containing the Serthri, or Golden Throne, of the Ganden abbots. This throne, like the building, has been rebuilt, but the abbot's hat on the throne beside the framed picture of the fourteenth Dalai Lama is the original. The next building to the east is Thritog *khang,* the former residence of the Ganden abbot.

On the right side of the cart track leading up to the Ser Dung is Ngam Chhö *khang,* a dark but interesting temple with an even darker *gön-khang.* (Women are not allowed into any of the *gön-khang,* or protector's temples, at Ganden, a rather unusual rule for Tibet.) Most of the other buildings are *khangtsaen,* and nearly every one contains at least one small temple within its premises.

Dayhikes near Ganden

Two fine hikes in the Ganden area are the pilgrimage circuits near the monastery: the high *kora,* which climbs above the monastery onto the ridge line of Angker Ri; and the standard, lower traditional *kora,* which encircles the entire ruins complex and leads to Je Drubphuu, Tsong Khapa's original meditation cave at Ganden.

The high *kora* requires 1¹/₂ **to 2 hours** to complete and initially follows the trail leading from Ganden toward Samye monastery. From the parking area, take the cart track up the hill for 200 feet (60 m) to where it swings back to the right. Don't turn with the cart track, but continue climbing up the hill in the same direction (south) along a footpath. In **less than 10 minutes** this trail forks. The lower left-hand branch leads on to Samye; the upper right fork is the pilgrimage route to the ridge top. Climb steadily up the dry slopes on this trail, reaching the Angker Ri summit in **less than 1 hour** from the monastery. The ridge line

*Stone image of Tsong Khapa on the wall of his meditation cave, Ganden
monastery*

resembles a serpent's backbone, undulating in a series of crests festooned with
streamers of colorful prayer flags. Pilgrims plod along the circuit quietly saying
their prayers, burning bundles of juniper or rhododendron incense bush, then
pouring offerings of *tsampa* and *chhang* on these fires for the gods.

Follow the pilgrims (they're especially abundant on Sundays) and the trail to
the right (west) along the ridge top, passing innumerable piles of stones stacked
by the devout Tibetans. Far below is the Kyi Chhu, weaving like the tangled roots
of an old tree through the vast gravel flats. On clear days the lone snowy summit
of the main Nyanchhan Thanglha peak (23,330 ft, 7111 m) rises to the northwest,
situated between the Yangpachan Valley and Nam Tsho. The *kora* stays along
the ridge of Angker Ri for **30 minutes,** then descends steeply for **15 minutes**
to rejoin the cart track near the south side of the monastery. You can return to
the temples from here or continue to the left (west) to join the *kora* behind the
monastery.

The pilgrimage circuit around Ganden is a fascinating walk. Hardly five
minutes goes by without groups of Tibetans stopping before a rock, a shrine, or a
crevice in a boulder to perform unusual rituals and exercises that "test" their
faith and help them earn religious merit, all in a carnivallike atmosphere. This
kora begins at the south end of Ganden and climbs up to a low ridge top behind
the ruins in **5 minutes.** You can also begin from the parking lot and follow the
cart track up the ridge. A large rocky cleft draped with prayer flags marks the
start of this circuit, which takes **at least 1 hour** to complete.

The *kora* traverses the rocky ridge side, providing outstanding views of the valley for the entire walk. Right from the start the rocks beside the trail are smudged with yak butter and bushes are decorated with tufts of yak and sheep wool. Throughout the rock fissures are small shrines filled with *tsha-tsha,* small religious offering tablets made of clay and deposited by the pilgrims. Farther along the pilgrims stop at particular rocks where they pass their hands carefully over a blackened surface, or reverently touch their heads, or perhaps rub their backs like a bear with an itch, all the while reciting their prayers. At several locations the pilgrims shout encouragement to one another as they each try to squeeze through the well-worn but narrow gaps between certain boulders. If you're walking alone and want to get in on the action, wait for a party of Tibetans to come along and show you all the intricacies of these rituals.

The trail eventually climbs to a rocky outcrop, then descends past a flat terrace on the left where sky burials are conducted. (This is a Western term for the practical Tibetan way to dispose of human corpses. The body is chopped into small pieces, then the bones and flesh are mashed into a paste with *tsampa* flour. The mixture is made into offering balls and fed to the flocks of vultures that have gathered, thus carrying the spirit of the deceased person closer to the heavens.) Continue descending around the back of Drog Ri, the ridge forming the northern wall of the Ganden amphitheater. Pass by more shrines and outcrops of well-worn limestone rocks to reach Je Drubphuu, the meditation cave of Tsong Khapa. Set in a hillside of scrubby juniper bushes, the cave now contains a small *lhakhang* with five self-manifested rock carvings on the wall. Many pilgrimage sites have stones or rock walls with a Tibetan alphabet letter on them, the prayer *Om mani padme hum,* or images of people or deities like the ones here, which are said to be *rangjön,* or self-manifested, because they appeared miraculously on their own. Tsong Khapa is the largest, central image, and according to the caretaker each of these figures is a "talking Buddha," meaning they also possess the power of speech. The caretaker may offer you the blessing from this temple, a handful of water from the long-necked urn on the altar.

The main pilgrimage route now traverses around the ridge to the monastery. When the trail branches near the ruins, take the left fork to return to the parking area, or the right fork to climb through the destroyed buildings. Another small trail scrambles up to the right from the cave temple to reach several isolated shrines and rock paintings. Farther up, on the summit of Drog Ri, is a white *chötaen* and fine views of the Kyi Chhu Valley. Watch out for the large stands of stinging nettles if you descend through the ruins to the monastery.

The hike up to Shark Fin peak, which is the solitary summit along the ridge line a few miles east of Ganden, is a full-day adventure requiring **10 hours or more** to complete, including rest breaks and a lunch stop. Bring enough water to last the entire day, for this is a dry ridge. There isn't much of a trail for this walk, but the route is straightforward, staying on the ridge top beyond Angker Ri the entire way.

Follow the cart track and then the footpath up to the south from Ganden as if you were heading toward Samye. When the trail forks, take the left branch and continue sidling across the flanks of Angker Ri. **About 1 hour** from the monastery reach a saddle in the ridge marked with a large *la-dzay* (14,800 ft, 4510 m). The trail to Samye drops down the south side into the next valley. The route to Shark Fin doesn't descend here. Instead, follow the ridge crest to the east, away from Ganden. It takes **around 4 to 5 hours** to reach the summit from here, and **another 3 hours or more** for the return walk back to the monastery. Use common sense on this hike; anyone with a bad headache or other preliminary signs of AMS should turn back rather than push on. Even if you don't reach the summit (nearly 18,000 ft, 5500 m, according to the NH 46-10 JOG map), the walk along the ridge line is still a beautiful hike.

THE GANDEN TO SAMYE TREK

The trail to Samye monastery heads south from Ganden along the side of Angker Ri, following the same route up the ridge as the dayhike to Shark Fin. From the monastery parking area, reach the saddle (14,800 ft, 4510 m) with the *la-dzay* in **1 hour.** The terrain along this ridge is a desert of rocks and lizards, with only a thin covering of vegetation. A peculiar plant growing near the trail is the alpine cushion plant, a compact colony of fleshy-leaved flowers growing in a humped, spongy green mound that may be a few inches or up to a few feet in diameter. Tibet has several types of cushion plants, including one from the carnation family and a species of cinquefoil. At lower elevations these cushions look more like typical wildflowers, with stems and thinner leaves. At higher elevations, the stems and leaves condense to help the plant reduce water evaporation and to protect it against the wind and cold.

Situated almost due south across the valley from the saddle is a steep drainage leading up to the first pass crossing, Shuga La (sometimes called Gokar La). The pass is hidden from this vantage point, tucked around to the left (east) behind a ridge. The monsoon's effects are considerable in this valley compared to the Ganden area. During the summer the hills below Shuga La are carpeted with greenery. Numerous *ba,* the woven yak-hair tents of the *drogpa,* and herds of yak are scattered across these slopes. The valley bottom is a patchwork of croplands with several settlements. Hebu, the first village along the trail from this saddle, cannot be seen from here.

Do as the Tibetans do when they reach the summit of a pass: toss three stones onto the *la-dzay* before starting your descent and shout "*Lha! Sö-sö-sö-sö!*" into the wind as an offering of thanks to the mountain spirits for a safe passage. The route to Ganden drops from the saddle on a well-defined trail that traverses along ridges and crosses several lower saddles. The first of these saddles, also marked by a *la-dzay,* is reached in **about 1 hour.** The higher rainfall in this region supports thick stands of brush where pairs of colorful rose finches enjoy singing from the branch tops. **Ten minutes** below this saddle is a walled-in, grassy oasis fed by a freshwater spring. This is often the first available water after Ganden. Descend steadily for **another 2 hours** to reach the village of Hebu.

If you had a late start from Ganden, consider spending the night here with a family. This small agricultural community is split into two groups of houses along the north (R) side of the valley floor. There are no shops, but if you ask around dairy products or vegetables should be available. This village is the last place before the Samye Valley where you can hire a pack animal. Besides their barley crop, these villagers tend herds of yak and some have a horse or burro. It could be a day or two before an animal is available, for they are usually up on the hills grazing. If necessary, go farther down the valley and ask at the other settlements. Some trekkers actually come to this valley first to arrange for pack animals, then return to Ganden with the guide to fetch their gear.

The route from Hebu to Shuga La crosses to the south (L) side of the valley. The houses and crops of this town are scattered over a mosaic of terraces separated by eroded gullies. Although the stream draining the valley runs beside Hebu, the gullies make it a bit difficult to find a way across. One solution is to follow the trail leading east between the two halves of Hebu to several red and white painted monuments and an egg-shaped incense hearth. Continue east beyond them for **a few minutes** to where the trail crosses a small creek bed. Leave the trail here and descend to the right into this gully. Soon a narrow path forms and leads to the stream. This is an excellent lunch spot with a few shade trees and the first good place for a wash.

Cross the stream to the south (L) bank and follow it downstream. Wherever it's convenient, angle to the left across the wet meadow to pick up the wide trail along the base of the ridge. Follow this path to the right (west) and climb gently along the curve of this slope. Ascend to the nose of the ridge in **20 minutes,** then continue climbing up to the left (south) above the stream draining from Shuga La. In **another 20 minutes** the trail passes under a large rocky outcrop. Set into the rocks a steep **5 minutes** of climbing along the upper right (south) side of this outcrop is a dusty rock overhang big enough to keep about four people out of the rain for a night. Lumpy campsites can be found in a series of rolling meadows located **30 minutes** farther up the valley. A *drogpa* encampment with six tents during the summer months is just above the top of these meadows. Several other herder camps are on the west (L) side of the stream. The mastiff guard dogs may not be chained, so call out before entering these camps. The total walking time from Ganden to the meadows and the *drogpa* camp is **5 to 6 hours.** This area is the last good place for camping before reaching the valley beyond Shuga La.

Finding the correct trail to Shuga La from the *drogpa* camp can be confusing due to the convergence of three drainage valleys from the right (east), center (southeast), and left (southwest) of the ridges surrounding this pass. The central drainage is the correct route. Ascend from the herders' camp on the east (R) side of the stream. In **10 minutes** cross the creek draining from the right, then immediately cross to the west (L) side of the central drainage. The trail climbs steeply up the ridge for a short way, but is soon lost in a maze of animal paths through thickets of dwarf rhododendron bushes. The central creek gully is too rugged to follow at first, so instead find a route that stays high above the west (L) bank of this creek. Climb steeply up to the left (southeast) up toward the obvious low point on the ridge, which looks like the pass but is not.

The hillside is dotted with marmot dens. These husky fellows are one of the larger members of the rodent family. The Tibetans do not eat them, but will hunt them for their pelts. While the marmots run for cover when intruders approach, their intense curiosity often stops them at their burrow entrance, where they stand dead still on their hind legs, much like pikas, to investigate who's passing by.

The chötaens *at Zurkar, commemorating the location where King Thrison Detsen first met the India tantric master Guru Rimpoche in the eighth century, near Samye monastery*

The dwarf rhododendron here are beautiful during the summer, blooming in fragrant miniature bouquets of pink, white, and purple flowers. The Buddhists prize these bushes for their aromatic scent and burn them like incense on religious occasions. Villagers from Hebu come here to harvest the incense bush, then carry their heavy loads up to Ganden for the pilgrims to buy.

It is a long, steep climb up from the *drogpa* camp to the pass. As the ridge becomes more rocky, the route eventually leaves the ridge crest and descends back to the central (southeast) of the three creeks. As the elevation increases the rhododendrons thin out, giving way to tall grasses and wildflowers. Just before reaching the low point in the ridge, cross to the east (R) side of the creek and continue climbing toward Shuga La. The terrain begins to level out and soon opens into a broad U-shaped valley littered with boulders and rock debris deposited by a long-ago glacier. It takes **2 to 3 hours** to reach here, not including rest stops, from the *drogpa* camp.

Water tumbles everywhere from these rocky slopes. Unfortunately, the ground is much too uneven for camping, for this would be a great place to pitch a tent. Shuga La is **at least another hour** from here, without breaks, and is still hidden around to the left; the pass cannot be seen until you are almost on top of it. Pick your way through the hummocks and rocks, staying along the east (R) side of the valley. There isn't much of a trail, but keep looking for a series of small stone cairns marking the route to the pass. A trail soon materializes near the first cairn. Contour up to the left through a jumble of rocks to reach Shuga La (17,200 ft, 5240 m), a broad summit clearly marked by a large *la-dzay* decorated with prayer flags.

Beyond the pass is a remote valley that must be entered to approach Chitu La. High across this drainage (south) is an impressive U-shaped tributary that sweeps upward into the mountains beyond. The ice field that scooped out this hanging valley must have flowed into a tremendous glacier that previously filled the entire gorge below. After the two glaciers receded, the larger ice floe left a trough so deep that the valley carved by the smaller glacier now appears to be suspended above the main defile.

Descend from the pass on a faint path that quickly becomes an easily followed, cairned trail. As you pick your way through a field of broken granite boulders, the upper reaches of this valley and a lake come into view. Like a setting somewhere in Kashmir, the meadows and tall ridges are vibrantly green with lush grasses during the summer. The trail is well defined and descends steadily along the ridge face. Reach the rushing creek on the valley floor in **1¹/₂ hours** from the pass. Before reaching the bottom, look up the valley (south) toward a tall ridge covered with shattered rock and gravel. Below this ridge, coming from the right (southwest), is a tributary drainage of the main valley you're about to enter. The route to Samye follows this tributary valley up to Chitu La.

The broad, flat meadows where the trail meets the valley floor are excellent campsites (16,200 ft, 4940 m). The closest of several scattered *drogpa* camps is **15 minutes** farther up the valley on the opposite west (L) bank of the stream draining this area. There is no bridge crossing here, and finding a suitable spot for rock-hopping during the rainy season can be difficult; shoes and socks may have to come off. Total time from the previous *drogpa* camp to this site is **4¹/₂ to 5¹/₂ hours.**

Rain and snow are frequent visitors to this area and the *drogpas* take full advantage of this unusually wet environment. The valley is heavily grazed, perhaps overgrazed; herds of yak and sheep are everywhere along the mountain slopes. Camping in this region means being lulled back to sleep all night by the tinkle of tin yak bells.

The route to Chitu La crosses to the west (L) bank of the stream. The *drogpa* camp is a good landmark, but if it has moved, head up the valley along the base of the west (L) ridge. There is no trail, so aim for the dip in a group of low hills near this ridge. A short climb up through this dip brings you to the top of the hills and to a good vantage point. The mouth of the tributary valley leading to Chitu La is just off to the right (south), below the ridge covered in rock and gravel. The lake is very near to the east and frequented by many waterbirds. It is not unusual to see formations of bar-headed geese or pairs of Brahminy ducks flying overhead. An alternative route to Samye continues up past this lake (southeast) for **2 to 3 hours** and crosses Gampa La (16,600 ft, 5060 m), the second pass crossing on the trek from the Gyama Valley to Samye monastery. This route is described in "The Gyama Valley to Samye Trek."

The mouth of the tributary leading to Chitu La is **45 minutes** above the base of the trail descending from Shuga La. This is another broad, glacially scoured area, lined with meadows and bursting with colorful wildflowers, including the large yellow poppy (*Meconopsis*). This valley ascends slowly and swings gently up to the left. Within **a few minutes** the rocky cleft of Chitu La can be seen at the far end. The long series of meadows leading toward the pass looks ideal for camping from a distance, but pools of water and huge networks of mounded tundra plates caused by frost heave and grazing animals make it almost impossible to pitch a tent. Walking is also a bit difficult, though the junction of the valley floor with the slope of the west (L) ridge is one of the drier routes. It takes **1¹/₂ to 2 hours** to pick your way up to the pass from the valley entrance.

The scenery from Chitu La (16,700 ft, 5090 m) is stunning and quite surprising for Tibet. Just before the pass is a small glacial lake. Beyond the summit to the south are two larger lakes set in a scoured, barren basin that could be part of the Rocky Mountains. There is a flat spot near the top large enough for a tent, and it is one of the most scenic campsites in Tibet.

The trail to Samye follows the drainage from these two lakes all the way to the mouth of the Samye Valley. Descend south from the pass to the far side of the lakes in **45 minutes.** A rough trail meanders through the jumble of rock along their west (R) shore. Proceed down the valley and eventually pick up a good trail that forms along the west (R) ridge side. **Forty-five minutes** below the last lake is a permanent *drogpa* camp with vicious dogs and a pleasant family. The interior of this *ba* is quite impressive, for it has the character of a well-established home: a wooden prayer altar with the seven offering bowls (*ting*) of water is behind the fireplace; pots and pans and cooking ladles are arranged neatly; and piles of attractive woven blankets and *tsampa* sacks line the edges of the tent.

Just beyond this camp the trail plunges into a narrow ravine, zigzagging under steep walls of broken rock. In **20 minutes** the valley opens onto the first of numerous flat meadows, offering an almost endless choice of campsites for much of the way to Samye. The willow groves and thickets of wild rosebushes are very dense in places, making it difficult to follow the trail. This part of the walk is like the Garden of Eden. Fat laughing thrushes bound through the undergrowth, redstarts perform aerial acrobatics, and colorful eared pheasants bustle about in the brush, gobbling noisily as they work over the ground. With luck you might find yourself in the company of some musk deer.

One hour from the *drogpa* camp a large creek enters the valley from the right. The meadow at the confluence is a fine campsite. A reasonably good trail heads downstream from here along the east (L) side of the stream until the first villages of the Yamalung Valley, above Samye monastery. Once in a while you must cross briefly to the opposite bank to avoid sections of thick brush, and sev-eral small creeks entering from the left must be crossed. The walk through this canyon is a delightful downhill stroll. Wildflowers are everywhere, warblers dart through the bushes, and stunted birch trees, along with a few rhododendron trees, cling to the steep valley walls. Even mosquitoes make an appearance.

One hour below the large creek confluence, a deep tributary valley enters from the left. (The trail from the Gyama Valley follows the south (L) side of this drainage and joins the trail to Samye here. This route is described in "The Gyama Valley to Samye Trek." The creek from this tributary is usually an easy ford, but during heavy rains the water level may be too high for a safe crossing. On rare occasions it may be necessary to wait here for a day or more until the water level drops. The trail to Samye remains on the east (L) side of the main stream. **A few minutes** below the creek ford is a big meadow camp (14,600 ft, 4450 m) suitable for large groups.

As the valley descends it narrows into a densely vegetated ravine. **Fifty**

A high camp on Chitu La, en route from Ganden to Samye monastery

minutes below the large camp it turns sharply to the right (west) as another big tributary enters from the left. A wooden bridge crosses this creek. Beyond here the valley opens up considerably. Tall juniper shrubs grow above the banks and giant, almost tree-size wild rosebushes are draped with yellow blooms during the summer. In autumn the colors of the changing season are brilliant: the barberry bushes turn deep red, the tall grasses become golden, and yellow-leaved willows are covered with delicate, fluffy white seedpods. Not far away, though, are the desert environs of the Samye Valley. The hills up ahead are very dry and speckled with only a scrubby vegetation.

The trail is wide and easy to follow, staying on the east (L) side of the main stream. Descend for **1 hour** from the small bridge crossing through winding, brush-engulfed meadows to reach an abandoned stone hut. Cross the creek coming in from the left just past here, and in **50 minutes** reach the first permanent settlement since Hebu, consisting of five or six houses and a small plot of cultivated fields. **Forty minutes** beyond these first houses the trail sweeps around to the left of an irrigation channel, then swings back to the right beside a large, grassy meadow. This is a great camp spot and a good place for a rest day.

Across the valley a trail climbs steeply up the west (R) ridge to Yamalung (also known as Emmaling), a historical hermitage hidden from view at this angle. To visit the temple, find the clusters of prayer flags showing above the tops of the bushes along the base of this ridge. These flags are strung across a small bridge obscured by the brush. Cross here and follow the trail up to the right; the steep climb to these caves takes **less than 1 hour.** Large patches of stinging nettles grow beside the trail.

Yamalung is a well-known pilgrimage site for Buddhists of the Nyingmapa sect. Guru Rimpoche, the founder of this school of thought, and his main disciple, Vairocana (the Tibetans call him "Berutsana"), are said to have meditated here twelve centuries ago. This site is particularly important because Guru Rimpoche also concealed religious texts here, known as *terma* ("hidden treasure"), which were discovered hundreds of years later. A new but rather sparse *lhakhang* has been built over the cave used by Guru Rimpoche, though the small *ani gompa* nearby still lies in ruins. Above the cave is the retreat of Vairocana, and scattered around the cliffs are five or six other caves used by various figures in Buddhist history. If you wish to spend the night, enquire with the monk tending the Guru Rimpoche cave. You need to bring your own food and bedding. A small donation is appropriate.

About 15 minutes beyond the Yamalung turnoff the trail to Samye crosses a solid wooden bridge to the west (R) bank of the stream. The cave temples can be seen quite well from here if you look back up the ridge. Nyango village (12,700 ft, 3870 m) is **15 minutes** beyond the bridge, situated under an impressive rocky outcrop at the confluence of a large tributary valley coming in from the right (west). This valley is the old trade route to Lhasa; it crosses Gokar La (17,200 ft, 5250 m) and enters the Lhasa Valley at the fortress town of Dechen Dzong. (The trek to Dechen Dzong takes **2 to 3 days** from here; see "The Samye to Dechen Dzong Trek.")

Nyango is the first of many villages and settlements located along this old trade route. Samye is still **a long 3 hours** away following a flat, sandy track wide enough for animal-drawn carts. If it's getting late, you should be able to find accommodation in these villages, and there are several large, flat meadows for camping. The track remains on the west (R) side of the valley all the way to Samye. **Twenty minutes** from Nyango a long meadow sprawls beside the track and a bridge crosses the stream, which is now big enough to be called a small river. **A few minutes** farther, the road to Samye crosses a wooden bridge at the mouth of a small tributary valley, then passes through the village of Wango. Several other settlements on the east (L) side of the river can be reached by a bridge farther downstream.

One hour below Wango the track enters a small settlement engulfed by poplars and willows. The valley is considerably broader now and the terrain becomes much drier as the track nears the Yarlung Tsangpo. **A few minutes** beyond these houses a good viewpoint overlooks the lower Samye Valley. The glittering golden roof of Samye's newly rebuilt main temple, known as the Utse, or the Tshog-*lhakhang,* rises impressively in the distance above a large forested area. The isolated ridge to the left of the monastery is Haypo Ri, and farther to the south are the sand dunes and ridges near the Yarlung Tsangpo. The Samye Valley would be a desert, like the shores of this river, were it not for the irrigation channels that direct the flow of water from the mountains. Crops of green barley alternating between plots of yellow and white blooming mustard contrast colorfully with the rocky desert and sand dunes lying just beyond the reach of these channels. If possible, walk this next section of the trail in early morning or late afternoon to avoid the heat, especially in the summer. The track to Samye threads from oasis to oasis along the west (R) side of the valley. Walking in this soft sand under a hot Tibetan sun can be torturous. Carry plenty of water.

Descend from the overlook for **15 minutes** to the base of a ridge spur topped by a fortresslike ruin. The remains of this building are decorated with prayer flags, for this is Dragmar, the birthplace of Thrisong Detsen, one of Tibet's most revered kings of the Royal Dynasty period. The small shrine erected among the crumbling walls is one of the main stops for prayer wheel–spinning pilgrims as they head up to the Yamalung caves.

Samye monastery is **1¹/₂ hours** from Dragmar across a long, sandy stretch of the valley. Stay on the cart track, using Samye's golden roof as a bearing. As the track approaches the monastery, numerous side trails and paths along the irrigation ditches can make the route confusing. Keep heading for the Utse, which is in the south part of town. Dormitory lodging is in a compound a little past the temple entrance, and sometimes the locals take in travelers. The best camping sites are to the south of town in the willow groves.

Samye

Samye was the first great Buddhist monastery in Tibet, founded in 775 A.D. during the reign of King Thrisong Detsen. On the advice of Guru Rimpoche and a visiting scholar from India, the king ordered Samye built as a three-dimensional model, or *mandala,* of the Buddhist universe. The original complex contained 108 chapels within a great circular stone wall. In the center of this *mandala* was the Utse, the main temple representing Mount Meru, the Mount Olympus of Buddhism. The three upper levels of this large building were built in Tibetan, Chinese, and Indian architectural styles. Symmetrically positioned around this center were four tall *chötaen,* each painted a different color; twelve temples representing the four major and eight minor continents of Buddhist cosmology; and two temples for the sun and the moon.

Many of these outlying buildings are now derelict or were destroyed during the Cultural Revolution. A few temples are being repaired and the Chinese government has helped finance the reconstruction of the Utse. By 1988 repairs on the upper three levels were well underway: the new roof was in place, teams of artists were painting frescoes and decorating the new wooden beams, and a

Guru Rimpoche temple on the second floor had been restored and opened to the public. The large circular wall surrounding Samye was also being rebuilt.

The candle-lit interior of the ground-floor Tshog-*lhakhang* has an ancient, musty atmosphere befitting its age. The figures contained within the long, raised cases to either side of the main altar are tributes to the founding fathers of Samye and to various personalities in the history of Tibetan Buddhism who have visited Samye. The large seated figure in the secondary room behind the altar is an eighth-century stone statue of the Buddha as a young boy. The room adjacent to the chanting hall is a dark *gön-khang* with a towering, shrouded statue of the protector Pehar. To the left of the main hall's entrance is a shrine with a thousand-armed figure of Chenrezig, the Tibetan god of compassion. The Dalai Lama is the human manifestation of this *bodhisattva*.

Samye monastery is unusual in that it is affiliated with more than one school of Tibetan Buddhism. Originally it was a Nyingmapa monastery, but after centuries of political and religious influences Samye is home to monks from the Sakyapa and Gelugpa sects as well.

Dayhikes near Samye

Although the town of Samye is rather grubby (it's one of the few Tibetan towns where pigs are raised), the region around Samye is worth exploring if you have a few extra days. The solitary, barren ridge just to the east is Haypo Ri, a former Bönpo ceremonial site now topped by a small square shrine. A residence palace for Tibet's kings during the Royal Dynasty period once crowned this ridge top; no sign of it remains today. The hike up Haypo Ri takes **less than 1 hour,** offering good views of the monastery and the surrounding valleys. The soft, sandy hillsides can make this a slow, hot climb. Try to walk in the early morning

Dragmar temple commemorates the birthplace of King Thrisong Detsen, near Samye monastery

or late afternoon, and fill your water bottles before setting off. The easiest approach from the monastery is to head east on the dirt track leading away from the Utse entrance gate. Reach the base of the ridge in **10 minutes,** then choose any of the numerous routes leading up the sides. One trail leads to an obvious saddle beside a white *chötaen,* then continues up the spine of the ridge toward the temple.

A more demanding excursion from Samye is the hike up to the Chimphu caves retreat, which takes **4 to 5 hours** each way. Set in a thickly vegetated amphitheater to the east of the monastery, this retreat is a surprisingly lush mountain oasis of birds, flowers, and tumbling creeks. Chimphu is also an important pilgrimage site, for this is where Guru Rimpoche meditated and taught his disciples when he came to Samye in the eighth century. Of the several routes leading here from Samye, one of the more direct ways skirts the left (north) end of Haypo Ri to enter an adjacent desert valley lying to the east. A cart track turns left (north) across the desert plain of this valley, leading into the hills toward Chimphu. In **1¹/₂ hours** the track ends at a ghost town of ruined buildings. A trail continues up the valley from here, passing abandoned crop terraces and another ruined village before ascending into the tangle of wild rosebushes and shrubs that engulfs Chimphu.

Dozens of caves and retreats built under overhanging rocks pepper the hills of this beautifully peaceful basin. Most of the caves have been reoccupied by meditating hermits, and at times even a few Western Buddhists have established temporary residences in some of the caves. The white temple that can be seen from a distance is Dragmar Kaytsang. A meditation cave of Guru Rimpoche and an associated *lhakhang* are on the lower level. Above it are a smaller building with residences for visiting *lamas* and the meditation cave of Guru Rimpoche's main disciple, Vairocana.

Directly below Dragmar Kaytsang, a solitary, conical outcrop of rock called Zangdog Paazer Ri, the "Glorious Copper-colored Hill," extends from the slopes. A pilgrimage route winds from cave to cave up to its summit. Towering above the entire Chimphu complex is the granite peak of Lonchen Gurgartse. A challenging pilgrim's *kora* that takes **8 hours or more** to complete climbs above the Dragmar Kaytsang temple onto the ridge top. At the summit is the cave where Guru Rimpoche is said to have meditated with his disciples. A small shrine with carved stone tablets of this Indian tantric master and his two consorts is at the back of the cave. The *kora* then continues down the eastern ridge of this peak to return to Dragmar Kaytsang.

If you plan to spend the night at Chimphu, bring sleeping bags and sufficient food for your entire stay; bring along a tent if you have one. The monks at Chimphu are in retreat, living on meager food supplies. They have little to spare, nor do they have facilities for accommodating foreigners. If you sleep on the floor of Dragmar temple, be sure to leave an appropriate donation.

About 1 hour to the west of Samye, on the road to the old ferry landing, are the five *chötaen* of Zurkar. Built upon the granite boulders along the ridge side, these monuments are said to mark the location where King Thrisong Detsen first met Guru Rimpoche. According to tradition, when the two great men initially faced each other, each believed the other should bow down in submission. When the Indian master raised his hand as if to salute, fire sprang out of his fingers, thunder rumbled overhead, and an earthquake shook the ground. Terrorized, the king and his ministers threw themselves in reverence at the guru's feet. As reparation for his error, Guru Rimpoche ordered the king to build the five "wonderful" *chötaen* at this site that now commemorate their meeting place.

―――――――

Other walks in the Samye area include the **2-hour** dayhike north up the Samye Valley to Dragmar, the birthplace of King Thrisong Detsen, and the **5-hour** hike to the Yamalung cave hermitage. Both walks are described, in reverse, in the section "The Ganden to Samye Trek."

Leaving Samye

Samye monastery is a fair distance from the Yarlung Tsangpo's northern shore, where ferries cross the river at two locations to connect with the Lhasa–Tsethang Highway. (See the section on Highway Kilometer Markers in the chapter "Using the Trek Descriptions.") A new tourist ferry went into operation in 1990, using a landing a number of miles downstream from Samye. Although the new boat is supposedly much quicker than the old local ferry, the bus ride to the landing takes so long that the total time for a crossing is about the same. The prices, however, are far from equal: the fast boat costs twenty-five times more than the old ferry. A recent government order forbids foreigners to use the old ferry. In practice, however, the tourist boat runs so infrequently that it may be necessary to take the old ferry, which is scheduled to depart each day at 9:30 A.M. and 1:30 P.M. for the forty-five-minute crossing to the highway. A truck or an amazingly rundown bus leaves for this ferry at 8 A.M. and 12 noon from the courtyard in front of the Samye Utse's main entrance. The ride takes around an hour. The **3-hour** walk to this ferry is typically a hot slog through soft sand or a gusty battle with the afternoon winds and sandstorms.

The old ferry lands near the highway between kilometer markers 89 and 90. Gongkar Airport is more than an hour's drive to the west, and Lhasa is another 2 hours or more beyond the airport. The tourist ferry landing on the south side of the river is near kilometer marker 112, only 7 miles (12 km) west of Tsethang.

THE SAMYE TO DECHEN DZONG TREK
(Map 2, page 119)

The trek from Samye monastery to Dechen Dzong takes **2¹/₂ to 3¹/₂ days** and follows an ancient caravan route that connected the residences of Tibet's kings in the Yarlung Valley with their summer camps in Lhasa. This route is the shortest and most direct of the various trails between Samye and the Lhasa Valley, crossing Gokar La (17,200 ft, 5250 m), the "White Eagle" pass. It can be combined with either of the treks from Ganden monastery or the Gyama Valley to create a scenic loop walk of **8 to 10 days** that visits Samye and returns to the Lhasa region.

The route from Samye initially follows the cart track north up the valley to Nyango village (12,700 ft, 3870 m). This walk is detailed in reverse in the section "The Ganden to Samye Trek." Nyango is the last settlement before the pass, situated at the confluence of the Yamalung Valley and a large tributary entering from the left (west). The trail to Gokar La leaves the main valley here, ascending the south (R) bank of this tributary. After weaving through a jungle of wild rosebushes, the trail crosses a bridge to the north (L) bank of the stream, below the junction with a creek entering from the north. A small meadow just above this bridge has room for several tents. Larger campsites are farther up the creek toward the pass.

The old trade route ascends along the west (R) side of this creek, and soon widens into a cobbled roadway. Apparently each Dalai Lama would pass this way on his once-in-a-lifetime pilgrimage to Lhamo Lhatsho, an "oracle lake" almost a week's journey by horse from here to the east. After the death of a Dalai Lama, the regents of the Gelugpa hierarchy would also come this way to the lake, seeking insight from its visionary waters to help locate the new, incarnate boy-*lama.* Some zealous administrator probably ordered the paving done for one of these occasions, but the stones that were used are so big that everyone opts to walk beside it.

The trail to Gokar La remains in this drainage, climbing steadily beside intermittent sections of pavement and past several remote *drogpa* camps before reaching the prayer flags and cairns on the summit (17,200 ft, 5250 m). The steep descent from the pass toward Dechen Dzong winds down the slopes into a vibrant, well-watered tributary valley of the Kyi Chhu. A friendly *drogpa* family has a summer camp near the base of the pass, with herds of yak and goats roaming the grassy hills. Farther north the pastures of wildflowers yield to barley crops, and the long but relatively flat trail to Dechen Dzong broadens into a dirt road as it nears the valley mouth. The first village is **about 4¹/₂ hours** from the pass. The track intersects the Lhasa–Chengdu Highway near a Tibetan tea house and several other buildings. If you wish to arrange for a vehicle to pick you up at the end of your trek, this tea house is a good meeting place. The actual town of Dechen Dzong, also called Dagze (km marker 4612), is a little farther to the east (right) along the highway. Lhasa is 14 miles (23 km) to the west. The old Dechen Dzong fortress, which was the residence of the *depa,* the administrator/tax collector for this area, is in ruins on a lone, rocky hill to the north of the town. A Gelugpa tantric college once shared the hilltop, but now only a small rebuilt temple occupies the site.

THE GYAMA VALLEY TO SAMYE TREK
(Map 2, page 119)

The Gyama Valley (km marker 4573) is a broad agricultural tributary of the Kyi Chhu situated about 45 miles (72 km) to the east of Lhasa on the Lhasa–Chengdu Highway. Barley fields sprawl across this valley floor, which is speckled with small villages, settlements, and temples, including the shrine commemorating the birthplace of Songtsen Gampo. The walk from Gyama to Samye via Tseb La (17,150 ft, 5230 m) and Gampa La (16,600 ft, 5060 m) takes **3¹/₂ to 4¹/₂ days** and is one of the finest moderate treks in Central Tibet. The approach to these passes is considerably easier than the crossings to Samye from either Dechen Dzong or Ganden, yet the valleys en route are just as remote and scenic. On about the third day of trekking from Gyama this route intersects the trail from Ganden to Samye in the upper Yamalung Valley.

The best time for this trek is generally from late April until the end of October, though if you are well equipped it is possible to cross Tseb La and Gampa La in the winter. All food requirements and other supplies should be brought from Lhasa, for there are no shops and only a few villages along the way. Because this trek is in a remote area, tents and fuel stoves are highly recommended, especially during the wet summer months.

If individuals are allowed to trek again in Tibet, the best way to reach the Gyama Valley by public transport is to take the Lhasa–Madhrogongkar bus. (The name of this town is Medu-Kongkar Dzong on the NH 46-10 JOG map, 1501 Series, and is sometimes spelled Maizhokunggar and Medrokongkar on other maps.) These buses operate almost every afternoon and gather passengers on the south side of Tsangnyu Shar Lam (the street running parallel to the Kyi Chhu), about 300 feet (90 m) to the west of the traffic-light intersection near the Himalaya Hotel. The Lingkor pilgrimage route around Lhasa turns from south to west at this same intersection. Tickets are sold on the bus. The driver should know where the Gyama Valley is, but get a seat on the left side of the bus anyway so you can keep an eye on the kilometer stones. Less frequent services to Madhrogongkar also leave from the bus stands near the Potala Palace. Private transport to Gyama can be arranged through your hotel or with any of the travel companies in Lhasa.

The turnoff for the Gyama Valley is to the south (right) of the highway. A small village called Nonda is perched on a hill at the southeast corner of this intersection. If you are with a commercial trek or traveling in a hired vehicle, you can drive 9 miles (14 km) up the Gyama Valley from the highway. The road ends at a bridge just past the village of Jogsumba (13,200 ft, 4020 m). This will save at least a day of walking, and Jogsumba is a good place for hiring yaks and a guide.

If you are walking this stretch of the road to Jogsumba, there are a number of camping sites en route as well as settlements and houses where accommodations can be found. About 3 miles (5 km) south of Nonda is the village of Dasha. I've been told that the site of Gyalpo Khang, the temple at Songtsen Gampo's birthplace, is near a *chötaen* on the left side of the valley from Dasha. The other temple and monastery sites scattered about the Gyama Valley mostly date back to the twelfth century and were formerly associated with the old Kadampa sect of Tibetan Buddhism.

Jogsumba is the last major settlement in the Gyama Valley. The people here are both farmers and herders. Not far up the valley, the last crops give way to the grassy hills and meadows where the villagers pasture their yaks. The road continues beyond Jogsumba, paralleling the tumbling river for **less than 1 hour** until ending at a wooden bridge. The route to Samye crosses the bridge to the west (L) bank and proceeds up the valley on a well-marked path. As the valley begins veering to the left, the first scrubby bushes appear beside the trail. During summer this area is vibrant with lush grass and wildflowers; by late September it is awash with brilliant autumn golds and reds.

Less than 1 hour beyond the bridge a tributary enters from the left. A *drogpa* family camps near the confluence. The first of the half-dozen stream crossings on this trek is just above this junction. The trail fords the river, now just a stream, to the east (R) bank. The valley swings back to the right and the distance between the ridges narrows. Climb steadily for **15 minutes** from the ford through rocks and brush, then rock-hop across a small tributary creek. A spacious meadow campsite (14,400 ft, 4390 m) is **a few minutes** up the valley. If you drove to Jogsumba and started your trek there, consider stopping at these meadows for the night, even if it's early in the afternoon. The next day's camp could then be in the pastures (16,000 ft, 4880 m) below Tseb La, allowing you two nights of acclimatization before you cross the pass.

The dense stands of brush and the willow groves through this part of the valley provide good cover for animals such as the little musk deer, which acts more like a giant rabbit than a deer; Tibetan partridges; Prince Henri's laughing thrushes; and occasional flocks of Elwes's eared pheasant, a large, plump, mostly grayish bird with striking metallic blue-green-and-purple tail plumage.

From this camp continue ascending along the east (R) side of the valley through the thick brush. Dwarf rhododendrons are common in this area, and are recognizable by their tightly packed bouquets of miniature flowers and fragrant leaves. During autumn the different willow species lining the meadows are draped in magnificent, feathery white seedpods that scatter in the wind like giant dandelion blooms.

Two hours beyond the meadow camp the trail fords the creek to the west (L) bank (15,500 ft, 4720 m). As the valley starts to open out again, the vegetation is noticeably thinner and more stunted. A rugged, rocky ridge dominates the head of the valley, but Tseb La remains out of sight, hidden by the ridges up to the right (west).

The trail continues to climb, rambling over rolling hills and gently sloping high yak pastures. The last good place for camping near water is beside several crumbling stone corrals (16,600 ft, 5060 m) near the base of the west (L) ridge, **1¹/₂ hours** above the last creek ford. Beyond this camp a faint trail angles up the ridge to the right (southeast) toward Tseb La. Don't head south along the valley floor toward the basin below the rocky ridge. Several trails in this area lead toward other passes, away from Tseb La and into tributaries of the Yon Valley, a major drainage farther to the east and away from Samye.

Sidle up the ridge from the corral camp for **15 minutes** to an obvious dip in the ridge. The terrain now opens onto an elevated plateau of grass hummocks and rolling hills. Tseb La is the gap in the ridge straight ahead (west) with a well-defined trail leading up to it. Angle toward this summit trail, keeping a good distance to the north and west of a beautifully blue glacial lake. Reach the top of the pass (17,150 ft, 5230 m) and the *la-dzay* in **1 hour** from the stone corrals.

Descend steeply from Tseb La into a broad, open basin dotted with yak herds in the summer. **Thirty minutes** below the pass cross to the west (L) side of a small creek (16,500 ft, 5030 m), then continue straight ahead (southwest) up the sloping pastures. The route to Samye is not well marked here, but as you follow the curve of the main valley up to the left (south), a trail forms along the base of the left ridge. Don't go down the main valley (north), which leads to a lake near the trekking route from Ganden monastery to Samye.

After **30 minutes** of easy climbing above the creek crossing, a cairn comes into view on a nearby hill sandwiched between two ridges. Gampa La (16,600 ft, 5060 m) is the boulder-strewn cleft with three *la-dzay* to the left of this hill. The

Monks practicing the gya-ling, *a ceremonial horn played during many tantric Buddhist rituals, Chimphu cave hermitage*

horizon beyond this summit is an etching of jagged ridges, and below them a deep, canyonlike tributary of the Yamalung Valley winds toward Samye. The trail from the pass drops steeply along a rocky course. **A few minutes** from the top the path divides. The route to the left stays high along the ridge side toward the Yon Valley, a fertile agricultural area across the Yarlung Tsangpo from Tsethang. Continue descending toward Samye via the right fork. In **20 minutes** pass a large *drogpa* encampment near the valley bottom (15,800 ft, 4820 m) where several families spend the summer months. These herders tend yaks and goats, so they may have some milk, buttermilk, yogurt, or meat to sell. Keep an eye out for their mastiff guard dogs. **A few minutes** below this camp is a stream crossing to the south (L) side. Follow the vague trail descending through the brush and dwarf rhododendrons along this bank. The valley quickly narrows from here, with towering rocky outcrops forcing the trail across the stream several times. These fords can get rather tricky during July and August, when the summer rains can swell this creek to a swift torrent.

The first crossing is **20 minutes** below the nomad camp. **A few minutes** later the trail recrosses to the south (L) bank near a tributary entering from the left, then quickly crosses again to the north (R) bank. The monsoon has more effect on this side of the mountains, supporting dense brush near the watercourses and small trees along the lower slopes. Scattered flocks of little warblers dart through the bushes and parties of laughing thrushes may be seen stealing about the undergrowth.

Continue descending along the north (R) bank. The valley starts to open out with several good meadow campsites near the trail. The largest of these is **30 minutes** below the last ford. Just beyond this camp the trail drops down to the stream and crosses back to the south (L) side. A smaller, higher trail stays on the north (R) bank above the camp, but eventually crosses to the south (L) as well.

Descend through this lovely canyon for **30 minutes** to the confluence with the main Yamalung Valley and the trekking route from Ganden. Continue descending for **a few minutes** below this junction to a sprawling meadow campsite (14,600 ft, 4450 m).

Samye monastery (11,800 ft, 3600 m) is still **7 hours** from this huge camp, not including rest stops. Although the monastery could be reached in a very long day of walking, the descent through this valley is such a fine journey that it is worth taking an extra day. The first village en route is Nyango (12,700 ft, 3870 m), **2 hours** downstream.

The remainder of the trek to Samye is detailed in "The Ganden to Samye Trek."

Dayhikes near Tsethang
(Map 3, page 141)

Tsethang (km marker 123/4; 11,650 ft, 3550 m), Central Tibet's third-largest city, is located less than an hour's drive east from either of the Samye ferry crossings, at the junction of the Yarlung Chhu Valley and the broad river plains on the Yarlung Tsangpo's southern banks. If you are flying into Tibet, the city is 60 miles (96 km) east of the Gongkar Airport, in a region of Southern Tibet known as Lhoka. Due to the relatively low elevation of the Yarlung Valley—almost 400 feet (120 m) lower than the Lhasa Valley—Tsethang is an ideal location to spend the first several days acclimatizing to the high altitude and getting in shape for a trek.

Few places have a historical and religious background as diverse as the Tsethang area's, particularly the Yarlung Valley and its tributary, the Chonggye Valley. According to tradition, the Tibetan race originated in the Yarlung Valley and the first king of Tibet descended from heaven onto a mountain overlooking the valley. The descendants of this king ruled Tibet from the fertile Yarlung region, and their burial tombs are located in the Chonggye Valley, the "Valley of the Kings." Notable religious personalities came to meditate in the caves tucked into Yarlung's hills. During the fourteenth and fifteenth centuries the Yarlung Valley was again the power base for the rulers of Tibet, this time the Phagmodhrupa family, who governed from their palace in Nedong, a few miles south of Tsethang.

Many of the historical sites and monasteries near Tsethang are now mostly in ruins or have disappeared. Still, there are numerous opportunities for dayhikes in the surrounding hills and valleys, ranging from easy strolls to serious, full-day efforts. A good warm-up walk near the city's main commercial area is the *kora* leading to Ganden Chhökorling, the largest monastery remaining in this part of the valley. A much longer outer *kora* circles Zodang Gampo Ri. This long, barren ridge, forming the eastern side of the Yarlung Valley, is one of the four most sacred peaks in Tibet. Near the summit is the cave where the *bodhisattva* Chenrezig, in the form of a monkey-king, mated with an ogress to create the first Tibetan people. The name Tsethang means "Playground," the place where their offspring played.

The inner pilgrimage *kora* begins along the highway to Nyingchi and eastern Tibet, the road leading east from the Tsethang traffic circle (km marker 123/4). The circuit takes **1 hour,** not including breaks or visits to the different monasteries en route. Allow **another 30 minutes** if you are starting from the

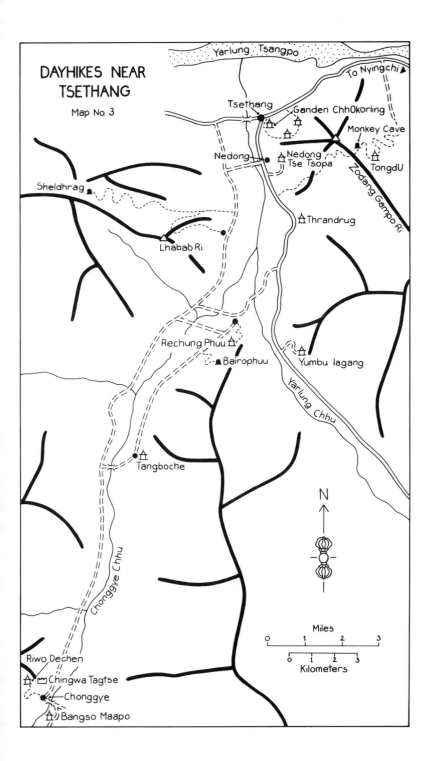

DAYHIKES NEAR
TSETHANG

Map No. 3

Yarlung Tsangpo

To Nyingchi

Tsethang

Ganden Chh0korling

Monkey Cave

Nedong

Nedong
Tse Tsopa

TongdU

Sheldhrag

Thrandrug

Zodang Gampo Ri

Lhabab Ri

Rechung Phuu

Bairophuu

Yumbu lagang

Yarlung Chhu

Tangboche

N

Miles

0   1   2   3

0   1   2   3

Kilometers

Chonggye Chhu

Riwo Dechen

Chingwa Tagtse

Chonggye

Bangso Maapo

Tsethang hotel (near km marker 125), where all tour groups stay. From the traffic circle, turn right (east) and follow the road for **10 minutes.** The tall, maroon-walled Ganden Chhökorling monastery rises above the other buildings up to the right. The pilgrim's circuit starts a little farther along the road, beyond a long cement wall dotted with occasional windows. When this wall ends look for a wide alley leading up to the right, in front of a white, three-storied building with unusual "wings" decorating the roof corners. (If you pass the kilometer marker 1 you've walked a couple of minutes beyond the turnoff.) After turning from the street, proceed about 100 feet (30 m) up, then take the second passageway on the left. The *kora* circuit is confusing for the next few minutes as it enters a labyrinth of Tibetan homes. Keep asking for Namjug *gompa,* the first monastery on the *kora.* It is **less than 10 minutes** from the street. Eight *dhrapa* have returned to this recently restored Gelugpa monastery. The wall frescoes in the assembly hall are particularly well done, and the room behind the altar has a darkened *gön-khang* beside a large figure of Tsong Khapa.

The *kora* does not drop down toward the larger building of Ganden Chhökorling, but circles behind (south) Namjug *gompa* on a path between more houses to approach the base of the ridge. A well-marked trail winds up a rocky gully lined with hundreds of stone offering cairns. The pilgrims rub certain stones en route devoutly with their hands, insert a knee in a large rock with a special depression, and rub their backs against another rock. One stone has the *zhabjay,* or footprint, of a former Dalai Lama.

The trail climbs out of the gully past a grove of willows and poplars, then turns right up to a scenic overlook with several large piles of offering stones and a tall pole topped by a banner. The pilgrims circle these piles twice, then continue across the ridge face to Sang-ngaa Semzi nunnery. This compact, well-cared-for monastery has a small but interesting *lhakhang* off the main courtyard, and two hidden chapels tucked into another building below the courtyard entrance. Twenty-five nuns, two monks, and a *rimpoche* are in residence at this temple, which is said to be one of the first Gelugpa *ani gompa* to have been established. Higher on the hill is a trail to a meditation cave and to the ruins of an old monastery.

The pilgrimage circuit descends from here, passing a red-painted shrine dedicated to the protectress Pelden Lhamo. Follow the small offering cairns to a road between some houses. This leads to Ganden Chhökorling *gompa,* a beautiful old building with detailed woodworking on all the structural beams. Although the building was once gutted, the restoration is nearing completion and some of the original wall frescoes can be seen in the *lhakhang* behind the assembly hall. Thirty-two *dhrapa* have returned to this Gelugpa monastery, which formerly had several hundred in residence.

The last leg of this pilgrimage walk descends west between more houses to end at the main street in Tsethang, just to the left (south) of the traffic circle. The Tsethang hotel is **less than 10 minutes** to the left.

The outer *kora* around Zodang Gampo Ri and to the cave shrine of the monkey-king takes **10 to 12 hours,** a tough dayhike that climbs into the mountains to the east of Tsethang. On the Saga Dawa festival, hundreds of pilgrims set off on this long but meritorious journey, for on this special day the effects of

Interior of Ganden Chhörkorling monastery, Tsethang

positive (or negative) actions are said to be multiplied ten million times. Because the circuit is so lengthy, many pilgrims come on foot and by vehicle the day before this festival and camp at the base of the trail, ensuring an early start the following day.

The pilgrim's *kora* around Zodang Gampo Ri begins about 5 miles (8 km) east of the Tsethang traffic circle along the highway to eastern Tibet. The turnoff is a few hundred yards past kilometer marker 6, near a lone, walled-in house on the right (south) side of the road. A dirt road leads about 1 mile (1.6 km) up the broad, barren plain to some ruined walls at the base of the hills. The wide *kora* trail, which is easily seen from the highway, climbs steeply from here to the top of the ridge. The ruins of Tongdü *ani gompa* are set back into these hills, and farther along the trail is the sacred shrine at the cave of the monkey-king.

The pilgrim's circuit returns to the Yarlung Valley from Zodang Gampo Ri by descending onto a ridge the locals call Digpa Ri, "Scorpion Hill." A good vantage point for seeing where this path winds down to the valley floor is the front steps of Nedong Tse Tsogpa, a Gelugpa monastery that has been rebuilt beside the former site of Nedong *dzong,* the old palace of the Phagmodhrupa family. The *kora* finishes to the north of Thrandrug monastery (km marker 129), a rambling, seventh-century temple founded by Songtsen Gampo.

Another ambitious dayhike is the full-day, round-trip journey up to spectacularly situated Sheldhrag (pronounced Shay-dhraa) cave, the "Crystal Rock" meditation cave of Guru Rimpoche. Nestled high into the craggy summits on the west side of the Yarlung Valley, this cave is one of the most sacred Nyingmapa pilgrimage sites in Tibet. Guru Rimpoche had been invited to Tibet in the eighth century by King Thrisong Detsen to subdue the demons that were plaguing the country, and it was here that he retreated to conjure up the terrific powers necessary to bring these beings under his control. In another cave the "treasure-finder" Orgyan Lingpa discovered this tantric master's biography, the *Padma Katang,* an important Nyingmapa text that had been concealed by the guru's consort some 600 years earlier. The Guru Rimpoche cave is enclosed by a shrine, and below is a small rebuilt *lhakhang* tended by several monks.

The trailhead for Sheldhrag cave is about 3 miles (5 km) to the west and south of the Tsethang Hotel. It is near another historical site in Tsethang, the Tsechhu Bumpa, an ancient, crumbling *chötaen* on a small plateau beside the Chonggye Valley road, at the base of the Yarlung Valley's western hills. Tsechhu Bumpa, the "Water of Life Receptacle," dates from the eighth century and contained a rock crystal image that had been presented to Thrisong Detsen. According to one legend, "life-giving" water issues from this *chötaen* on the full moon. The route to Sheldhrag follows a wide trail into the valley opening behind the Bumpa, then ascends the ridge on the right (north), taking **5 to 6 hours** of steep climbing to reach the cave.

A less demanding hike with equally panoramic views of the valley is the climb up Lhabab Ri, the next ridge to the south of Tsechhu Bumpa. Trails wind up both sides of this ridge, from behind the *chötaen* as well as from a small settlement of houses less than 1 mile (1 km) farther south. Lhabab Ri, the "God/King Descending Mountain," is where Tibet's legendary first king (fourth to third century B.C.?), Nyathri Tsaenpo, descended to earth from the heavens. According to tradition, the shepherds who first discovered the newly arrived stranger asked him where he was from. Not understanding Tibetan, the man simply pointed to the sky, which was interpreted to mean he came from heaven. The shepherds responded with reverence, claiming him as their king. They carried him on a palanquin upon their shoulders to the valley below, earning him the name Nyathri Tsaenpo (the "Neck-throne King"). The palace he built is believed to be Yumbu

Yumbu lagang, the palace of Tibet's first king and the oldest building in Tibet, near Tsethang

Lagang (km marker 135/6), a medieval-looking castle 7 miles (12 km) up the Yarlung Valley from Tsethang. It is reputed to be the oldest building in Tibet.

High on a ridge spur separating the Chonggye and Yarlung valleys are the ruins of Rechung Phuu monastery. This prominently situated Kargyü/Nyingma sect *gompa* was built around the meditation cave of Rechungpa, a disciple of the ascetic Milarepa. Several small temples have been rebuilt adjacent to the original cave, where Rechungpa spent three years, three months, and three days in retreat. His figure, along with those of his spiritual masters, Milarepa and Marpa, are honored in the shrine built over the cave. The monastery is best approached from Tsethang by way of the road up the Yarlung Valley. The turnoff is on the left a few hundred yards past kilometer marker 131. The village of Rechung is about 2 miles (3 km) along this road at the base of the ridge. A couple of trails lead up from different parts of the town, taking **less than 1 hour** to reach the cave temple. A trail continues up the ridge to the massive stone walls of the former monastery. The view across the valleys is stunning.

The Chonggye Valley is where most of Tibet's kings were buried until the Royal Dynasty collapsed in the ninth century. The main group of tombs is near the town of Chonggye, 17 miles (28 km) south of Tsethang. The most prominent tomb is Bangso Maapo, a large earthen mound in the middle of the valley containing the remains of Songtsen Gampo. It is the only tomb with a temple crowning the summit. An interesting hike in this area is the climb up to Riwo Dechen *gompa* and to the ruins of Chingwa Tagtse, the "Tiger Peak" castle, on the ridge directly behind (north) Chonggye village. There is a good view of this ridge looking across (north) from Bangso Maapo.

The monastery is **less than 1 hour** from the center of the village. A road leads toward it between the rows of white-washed houses, then a trail ascends from the base of the hill to an entrance on the left side of the monastery compound. This fifteenth-century Gelugpa *gompa,* now a fraction of its former size, was designed after the great Ganden monastery near Lhasa. When the Italian scholar Guiseppe Tucci visited here in 1948, he noted that "the temples and chapels were nearly drowned among the houses accommodating the monks." The monastery was completely destroyed in the 1960s; one main building with two temples and a *gön-khang* has been rebuilt above an enclosed courtyard.

A **15-minute** walk along the ridge will bring you to the ruins of the old assembly hall. Its magnificent cobbled courtyard is inlaid with a large white swastika, an ancient symbol favored by both the Bönpo and Buddhists in Tibet. Farther up the barren slopes are the ramparts of Chingwa Tagtse, a palace of the early Tibetan kings until Songtsen Gampo shifted his residence to the Lhasa Valley. The tomb of an early king is said to be under the ruined tower near the ridge top. In later years the castle became the home of the Chonggye princes, the feudal landlords who ruled over this valley. In the early seventeenth century a son of these lords was recognized as the fifth Dalai Lama. Lower on the ridge, below an ill-placed cement pagoda, are the ruins of the old Chonggye *dzong*.

Other excursions around the Chonggye region include visiting the various burial mounds of the kings, or hiking 1¹/₂ **hours** farther up the main valley to Paari *gompa*. The monks are the caretakers for the Bangso Maapo temple on Songtsen Gampo's tumulus. Paari's recently rebuilt *lhakhang* overlooks the upper Chonggye Valley, where a pass leads west to the Drachi Valley and to Mindhroling *gompa,* one the main Nyingmapa monasteries in Central Tibet.

Tshurphu and the Yangpachan Valley
(Map 4, page 147)

Except for the Western Buddhists who come on regular pilgrimages to the home of their spiritual leader, the Karmapa ("Man of Karma"), few trekkers have discovered the powerful beauty of Tshurphu monastery. The sprawling ruins of this monastic complex are set high in a tributary of the Tölung valley, just 40 miles

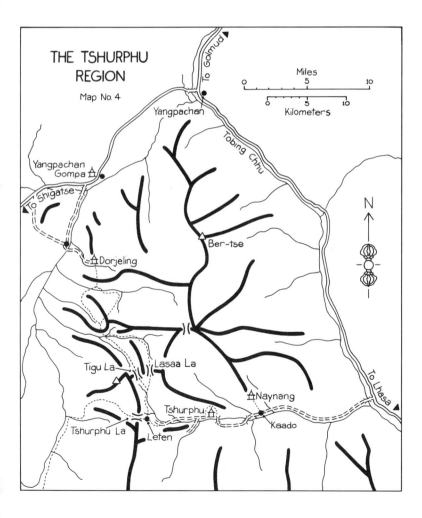

THE TSHURPHU
REGION

Map No. 4

To Golmud

Miles

Kilometers

Yangpachan

Tobing Chhu

Yangpachan
Gompa

To Shigatse

Ber-tse

N

Dorjeling

Tigu La

Lasaa La

Naynang

To Lhasa

Tshurphu

Kaado

Tshurphu La

Leten

(64 km) by road from Lhasa. A wild and scenic trek of **3 to 4 days** originates from Tshurphu, crosses Lasaa La ("New Pass"; 17,500 ft, 5330 m), then winds through a series of remote valleys to the seldom-visited Dorjeling *ani gompa*. The trek ends at the Yangpachan monastery, set in the vast Yangpachan Valley at the foot of the Nyanchhan Thanglha. Despite its proximity to Lhasa, this sparsely populated area provides a relatively undisturbed habitat where herds of blue sheep, Tibetan antelope, and an occasional fox are not uncommon sights.

Arriving in Tshurphu

To get to Tshurphu, take the Golmud Highway, which turns west from the Lhasa–Kathmandu Highway near kilometer marker 3879, about 6 miles (10 km) to the west of the Lhasa Holiday Inn. (This is the same turnoff for vehicles using the Northern Road to Shigatse.) The turnoff for Tshurphu is 21 miles (34 km) to the northwest of Lhasa on the road to Golmud, a major Tibetan supply artery. The route then follows the Tobing River's east (L) bank (a tributary of the Kyi Chhu) for 16 miles (26 km) before leaving the highway at kilometer marker 3583 and crossing a steel girder bridge to the west (R) side of the river. The monastery is another 17 miles (27 km) up a side valley on a road accessible only by four-wheel-drive vehicles or trucks. Unlike the road access to Ganden monastery, this route is too rough for minibuses.

If you are an individual traveler, the best way to reach the Tshurphu bridge turnoff by public transport is to take the Lhasa–Nagchhu bus, which leaves almost every day about 8 A.M. from the front of the Potala Palace. The ticket booths are on the sidewalk just east of the Potala along Dekyi Shar Lam, the main street through Lhasa. Buy your tickets a day or two before departing. Because the ticket seller probably has no idea where Tshurphu is located, you may have to pay a nominal difference for a ticket to Yangpachan (km marker 3804/5), the next major town to the north. Try to get a seat on the left side of the bus so you can watch the roadside kilometer stones and tell the driver when to stop.

The season for trekking in the Tshurphu area is generally from April through October, though the summer rains can cause the river and stream crossings to be somewhat troublesome in July and August. Winter treks are also worth considering, for the snow seems to skirt this region and falls instead on the Lhasa hills and the Nyanchhan Thanglha. My first time over this route was early in 1986; all of the streams were frozen, making the crossings quite easy compared to my next visit, which was a mid-September trek several years later.

All food for your stay at Tshurphu and your trek to the Yangpachan Valley should be purchased in Lhasa. There are no shops en route nor facilities for feeding visitors at any of the monasteries. Due to the remote nature of the trek, tents and fuel stoves are recommended, though it is possible to obtain lodging at the monasteries and the few isolated herders' settlements along the way.

Tshurphu monastery is **2 days** from the steel bridge over the Tobing River. Even though this walk follows the road, few vehicles use it and there's great scenery the entire way. If you want to hire a pack animal to carry your gear to Tshurphu, ask around at the various settlements near the bridge. Finding accommodation en route to Tshurphu is usually no problem, for this is a rich agricultural area with houses most of the way up the valley. If you are short of time, it may be possible to get a lift with the occasional truck taking supplies and building materials to the monastery.

The village of Kaado is **3 to 4 hours** (7 miles, 11 km) from the bridge, set at the base of the Tshurphu Valley's left ridge. In the hills behind this town is Naynang *gompa,* a Kargyüpa monastery dating back to the fourteenth century. Naynang was the original seat of power for the Zhamaapa *truku,* who were known as the "Red Hat" *lamas* because of the ceremonial red crowns that they wore. The *gompa* began as a small meditation retreat and has always had a close affiliation with nearby Tshurphu, also a Kargyüpa monastery. Naynang eventually became the seat for the Pawo *rimpoche,* a line of incarnate *lamas* that began near the middle of the fifteenth century; the current Pawo *rimpoche* lives in a monastery at Bodhnath, a Tibetan community on the outskirts of Kathmandu. (A little-known trek of **3 to 4 days** crosses Nyang-ring La to the north of Kaado, following the old route between the Naynang and Yangpachan monasteries.)

Beyond Kaado the valley narrows and the road begins the steep ascent to Tshurphu. About 1 mile (1.6 km) below the monastery the road passes to the right of Tshurphu's old summer palace, the Lingka Wog, a high-walled compound surrounding several ruined buildings and a grove of poplar and willow trees. The wooden main-entrance gate on the north side is usually locked. To enter this *lingka,* go to the far left (east) end of the enclosure, where a section of the wall is missing beside the groundskeeper's house. Inside is a peaceful private park with a small creek tumbling between hilly meadows. Some weathered frescoes can still be found on the crumbling walls.

Upstream from the summer palace the road crosses on a wooden bridge to the north (L) bank of the river. It then climbs a short way to reach the walls and entrance gate of Tshurphu.

Tshurphu Monastery

The grand ruins of Tshurphu monastery (14,700 ft, 4480 m) stretch magnificently across the base of a steep, scrub-covered ridge. This complex was once the seat of the Karmapa, the incarnate spiritual head of the Zhanagpa, or "Black Hat" Karma Kargyüpa school of Buddhism. (The name is derived from the legendary black crown worn by the Karmapa, said to be made from the hairs of a million fairies and to possess magical powers. The crown is now stored at Rumtek monastery, in Sikkim.)

Tshurphu, one of the many great monastic institutions established around Central Tibet's leading religious teachers during the eleventh and twelfth centuries, was founded as a meditational retreat circa 1187 by Dusum Kyenpa, a *lama* from Kham who received his teachings from a disciple of the hermit ascetic Milarepa. Dusum Kyenpa is now regarded as the first Karmapa, beginning a lineage of *truku* that continues to this day. During the next five centuries Tshurphu grew into a great religious center. Like most of Tibet's large monasteries, it was eventually drawn into the political arena, leading to its destruction by Mongol armies in 1642 during a lengthy war between rivaling noble familes in Ü and Tsang provinces. Tshurphu slowly rebuilt and gradually restored its status as an important Kargyüpa center; nearly a thousand monks were in residence when the Chinese army arrived in the 1950s. Foreseeing the plight of Tibet, the sixteenth Karmapa fled to Sikkim with a large retinue of disciples and many of the monastery's most important treasures. His new seat of power is at Rumtek monastery, 25 miles (40 km) from Gangtok, Sikkim's capital city.

According to a former monk from Tshurphu, a Chinese artillery unit came up the valley in 1966, during the Cultural Revolution, with intentions of destroying the monastery. But the thick temple walls were so solidly built that they withstood the cannon fire. The soldiers went back down the valley, but later a demolition team came to the monastery with explosives. For one week they drilled holes in the walls and planted charges, systematically working their way from one end of the complex to the other until all the buildings were razed.

Nuns sharing a quiet moment at Tshurpu monastery

Despite the extensiveness of the destruction, Tshurphu remains a stunning location. The valley is quite narrow here, with an abundance of leafy trees and meadows lining the rushing stream below the old boundary walls. Perched on the cliffs above the monastery is a retreat center built over the former meditation cave of the third Karmapa, and nearby is the meditation cave of Karma Pakshi, the second Karmapa. A breath-grabbing pilgrimage *kora* climbs 500 feet (150 m) above Tshurphu to these caves and other shrines. The views overlooking the valley are superb, and this walk is a good way to acclimatize for the high crossing over Lasaa La to the Yangpachan Valley. The unusual terraced area built into the right-hand ridge side across from the monastery was formerly used for laying out a giant *thangka* during religious festivals.

The rebuilding at Tshurphu is remarkably advanced considering its remote location and the fact that it is not a major tourist site. The Chinese government initially helped to rebuild the residence hall and the Dhra-tshang temple at the north end of the monastery. The *lhakhang* on the first floor of this temple has images of the Kargyü lineage, including the goateed Karma Pakshi. Upstairs a droning drumbeat resonates from a black-walled protector's temple decorated with delicately painted line drawings of wrathful deities. The huge skeletons of multistoried, red-ochered stone walls are the remains of Dukhang Chhempo, a temple founded by Karma Pakshi. In 1988 the reconstruction of Tshurphu Labrang, an impressively large and ornate structure in the center of the complex where the Karmapas formerly resided, was well under way.

Accommodation at the monastery can be arranged through the monks. There are no shops here, so it is necessary to bring all of your own food. A number of good camping sites are available, the closest being in the large meadow below the monastery walls. If you do camp here, be sure to establish a toilet away from the creek and away from the monastery grounds.

The monks at Tshurphu have unfortunately been spoiled by the Western pilgrims who freely distributed huge quantities of Karmapa pictures and other religiously oriented handouts during their visits. The unpleasant result is that foreign visitors are now inundated with monks, villagers, and visiting Tibetan pilgrims who relentlessly beg for *kupaa,* or religious pictures. Giving away a few photos doesn't help because they tell others, who will be even more persistent. It's a vicious circle that can be resolved only by not giving out any pictures. Away from the monastery, though, a Karmapa picture is an excellent thank-you gift, along with an appropriate payment, if you spend the night in someone's home.

If you stay a night or two at Tshurphu, there's a good chance some of the monks, especially the younger ones, will try to sell you a small packet or a handful of pearl-like bits and pieces, known locally as *pidung* or *ringsay.* They are said to be the relics, or bone fragments, of former Karmapas, salvaged from the ashes after their bodies were cremated!

The Tshurphu *Kora*

Before starting the trek from Tshurphu to the Yangpachan Valley, consider spending at least a full day and two nights acclimatizing at the monastery, particularly if you arrive by vehicle rather than on foot. The pilgrimage circuit up to the cave shrines is a challenging warm-up walk that offers excellent opportunities for photographing Tshurphu's mountainous setting, wandering the ruins, and visiting the temples. The *kora* takes **about 1¹/₂ hours** of actual walking, so allow **a minimum of 3 hours** for rest stops, picture taking, and encounters with pilgrims and monks. The *kora* is walked clockwise and starts beyond the western boundary wall of the monastery. The white *chötaen* near this wall has been erected as an offering to help protect Tshurphu from falling rocks and other calamities.

Follow the road west past the monastery for **15 minutes,** taking the left fork around an extensive succession of *mani* walls piled high with beautifully crafted prayer stones. To the left of the *mani* wall is a crumbling, lichen-covered stone wall enclosing the Karmapa *lingka,* another parklike summer residence associated with Tshurphu. After the *mani* wall ends the road swings around a low, flat-topped hill on the right where sky burials are conducted. Bone chips can be found scattered among the rocks. The *kora* leaves the road near here and ascends this same hill a little beyond the burial site. The turnoff is rather obscure; near the place where the left fork around the *mani* wall rejoins the road, look for the small rock cairns and a thin trail to the right leading up the hillside. The path soon becomes well defined, climbing through several switchbacks before reaching a saddle in the ridge. **Thirty minutes** above the road pass some ruined walls on the point of a ridge spur; the ruins along the base of the cliff are where a *lhakhang* was built over the first Karmapa's meditation cave. Some of the old frescoes are still visible. The streamers of prayer flags just beyond here mark the location of Karma Pakshi's meditation cave. It is situated **5 minutes** above the stone-walled Khyung Dzong hermitage ("Garuda Fortress"; 15,200 ft, 4630 m), built over the third Karmapa's meditation cave. There are shrines at both of these sites.

The *kora* descends to the east from the hermitage into a creek gully. Several shortcuts plunge down the ridge side, though the main pilgrimage route traverses to a small, red offering temple. Below here the trail descends steeply through stands of wild rose and barberry bushes decorated with tufts of yak and sheep wool. **Ten minutes** below the temple is a red-painted shrine for the protectress Pelden Lhamo. The *kora* continues its steep descent to meet the road beside the far eastern wall of the monastery. The main entrance is **a few minutes** to the right (west).

TSHURPHU TO THE YANGPACHAN VALLEY TREK

Due to the lack of villages near the monastery, arranging pack animals for the trek to the Yangpachan Valley can be a problem if you are not with a commercial trekking group. Probably the best place for hiring a guide and a pack animal is the village of Leten (16,700 ft, 5090 m), a small herders' settlement **2¹/₂ hours** above (west of) Tshurphu. If you're not prepared to carry your own gear to Leten, ask around at the monastery and wait for word to get out that you need a pack animal. Or else hike up to Leten (directions below), make arrangements with a herder, then return to Tshurphu to collect your packs.

The trek to Yangpachan initially follows the road to the west from Tshurphu. Not far past the Karmapa *lingka* the main valley splits. Don't take the turnoff to the left; stay on the road paralleling the north (L) stream bank. Climb steadily into the valley on the right (northwest), which soon narrows into a rocky chasm. Cross a small creek, then pass below a summer *drogpa* camp with snarling dogs. Great bastions of eroded rock tower over the tumbling stream course. **One hour and 15**

The spectacular setting of Dorjeling nunnery, en route from Tshurpu monastery to the Yangpachan Valley

minutes above the monastery a large tributary enters from the right (northwest). Several *drogpa* encampments are situated above the road. Cross this creek, then in **a few more minutes** ford the main stream to the south (R) bank. The rocks here are extremely slippery.

The valley levels out and the road follows the south (R) side of the stream. **Thirty minutes** beyond the ford a wide path angles up the south (R) ridge. Leave the road here and turn left, for this trail leads to Leten village. Climb steeply through several switchbacks, reaching the top of the ridge (16,900 ft, 5150 m) in **30 minutes.** The scattered houses of Leten (16,700 ft, 5090 m) are **less than 10**

minutes below on an elevated plateau. The broad trail continuing west along the south (R) ridge side is the route to Tshurphu La, a pass that leads into an upper tributary of the Yangpachan Valley. The locals say the Yarlung Tsangpo is **2 to 3 days** away via this route. Lasaa La, one of several passes on the way to the Yangpachan Valley, is approached by a wide braid of animal tracks leading into the tributary valley to the right (northwest).

Leten must be one of the highest "permanent" settlements in the world. It is inhabited by families of herders who, during the summer months, move into adjacent valleys to graze their herds of yak, goats, and sheep. They return to the shelter of their rock-walled homes in the winter.

Leten is a good place to spend the night. It is the last settlement before Lasaa La and is well positioned to help the acclimatization process. Reaching Lasaa La requires **2 hours or more** of walking through undulating hills, and the next camps are **at least another hour** beyond the pass. One bonus of staying in Leten is the opportunity to consume huge quantities of fresh milk, buttermilk, and yogurt.

If you are trekking as an individual, I recommend hiring a guide and a pack animal for at least the walk up to Lasaa La, because the terrain beyond Leten is confusing. Although this pass is rather high in elevation, it is a broad, unmarked summit that can easily be confused with other crossings. The herders may be reluctant to go much beyond Lasaa La and on to Yangpachan *gompa,* so it may be necessary to hire guides and pack animals in two or three half-day stages during your trek if you want your gear carried to the monastery and the highway. This allows your guide to return home on the same day.

To get your bearings before setting out for Lasaa La, look across the valley (north) from Leten. The route skirts the left (west) side of the prominent, domed mountain rising to the north, then crosses the low ridge behind it. From Leten, descend in **a few minutes** into the main stream channel, cross to the north (L) bank, and climb the ridge on one of the many animal trails leading to the top. The tracks lead beyond the last settlement into a shallow drainage basin, but soon become obscure near the base of the domed peak. Look for a *la-dzay* (cairn) up to the right (north) on the low ridge that extends behind this peak. The trail leading up to this *la-dzay* is the route to Lasaa La. Reach the cairn in **30 minutes** from the stream crossing. This is a false summit; you must pass three more *la-dzay* to reach the top of the ridge spur (17,000 ft, 5180 m), **a few minutes** beyond. A number of mountainous ridges and ranges now come into view, but Lasaa La is still out of sight and **1¹/₂ hours** farther to the north. The access to the pass ascends the drainage to the right (east) of an obvious, deep red ridge. Another pass to the Yangpachan region follows the valley up to the left of the red hills.

Descend north from the ridge spur for **10 minutes** into the stream gully. Climb easily along its west (R) bank and in **another 10 minutes** cross a creek that enters from the left. Continue following this main stream as it winds a long S-shaped course into the barren hills. Jagged peaks emerge on the horizon and the terrain begins to open out. Wherever water flows, the ground is covered in plates of thick tundra; some of the large meadows near the stream would make fine campsites. Chubby little pikas race about on the drier patches of ground, but remind yourself to look up onto the ridges. The steep, rocky hills are perfect habitat for the herds of blue sheep that roam this area.

Continue ascending along this drainage, using whichever side is more suitable for walking. **Less than 1 hour** above the last creek crossing another small creek sweeps in from the right (east). Just beyond here the main stream angles sharply to the left, but the route to Lasaa La continues straight ahead (north). Cross the small creek and climb for **a few minutes** toward a cairn of red rocks (17,300 ft, 5270 m) atop a low morrainal hill. Lasaa La is **20 minutes** farther to the north across a flat, wet plateau of tundra hummocks. Another pass to the Yangpachan Valley, Tigu La (17,500 ft, 5330 m), is several hundred yards to the left (northwest) and is marked by a tall, narrow cairn. Either pass can be used; the drainages descending from them merge to form one large valley on the other side.

The actual summit of Lasaa La is not easy to pinpoint, though a pond and a small pile of rocks are near what appears to be the highest point. Keep heading north. The plateau eventually drops into a U-shaped, glacially carved valley. The large range of snowy peaks in the distance (north) are the Nyanchhan Thanglha mountains, which border the Yangpachan Valley. As you descend, stay to the west (L) side of the gully cutting into the plateau. The terrain is more rugged on this side of the pass; jagged peaks loom in a side valley to the right. A trail forms along the base of the west (L) ridge, avoiding the meadows of deep hummocks on the valley floor. Pass a herders' camp near the stream, then reach a stone goat corral (16,400 ft, 5000 m) **1 hour** below the summit. The valley now enters a long, almost 90-degree bend to the left (west) as a large tributary spills in from the right.

Descend **another 20 minutes.** Before reaching the confluence, ford the main stream to the north (R) bank, then cross to the north (R) side of the tributary creek. Follow one of the many animal tracks for **30 minutes** below the last ford to reach a small *drogpa* settlement (15,900 ft, 4850 m). If you are not part of a trekking group, I recommend having a guide for this final portion of the trek to Yangpachan *gompa,* as the route is obscure and there are few people around to give directions.

With no trees and few shrubs growing in these valleys, the inhabitants are forced to use other resources for building materials and cooking fires: yak dung is the common source of fuel, but it is also used to construct goat corrals. These are made from great stacks of chips piled with rocks and clumps of sod to help keep predators, mainly wolves, from preying on the herds at night.

There are several ways to reach Dorjeling monastery from here, though the most direct and scenic is a high route that leaves the valley near this settlement. Continue descending on the north (R) side of the valley, using the trail leading past a nearby *mani* wall; among the prayer stones are the skull and rack of a large blue sheep. Following the trail soon becomes a battle with the grass hummocks. Try to find the path of least resistance, which means staying along the base of the ridge rather than close to the stream. As the valley starts bending again to the right, more of the Nyanchhan Thanglha peaks come into view. The locals call the most prominent of these summits Da-tse (20,180 ft, 6150 m). A tributary enters from the right **30 minutes** below the *drogpa* houses. Just beyond this crossing a heavily braided track climbs for **10 minutes** up the dry north (R) ridge to a low saddle (15,850 ft, 4830 m). This is the route to Dorjeling monastery.

Although another ridge must still be climbed, views of the mountains span from the west to the south: due south (behind you) is a tall peak known as Ra-tse; the distant, snowy mountains to the right (southwest) of Ra-tse form the border between Bhutan and Tibet; and Da-tse dominates the Nyanchhan Thanglha to the west. The meadows near the saddle, clipped short like putting greens by grazing animals, make remote, scenic campsites. Depending on the time of year, water can be found in several shallow ponds between the sculpted tundra plates.

A high route to Dorjeling ascends without a trail onto the ridge rising straight ahead (north) from the saddle. An alternative, lower route to Dorjeling *gompa* descends via the drainage that forms to the left (northwest). After **1 hour or more** this lower route turns right (north) near the first settlements in the valley below. It then leads into a series of rolling hills and ridges to reach Dorjeling in **about 2 more hours.** If you are trekking as an individual, a guide is also recommended for this route.

If the weather is good, consider taking the high route for the panoramic views from the top. Use whatever course you can from the saddle to find a way across the eroded sections of tundra. Stay to the right of a ruined herders' settlement and keep aiming for the obvious low point in the ridge crest. There's no trail, but as you ascend keep to the right of a deep gully cutting into the slopes. Reach a false summit in **30 minutes,** not including breaks, from the meadows near the previous saddle. Continue heading north for **5 minutes** to a *la-dzay* and the spectacular ridge summit (16,100 ft, 4910 m). The large peak to the right (northeast), with the impressive glacial icefall pouring from its shoulder, is called Ber-tse (19,000 ft, 5800 m) by the locals. The rugged summits and deep valleys of the Nyanchhan Thanglha range stretch majestically from north to south across the entire horizon. Da-tse is to the left (west) and the huge massif of the main Nyanchhan Thanglha peak (23,330 ft, 7111 m; this is the peak marked 6955 m on the NH 46-5 JOG map, series 1501) rises in the distance to the north. If you camp on the meadows near the saddle, try to hike up here early in the morning for the sunrise.

To reach Dorjeling, descend to the right (northeast) from the *la-dzay*, using Ber-tse as your bearing. Soon a set of braided animal tracks forms, leading off the tundra plates to the east (R) side of a drainage gully. Follow this drainage to reach the bottom of the next valley (15,400 ft, 4700 m) in **30 minutes** from the ridgetop.

Don't cross the stream draining this valley. Instead, stay high on the trail along the south (L) bank, then walk cross-country, still heading downstream, for **30 minutes** to a lone herders' house. Descend from this house to a broad trail alongside the stream. A *mani* wall sits at the entrance to a small gorge. Once the valley opens out again, cross to the north (R) side of the stream (shoes and socks may have to come off), **30 minutes** beyond the herder's house. Several *drogpa* families establish camps here during the summer months, and near the stream are a few small meadows good for camping or picnics. The elevation is noticeably lower now; the scrub juniper bushes on the ridges are the tallest vegetation since Tshurphu.

The route to Dorjeling leaves the valley from here on a wide trail climbing up the north (R) ridge. Reach the saddle (15,000 ft, 4570 m) in **less than 30 minutes** from the stream crossing. The *gompa* is **another 40 minutes** to the north across a dry plateau wrought with mine fields of pika burrows. Aim for the group of rounded hills that end with deep, vertical clefts of exposed rock; Dorjeling is set at the base of these cliffs.

Dorjeling monastery (14,600 ft, 4450 m) has been built in a spectacular setting, with a soaring backdrop of weathered rock and the twin sentinels of Ber-tse and Da-tse rising on either side. Locations such as this deserve being called a *naychhan,* or "power place," by the Tibetans. (Dorjeling is incorrectly marked on the NH 46-9 JOG maps. The correct position is about 2 inches (5 cm) farther up to the northeast, at approximately 29 degrees 53 minutes north latitude, 90 degrees 26 minutes east longitude.) At least a half-dozen new residence buildings have sprung up in the past few years at this Kargyüpa *gompa* to accommodate the growing number of *ani,* at last count almost sixty. The central building with the stone stairway and the covered porch is the *lhakhang.* It is decorated simply but reverently. Visitors are warmly greeted with copious cups of butter tea and accommodation is usually easy to arrange. Donations will be very appreciated.

The remainder of the walk to Yangpachan *gompa* follows the access road to the left (west) from Dorjeling. Pass several houses near the first cultivated fields seen since the villages below Tshurphu, then cross to the south (L) side of a creek **30 minutes** below the monastery. The valley swings to the right and soon opens out onto the huge expanse of the Yangpachan Valley and the Nyanchhan Thanglha range. During the wetter summer months the valley floor is a patchwork of grass, wildflowers, and barren desert, speckled with thousands of grazing yaks, goats, and sheep. The *drogpa* of the Yangpachan region were one of the four main northern tribes of Tibetan nomads and had their own internal organization, like a gigantic extended family. Their patronage and financial support probably played a major role in the fourth Zhamaapa's decision to move his monastery to the Yangpachan Valley at the end of the fifteenth century.

As the ridges melt into the plains, the road veers off to the left toward the river that drains this end of the Yangpachan Valley. The ford used by locals is about 200 yards (180 m) upstream from Tsabarung (it may have other names), the settlement of bright, whitewashed houses on the west (L) bank. Leave the road and walk cross-country toward this village, reaching the river in **1 hour** from the monastery. The preferred crossing point is at the beginning of a tight S bend, though the water will come at least halfway up your thigh. (During July, August, and early September the river might be too deep to ford.) Find out where the locals cross, or try to catch a lift with a truck farther upstream where the road crosses.

Tsabarung (14,200 ft, 4330 m) is the main trading center and the road link to Lhasa and Shigatse in this part of Yangpachan. The courtyards of each house are heaped with goat- and sheepskins and piles of precious lumber; inside great mounds of dried goat carcasses, yak heads, and dozens of bags of *tsampa* are stacked along the walls. If you're walking this trek in the opposite direction, from Yangpachan to Tshurphu, this is a good place to enquire about hiring a guide and a pack animal (expect a horse or a burro). Accommodation can often be arranged with one of the families here.

The road to Yangpachan *gompa* initially skirts the base of a long, gravel-covered hill just north of Tsabarung. Pass to the right of a pond, then follow the road to the top of this hill. The road now heads almost due north above the west (L) bank of the river. Another road leads west from Tsabarung, but it goes to a different part of the valley. The terrain beyond the village quickly changes to stony desert, yet along the river are tall stands of grass and small green meadows. **Two hours** from Tsabarung a new bridge spans the wide braided stream joining the

Nuns gathered on the steps of Dorjeling nunnery

river from the left.

The Northern Road to Shigatse is **5 minutes** beyond this bridge (near km marker 20). Yangpachan *gompa* (marked Angchen Gompa on the NH 46-9 JOG map) and the junction with the Lhasa–Golmud Highway are to the right (northeast), and Shigatse is 137 miles (221 km) to the left. Follow the road to the right for **10 minutes** into a rocky gorge. The white-walled *gompa* (near km marker 19) is perched in the hills to the left. A steep trail leads directly up to the monastery in **another 10 minutes. A few minutes** farther along the road a cart track winds up to the monastery from a nearby village.

Yangpachan Monastery

This Zhamaa Kargyüpa monastery (14,200 ft, 4330 m) overlooks the northern half of the Yangpachan Valley. The Nyanchhan Thanglha mountains march into the distance and another range of peaks, including Ber-tse, forms the impressive eastern boundary of the valley. Yangpachan was quickly transformed into one of Tibet's major political centers when the fourth Zhamaapa moved here from Naynang *gompa*. Destroyed during the Cultural Revolution, the *gompa* now consists of a rebuilt *Ibalchang* and courtyard overshadowed by the immense boundary walls and ruins of the former complex. Nearly sixty *dhrapa* were associated with Yangpachan in 1988, and workers were repairing the inner rooms of the main temple. The seat of the present Zhamaa *truku*, the thirteenth, is the Buddhist monastery atop the Swayambunath hill in Kathmandu.

If you have not arranged for transport to meet you at Yangpachan *gompa,* the only way to secure a ride back to Lhasa or Shigatse is by hitchhiking. The monastery is 12 miles (19 km) west of the Lhasa–Golmud Highway junction (km marker 0), and Lhasa is another 52 miles (84 km) to the southeast. No local buses serve this part of the valley, though it's fairly easy to get rides with local traffic to the highway or to the town of Yangpachan (km marker 3804/5), located less than a mile (1 km) south of the Lhasa–Golmud Highway junction. Yangpachan has a hotel and several eating establishments. An unusual domed, geodesic-style building, the steam release towers, and many of the other modern-looking buildings in this region are part of a large geothermal project that supplies Lhasa with most of its electricity.

The Nyanchhan Thanglha–Nam Tsho Trek
(Map 5, page 160)

The loop walk across the Nyanchhan Thanglha mountains to the pebbled shores of Nam Tsho (also known as Tengri Nor, the "Heaven Lake" mentioned by nineteenth- and early-twentieth-century explorers in Northern Tibet) takes **7 to 8 days.** The trail for this circuit begins and ends at Damzhung (km marker 1774/3; old system), a small roadside town 99 miles (160 km) to the north of Lhasa on the Lhasa–Golmud Highway. This spectacular route climbs out of the Damzhung Valley via Lagaen La (17,000 ft, 5180 m), then descends to the mystical environs of Tashiy Do hermitage and the vast Nam Tsho, the second-largest salt lake in Tibet. The final leg of the loop enters a remote region of the Nyanchhan Thanglha range, crosses Kong La (17,200 ft, 5240 m), and winds through deep glaciated

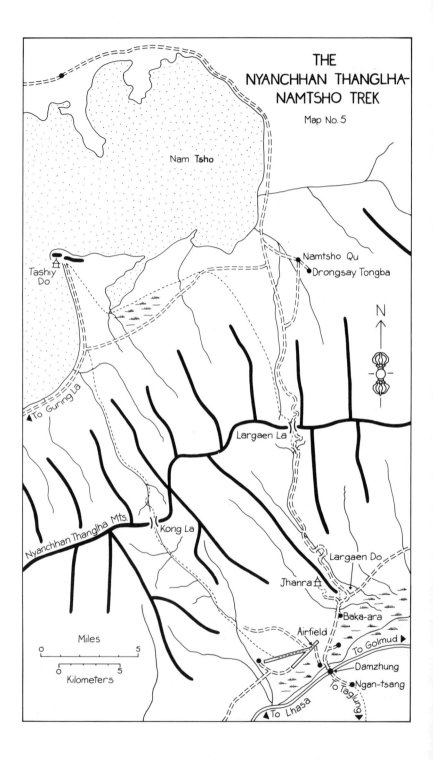

THE
NYANCHHAN THANGLHA-
NAMTSHO TREK

Map No. 5

Nam Tsho

Namtsho Qu
Drongsay Tongba

Tashiy
Do

N

To Guring La

Largaen La

Nyanchhan Thanglha Mts.

Kong La

Largaen Do

Jhanra

Baka-ara

Miles

Airfield

To Golmud ▶

0   5

Damzhung

0   5

Ngan-tsang

Kilometers

To Taglung

▲ To Lhasa

valleys on the return to the Damzhung area.

Damzhung ("Center of the Marsh") is an unremarkable, windblown gathering of *chhang* halls, shops, and a few Chinese restaurants. The largest building in town is a multistoried tourist hotel with few amenities. Cheaper accommodation can be found in a small rest house across the river near the cinema. **Thirty minutes** to the south of Damzhung is Ngan-tsang, a small village where families will put up travelers for the night. This settlement is also the best place to rent pack horses or yaks to carry your gear to Nam Tsho. All of the residents here are herders, as the climate in this valley is unsuitable for growing crops.

The best season for trekking in this area is late May to mid-October, though you must be prepared at all times for wet weather, snow, and cold winds. Nam Tsho is a very high lake (15,060 ft, 4590 m), situated at the edge of the severe-weathered Jhang Thang plateau. During July and August the monsoon rains can be quite persistent. Also, snows of up to a foot or more can fall on the mountains during any of the summer months, blocking the road over Lagaen La for several days at a time.

Tents and fuel stoves are a must for this trek and most provisions should be purchased before arriving in Damzhung or Nam Tsho Qu. Noodles, powdered milk, and a few other basics are usually available in these towns, but don't count on finding much more. The roadside Chinese restaurants in Damzhung will probably sell a few fresh vegetables if you ask.

Arrangements for private transport to Damzhung, Nam Tsho Qu, and even to Tashiy Do can be made through any of the hotels or travel companies in Lhasa. The only local buses offering service to Damzhung from Lhasa are the through buses going to Nagchhu, a large town another 105 miles (170 km) to the northeast of Damzhung. Purchase tickets in Lhasa from the ticket desks on the street near the Potala and be sure to specify a seat to Damzhung. It's a beautiful **4¹/₂-hour** ride through the Yangpachan Valley and along the base of the main Nyanchhan Thanglha peak. If you are short of time, trucks and tractor carts regularly cross from Damzhung to Nam Tsho Qu via Lagaen La; they usually gather passengers in front of the shops along the highway.

An alternative trek from Damzhung is the **3-day** walk to the south on a mountainous pilgrimage route to Taglung *gompa*. This ancient monastic site, formerly the seat of power for the Taglung Kargyüpa sect of Buddhism, dates back to the twelfth century. Another walk from Damzhung is the **3- to 4-day** journey east to Reteng *gompa*. This famous Gelugpa complex was originally a Kadampa monastery founded in the eleventh century by Dromton, the main disciple of the Indian religious scholar Atisa. Since these two monasteries are only a long day's walk apart along a jeep road, the treks to Taglung and Reteng can be combined into a **7- to 9-day** loop that originates in Damzhung. Lhasa is only a **3-day** trek south from Taglung on the old northern trade route via Chag La (15,910 ft, 4850 m) and Pembogo La (16,570 ft, 5050 m). At times it is possible to find a truck going back to Lhasa from either of these monasteries.

A large marsh visited by the black-necked crane and other migratory birds is **about 1 hour** to the north of Damzhung. According to the locals, the best time to observe these tall cranes, which are an endangered species, is mid-May to mid-

Yangpachan Valley and the Nyanchhan Thanglha mountains

July. Another dayhike from Damzhung is the **2-hour** walk to Jhanra *gompa*, a small hermitage along the road to Nam Tsho. Details of this hike are included in the trek description that follows.

The walk to Nam Tsho initially follows the dirt road from Damzhung over Lagaen La. Plan on **2 to 3 days** to reach the lake and **another long day** of walking to arrive at the Tashiy Do cave hermitage. Hiking along roads is usually unpleasant, but this track is an exception: most of the traffic consists of yak herders and people on horseback. Years ago this was the old caravan route for the salt traders of the Jhang Thang, Tibet's great northern plateau. From May until July it is still possible to see loaded yaks setting off on the forty-day journey across this plateau, taking tea and other goods to remote herding settlements and returning with salt, butter, and animal hides.

The road to Lagaen La leaves the highway about 100 yards (90 m) to the west of the hotel and crosses a bridge to the north (R) side of the river. Before leaving the highway, take a few minutes above the bridge to get your bearings, for this is a good vantage point. The Nyanchhan Thanglha mountains rise steeply from the plains; the main snowcapped summit rises impressively to the left (west). Three deep valleys drain from these mountains into the Damzhung area. The one farthest to the left (northwest) and beyond the airfield is the drainage from Kong La. Almost due north is the mouth of a dry valley with Jhanra *gompa* perched on a barren ridge, and the next valley to the right (north-northeast) is the route to Lagaen La.

Just across the river and up to the left is a large, walled compound with an arched entrance. A rest house and cinema are on the premises, set back and to the right of the paved road running through the center. The road to Nam Tsho does not enter this compound. Instead, turn right after the bridge along an orange-colored mud wall. After **5 minutes** this road jogs left (north) between two walled compounds. Continue north past more walled-in houses, reaching the last compound in **another 20 minutes.** In **a few minutes** more the road forks, the smaller right-hand track leading to a nearby settlement. The main road heads north, angling toward the hills across a scrubby desert plain. **Thirty minutes** beyond this fork the mouth of a valley opens on the left; Jhanra *gompa* and its many cave hermitages are above the north (L) side of this drainage. This Kargyüpa temple is built into an eroding ridge dotted with stunted juniper bushes. The cart track turning off for this retreat is still a fair distance away, but the quickest approach from Damzhung is to walk without a trail across the flat plain from the road. The *gompa* can be reached in **1 hour or so.**

The road to Lagaen La continues north, passing the *drogpa* village of Baka-ara **1 hour** beyond the fork. **Fifteen minutes** farther a bridge crosses the creek draining the valley. Beyond this crossing the road veers to the right to avoid a ridge spur. The braided animal track that continues straight ahead (north) is a shortcut that climbs onto the spur. Following this broad trail, cross another creek in **15 minutes** beyond the bridge. After passing behind the last houses in this part of the valley, the track intersects the east-west road leading into the hills toward the *gompa*. Stay on the animal track and climb up the ridge for **20 minutes** to the summit *la-dzay* (14,400 ft, 4390 m). From this viewpoint it is possible to see the gap where the road to Nagchhu and Golmud crosses the Nyanchhan Thanglha range at the far eastern end of the Damzhung Valley. According to the NH 46-5 JOG map for this area, the tall peak that rises across the valley (southeast) above all the other summits is about 20 miles (32 km) away and very close to Reteng monastery. My yak man said it is called Bagandam (18,790 ft, 5727 m).

The trail descends north from this desert ridge into a well-watered valley of green meadows known locally as Lagaen Do. Rejoin the road to Lagaen La in **5 minutes.** Beside the stream draining this area are several good campsites with plenty of room for large groups. The *drogpa* that populate the meadows throughout this valley bring their herds here in May; by late October most of the camps have been packed up.

The road winds up the Lagaen Valley, climbing gently under dry hillsides vegetated with barberry and juniper bushes. This area is prime territory for the lammergeier, the monstrous but elegant bearded vulture of Tibet and the Himalaya. Its abdomen and head are a beautiful golden color; a streak of dark brown feathers extends down from the eye to form a beard under its beak. As the birds glide overhead, the wind rushes noisily across their enormous wings, which can reach 9 feet (2.8 m) or more in length. No other bird in Tibet has a wingspan this long, though another vulture, the Himalayan griffin, is actually larger. The griffin's head lacks feathers, like most other vultures, and its white abdomen and the white leading half of its underwing help to distinguish this bird from the lammergeier.

One hour beyond the meadow campsites the valley narrows into a gorge where the road crosses a bridge (14,900 ft, 4540 m) to the east (L) side of the stream. White-throated dippers dive for insects here, then bob up and down on the rocks beside the water. The high, steep slopes enclosing this gorge are ideal terrain for the noisy Tibetan snow cocks. These giant partridges glide in tight, fixed-wing formations like a squadron of fighter jets, filling the air with their unusual high-pitched gobbles.

Twenty minutes above the first bridge is a second bridge crossing, and **10 minutes** farther is a double ford where a tributary meets the main stream. The road now ascends the east (L) side of the valley; the sheer walls begin to open out and the ridges soon become more rounded. **Two hours** above the fords the road crosses a bridge (16,600 ft, 5060 m) to the west (R) side of the stream. Above the west (R) stream bank before this bridge is a grassy plateau flat enough for camping, though it is rather exposed to the wind. The next good campsite is a couple of hours away and over the pass.

Just beyond the bridge a large valley enters from the left (west). Lagaen La is straight ahead to the north. While the road swings off to the right in long switchbacks to reach the summit, a wide animal track continues straight up the gravel slopes toward a large outcrop of red rock and Lagaen La. The pass (17,000 ft, 5180 m) is a **30-minute** climb from the last bridge.

Nam Tsho lies to the north of Lagaen La, looking like a deep blue iceberg. Though only its easternmost tip is visible through the rounded hills and ridges, it is still an impressively huge body of water. The town of Nam Tsho Qu is on the plains to the right (east) of the lake, but cannot be seen from here. The caravan route skirts this end of the lake, entering the low hills beyond for the journey across the northern plateau.

From Lagaen La the road weaves down onto the lakeside plains. If you are not going to Nam Tsho Qu you may want to use a shortcut that avoids the long bends in the road. This alternative route drops down the side of the ridge to the left (northwest) from the summit *la-dzay* and prayer flags. Descend the slope in an arc along the ridge side to reach a creek bed in **20 minutes.** Cross to the west (L) bank, then descend for **45 minutes** on braided animal trails to a series of large, flat meadows. These are excellent campsites, well protected from the winds that can buffet the Nam Tsho basin. *Drogpa* families like this area and often erect tents here in the summer.

The road here is only 100 yards (90 m) from the creek, squeezed toward these meadow camps by the foothills to the east. The road to Nam Tsho Qu (15,400 ft, 4690 m) branches off just to the north of these hills. This small settlement, **1½ hours** from here, consists of a few poorly stocked shops, a rest house, a handful of residences, and a bizarre "planned community" of several identical cement houses, all white, all rectangular.

Trucks and tractors going to Damzhung usually park in front of the shops to take on paying passengers. The "cadre" (a Chinese title for the administrative head of an area, similar, in this case, to being the mayor) in Nam Tsho Qu is a helpful young man with a reasonable knowledge of English. If you need to hire yaks, ask him or enquire at Dhrongsay Tongba, the village where the *drogpa* live, which is a **30-minute** walk to the southeast of Nam Tsho Qu. Tashiy Do hermitage is **1 long day** due west from Nam Tsho Qu, at the far end of what looks like the Ayers Rock of Tibet.

If you don't choose to visit Nam Tsho Qu, there are two ways to approach the lake and Tashiy Do from the creek meadows below Lagaen La. Both choices take about the same amount of time.

The more direct route follows a trail that leads north from the meadow camps along the creek's left bank. In **a few minutes** the trail skirts the base of a rocky ridge. Beyond these cliffs the stream turns away to the right, but the route to the lake continues straight ahead (north), without a trail, along the base of these hills. Because the ground here is covered with tall grass tussocks and pools of water, the best terrain for walking is along the junction where the plains and the hills meet. **About 1 hour** beyond the meadow camps the hills start fading into the plains and Nam Tsho finally comes into view. There are a few herders' campsites, but the only sources of water are the small meadow pools. Nam Tsho Qu, Dhrongsay Tongba, and several other clusters of houses can be seen across the plains to the right (northeast). Two prominent snowy peaks in the Nyanchhan Thanglha range jut high above the other mountains beyond these settlements. The locals call the taller, more pointed summit Samteng Ghangsang (20,505 ft, 6250 m). The large mountain to the right (south) is known as Hargu Dungtse (19740 ft, 6016 m).

Continue walking along the base of the ridge. As the hills recede, thin desert vegetation replaces the grass hummocks and the plains become much easier to walk on. Instead of aiming for the lake, angle across the flat expanse toward Tashiy Do, the lone humped hill to the left (west). Although you might want to walk along the lakeshore, it is not a very practical way to reach Tashiy Do; a broad arm of land extends into the lake, and beyond this is a long, narrow bay that must be skirted before you reach the cave hermitages.

Three hours past the meadow camps the plains end abruptly, dropping about 6 feet (1.8 m) over a steep embankment that stretches for miles. A jeep track to Tashiy Do parallels this shelf, a former shoreline of Nam Tsho. All of the lakes

Kyung Dzong ("Garuda Fortress") hermitage, perched high above Tshurpu monastery on the pilgrimage kora

The Nyanchhan Thanglha mountains and the sparkling waters of Lake Nam Tsho, the second largest salt lake in Tibet

in Northern Tibet are ringed by similar embankments, some as much as 660 feet (200 m) higher than their present level. Apparently the lakes here were considerably larger two to three million years ago, but changes in the climate made the region more arid.

The jeep track to Tashiy Do can also be reached by following the road north from the meadow camps. The turnoff for Nam Tsho Qu is just beyond the foothills to the right (east). Don't turn here, but continue straight ahead on the main road, which gradually angles away from the hills that lie to the left. **About 2 hours** beyond the meadow camps the road passes to the right of the only houses along this entire stretch. The jeep track heading west to Tashiy Do runs between the main road and this scattered settlement, though the turnoff is farther ahead (north). Once you are near these houses, leave the main road and turn left (west) across the plain for **a few minutes.** The jeep track is at the base of the old shoreline. Follow it west for **about 1 hour** from the last houses until the embankment and the jeep track start angling away from the lake to the left. This is approximately where the cross-country route from the meadow camps intersects with the track.

Although the track leads to the cave hermitages, it is a very roundabout journey that is unnecessary if you are on foot. Instead, walk cross-country over the plains toward Tashiy Do, a very obvious landmark. It is best to aim a bit to the left (south) of this hill to avoid a long detour around the bay. The terrain is generally quite good for walking, but if the ground becomes too wet or uneven with hummocks, adjust your course toward the mountains and higher ground.

During the wet summer months the plain around the lake is lush with grass and speckled with black tents. Surrounding these handspun, hand-woven tents are hundreds, possibly thousands, of grazing yak. If the *drogpa* invite you in for a cup of butter tea, accept the offer even if you're not keen about the taste. It's a great opportunity to meet some of these hearty people and have a glimpse of their rugged life-style. The nomads' tents are usually well equipped, often containing a few pieces of furniture, trunks of gear, and elaborate Buddhist altars graced with butter lamps and possibly even a *thangka* or two. The *drogpa* on this side of Nam Tsho are either from the villages near Nam Tsho Qu or from the Damzhung Valley.

These plains are also home to vast numbers of black-lipped pikas, small members of the rabbit family that resemble guinea pigs. Some of their colonies are so huge that you might not be able to find an area 10 feet (3 m) across without at least a few burrow holes, and large tracts of ground may be perforated with hundreds upon hundreds of holes. If you're lucky you might see Eversmann's polecat, a black-masked, reddish brown ferret that closely resembles the critically endangered black-footed ferret of the North American prairies.

Two and a half hours beyond the last houses, a fairly large stream flows through a series of low sandy hills. Depending on where you cross this stream, you should find several flat areas suitable for camping at the base of these hills. Except for the mud-walled ruins scattered across the plains, few campsites can offer protection from the wind. Tashiy Do appears very close from here, though the long finger of water cutting inland will block the way if you walk directly toward this hill. Instead, head left (southwest) across the plain until the bay can be seen over the hills to your right. The inlet for the bay is **1^1/$_2$ hours** from the stream. Two creeks converge near the inlet, making the ground quite swampy.

Large flocks of migratory birds—including bar-headed geese, mallards, Brahminy ducks, brown-headed and black-headed gulls, black-necked cranes, cormorants, terns, and several types of pochards—congregate along the shores of this bay, resting during their long journeys across Asia, especially from April until November. Perhaps the most interesting terrestrial birds in these parts are the sand grouses. They fly in swift, acrobatic formations, swooping noisily over the plains with their long, pointed tails trailing behind. Sand grouse are pale tan and gray, with very fine black stripes on the head, neck, and across the breast. They act much like quail when feeding and can be surprisingly fearless when intruders pass nearby.

Once you have found a suitable route around the bay, head toward Tashiy Do. Not far from the end of the bay is a pale, pink-walled ruin that may have been a small monastery. The stonework here was very well crafted and many *mani* stones grace the site. Another mud- and rock-walled enclosure is on a nearby hill.

The bulk of Tashiy Do now lies to the north, a **1-hour** walk from these ruins. Eventually it's possible to distinguish that this outcrop consists of two separate hills. The larger, Tashiy Do Thuujhe ("Merciful Lucky Rock"), is to the right (east); Tashiy Do Chhungchhung ("Little Lucky Rock") is to the left. There are caves within the rock walls of both hills, though the main hermitage site is located in Tashiy Do Chhungchhung.

The plain between the bay and the Tashiy Do hills is flat and arid, with pockets of soft sand and a wispy covering of vegetation. The jeep track can be seen coming in from the left, paralleling the lakeshore and leading directly to a pair of immense limestone monoliths at the entrance to Tashiy Do Chhungchhung.

Few hermitage sites can rival the power and grandeur surrounding Tashiy Do. The unusual twin pillars of rock are the watchtowers for a myriad of cave temples and grottos lying within the folds of the red limestone cliffs. Most of the caves' facades have been destroyed, and some caves are littered with goat droppings, but the sanctity of Tashiy Do remains intact. Remnants of a few wall paintings and the stone and plaster altars can still be seen. The blackened ceilings attest to centuries, perhaps millennia, of use. Although the caves were uninhabited when I visited late in 1988, some altars seem to be in use and new prayer stones and clay *tsha-tsha* have been deposited about the area. One fire pit has been reconstructed, with conical adobe cooking-pot supports and a backdrop decorated with a three-sided yin-yang symbol.

The main summit of the Nyanchhan Thanglha range dominates the southern horizon of peaks. Nam Tsho's 70-mile (113 km) length can now be appreciated, although the far end is still lost from sight. Nam Tsho is considered a salt lake, but there are times when its water is deliciously free from a saline taste. The main fish here are high-altitude scaleless carp, which apparently exist in sufficient numbers to be harvested commercially.

The main campsites are on the south side of Tashiy Do Chhungchhung near the caves, though a fair amount of trash and broken beer bottles has been scattered around. One of the nicest campsites is beside the long, Ladhaki-style *mani* wall stretching between the Tashiy Do hills. The lake water on this side of the peninsula is very clear and the site is reasonably protected from the wind.

The *kora* around Tashiy Do Chhungchhung is a **2-hour** lakeside walk under sculpted limestone cliffs. The climb to the summit (15,500 ft, 4720 m) takes **less than 30 minutes** and is best approached from the east side near the *mani* wall. Piles of carved prayer stones decorate the summit and the views are outstanding in all directions. Almost due south from Tashiy Do is the broad-mouthed valley that leads to Kong La (17,200 ft, 5240 m). Several valleys farther to the right (west) is a little-known route over the mountains via Chag La (17,200 ft, 5240 m); to the west of the massive Nyanchhan Thanglha peak is a higher crossing over Guring La (19,590 ft, 5970 m). The trek from Tashiy Do over Guring La to the Yangpachan Valley is a difficult trek of **7 to 8 days** that involves crossing a glacier. The Austrian climbers Heinrich Harrer and Peter Aufschneiter crossed here in 1945 during their daring two-year escape to Lhasa from a British P.O.W. camp in India.

The return to Damzhung via Kong La can be trekked in **2 long days.** The route begins with a scenic lakeshore walk on the jeep track leading south from Tashiy Do. **Two hours** from the hermitage this track reaches a T intersection. Nam Tsho Qu is along the road to the left (east) and the approach to Guring La is to the right (west). The valley opening onto the plain due south from this junction is *not* the way to Kong La. The correct route is up the next major valley to the right. The west (L) ridge of this drainage from Kong La is a steep, sweeping wall that curves back

Hip yak herders near Lake Nam Tsho

into the mountains, with a tall, pyramid-shaped peak looming behind.

From the intersection, angle to the right (southwest) across the plain toward the mouth of this valley. The old lakeshore ledge is only **10 minutes** away. Continue climbing gently, staying to the right (southwest) over the grassy alluvial plain. There is no real trail to follow, but as you enter the valley keep to its east (R) side. **One and a half hours** beyond the jeep track cross a large gravel wash spilling from the talus slopes of the east (R) ridge. Near the stream draining this valley is a plateau of narrow meadows where *drogpa* may be camped.

Not far from here the valley bends to the left and the meadows are interrupted by large, rolling morainal hills. To avoid climbing one hill after another, stay close to the base of the east (R) ridge. As the hills smooth out, the valley turns back toward the right, widening into a broad basin of red mountains and green meadows with several herders' camps. Reach the largest of these camps (16,000 ft, 4880 m) **2¹/₂ hours** after leaving the jeep track. Kong La is a long climb of **1¹/₂ hours** from this basin, and there are no suitable campsites for **another 1¹/₂ hours** after crossing the pass, so if it is getting late, camp here for the night.

The route to Kong La remains on the east (R) side of the valley for **30 minutes** past the last *drogpa* camps, then crosses to the west (L) bank to avoid a steep slope of moraine. The vegetation is now very sparse and the valley quickly assumes a high alpine feel as it turns sharply to the right (southwest). Follow the livestock tracks near the stream for **10 minutes** until the drainage forks. Recross to the south (R) bank above a junction with another creek, then ascend a narrow red rock gully, which is the fork from the left (south). Climb for **another 10 minutes,** then cross to the east (R) side of the small creek bed. The gully soon opens into a steep catchment area with several small tributaries spilling through the red crags. If the route is obscure in places as it weaves between the boulders and talus, yak droppings are as good as cairns for relocating the trail.

Kong La (17,200 ft, 5240 m) is **25 minutes** above this last creek crossing, with *la-dzay* marking the broad summit at either end. The mountains are strikingly rugged here, unlike the gently rounded ridges near Lagaen La. The descent follows a stunning valley system that has been scoured by repeated glacial advances and retreats. Initially a trail leads down from the summit, though it is not easy to follow as the valley widens. Stay to the west (R) side of the creek that forms to drain this area. After **15 minutes** pass the mouth of a large glacial tributary entering from the left (east). The main valley becomes noticeably U-shaped and the terrain is littered with pieces of rock torn from the ridges by old glaciers. Continue descending, choosing the path of least resistance around the hills and boulders. **One hour** below the pass the piles of morraine are especially jumbled and difficult to negotiate. When it is convenient, cross to the east (L) side of the creek. Soon it becomes obvious that this large drainage is merely a tributary for a much greater valley coming in from the right (west). The easiest route down hugs the base of the east (L) ridge. Descend steeply along a trough between the ridge and the hills of morraine. Where a tumbling creek cuts across this trough, veer right and follow it down the steep embankment, reaching the broad valley floor in **1¹/₂ hours** from the pass. A herders' camp (16,300 ft, 5970 m) and stone corrals are above the junction of this creek with the stream draining the larger, main valley.

This sensational spot makes a spectacular campsite, wonderfully remote and with several isolated meadows for camping, but most impressive is the enormity of this location. Four gigantic glacial valleys converge around this camp to form a fifth, a geological rarity made even more unusual by the extreme elevation. The western glacier was the main ice floe, for the mouths of the other drainages have been left hanging with great vertical walls of morraine spilling from them. For those who are walking this route in the opposite direction, the second valley on the right from this camp, up to the northwest, leads to Kong La.

Damzhung is only **5 hours** of steady walking away, but the terrain below this camp is rather demanding. Stay to the east (L) side of the main valley, for soon another large tributary enters from the right with a towering morraine sweeping from its mouth. The descent is more a route than a trail, though at times there is a good path to follow near the base of the east (L) ridge. At first the walking isn't bad, but as the valley narrows numerous hummock fields must be conquered and piles of rock rubble are everywhere. **One and a half hours** beyond the herders' camp a long, unstable rock slide spills from the east (L) ridge. Don't try to negotiate the thin trail winding through it. Instead, rock-hop to the west (R) bank of the stream: the trail on this side is much easier to follow, though the valley remains quite rugged. This area becomes noticeably more green and alive as you descend; dwarf rhododendron and barberry bushes start cluttering the slopes, brilliantly colored rose finches sing from the bush tops, and brown dippers bob beside the stream. The Damzhung area soon comes into view, enclosed by a parade of rocky peaks.

Forty minutes below the rock slide the trail climbs out of the valley to skirt a narrow gorge. **Less than 10 minutes** away is a viewpoint (14,700 ft, 4480 m) overlooking the Damzhung region. An airfield (marked LA SA on the NH 46-5 JOG map and the ONC aeronautical maps) stretches in two oblique swaths across this end of the valley. The jagged summits along the skyline are the neighbors of Reteng and Taglung monasteries. A beautifully situated campsite is set in the rolling hills below this viewing spot, and is the first decent flat area for camping since the high herders' camp, though the only source of water is a long walk back to the stream.

The route to Damzhung drops quickly from this ridge down a steep grassy slope. On the next ridge to the left are several ruined walls, probably an old fortress or a well-chosen hermitage site. Angle to the right as you descend, following the network of trails for **10 minutes** through scrubby patches of barberry and juniper to reach the stream gully. There are several potential campsites along here as well. Descend on the west (R) bank for **5 minutes,** then cross to the east (L) side below a powerhouse. Damzhung is **2¹/₂ hours** to the left (southeast) across the valley floor. The main part of town is easily recognized by the tall blue hotel rising above all the other buildings. The most direct route is to aim straight for the hotel, though a fenced area causes a detour near the airfield.

Ascend the embankment on the east (L) side of the stream to reach the outflow from the powerhouse. Beyond here the valley is quite flat with a gentle downward slope, making it easy to walk cross-country toward Damzhung without a trail. Cross a jeep road **less than 30 minutes** beyond the outflow. This road eventually leads into Damzhung, but it is a circuitous journey. Instead, continue toward the town for **10 minutes** to the fenced enclosure. Walk to the right (south) along the fenceline to meet the runway of the little-used airfield. To avoid marshy ground and another fenced area, follow the runway to the left (east). When it ends, turn left onto the second runway. At the end of the fence paralleling this runway a road leads off to the right (south) toward the first houses of Damzhung. Don't follow the first turn into these compounds, but continue straight ahead. This road eventually swings to the left between several other compounds and onto a cement-paved avenue with army posts and fancy gates. The rest house and the cinema are about halfway down on the left. Just below the gate at the end of the pavement is the bridge crossing to the highway and the tourist hotel.

Unless you have made arrangements in Lhasa for a vehicle to meet you in Damzhung, the best way to get a ride back to Lhasa is to hitchhike on a truck or go by local bus. The restaurants along the highway are good places to meet truck drivers, and the buses from Golmud and Nagchhu sometimes stop here briefly before continuing on to Lhasa.

Pilgrim stopping before one of the many special rocks and shrines on the Tashilhumpo kora

8   The Shigatse Region

(Map 6, page 173)

Shigatse

Shigatse (12,800 ft, 3900 m) is Tibet's second-largest city and the capital of the western province of Tsang. Situated near the confluence of the Nyang Chhu and the Yarlung Tsangpo, about 200 miles (330 km) west of Lhasa, the city is a standard stop for groups touring Tibet. The main attraction in this sprawling town of tree-lined avenues is the monastic complex of Tashilhumpo, the seat of the Panchhan Lamas and the largest Gelugpa monastery west Lhasa and Ü province. Shigatse (km marker 0/4903) is also a market town, straddling the crossroads of the Lhasa–Kathmandu Highway and the Northern Road to Golmud and Lhasa.

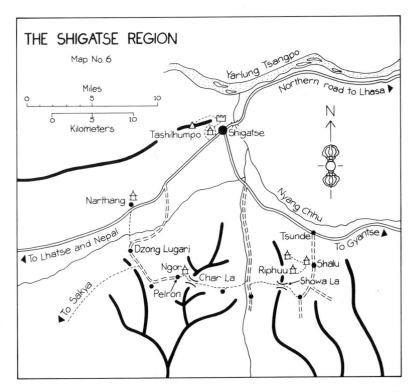

In former times Shigatse was called Sam-dhrubtse, and was the seat of the Tsang kings who ruled much of Tibet in the late sixteenth and early seventeenth centuries. Their rule came to an abrupt end in 1642 when Mongol armies fighting for the Gelugpas and the fifth Dalai Lama invaded Sam-dhrubtse, captured the king and killed him. The palace, located on the hill that towers over the Tibetan market area, was converted to a military garrison by the Chinese in the first half of the eighteenth century. During the first half of the twentieth century it became the residence for the governor of Western Tibet, but was reduced to its present condition after the 1959 Lhasa Uprising. A mural in the Shigatse Hotel's dining room portrays this Potala-like *dzong* in its former grandeur.

If you spend a day or two in Shigatse before your trek begins, be sure to venture beyond the Tibetan curio market and get into the hills. The area around Tashilhumpo monastery offers several fine hikes, including the *kora* encircling the outer boundary walls, a trail to the ruins of the Shigatse fortress, and the demanding hike to the summit of Drolma Ri (also known as Nye-zayra Ri), the rocky ridge rising directly behind the monastery; all are described below.

The most accessible Bön monastery in Central Tibet is Yungdrungling, located only a few hours by vehicle from Shigatse on the Northern Road to Lhasa. After crossing to the left bank of the Yarlung Tsangpo at the Tagdhrukha ferry (km marker 4821, new system; marker 158/9, old system), continue about 1 mile (1.6 km) along the highway to where a dirt road turns off to the right. The monastery is across a tributary valley, perched on a plateau overlooking the river. Several temples have been rebuilt at this 150-year-old site, which housed several hundred monks in the 1950s.

DAYHIKES IN AND NEAR SHIGATSE

Tashilhumpo Monastery *Kora*

Tashilhumpo is the oldest and largest Gelugpa monastery in Tsang province. This impressive city of temples and monks' residences sprawls across the foot of Drolma Ri, at the western end of Shigatse. The main entrance gate is along the lower south wall, beside the highway to Lhatse and Nepal. The entrance is a **20-minute** walk from the market area, a bit longer if you're starting from the Shigatse Hotel.

This Gelugpa monastery was founded by one of Tsong Khapa's main disciples, Geden Drub, during the fifteenth century. He was the first abbot of Tashilhumpo and his tomb is a major shrine in the Tshokhang temple. Geden Drub is now revered as the first Dalai Lama, though the first person to actually receive this title, Sonam Gyatsho, is regarded as the third Dalai Lama.

Tashilhumpo's role in the Gelugpa hierarchy changed dramatically in the seventeenth century when its abbot, Chokyi Gyaatsan, was recognized by the fifth Dalai Lama as an incarnation of Opaame (Amitabha), the Dhyani Buddha of Infinite Light and the spiritual teacher of Chenrezig, the patron saint of Tibet. Along with this recognition came the title Panchhan Lama: Panchhan is the shortened form of Pandita Chhempo, meaning "Great Scholar." Like the title of Dalai Lama, the honorific title of Panchhan Lama was retroactively given to the three previous abbots of Tashilhumpo, making Chokyi Gyaatsan the fourth *truku*

Young monks at Tashilhumpo monastery, Shigatse

in this lineage. His burial *chötaen* is in the Labrang temple, beside the tall red building containing the 85-foot (26 m) statue of Dawa Jhampa, the Future Buddha. The most recent Panchhan incarnation, the tenth, died at the beginning of 1989, and the eleventh incarnation has yet to be recognized.

The *kora* at Tashilhumpo takes **less than 1 hour** to complete, not including breaks, though more time should be allowed to enjoy all the pilgrim activities along the way. Like the *kora* around the large Gelugpa monasteries near Lhasa, this walk provides fine views of the entire monastery and the outlying valley. Remember to walk in a clockwise direction.

Starting from the monastery entrance, follow the main boundary wall away from the gates and turn right (west) onto the road. Continue alongside this wall for 100 yards (90 m), then turn up the first alley on the right (north). The *kora* now ascends toward the hills between the boundary wall and a row of houses. After **a few minutes** the trail opens out, with the old mud walls of Tashilhumpo on the hills to the left and the tall Dawa Jhampa temple just beyond the new walls on the right. The tenth Panchhan Lama helped spare Tashilhumpo from total destruction during the Cultural Revolution; the old walls are one of the last reminders of the monastery's former size.

After passing an incense burner and a wall of prayer wheels, the pilgrim trail climbs into the hills and angles behind the northern boundary wall. Along this stretch of the *kora* are little holes dug by dogs who have taken up residence near the monastery. The monks and pilgrims put out water bowls for these "fallen monks" and feed them offerings of *tsampa* dough balls.

The next section of the *kora* is an avenue of merit-earning sites where pilgrims rub parts of their bodies against certain rocks and place offerings of incense bush, *tsampa,* or *chhang* onto smoldering hearths. At one spot the pilgrims line up to watch each other test their skill at directing a finger into a small hole in a rock, which is done blindfolded. If no one happens to be present while you're walking this portion of the trail, find a seat and enjoy the scenery until some pilgrims come along to guide you.

The circuit climbs to its highest point behind the Kiy-ku, the tall, windowless building resembling a drive-in movie screen where giant appliquéd *thangka* made of silk (the intricate designs are entirely hand-sewn) are hung on special occasions. During one of the biggest yearly festivals at Tashilhumpo, held in the middle of the fifth Tibetan month (usually in June or July), three different *thangka* portraying Sakyamuni, Opaame, and Dawa Jhampa are displayed on three consecutive days before huge crowds.

On the far side of the *thangka* wall the trail forks, with the upper route traversing the ridge toward the Shigatse *dzong.* These ruins are **15 minutes** away, and many pilgrims opt to finish their circuit along this trail. The lower route, the traditional *kora,* descends steeply from this junction, following the eastern boundary wall before intersecting a cart track leading from the market area. The *kora* continues straight ahead (south) along the boundary wall, entering a twisting corridor between tall stone walls before emerging onto the road. Turn right to complete the circuit, reaching Tashilhumpo's entrance gate in **a few minutes.**

Shigatse *Dzong*

The immense ruins of the old Shigatse fortress dominate the skyline of the city. Although nothing remains at the site but crumbling stone walls and a horrific loudspeaker that blares across Shigatse in the early morning hours, the *dzong* is worth a visit for its commanding views of the valley and Tashilhumpo. If you're planning to walk the *kora* around the monastery, the fortress is an easy side trip from the highest point behind the *thangka*-hanging wall. An alternative trail leads up (north) from the vicinity of the market, twisting through alleys between Tibetan homes. Just keep asking for the *dzong lam,* or fortress road. In **20 minutes** you should end up on a saddle in the ridge graced with *la-dzay,* just to the left (west) of the ruins.

Drolma Ri

Drolma Ri ("Tara's Mountain") is the highest ridge near Shigatse, running west from the Shigatse *dzong* behind the monastery. Pilgrims climb to its top to burn incense offerings, especially on festivals such as Saga Dawa and at Tibetan New Year. The most direct approach up this ridge is from the saddle below the fortress. The main offering site on Drolma Ri (13,700 ft, 4180 m) is a steep climb taking **less than 1 hour** from the fortress, though the highest point along the ridge line is **another 30 minutes** or more farther to the west. Bring plenty of water, for this is a dry ridge.

Once you reach the saddle, the route to Drolma Ri follows the obvious trail west up the crest of the ridge, away from the fortress. In **less than 10 minutes** the main trail peels off to the right side of the ridge. It leads to a popular weekend picnic area and clothes-washing site, but is not the way to the ridge summit. Instead, ascend the left side of the ridge's central spine on a smaller, rather indistinct trail. This route quickly leads onto a narrow, layered outcrop of rock. The trail disappears, but continue ascending along this rocky pathway. When these rocks end, a well-defined trail forms and leads to a higher saddle in the ridge where pilgrims have erected prayer flags and devotional piles of stones.

The trail does not continue from this higher saddle to the top of the ridge. The easiest way seems to be up the steep grassy slope farther to the right. Choose your own route among the crosshatching animal trails, reaching the summit monument and prayer flags in **10 minutes** from the saddle. A trail traverses west along the ridge crest to the highest point (14,100 ft, 4300 m), which is marked by a cluster of rocks decorated with prayer flags.

Shalu, Ngor, and Narthang

The **2- to 3-day** walk from Shalu monastery to Narthang monastery is a good choice if your time is limited or if you want a taste of trekking in Tibet without the commitment of a longer or more difficult route. There are two pass crossings, though neither is particularly high compared to most other walks in Tibet. The route travels through the hills to the southeast of Shigatse; Shalu monastery is only 14 miles (23 km) from Shigatse on the way to Gyantse, while Narthang monastery is 9 miles (14 km) west of the city beside the main road to Lhatse and the Nepal border. Ngor monastery is in the hills between them.

If you are in a hurry, you can complete the trek in **2 days; 4 days** are recommended if you wish to spend time at the monasteries and dayhike into the hills above Shalu. Overnight accommodation can be arranged in the monasteries and the settlements along the trekking route, so a tent is unnecessary. There are no shops along the way, so purchase all of your food requirements in Shigatse or Lhasa. If you are camping, bring a fuel stove. Wood is almost nonexistent in this region.

This trek is best accomplished between March and November, though late May and June can be stifling hot, with gusty dust storms blowing on many afternoons. India's monsoon does not really penetrate into the Shigatse region, though enough rain falls in July and August to give the hills a pastel green frost-

The tiled, peaked roofs of Shalu monastery reflect the strong Mongol influence in Tibet during the thirteenth and fourteenth centuries

ing of grass. Snow is not usually a problem here, so you could also consider taking this route during the winter. This relatively unknown circuit was suggested to me by Keith Dowman, author of numerous works on Tibet and Buddhism.

Shigatse to Shalu

Shalu monastery is situated in a tributary valley of the Nyang Chhu, 2¹/₂ miles (4 km) south of the Shigatse–Gyantse Highway. The turnoff is a few hundred yards beyond kilometer marker 19 and a small village called Tsunde, near the base of a barren ridge. The peaked roofs of Shalu can be seen rising above the flat plain from the highway. A large tree beside a rock outcrop topped with prayer flags and a white stone monument is a good reference point for finding the turnoff.

If you are trekking as an individual, arranging local transport from Shigatse to the Shalu turnoff can be somewhat difficult because there are no advance ticket sales for people traveling short distances on the buses. The best alternative is go to the bus station near the Shigatse Hotel about 8:00 A.M. Find the Gyantse–Lhasa bus, then politely ask the driver if you can have a seat or an aisle space for the ride to the Shalu turnoff. Be sure to explain that you want to get off at kilometer marker 19. The driver will usually want a few *yuan* for the ride. The buses to Gyantse and Lhasa leave at 8:30 A.M. Once you're on the road, pay attention to the kilometer markers or you could end up having breakfast in Gyantse (km marker 90).

If you walk to Shalu from the highway turnoff, the monastery is **1 hour** from Tsunde. Before reaching the monastery, note the column of mud brick utility poles crossing the plain from the east. Where the poles intersect the road, look to the right (west) up the deeply eroded wash cutting into the main ridge. The mud-walled ruins in this gully, which can be difficult to see against the backdrop of barren hills, are the remains of Chambaling *ani gompa*.

To the right (west) of the road, **about 10 minutes** before reaching the walled village of Shalu, is a small rebuilt tenth-century shrine for Rabtanma, a form of the protectress Pelden Lhamo. In the thirteenth century the great abbot of Sakya monastery, the Sakya Pandita, was ordained here. A large stone basin used for washing the Pandita's hair during his ordination is now in the upper courtyard of Shalu monastery.

To enter Shalu village (12,900 ft, 3930 m), follow the road to the left (east) around the walled complex. The entrance gate to the village and the monastery is on the right.

Shalu Monastery

The courtyard of Shalu monastery is a dazzling display of color amidst the naked reddish brown hills surrounding the valley. The site was established as a religious center in the eleventh century, though the main temple in the courtyard, all that remains of the monastic complex, was built in the early fourteenth century. The tiled, peaked roof lines and intricate woodworking of Shalu are not typical of Central Tibetan architecture and reflect the strong influence of the Mongol dynasty during that era. The interior of the *dukhang,* or chanting hall, the large building facing into the courtyard, is locked and in disrepair. Three smaller *lhakhang* tucked behind the *dukhang* on an upper level are open to the public and contain the best-preserved examples of fourteenth-century art in Central Tibet, as well as an impressive array of ancient statues. A flashlight is useful for examining the details of the frescoes and the geometric *mandala* designs.

The central figure in the two *lhakhang* facing each other across the upper courtyard is Buton Rimpoche, a fourteenth-century abbot at Shalu and one of the greatest scholars in the history of Tibetan Buddhism. He edited a vast, authoritative collection ot Tibet's Buddhist and tantric texts, known as the Tangyur, "Translation of the Treatises," and helped compile an important set of doctrinal texts called the Kangyur, "Translation of the Buddha's Words." Together these massive volumes form the backbone of Tibetan Buddhist thought. The monks at Shalu today call themselves Bu-*luu,* the "Buton sect." In later centuries, Shalu was recognized as a center for mystical and psychic training.

A walk around the walled village will reveal the ruined walls of the former monastery, which once consisted of eleven *lhakhang* and several chanting halls. Overnight accommodation can be arranged at the monastery; villagers will put up travelers as well. There are no shops here.

DAYHIKES NEAR SHALU

Try to spend an extra night or two at Shalu, especially if you plan to hike into the hills. Riphuu hermitage (13,300 ft, 4050 m) is the largest of the retreats associated with Shalu, and is **1 hour** southwest of the village. Although now mostly in ruins, this hermitage once rivaled Shalu, with seven *lhakhang,* two main chanting halls, and more than 300 monks. Two smaller retreats, Chug hermitage and Galung hermitage, are located nearby.

Despite its size, Riphuu is well hidden from Shalu by the rolling, naked ridges. If you walk to the far west side of Shalu village, the wide trail to the hermitage can be seen snaking up an alluvial fan spilling from the hills. The Tibetan letters *Om mani padme hum* are written on an adjacent ridge. There doesn't seem to be a specific trail leading from the village toward Riphuu, so choose a path between the barley plots toward the track leading up the alluvial fan. Once you are beyond the fields you can see the whitewashed walls of a small temple–cum–monk's residence at Riphuu. The track leads up to this building.

The devastation at Riphuu is extensive, but springs flow through the ghostly reddish brown ruins and down the hills, nourishing willow trees, bushes, and wildflowers. One spring under a rock overhang is the residence of a *lu,* or water spirit; the blessing a pilgrim receives at this site is three pitchers of chilly water poured over his head. A *kora* climbs into the hills around Riphuu, taking **1 hour or more** to complete. The two kindly caretakers will point out the route. The Chug and Galung hermitages are set in the hills to the north of Riphuu.

———————

The remains of Chambaling *ani gompa* (13,300 ft, 4060 m) are in a steep drainage gully to the north of Shalu. These ruins are also hidden from the village and monastery, though they can be seen while approaching Shalu from the Shigatse–Gyantse highway. It is **1 hour** to these ruins. Starting from the north side of Shalu village, follow a cart track through the barley fields toward the base of the ridge. The track makes a few jogs, then parallels a stone retaining wall along the edge of the crops. After passing the end of a rocky ridge, it skirts the base of a broad gravel wash dumping out of the hills. Chambaling is above this alluvial outflow. About halfway along the gravel wash a turnoff leaves the main track and leads up to the old *gompa* site.

Woodworking repairs at Ngor monastery, near Shigatse

The first ruins are **30 minutes** from the turnoff. These mud-brick walls and foundations were part of a small hermitage tended by a lone monk. The walls with traces of red paint were the former *lhakhang;* the kitchen area still bears the black soot of cooking fires. The *ani gompa* is another 100 yards (90 m) up the hillside. The remains of nine *chötaen* are immediately below the ruins. Chambaling once had six or seven buildings with twenty nuns in residence, but is presently uninhabited. The monks at Shalu said the tall, red stone walls were the main assembly hall, and another building was a *lhakhang.* Climb **another 45 minutes** above Chambaling for panoramic views overlooking Shalu monastery and the upper Nyang Chhu Valley. The highest point on the main ridge (14,606 ft, 4452 m) is perhaps **another hour** farther.

The dayhike to the ruins of Potangtse *dzong* (13,200 ft, 4020 m) is also scenic. This old fortress is $1^1/2$ **hours** from the monastery, perched upon a solitary hill across the valley (southeast). The most direct approach is to walk cross-country over the plains. A more roundabout route follows the road up the valley (south) from Shalu for **20 minutes,** then turns off to the left on a smaller track toward the hill. After you reach the base of Potangtse hill, the easiest way to the summit is along the ridge spur leading up the far (east) side. During June, July, and August this is a beautiful picnic spot, set high above the geometrical configurations of circular and oblong barley fields in the Shalu Valley.

THE SHALU–NGOR–NARTHANG TREK

The walk from Shalu to Ngor monastery takes **10 to 12 hours,** including the crossing of two passes. Although this can be completed in one long, hard day, I recommend staying somewhere in the valley between the two passes, then continuing on to Ngor the following day. If you want to hire a burro or horse, inquire at Shalu village.

The route to Ngor follows the dirt road up the valley (south) from Shalu past several small settlements and extensive farmlands. During the summer these fields are alive with busy villagers, whistling and singing, but always quick to note a visitor. After **45 minutes** a cart track turns off to the left (southeast) across the broad valley. Continue straight ahead toward two small groups of houses at the base of a tall rocky prominence topped by ruins. Reach these settlements in $1^1/2$ **hours** from Shalu.

The trail to Ngor now leaves the road and turns right (northwest) toward the dry environs of Showa La (13,600 ft, 4150 m), the first and lower of this trek's two passes. Top off your water bottles before starting the ascent; except during the rainy season, little water is available until the next valley.

Showa La cannot be seen from these settlements, but the route toward the pass climbs the gravel wash spilling from the hills to the right (west). Walk along the edges of the barley fields, staying toward the south (R) side of the drainage where a path eventually forms. **One hour** beyond the settlements the gravel wash narrows into a deep gully. The trail generally follows the gully as it slices through deposits of red volcanic mud embedded with river rocks, but occasionally climbs up and around the steeper sections. The final route up to the pass can be a bit tricky to find. Watch for a trail that leaves the gully and ascends the north (L) embankment. Sheep and goat droppings are good route markers, for the shepherds go this way with their herds. If the gully begins branching and you need to scale small rock ledges to continue, you've gone too far up the stream bed and have missed the easier path along the north (L) side. The summit of Showa La is **1¹/₂ hours** from the last settlements, marked with a small pile of white *la-dzay* rocks and carved prayer stones. Above the pass to the right are several ruined walls, perhaps the remains of an old *dzong*.

Char La (14,800 ft, 4510 m), the last pass before Ngor monastery, is in the obvious cleft in the next succession of mountains directly west across the valley. Several settlements and a braided trail can be seen on the broad alluvial fan leading toward this summit, but the actual pass is tucked out of sight behind several ridges. The dirt road on the valley floor connects with the Shigatse–Gyantse Highway.

The descent from Showa La to the road takes **1¹/₂ hours.** Stay on the south (L) side of the main gully forming below the pass, winding down through a world of heavily eroded hills. Despite the bleakness of this area, a few brilliant wildflowers manage to pop out between the pieces of broken rock. If you are here early in the morning or in the evening, the gobbly calls of Tibetan snow cocks echo throughout the hills. Judging from the droppings near the trail, fox or lynx frequent this region as well.

As you near the valley bottom, the trail from Showa La jogs left and climbs over a small rocky outcrop marked by piles of stones. Do not follow the trail over this low hill. Instead, continue walking straight ahead (west) without a trail for **5 minutes** to reach the road. If you want to return to Shigatse, the highway is **3 hours or more** to the right (north) along this road. The valley floor is a stony desert, a remarkable contrast to the fertile expanses near Shalu monastery. The only greenery in sight is farther up the ridge toward Char La, where creeks flowing out of the hills support stands of willows and thriving barley fields.

The route to Ngor follows the road to the right (north) for **less than 10 minutes,** then turns left onto a smaller cart track leading up a broad alluvial fan. Reach the first of several settlements in **45 minutes** from the road. This is the group of houses that could be seen from Showa La. **Another hour** up the valley is a small village, the last settlement in this area before Char La. As you ascend, stay toward the north (L) side of the valley, ignoring any trails leading toward the opposite side. Just below the village is a welcome picnic spot/campsite in a row of poplars near an irrigation pond. The walking time to these last houses is **6 hours or more** from Shalu monastery. With Ngor monastery at least **another 4 hours** away and the long ascent to Char La en route, consider spending the night here if it is late in the afternoon.

The track leading to this village is easy to follow, but beyond here the route to the pass is not so obvious. As you approach the settlement, the cart track reaches a stone wall enclosing a dense grove of poplars. The track stays to the left of this wall, but the trail to Char La turns off to the right, away from the village and onto a more narrow footpath. In **a few minutes** this trail skirts the end of a small ridge, then drops steeply into a gravel stream bed. Cross to the north (L) side, but don't follow the trail into the terraced fields. Instead, continue up the north (L) edge of this gravel wash for **10 minutes.** The route now leaves the stream bed to avoid a narrow gorge. Look for a network of well-trodden animal trails leading up from the stream onto the north (L) bank. This turnoff can easily be missed. If you keep walking up the gully, you will come to the mouth of the gorge.

The animal tracks wander away toward the left (northwest) from the stream across a hilly plateau, eventually combining into a single path. The trail ascends above the gorge, reaching a stone-reinforced pond in **15 minutes** from the stream bed. This is the last campsite before the pass, with room for only a few tents. In **several minutes** the trail descends into the gorge. Head upstream briefly, then cross over to the south (R) side and begin climbing out of the gorge on a series of switchbacks. Where the trail levels out, Char La can be seen farther up the valley. Look for several small cairns beside a flat-topped rock outcrop on the ridge line. After crossing a tributary drainage coming in from the left, the trail begins to ascend steeply to the pass. The route is often obscure where it crosses stretches of barren rock, but with a little scouting Char La can be reached in **1 hour** from the tributary crossing, and in **3 hours** from the last village. The large cairn of stones on the summit is an accumulation of offerings placed here by pilgrims and travelers to ensure a safe journey through the mountains.

The view from Char La is a delightful surprise. Barren hills of red soil and rock, speckled with stands of willow and poplar, are etched with numerous ravines. Stretched across the middle of these badlands are the red-walled ruins and buildings of Ngor monastery.

Descend to the monastery in **45 minutes** from Char La, following the trail along the south (L) side of the gully forming below the pass. From a group of ruined *chötaen* cross the creek to the north (R) bank, then climb up the ridge for **a few minutes** to the main buildings of Ngor (14,100 ft, 4300 m).

Ngor Monastery

Ngor was founded in 1429 by Ngorchhan Kunga Zangpo, a prolific writer and Buddhist scholar who was educated at Sakya monastery. Through his writings and teachings a separate school of Buddhist thought, closely related to the doctrines of his Sakyapa masters, developed and took the name of this monastery: the Ngor-pa sect. Ngorchhan's following grew rapidly, and at one time these ruined walls supposedly contained 100 temples and housed 1000 monks. The rebuilding project here is perhaps the most enthusiastic renovation in Central Tibet, and is being conducted without the aid of Chinese money. When I visited in 1987, several residence halls had been built, the main chanting hall and its upper-level *lhakhang* were nearing completion, and the fifteen large *chötaen* down the hill from the monastery were being prepared for renovation. The long-haired, bespectacled head *lama,* always dressed in golden robes and carrying a long walking staff, was also the construction foreman. Each day he examined the progress, joking and offering encouragement to the large assembly of people who were shoveling and carrying dirt, tamping earthen walls, carving and painting beams, making mud bricks and laying them in place, all in an organized flurry of activity.

Behind the altar in the rebuilt *lhakhang* is a Sakyamuni Buddha statue, and to the right is the figure of Ngor's founder. To either side are wooden cases containing numerous statues from Dege and Nepal. The most interesting piece is a very large, dark egg, said to be a *druu go-nga,* a dragon's egg.

Accommodation can be arranged at the monastery or in the village of Pelron, **20 minutes** down the hill from Ngor.

On to Narthang Trek

The trail to Narthang monastery is easy to follow and takes **4 to 5 hours.** Descend to Pelron by heading down the gully beside the monastery. Cross to the west (R) side of a small creek, then pass an irrigation pond and a crumbling *mani* wall before entering this attractive village. The trail twists between smartly whitewashed walls decorated with thick maroon and gray stripes, much like those on homes in the Sakya monastery and Dingri regions. **A few minutes** past Pelron the trail meets a motor road that winds down to the valley floor. Sometimes it is possible to get a ride from here on trucks bound for Shigatse.

The motor road leads down the valley, dropping into a gravel wash that broadens quickly as the valley descends. Groves of willows flourish in the moisture of this wide river plain. **Forty-five minutes** beyond Pelron a steep-sided tributary enters from the left. A very Ladhaki-looking village called Day-thomba stands at the confluence, its flat-roofed houses stacked upon each other, fortress-like against the ridge. As the valley starts bending to the right, the road angles across the river plain toward the south (L) ridge and a hill of multicolored rock. The old pilgrim and caravan route from Ngor to Sakya monastery, a **5- to 6-day** trek, climbs out of the valley in a gravel wash below the colorful hill.

One hour past Day-thomba a solitary three-humped hill rises in the mouth of the valley. The village along its base is Dzong Lugari, named for a fortress that is now gone. Before reaching this settlement, the square-walled ruins of Narthang monastery can be seen in the distance to the north. The monastery is **1¹/₂ hours** from Dzong Lugari across the flat, dry plain. Fill your water bottles and enjoy some butter tea with the locals before resuming your walk. Continue for **10 minutes** along the road leading north from town to where it veers right (east). At this bend a smaller cart track leads straight (north) toward Narthang. Follow this smaller track between vast tracts of barley and across the sandy river bed (unless it is the rainy season). Pass under the mud brick utility poles and soon arrive at the highway, Narthang village (13,100 ft, 4000 m), and the monastery.

Narthang Monastery

Narthang monastery (km marker 4917) is beside the Lhasa–Kathmandu Highway, directly behind the village of Narthang. The immense mud walls look more like ruins of 300 years, not twenty-five. The lifeless moonscape within these walls creates an eerie atmosphere, far removed from the vitality and beauty surrounding Ngor monastery. Narthang dates back to the mid-twelfth century. The Kadampa school of Tibetan Buddhism originated here through a disciple of Atisa, the highly regarded eleventh-century Buddhist master from India. This sect was one of the first organized schools of Buddhism to evolve in Tibet after the dark ages of the tenth and eleventh centuries.

Narthang was once renowned for its religious printing, particularly for pro-

Work crews tamping earthen walls during the reconstruction of Ngor monastery, near Shigatse

ducing the voluminous copies of the Tibetan Buddhist Canon, the *Kangyur* and the *Tengyur*. One hundred and twenty-five thousand blocks were hand carved to print these texts, but most of the printing blocks were destroyed along with the monastery in 1966. Despite its history, Narthang is no longer a Kadampa monastery. The two monks tending the recently rebuilt *lhakhang* within the ruined walls are from the Gelugpa sect.

The facilities at the monastery are very limited. If you are considering spending the night here, make arrangements with a family in the village. There are no shops nor small eateries in this town, but the hotels and restaurants of Shigatse are only 9 miles (14 km) to the east. If you haven't arranged for transport to meet you in Narthang, the best way of securing a ride to Shigatse is to wave down a truck or bus on the highway. Late afternoon is a good time to try, for most vehicles will be heading to Shigatse for the night.

Tibetan women in the Everest region

9   The Everest Region

(Map 7, pages 188–89)

Introduction to the Everest Region

Nowhere in the Himalaya can the immense height of Mount Everest, the highest point on earth, be appreciated as it can be from Tibet. The northern half of this grand mountain is unobstructed by neighboring peaks or ridges, allowing excellent views of the entire massif from both the Rongphu (often spelled Ronbguk) and Kangshung Face base camps. A good portion of the summit is even visible from several points along the Lhasa–Kathmandu highway, particularly from the Dingri (or Tingri) plains.

The Tibetan name for Mount Everest is Chomolangma, also spelled Chomolungma and Qomolangma. The mountain was first recognized as the world's tallest in 1840, when it was labeled Peak XV during the Great Trigonometrical Survey of India and the Himalaya. In 1865, after attempts failed to discover a local name, the survey named it Mount Everest in honor of the genius behind this huge project, Sir George Everest. A great debate has raged for decades now over the correct local name and its meaning. "The Abode of the Mother Goddess of the Universe" is a common interpretation; "Mother Goddess of the Five Fairies" is another. The most accurate literal translation is "Lady Cow," for *langma* means a cow or female ox.

The North Face of Mount Everest is arguably its most spectacular side, rising in a sheer wall of rock and ice 2.5 vertical miles (almost 5 km) above the Rongphu base camp and the picturesque environs of Dza Rongphu monastery. This small rebuilt temple in the upper reaches of the Dzakaa Chhu Valley is said to be the highest monastery in the world (16,350 ft, 4980 m).

The stunning scenery in this area has been acclaimed since the first British expeditions attempted to climb Mount Everest in the 1920s. With the advent of tourism and trekking in China during the early 1980s, Dza Rongphu monastery and the nearby base camp quickly became Tibet's most popular trekking destination.

An interesting topographical feature on the Tibet side of Mount Everest is the unusually gentle slope of the valleys descending from this mountain. The glaciers that fill these drainages are not wrought with impassable crevasses, nor do they tumble in steeply broken icefalls. Well-prepared and well-acclimatized trekkers can continue beyond the Rongphu base camp without ice axes or crampons and reach the higher advance camps used by the climbing expeditions.

The best time for trekking to Mount Everest is generally between May and October, though in the Rongphu area it is possible to trek throughout most of the year. The wall of peaks stretching from Makalu to Everest and across to Cho Oyu

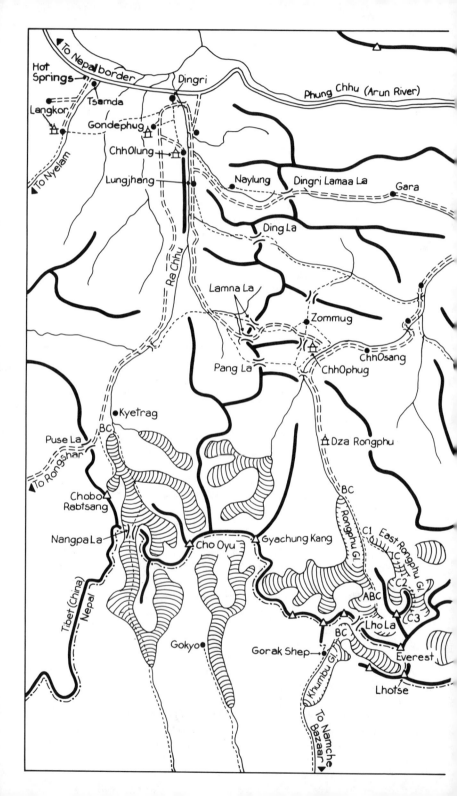

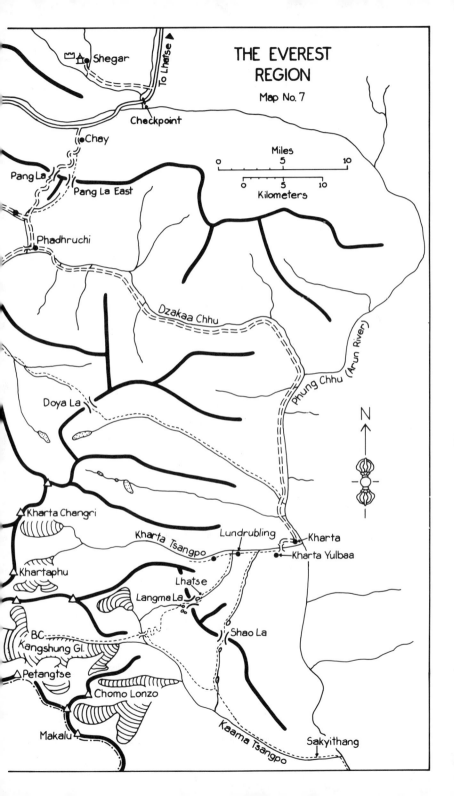

creates a particularly effective rain shadow over this region, blocking most of the moisture that would otherwise cause snow in the winter and heavy rains during the summer. The high passes between the main road and the Rongphu base camp are all 16,000 to 17,000 feet (4900 to 5200 m) in elevation and remain relatively snow-free throughout the winter. The temperatures from May to October are fairly mild and at times surprisingly hot, though it is a good idea to carry warm clothing and waterproof gear. Between July and early September the monsoon still manages to push over the mountain barrier, draping Everest in clouds and occasionally dropping snow on the high ridges. The lower valleys receive rain, and at times the road from Phadhruchi to Dza Rongphu monastery is a quagmire of muddy ruts deep enough to swallow a four-wheel-drive vehicle up to its frame.

During the winter months the weather pattern over Tibet is often very stable. The days are typically clear and brisk, the snowfall is negligible, and Everest often displays its summit day after day. Although major storms will sometimes dump a foot or more of snow on the ridges and in the higher valleys, the biggest obstacle to trekking this time of year is the incessant, numbing afternoon wind. During the mornings the weather is often pleasant though cold, the sun's warmth taking the bite out of the chill. After midday the winds begin to howl and often increase in intensity until sunset. Night temperatures are well below freezing but tolerable with the proper gear. On my first visit here, in midwinter, the food on our plates kept freezing before we could finish eating.

The trekking season for the East Everest base camp/Kangshung Valley area is much shorter than in the Rongphu area. The Himalayan rain barrier that keeps the Dzakaa Chhu Valley and the Dingri plains so dry is severed to the east of Makalu by the Arun River Valley, one of the deepest canyons in the world. The Arun acts like a funnel from late June until early September, channeling the monsoon past the Himalaya and into the Kangshung area. Commercial trekking companies consider mid-May until late June, and September until mid-October to be the best times for trekking here. With good rain gear and waterproof tents, however, trekking to the Kangshung Valley during the July and August monsoon is an unforgettable wilderness experience of misty glacial valleys, brilliant wildflowers, and very soggy hiking boots. By late October winter weather usually returns to the high ridges. Lamna La and Shao La, the two main accesses into the Kangshung region, become so choked with snow that the locals don't attempt to cross again until the following May.

Regardless of the season, trekking in the Everest region requires being prepared for extreme conditions. The sun is very strong at these elevations, especially if it reflects off snow. Sun hats and plenty of sunblock are a must throughout the year. During summer it is a good idea to have a warm jacket or coat, even a down parka if you chill easily, and bring knitted gloves, a wool cap, and a wool scarf as well. During the summer it's also a good idea to have a warm jacket or a coat, even a down parka if you chill easily. The Dingri area and the upper stretches of the Dzakaa Chhu near Dza Rongphu monastery are notorious for their gusty conditions, particularly when the afternoon winds descend from the mountains. On a cool evening, with the sun down and a stiff breeze blowing, a hat and gloves can be a blessing, especially if you are camping.

The town of Dingri (km marker 544) and the turnoff near kilometer marker

494 on the Lhasa–Kathmandu Highway are the main trailheads for treks into the Everest region. They are approximately 400 miles (650 km) by road to the west of Lhasa. Whether you're in a four-wheel-drive vehicle or coming by local bus, the journey is a long 2-day trip over a rugged, dusty, unpaved road. For treks into the Kangshung Valley, plan on an additional day's drive to reach the trailhead at Kharta. Organized groups coming from Lhasa usually stop in Gyantse and spend at least a day in Shigatse for sightseeing and acclimatization before beginning their trek.

If individual trekking is permitted again, the local bus is the cheapest way to reach the Everest region, though the bus schedule can be downright inconvenient, especially if you're starting from Shigatse. For some reason, the buses (departing on Saturday and sometimes Tuesday mornings) from Lhasa to the Nepal border (Khasa) are the only scheduled buses that go west of Shigatse. Once these buses from Lhasa get rolling, they stop in Shigatse for just one night before continuing on to the border. The local buses originating in Shigatse do not continue west beyond the Sakya monastery turnoff (km marker 5028/9). If you are staying in Shigatse, the best way to secure a reserved seat on the bus to the Everest trailheads is to go back to Lhasa, or take a chance that the driver in Shigatse will sell a vacant seat or a place in the aisle on the morning of departure (usually Sunday and Wednesday).

If you are coming from Nepal, the Everest base-camp turnoff at kilometer marker 494 and the town of Dingri are less than a day's drive from the border. However, the rapid ascent by road from Khasa (7300 ft, 2230 m) to Dingri (14,300 ft, 4360 m), followed by a trek that quickly crosses one of the high passes into the Rongphu or Kangshung area, is not recommended unless you have recently been to high elevations. To properly acclimatize, continue on to Shigatse or Lhasa for 3 days or more, then return to the Everest region for your trek. To stay in shape, take warm-up walks around Shigatse (see "Dayhikes in and near Shigatse") and near Shalu monastery (see "Dayhikes near Shalu").

The Everest region is a long way from the nearest major medical facility, in Shigatse. There is a small hospital with a few doctors in Shegar (km marker 488) and a health post in Kharta. If anyone in your party experiences elevation-related problems while crossing any of the high passes en route to Everest, turn back to lower ground toward the highway rather than pushing on for the Dzakaa Chhu or Kangshung valleys. Keep in mind that traffic is sporadic in this part of Tibet, even along the main road.

Chomolangma Nature Preserve

The entire Tibetan side of Mount Everest is part of the Chomolangma Nature Preserve, a huge protected area covering approximately 10,400 square miles (27,000 sq km; about the size of Massachusetts) along the north slope of the Himalayas. It is the first nature preserve in Tibet or China to include people and their cultural heritage in its preservation agenda, and the first to accept international collaboration in its planning and management. Through the efforts of the Working Commission of the Tibet Autonomous Region, the Tibet Academy of Social Sciences, the Chinese Academy of Sciences, and the Woodlands Mountain Institute of the United States, the Chomolangma Nature Preserve became a reality on March 18, 1989.

The boundaries extend west to the headwaters of the Trisuli River, which flows into Nepal, and include the whole Shishapangma–Peghu Tsho region. The northern boundary lies to the north of the Lhasa–Kathmandu Highway to include the headwaters of the Phung Chhu (the major source of Nepal's Arun River), and the eastern limits encompass the southward sweep of the Phung Chhu toward Nepal but do not include this river's easternmost tributaries. The southern boundary is the Tibet–Nepal border, linking the preserve with the Langtang and Sagarmatha national parks, and the Makalu–Barun Conservation Project in Nepal. Within the perimeters of the preserve are five of the world's tallest mountains.

The Chomolangma Nature Preserve is administered within Tibet by the Shigatse prefecture. (A prefecture is an administrative region larger than a county. There are four counties within the preserve.) The main headquarters are in Shigatse, with a branch office in Shegar and a preserve officer/warden stationed in Dingri. An ambitious master plan includes development of educational, cultural, and public health services to raise the local people's quality of life; protection and rehabilitation of the unique mountain, forest, and grassland ecosystems; protection of wildlife including a ban on hunting; protection of the area's cultural heritage, which will include financial aid for the reconstruction of Dza Rongphu monastery; and environmental cleanups in places such as Everest base camp. The creation of the preserve has already been instrumental in halting the construction of a major logging road that was to link the town of Kharta with large stands of virgin forest near the Tibet–Nepal border.

The Woodlands Mountain Institute is a nonprofit conservationist institute that coordinates international support for the Mount Everest region in both Tibet and Nepal. If you would like more information on Chomolangma Nature Preserve, or on how you might help support it, write to: Woodlands Mountain Institute, Chomolangma Nature Preserve Project, Dogwood and Main Street, Franklin, West Virginia 26807.

The Trek to Everest Base Camp via Pang La

The shortest route into the Everest region is the approach over Pang La (16,900 ft, 5150 m) from the Lhasa–Kathmandu Highway. This trek of **3 to 4 days** begins in a desert valley that lies to the south of the main road between kilometer markers 494 and 495, about 7 miles (12 km) west of the relocated Shegar checkpoint (km marker 488/9). Although this route to the base camp follows or remains near the road constructed for the 1960 Chinese Everest expedition, traffic is almost nonexistent. (You can also drive to base camp if you're short of time.) The scenery is outstanding and a number of villages are spread along the route, with some of Tibet's first trekking lodges; it is possible to find food and shelter for the entire journey up to Dza Rongphu monastery. The monks at the monastery now hire out basic but fairly comfortable rooms with wood stoves. Due to their limited facilities they are unable to sell or prepare food for travelers. Bring all of your own food for the latter part of this walk. A tent and a stove are not necessary, but they do provide freedom from constantly relying upon the villages for food and lodging.

The turnoff for Pang La near kilometer marker 494 is a minor junction that

Passum village in the Dzakaa Chhu Valley looks like a setting in the southwestern United States

can easily be overlooked; there are no road signs nor buildings in the area at this time. If you are coming from the Shegar checkpoint, look for a small bridge crossing after kilometer marker 494. The road to Everest turns south into a dry tributary valley a few hundred yards farther to the west and follows the base of a sweeping rocky ridge. Chay (14,600 ft, 4450 m), the only village before the pass, is **1 hour** from the turnoff. This town of forty houses and its concentric rings of terraced barley fields are situated above a deep stream channel near the junction of two large valleys. Pang La is a climb of **3 hours** from Chay into the barren hills to the south. Unless you had an early start, consider spending the night here with a family or camping above the town near the stream. Camping lower in the valley can be a problem because the stream tends to disappear into the sand and rocks lining its gully. Unless it has rained heavily, the only available water in this valley is near Chay. The people here are very accommodating and one of the treats of staying with a family is the chance to sample the local *chhang*. They make a rather tasty brew here, served by pouring hot water over fermented barley berries, then drunk with a wooden straw in much the same way as millet *tongba* is served in eastern Nepal and Sikkim.

Burros can usually be hired in Chay to carry gear to the top of Pang La. For a burro and guide to continue beyond the pass to Phadhruchi, the next major village, you might have to pay at least an extra day's wages for their return journey. The folks in Chay are less than enthusiastic about taking their pack animals all the way to Rongphu; plan on hiring another animal and guide in Phadhruchi for the rest of the journey.

As of 1990 a toll booth erected at Chay was charging foreigners a fee for using the road. Apparently the local people living between Chay and Dza Rongphu monastery are responsible for maintaining the road. I've been told the toll is used to reimburse the villagers for their labor. A lot of work must go into the road, for the toll is stiff. Groups must pay 200 *yuan* (in 1990, about $40 U.S.) per vehicle, plus fifty *yuan* per person. For supply trucks the fee is 1000 *yuan* ($200 U.S.). Walking provides no exemption; the toll is still fifty *yuan* per trekker. However, rumor says the fee can be bargained down to about half of the initial demand.

The road to the base camp continues south beyond the last few houses of Chay, and in **less than 10 minutes** veers east to begin a long series of switchbacks up a wide alluvial fan. Instead of following this bend in the road, continue climbing straight ahead (south) up a well-defined rocky trail. Although it may be faint in places, this route is much more direct and avoids several large turns in the road. Continue ascending in a southerly direction up the valley.

As the trail climbs higher, the ridges close in on the broad alluvial slopes. Gradually the valley starts bending to the right (west) toward Pang La (16,900 ft, 5150 m). When locals travel by foot in this area they often use an adjacent pass also called Pang La (16,800 ft, 5120 m), located farther to the left (east) of the road. This is a much better route with several good, remote campsites along the way. To avoid confusion, this pass will be referred to as Pang La East in the text. It rejoins the road a few hours above Phadhruchi. If you're trekking on your own, it's worth hiring a guide and a pack animal to take you to the top of the pass because the approach is obscure in places. From the summit the route to Phadhruchi is easy to follow.

One hour beyond Chay the walking route to Pang La East crosses the road for the last time. The road now leaves the valley floor and begins a long series of switchbacks up to Pang La used by vehicles. The foot trail over Pang La East does not follow the road, but continues up to the south toward the stream flowing along the far eastern side of the valley. During July and August the meadows near this stream are thick with green grass and bursts of wildflowers, though elsewhere the terrain is sparsely vegetated with wispy herbs, tundra-type flowers, and occasional clusters of cushion plants. **Twenty minutes** above the last road crossing, rock-hop to the east (R) bank of the stream. A small creek draining from the steep east (R) ridge joins the stream here, though it might not be flowing in the drier seasons. This is a good landmark, for it is the only tributary entering the stream in this area.

The trail to Pang La East leaves the valley bottom and ascends the ridge beside the narrow creek gully. **Ten minutes** above the stream-ford an unfinished road spur cuts across the face of the ridge. Don't turn onto this road, but cross it and continue climbing steeply beside the small gully. **Half an hour** above the stream crossing, reach the rounded top of this ridge (16,500 ft, 5030 m). The scenery from here is worth a break; the snowcapped peaks far to the north are part of the Nyanchhan Thanglha range. Pang La East is still **30 minutes** away on the trail leading around the ridge to the right (south).

To reach Pang La East, follow the trail to the right (southwest) across the flat ridge top. In **10 minutes** pass several *la-dzay*. From here the trail leaves the ridge top and traverses south across the slope of the ridge. Reach the cairns on the Pang La East summit (16,800 ft, 5120 m) in **another 20 minutes.** The pass for vehicles is farther to the right (west) and hidden by the ridge.

If the weather is clear the giants of the Himalaya range can be seen marching majestically across the southern horizon. Makalu (27,805 ft, 8475 m) is the large, pale, snowy peak on the far left (east). After a few intermediate mountains, the next large peak to the right is the massive triangular summit of Everest (29,028 ft, 8848 m). Farther to the right is a huge, snowy massif that includes Gyachung Kang (25,990 ft, 7922 m) and Cho Oyu (26,748 ft, 8153 m). Several breaks in the ridges below the pass yield views of the Dzakaa Chhu and its broad, flat valley.

Only **10 minutes** below the pass is a grassy campsite (16,600 ft, 5060 m) beside a freshwater spring. Although this site is only big enough for a couple of tents and offers limited protection from the wind, it's a great location for viewing the mountains. In summer look for the obvious flat patches of green vegetation contrasting with the otherwise barren ridge side to the right (west) of the main trail. The nearest settlement is **less than 2 hours** below Pang La East. The town of Phadhruchi, which has a hotel and a *thugpa* shop, is **about 4 hours** from the pass.

The trail from Pang La East descends along the east (L) side of a gently curving valley. There is little vegetation near the pass, but as you descend grass and wildflowers appear on the banks above the stream. **Forty-five minutes** below the pass a small tributary enters from the left. Beyond here the valley turns sharply to the right (west). Cross this small creek and in **15 minutes** meet the road from Pang La. The route to Dza Rongphu monastery and Everest base camp now follows the road to Phadhruchi and the Dzakaa Chhu Valley. Look for the trails that short-cut some of the longer switchbacks. Descend steeply beside a rushing torrent that crashes through a narrow gorge of upended rock. **Forty minutes** after meeting the road, cross to the west (R) side of this stream. **A few minutes** farther a small cluster of houses is tucked into a bend on the east (L) bank. Despite the parched hillsides, irrigated barley crop is vibrantly green here during the summer.

The road continues to descend, crossing the stream twice and passing the extensive mud-walled ruins of some ancient fortification. **Ninety minutes** beyond the small settlement a road turns off to the right (west) into a broad valley. This is the old trade route up the Gara Valley to Dingri Lama La (16,000 ft, 4880 m). The trek over this pass from Phadhruchi to the Dingri plains is described later in this chapter (see "Return to Dingri via Dingri Lama La") as an alternative exit from the Dzakaa Chhu Valley.

Phadhruchi (13,800 ft, 4210 m) is **30 minutes** farther down the road, at the edge of the Dzakaa Chhu Valley. (Phadhruchi is known as Paru to the Chinese. On some maps it is spelled Pa-drug or Pharuk. Older Tibetans sometimes call it Tashiy Dzum, "Lucky Fortress.") The residents in this town as well as in other settlements near the Dzakaa Chhu are not as friendly nor as helpful as people elsewhere in Tibet. You might think that their attitudes have been influenced by the great influx of tourists and climbing expeditions over the past decade—until you consider the Sherpas, who have had even greater exposure to trekkers and climbers for a longer period of time, yet remain warm and receptive. How can there be such a difference between these neighboring people? A fellow from India once told me that people are like the soil they live on; when the soil is hard, so are the people. The ground here is definitely hard. There is also a strong Chinese influence in Phadhruchi, for this is the area's main administrative post.

Just inside Phadhruchi the road splits at a small bridge crossing. The left fork leads east to Kharta, the starting point for the East Everest base-camp trek. The road to the right crosses the bridge and continues up the valley toward Dza Rongphu monastery and the Everest base camp.

Just past the bridge and on the left is the walled compound of the Chomolangma Hotel. This ill-kept, Tibetan-run lodge, the only hotel in town, has distressingly filthy bedding and rooms that cannot be locked from the inside, yet it can seem like paradise after a long walk without a proper wash. To get a room late at night, contact the manager at his house across the street. A dining hall/restaurant and a small shop are located in the central building of the compound, though these open only upon request. Directly across from the hotel is a tea and *thugpa* restaurant with erratic business hours. A second shop is hidden among the cluster of Tibetan homes on the east (L) side of the stream.

The usual array of Chinese army sneakers and panda-covered tea thermoses graces the shelves of both shops. Noodles, candies, yak butter, and some canned fruits are available too. Potatoes, peas, spinach, and turnips are grown locally; some houses have rice, eggs, or kerosene for sale. Ask if a local family will make you a stack of *bhalay,* an unleavened chapatti-like bread that usually keeps for days.

If you spend a day in Phadhruchi, the ruined walls with a stone monument and prayer flags on the ridge directly behind the town are worth climbing to for the view. This site could have been the "Lucky Fortress." West of town and hidden high on the ridge across from these ruins is Gyedong *gompa,* an isolated hermitage that has yet to be repaired. The easiest approach to it is to walk **15 minutes** back up the valley toward Pang La, but on the west (R) side of the stream, not along the road. The *gompa* is set into a cleft in the twisted rock formations that tower over Phadhruchi. An obscure trail leads to the ruins starting from the base of the ridge.

Located at a major crossroads, Phadhruchi is the main transport junction for this area. Intermittent trucks and tractor-pulled carts carry passengers to Kharta, Dza Rongphu monastery, and Shegar. Burros and horses can usually be hired here to carry gear, though prices can be frustratingly steep and the guides are notorious for demanding hidden charges once on the trail. Don't be bullied into paying extra for the guide's food, lodging, or animal feed.

The trek to Dza Rongphu monastery from Phadhruchi takes **2 days.** For most of the journey it follows the vehicle road along the west (L) side of the Dzakaa Chhu. Initially the valley is flat and remarkably fertile compared to the dry desert ridges rising thousands of feet above the river. With the help of irrigation, the predominant crops are barley, wheat, peas, and mustard. Because the road tends to wander between numerous small settlements, you can save considerable time by following the shortcuts that bypass the wide bends in the road.

Two hours beyond Phadhruchi the road squeezes between the river and a prominent rocky outcrop capped by Chetöng, a large, mud-walled ruin that is the former residence of a highly regarded *lama* who was probably the feudal landlord of the area. It is a worthy side trip offering good views of the valley. Throughout the ruins are hundreds of stone offering piles erected by visiting pilgrims. Fading frescoes can still be seen on a few inner walls.

Another 40 minutes up the valley is Passum, the largest settlement above Phadhruchi. A local resident has established a trekking lodge/tea shop in the middle of town. It has a few beds and the kitchen serves sweet or salted tea, *thugpa,* and *momo.* Watch out for the kids in Passum and farther up the valley; they sometimes chuck rocks at trekkers passing through who don't yield a pocketload of *jhiri,* or sweets. Don't encourage this bad habit by complying with their requests.

Beyond Passum the terrain is much drier than near Phadhruchi. The agricultural plots are smaller and large portions of the valley floor are covered with little more than thin grasses and scrub. The towns and the topography along this stretch of the Dzakaa Chhu have an uncanny resemblance to the scenery of the southwestern United States: flat-roofed, white adobe houses; people with dark, braided hair who wear turquoise jewelry; grand ridges of swirling rock formations; and clear, dry desert air. The swirling flocks of gray-and-white snow pigeons fluttering across the fields seem out of place here.

The valley now turns south as the river sweeps around the contortions of ridges that radiate from Mount Everest. **A few minutes** past Passum on the ridge to the west is Zaphu *gompa,* an affiliate of Dza Rongphu monastery and the only active temple in this area. Four *dhrapa* have returned to this *gompa* and two buildings have been rebuilt, including a rustic *lhakhang* with simple earthen walls. The raised platform presiding over the floor cushions is for the Dza Rongphu *rimpoche,* who fled his monastery in 1959 and is now the head *lama* at Thubten Chhöling *gompa,* near Junbesi in Nepal. Beside the rows of cushions is a colorful rack of prayer texts with twelve volumes of the Yum, a metaphysical text of Indian origin that is an important part of the Nyingmapa religious tradition.

Half an hour beyond Passum the road crosses a small bridge. The large tributary entering from the right (west) is the Ding Valley. Dingri, via Ding La (16,400 ft, 5000 m), is a long **2 days** away. A series of lush meadows at the upper end of this valley offers some of the nicest wilderness camps in the Everest region.

Another large tributary enters a little farther up the Dzakaa Chhu on the east (R) side of the valley. In 1921 the British Reconnaissance team followed this drainage on the approach to Kharta from Dingri during their survey of Mount Everest. This trek to Kharta and to the upper stretches of the Arun River crosses Doya La (16,810 ft, 5124 m) and takes **3 to 4 days.**

One hour beyond the bridge crossing, pass the settlement of Zaphu, which is split into two small clusters of houses. The second group of houses is **another 10 minutes** farther, located below a large cliff face. The river runs very close to the ridge here and is often so shallow that vehicles and people can ford it to the east (R) bank. In 1988 a large cement bridge was built **a few minutes** upstream from Zaphu to facilitate the Tri-Nation (Japan, China, and Nepal) Everest expedition, which placed climbers from both sides of the mountain on the summit at the same time.

Chhösang (14,800 ft, 4510 m), the last village along the Dzakaa Chhu, is on the east (R) side of the river **1 hour** upstream from the new bridge. Within the village are the remains of a crumbling monastery now used as a goat pen. A small semi-functioning *lhakhang* has been built above the town on its southern out-skirts. The former center for religious activities in this area was Chhöphug (or Chobuk) *gompa,* a Nyingmapa cave hermitage built into limestone cliffs above the west (L) bank of the river a few miles farther upstream. Despite the *gompa's* sad condition, ten monks are presently associated with this retreat, though none reside there. Chhöphug *gompa* can be approached by a footbridge near Chhösang; locals say that the steep trail is suitable only for foot traffic and sure-footed yaks.

Dza Rongphu monastery is a steady climb and **1 long day** of walking from Chhösang. If you don't plan to camp, Chhösang is the last possible place to spend the night before reaching the monastery. Finding a family to stay with in this town is not a problem; finding a family that isn't greedy or prone to pinching bits of your gear is. I would rather walk an extra hour or stop an hour early at Zaphu than take the chance of staying with one of the unpleasant households in Chhösang.

Above Chhösang the river gradient steepens considerably. The Dzakaa Chhu spills through a rocky canyon and the valley arcs to the left. The monastery is **5¹/₂ hours** from Chhösang. Initially the road climbs west from the town, past the small *lhakhang* and onto a low escarpment covered with rounded river rocks. After **1 hour** the road splits, the larger fork turning right onto the gravel plain beside the river. The left fork is a shorter route that contours gently through a series of low, scrubby hills before rejoining the road in **1¹/₂ hours.** The valley begins to angle south and the desert vegetation becomes considerably more sparse. On the west (L) side of the river is the Zommug Valley mouth, a broad drainage with grassy meadows and a large *drogpa* population based out of Zommug (or Zombuk) village. Dingri is **2¹/₂ days** from this town via Lamna La (sometimes referred to as Tambo Pang La; 16,800 ft, 5120 m). A little farther upstream is a wall of cliffs and the cave hermitages of Chhöphug *gompa.* Several snowy peaks come into view up the Dzakaa Chhu, but Everest remains elusive.

The trail leaves the low hills, then follows the base of a tall cliff. Shortly before rejoining the road, pass a long wall of *mani* stones. These rocks have Tibetan prayers, or *mantras,* carved onto their faces. They are very common in the Dzakaa Chhu area and typically have the phrase *Om mani padme hum* etched into them.

On the west (L) side of the river a steep drainage spills into the Dzakaa Chhu. This valley leads to yet another pass called Pang La (17,100 ft, 5210 m), the southernmost of the four passes that connect the Rongphu area with the Dingri plains. The road climbs steeply from here as the valley walls close in to form a narrow gorge. **Twenty minutes** above the trail junction with the road a wide path to the right descends to a wooden bridge. This is the last bridge in the valley and the best place to cross if you're heading to Dingri over Langma La or Pang La. The trek from Dingri to Dza Rongphu monastery via these passes is described in "The Dingri to Dza Rongphu Monastery Loop." A short distance upstream from this bridge a large tributary drains from the glaciers of Gyachung Kang (25,990 ft, 7922 m), a massive ridge spur to the east of Cho Oyu (26,748 ft, 8153 m).

The road to the base camp continues climbing steadily through the canyon. **Less than 30 minutes** above the bridge a spring emerges from a grassy knoll to the left of the road. Except during the rainy season, this is often the only fresh water available other than the river until reaching the monastery. **Twenty minutes** farther, high in a side valley up to the left (northeast), is Gyelung Dezeng Chhöling, former retreat for Dza Rongphu's senior monks. Very castlelike in design, this building was only seven years old when it was destroyed during the Cultural Revolution. The meadows near here provide one of the few good campsites in this area, though it takes **30 minutes** of climbing along a steep side trail to reach them.

The main road continues its ascent, twisting away from the river through arid hills and rocky plains to pass beside a large stone *chötaen*. Thrulzhig Rimpoche (pronounced Thrü-zhiy), the former head *lama* of Dza Rongphu, says this monument was probably built nearly two centuries ago when the Sherpa people of Nepal supposedly used Lho La (19,700 ft, 6006 m) instead of Nangpa La (also known as Khumbu La; 18,750 ft, 5716 m) as their trade route between the Khumbu Valley and Tibet. It is known locally as the Khumbu or Bhay-yü (Nepal) *chötaen*. Climbers who are familiar with the sheer 1500-foot (460 m) cliffs on the Nepal side of Lho La find it hard to believe that a glacier large enough to cross on foot could have existed there only 200 years ago.

Throughout this area are hundreds of small rock piles erected by devout Tibetans who have made the journey to Dza Rongphu *gompa* and the abode of the Mother Goddess. **About 20 minutes** past the Bhay-yü *chötaen*, Everest finally comes into view. Numerous trails now shortcut the long bends in the road along this final stretch to the monastery. **One hour** above the *chötaen* the road descends into a deep creek bed. During the winter this entire gully is a huge sheet of sloping ice that can be difficult for trekkers to negotiate and impossible for vehicles. A few dozen handfuls of gravel thrown across the ice should provide enough traction for everyone to cross safely, even a pack animal. Though it is now mostly obliterated, the Chhu Ara *ani gompa,* also called Samding Chhöphug *gompa,* was at the base of the cliffs where this creek emerges from the cleft in the ridge.

Ascend from the creek gully, then follow the road for **another 20 minutes** into a series of morainal hills. Just **a few minutes** beyond a shallow basin with several stone buildings, the road arcs around a rocky ridge spur and Dza Rongphu monastery explodes into full view, with the massive North Face of Mount Everest dominating the entire head of the valley.

Dza Rongphu Monastery

Situated at 16,350 feet (4980 m) elevation, Dza Rongphu *gompa* and its accompanying hermitage retreats were introduced to the world in the 1920s through the accounts of the first British mountaineering teams. Their descriptions of this secluded monastic hideaway, where "every animal that we saw in the valley was extraordinarily tame," could have been the inspiration for the mysterious lamasery of Shangri-la in James Hilton's well-known novel *Lost Horizon.*

Today most of the retreat cells are abandoned and only one of the six monasteries scattered at this end of the valley is functioning. According to Thrulzhig Rimpoche, the Rongphu area was first established as a religious site 250 to 350 years ago.

The first *gompa* at this site, a Buddhist nunnery, was established about 200 years ago. By the 1950s there were nearly 250 residents, most of them nuns. The two largest *ani gompa,* Shanju Töling and Runjung, were located a little farther up the valley along the ridge side. Many nuns fled from Tibet in 1959 together with

Known as "the highest monastery in the world," Dza Rongphu monastery (16,350 ft, 4980 m) lies near the foot of Mount Everest

Thrulzhig Rimpoche to Nepal.

The present Dza Rongphu monastery is located where the *lama* Ngawang Tenzing Norbu built a Nyingmapa temple called Donga Chhöling in 1901–02. (His image is the central figure in the rebuilt *lhakhang*.) The new temple is small and simple, though the wall frescoes are brilliantly painted. In the entrance foyer the Four Guardian Kings glare down alongside a painting of Guru Rimpoche, the Indian sorcerer/magician who came to Tibet in the eighth century. The statue on the central altar next to the image of Ngawang Tenzing Norbu is the Mindhroling *rimpoche,* one of Thrulzhig Rimpoche's spiritual teachers.

Accommodation is available at the monastery in the long building adjacent to the *lhakhang.* Several years ago the rooms were pretty rough, but they have been spruced up: Tibetan carpets serve as mattresses and wood-burning stoves have been installed for heating and cooking. The area below the *chötaen* is large enough to accommodate a number of tents, though it is exposed to the gusty winds that regularly blow down the valley. The water source is a spring a few minutes to the south of the monastery along the ridge. A few small tent sites can be found on the grassy patches below it.

There is no village nor any type of shop selling goods at the monastery. The monks sustain themselves primarily on *tsampa* and butter tea. Although they occasionally will sell a few packets of freeze-dried food left by the expeditions, please don't rely upon the monks or any of the mountaineers as a potential source of food at Rongphu. It's not fair to the monks and some expeditions have become so tired of trekkers trying to scrounge food and equipment that they have posted signs telling unauthorized visitors to stay away.

Most vehicles that come to the monastery or base camp have been hired by tour groups or by the climbing expeditions. If you are refused a ride, remember that the decision to accept extra riders is often up to the driver, not the group.

FROM DZA RONGPHU TO EVEREST BASE CAMP

Everest base camp (16,900 ft, 5150 m) and the Rongphu Glacier are **less than 2 hours** (not including rest stops) above the monastery. The road to the base camp, which takes **about 40 minutes** by vehicle, can be bypassed for the first **30 minutes** by taking a path that stays high along the east (R) side of the valley. From the entrance gate of the *lhakhang,* follow the trail from the monastery toward the freshwater spring. Continue past the pipe and traverse along the ridge. In **less than 10 minutes** reach two stone monuments at the top of a ridge spur. The path forks here; the right branch descends to the base-camp road in **20 minutes.** The left fork stays on the ridge, leading to the ruins of several old nunneries and past an unusual gathering of small, crudely built stone huts. The Rongphu Valley was once a well-known meditational retreat where Buddhist hermits would have themselves sealed into one of these huts for a year, three years, or even a lifetime. Food and water were passed to them daily by an unseen servant through an opening in the wall.

A trail descends to the road from the lower retreats in **15 minutes.** Initially the road parallels a tumbling but much smaller Dzakaa Chhu, though as the valley opens out the road and the river diverge to opposite sides of a broad gravel plain. The stones and glacial debris here are beautifully patterned; some pieces look like painted works of art rather than ancient layers of sedimentary deposits. With Everest so close, chances are that some of these rocks are actually pieces of the mountain that have been carried down to the plain by grand glaciers of the past.

Before reaching the low morainal hills separating this part of the valley from the end of the glacier, the road swings around a large rock slide that has fallen from the east (R) ridge. At the base of this slide are two mud-and-stone monuments and a *chötaen.* This is a particularly good location for viewing Everest. The mountain is very close and the broad yellow band of rock across its North Face almost glows with its geologic antiquity. These colorful layers of compressed clay, silt, and limestone near the summit are a tribute to the cataclysmic forces that shaped the Himalaya range, for they were once sediments at the bottom of an ancient ocean.

Along the top of the rock slide are the ruins of Sherab Chhöling, a small nunnery. Numerous square *chötaen* have been reconstructed between the gigantic boulders; a hermit monk now tends a small rebuilt *lhakhang.* A trail leading to this temple climbs the north side of the slide. Beyond here the road enters a series of gravel hills that mark the advance and retreat of the Rongphu Glacier. At the far side of these deposits, within the elbow of the last hill before the glacier's terminus, is Everest base camp. This is the most popular site used by expeditions, for it is protected from the wind and is supplied with fresh water from a natural spring. It was the base camp for the 1924 British Everest Expedition.

Rongphu Glacier Dayhike

Many base-camp sites are scattered between the old British site and the Rongphu Glacier, including the 1960 Chinese base camp near the glacier on the far west (L) side of the valley.

The terminal moraine of the glacier is a walk of **15 minutes** across the gravel flats from the British campsite. Follow the road past this base camp for **5 minutes** to a creek crossing. Early in the morning this ford is often just a rock hop; by evening, especially during the summer months, the current quickens and the water level can be well above the knees in many places. If this is the case, remember that the widest part of the creek is usually the shallowest. The road continues a short distance beyond this crossing before it disappears into the gravel.

The Rongphu Glacier is an impressive frozen ocean of ice waves and should not be missed if you took the effort to reach base camp. The views of the glacier and the Himalayan peaks are some of the most dramatic in Tibet. Along the east (R) side of the glacier is the trail that expeditions use to begin their climbs. The terrain is rocky but easy enough to negotiate, for this track follows a relatively flat, natural trough between the glacier's lateral moraine and the side of the ridge. **One hour** above the end of the glacier is a flat campsite; nearby is the gully of a rushing creek. This is often a dangerous crossing, making it a good place to turn back to the base camp or the monastery.

Beyond this creek, the route leads to the advance base camp (18,900 ft, 5760 m) for expeditions climbing Everest's North Face or Changtse (24,780 ft, 7553 m), the North Peak of Everest. Another trail ascends steeply to the left (east) up the ridge toward Camp I (17,900 ft, 5460 m) and the East Rongphu Glacier. This is the route to Camp III (20,800 ft, 6340 m), the advance base camp for expeditions climbing the North Col or Everest's Northeast Ridge. This trek, which should be attempted only by extremely fit and thoroughly acclimatized parties, is described in "Beyond Everest Base Camp."

LEAVING DZA RONGPHU

If you have come to the Rongphu area from Dingri and have plans to return there, at least three different routes loop back to Dingri and the Lhasa–Kathmandu Highway. The trek from Dza Rongphu to Dingri takes **3 to 4 days** regardless of which pass you cross. If your food supplies need replenishing, the routes through Passum or Phadhruchi crossing Ding La or Dingri Lama La, are the best choices. For those who walked over Pang La from the kilometer marker 494 turnoff, there are four passes to choose from that connect the Rongphu Valley with the Dingri plains. The most scenic but also the most demanding route is to walk to the village of Zommug, via a high ridge shoulder with good views of Everest, then cross either Lamna La or Ding La to reach Dingri. Zommug is also the best place to arrange for a burro or a horse to carry your gear; pack animals are rarely available at Rongphu. The various crossings between Dingri and Rongphu are described in "The Dingri to Dza Rongphu Monastery Loop."

Transport from the Rongphu Valley to the highway and Shegar typically originates in Phadhruchi, which is 2¹/₂ **hours or more** by four-wheel-drive vehicle from the monastery. The highway junction at kilometer marker 494 is **at least another 2 hours** away. With an early start and optimum road conditions, a vehicle can reach Nyelam (km marker 694), and sometimes even Khasa (km marker 731), from Dza Rongphu in **1 day.** Occasionally a truck or a tractor-pulled cart will take passengers from Rongphu to Phadhruchi and Shegar, though the travel time will be considerably slower. A tractor heading to Shegar from Rongphu will often take **2 days,** including an overnight in Phadhruchi.

Mount Everest and the North Face base camp

The Dingri to Dza Rongphu Monastery Loop

Dingri village (km marker 544) is the trekkers' gateway to Mount Everest. This former staging point on the Lhasa–Kathmandu caravan route, situated within sight of Everest's northern slopes, is in the middle of an expansive plain not far west of the Rongphu Valley. Between these two drainages is a long dividing ridge with four main passes, all 16,000 feet (4880 m) or higher. The highest and most southern of these crossings is called Pang La (not to be confused with the Pang La along the vehicle road to Everest base camp). About 1 mile (1.5 km) to the north is Lamna La (16,800 ft, 5120 m), a more traveled and slightly lower pass that has become the standard route used by organized trekking groups to approach the Everest region. There are few villages en route, so it's advisable to carry tents, stoves, and all your food requirements. As the sign at Danda's general store in Dingri suggests ("The last shop before Everest"), there are no shops or lodges in the villages beyond Dingri.

An old trade route from Dingri to the town of Phadhruchi crosses Dingri Lama La (16,000 ft, 4880 m), the lowest and the northernmost of the passes into the Rongphu region. The trek from Phadhruchi to Dza Rongphu up the Dzakaa Chhu Valley takes **2 days.** If this route is walked in the opposite direction (from Dza Rongphu to Phadhruchi and on to Dingri), it can be combined with the trek

Dingri village and Cho Oyu peak

over Lamna La to create a scenic loop of **8 to 10 days** that requires only a half day of backtracking. By starting in Dingri and walking this loop counterclockwise, the few amenities available in Phadhruchi will come at the end of the trek rather than at the beginning.

The least known of these four passes is Ding La (16,400 ft, 5000 m), a remote approach to Everest via a tributary valley rising east behind Lungjhang village. Several infrequently traveled high passes also connect the Ding Valley with the Gara and Zommug (or Zombuk) valleys.

DINGRI

Dingri (14,400 ft, 4390 m) is a windblown settlement with a hundred houses or more bunched along the base of an isolated hill. Its true name is Ganggar, but people from outside the region know it as Dingri (Tingri). Despite the high-walled Chinese compounds near the Lhasa–Kathmandu Highway, the town and the surrounding area offer a fascinating glimpse of Tibetan village life. Legends claim that the area earned its name when the Indian tantric master Padampa Sangye came to these plains near the end of the eleventh century on his search for a special black rock. A manifestation of the Buddha Sakyamuni had used his great powers to throw this rock all the way from India to Tibet. The rock first landed on a frozen body of water, near the present site of Dingri. It struck the ice with a loud "ding," said to be like the sound of a hammer hitting steel. Since that time this region has been called Dingri, the hill of Ding. After bouncing off the ice, the magically lofted stone settled upon a spot at the far western edge of the Dingri plain, where Padampa Sangye recovered the rock and established Langkor *gompa*. All that is left of this famed monastery is a small, walled-in *lhakhang* within the village of Langkor, **5 hours** west of Dingri.

The crumbling walls on Ganggar Ri, the hill above Dingri, are the remains of a *dzong*. This Chinese-built fortress was erected as a line of defense after the Nepalese army captured the area in the late eighteenth century. Many of the dissolving mud-walled ruins scattered along the highway between Gutsuo (km marker 581) and the checkpoint near Shegar are testimony to this attack by the Gurkha armies.

The villagers say a small monastery was also located on Ganggar Ri, and local businessmen and people with illnesses would come to seek insight regarding their problems and needs. The monks would vigorously shake a handful of dice, then spill them out before the visitor to determine his or her fortune. The small shrine recently rebuilt amid the hilltop rubble has become the dwelling of an unusual hermit caretaker. The top of Ganggar Ri is also one of the finest places for watching the sunset on Mount Everest and the huge massif of Cho Oyu. One of the locals told me the large summit just to the southeast of Dingri is called Dunza (23,092 ft, 7038 m), though it is unnamed on maps.

The availability of accommodation in Dingri has been in a state of flux over the past few years, though recently a lodge and restaurant catering to locals and foreigners was established on the Lhasa–Kathmandu Highway, across from the turnoff for the town. The menu is simple, the meals are family-style, and the atmosphere can be quite lively. This is a good place to arrange reasonably priced pack animals and guides. They also have saddle horses for hire for day rides to the

Tsamda hot springs (km marker 555) or Langkor *gompa,* and they outfit groups for **7- to 8-day** round-trip horseback trips to Dza Rongphu monastery.

Although there are a number of little shops in Dingri, the goods on their shelves are mostly an odd assortment of canned fruit, noodles, candies, and army sneakers. Purchase all of your food requirements in Shigatse or Lhasa.

Unless transport has been prearranged with a travel agent in Shigatse or Lhasa, the usual procedure for arranging a ride out of Dingri is to stand by the highway at the lodge and try to wave down passing trucks and buses. If the local buses heading to the Nepal border from Lhasa have not been delayed, they usually pass Dingri on Sunday and Wednesday afternoons. Local buses returning to Lhasa from the border seem to have no fixed departure schedules.

If you plan on spending a day or two in Dingri acclimatizing before your trek, a good warm-up walk follows a cart track south from Dingri to the village of Gondephug. Set below a low hill with a ruined *gompa* on its slopes, this settlement is **1 to 1¹/₂ hours** away across the flat plain. The walls of a *lhakhang* are all that remain of this Nyingmapa monastery.

If you have a full day free, a long but flat loop walk continues southeast from Gondephug for **about 2 hours** to Chhulung village, situated at the base of a tall, narrow, and rocky ridge. The ridge is a good bearing to aim for and can be recognized by the extensive ruins crowning the top. A new *lhakhang* has been built among the crumbling walls. The return walk to Dingri takes **3 hours** along a cart track leading north from Chhulung.

DINGRI TO CHO OYU BASE CAMP

An alternative trek from Dingri is the walk south to Cho Oyu base camp (16,300 ft, 4970 m), located at the foot of high gravel moraines below the Kyetrag Glacier, in the Ra Chhu Valley. A dirt road threads for 27 miles (44 km) across the expansive Dingri plains to the base camp, **1¹/₂ to 2 days** from Dingri, then continues to the southwest over Puse La ("Mouse Pass"; 17,500 ft, 5300 m) to the fertile Rongshar Valley, a frontier trading post with Nepal. Not far north of the base camp on the east (R) side of the Ra Chhu Valley are the ruined buildings of Kyetrag, a former salt depot on the Nepal caravan route that crosses glaciated Nangpa La (18,753 ft, 5716 m). The trail to Advance base camp follows this trade route up the east (R) side of the glacier.

A beautiful dayhike from the base camp, with panoramic views of Cho Oyu (26,748 ft, 8153 m), Chobo Rabtsang (21,870 ft, 6666 m), and towering overviews of the Kyetrag Glacier and its huge lake, follows the road toward Puse La for **1 hour.** When the road swings to the right (west) to start the steep ascent to the pass, continue straight ahead up the trough along the west (L) side of the glacier. Ascend onto the high lateral moraine whenever convenient. Follow the crest until it joins the side of the mountain (17,400 ft, 5300 m), below the ice falls of Chobo Rabtsang, **2 hours** from the base camp.

The Everest–Rongphu base camp can be reached in **2¹/₂ days** from Cho Oyu base camp via a trail that climbs out of the Ra Chhu Valley, then turns east across the hills to join the cart track crossing Lamna La. The route over this pass, starting from Dingri, is detailed below in "Dingri to Dza Rongphu via Lamna La."

DINGRI TO DZA RONGPHU VIA LAMNA LA

This trek takes **4 days,** though strong, well-acclimatized parties can reach the *gompa* in **3 days.** The route begins at the bridge on the southeast edge of town and follows a well-graded cart track for most of the way to Lamna La. Cross the wooden bridge to the east (R) bank of the Ra Chhu and follow the track across the grass- and scrub-covered plains. (**A few minutes** beyond the bridge are several good camping areas, but they are rather exposed to the wind.) The track soon angles toward the south, with Cho Oyu straight ahead like a gigantic directional beacon on the horizon. Several trails shortcut some of the long bends in this road. The plains here are a strange mixture of silence and activity: the wind rustles the grasses, young boys whistle at their herds of miniature goats, and groups of women bent over from the waist chat and sing as they tend the barley.

One hour from Dingri the track passes the settlement of Ra Chhu, a distant cluster of white buildings in the hills rising to the east. As the road continues south the grasses gradually yield to sparsely vegetated gravel expanses. Somehow barley can be coaxed to grow in these conditions. **About 45 minutes** beyond Ra Chhu the line of hills edging the plains is interrupted by a broad valley mouth. The route over Dingri Lama La to the Gara Valley follows this wide tributary up to the left (east). Finding the proper approach to this pass can be somewhat confusing from this direction, for there are actually three different drainages converging here through the jumble of dry hills. The correct route leads up the valley to the far right (southeast), reaching the village of Naylung (14,900 ft, 4540 m) in **1¹⁄₂ hours.** Another graded cart track originates near Lungjhang, a settlement farther to the south, and runs along the north (L) side of the Naylung Valley and over Dingri Lama La to Phadhruchi. This route is described in reverse in "Phadruchi to Dingri via Dingri Lama La."

The cart track from Dingri to Lamna La continues south toward Cho Oyu. **One and a half hours** beyond the valley entrance to Naylung a prominent rocky ridge erupts from the plains along the west (L) bank of the Ra Chhu. Chhölung village is situated at the base of this outcrop; scattered across the ridge crest are the extensive ruins of Chhölung *gompa.* A small temple has been rebuilt amongst the rubble. A footbridge sometimes spans the river near this settlement.

The open plains are eventually squeezed between this ridge and the hills to the left (east). **Thirty minutes** past the end of the Chhölung ridge the track from the Naylung Valley comes in from the left to join the Dingri–Lamna La road. In **another 30 minutes** the road passes through Lungjhang (14,800 ft, 4510 m), the last village in this part of the Dingri plains. A wind-generator farm in Lungjhang could supply half of Western Tibet with electricity. It is a bleak region surrounded by barren gravel flats, yet the people manage to harvest barley. Most of the villagers are also herders, and yaks can be arranged here for large groups heading to Everest. If you are coming from Dingri with pack animals and a guide, this is probably where you will stop for the night. A house–cum–*chhang* hall in Lungjhang will put up travelers, but it's best to find a family to stay with for the night. Unless you have a tent for your guide, the next available shelter where he could sleep is at a *drogpa* camp **2 hours** farther south. Enquire in Lungjhang regarding the whereabouts of these herders.

Unfortunately, hospitality in this town is a bit lacking. Beware of greedy hosts, keep your belongings close at hand, and make sure prices are established before you consume any food or drink.

The cart track continues south from town beyond a mud brick wall and a huge circular stack of *mani* stones. **A few minutes** from this prayer wall the track forks, the left half angling into a large tributary valley. This is the route to Ding La (16,400 ft, 5000 m), the most difficult and remote of the crossings into the Dzakaa Chhu Valley. The journey over this pass to Dza Rongphu monastery takes **3 long days** but it is a beautiful walk.

The right fork stays on course with Cho Oyu's diminishing summit. In **20 minutes** it passes to the right of a rocky crag topped with ruins, which may be an old *dzong*. The high ridge extending along the Ra Chhu's west (L) bank now closes in on the river to form a gorge. **One hour** past Lungjhang the gorge forces the track to turn left into the scrubby hills. In **20 minutes more** climb to a ridge summit with panoramic views looking across the gorge to the Himalayan peaks.

Descend from here onto an unusually straight section of the track neatly bordered by white river rocks. **Forty-five minutes** from the ridge top the road begins climbing into the hills again. To the right at the base of these hills is a *drogpa* camp with stone corrals. If you don't mind sleeping beside a few hundred sneezing goats this is one of the more sheltered campsites before the pass.

The track ascends past this camp and over the eastern hills that guard the entrance to a tributary valley. Cho Oyu, massively close, soon disappears behind its foothills. To the west is an endless succession of morainal ridges dumped by the glaciers of past ice ages. A bit of geological history lies scattered on the gravel slopes near the track: the shell fossils are remnants from the ancient Tethys Sea that once covered Tibet.

One hour from the *drogpa* camp the track descends into the new drainage, passing a stone corral and several grassy meadows. As the valley starts veering left (east) the road crosses the creek to the north (L) bank. Just beyond this ford are a large corral and *drogpa* camp (15,600 ft, 4750 m) up to the right. Used almost year-round, this is often the last inhabited herders' camp and one of the better places to stop before the pass. The next village is Zommug, but it is still **3¹/₂ hours** away, including the crossing of Langma La. The corral walls provide a welcome windbreak.

Not far from this camp the valley opens out but quickly divides into two separate drainages. The cart track hugs the base of the far north (L) ridge and ascends the larger valley to the right (southeast) toward both Lamna La and Pang La. (Lamna La is also known as Zommug La and Tambo Pang La, although the latter does not seem to be a common name.) If you plan to cross the more remote and somewhat higher Pang La (17,100 ft, 5210 m), stay on the cart track for **about 1 hour** past the *drogpa* camp. When the track starts angling to the left (northeast) toward Lamna La and the Zommug Valley, the cross-country route to Pang La leaves the road and continues right (southeast) toward a network of high, gravel-covered ridges.

Although this is a shorter approach to Dza Rongphu monastery, it is a steep ascent and the area is mostly uninhabited; it is too rugged for crossing with pack animals and even the herders are absent. If you remain on the cart track, Lamna La is a **1¹/₂-hour** climb to the left (northeast).

When the locals travel between Dingri and Zommug, they typically use a shortcut that also goes over Lamna La but at a slightly higher point on the ridge than where the cart track crosses. This shorter route follows the road for **about 15 minutes** past the last *drogpa* camp. It then leaves the track where the valley divides and follows the smaller drainage up to the left (northeast). There isn't a trail at first, so choose a convenient cross-country route over the wet tundra and grass hummocks. Aim for the hills on the south (L) side of this drainage. Not long after you enter the mouth of this side valley the walking becomes much easier and a trail forms along the base of the south (L) ridge. The terrain beside this ridge is very dry and supports large colonies of pikas. They're everywhere, scurrying into their burrows and quickly reappearing to inspect whoever is approaching. Several small piles of *mani* stones grace the trail along here. **Forty-five minutes** beyond the last herders' camp is a stone corral (15,900 ft, 4850 m) at the base of the ridge. The area around this enclosure is the last good campsite before Lamna La. Grazing grass and water are nearby.

Only **10 minutes** beyond this camp the valley floor turns into a stony desert plain. The trail is easy to follow at first and stays near the south (L) ridge. The actual pass crossing is not visible from here, though a saddle in the ridge marked by a rock cairn can be seen to the southwest near the summit. Occasionally a lone *kyang,* the wild ass of Tibet, can be spotted in this region. It looks like a small horse from a distance, with a reddish brown coat and black markings.

As the valley turns to the right (south) the trail leaves the base of the ridge. The path becomes faint but continues to the southwest across the rocky flats and into a group of low hills. **Twenty minutes** beyond the stone corral these hills drop away steeply into a narrow creek bed. Descend the slopes of broken shale and cross to the west (L) bank of the creek. The last stone corral before the pass is **a few minutes** above this embankment. The cairn on the saddle is directly above on the ridge. Farther to the right (west) are views of the adjacent valley and the cart track leading to Zommug.

The trail is faint above this final corral until just below the top of the saddle. Route finding, however, is not a problem if you aim for the cairn. During the summer, high-altitude blue poppies (*Meconopsis*) dot these rocky slopes and *gowa,* the Tibetan gazelle, may be grazing along the high ridges near the pass. The cairn is a breath-grabbing **40-minute** climb, without rest stops, from the creek crossing. Lamna La (16,900 ft, 5150 m) is only **5 minutes** farther and is marked by a *la-dzay.* The cart track is out of sight and crosses a few hundred feet below this point. The snowy peaks off to the south are the foothills of Gyachung Kang and Cho Oyu. Pang La crosses the large ridge system in front of them.

The trail swings gently to the left (east) before starting its steep descent, intersecting the cart track **15 minutes** below the summit. The track stays on the north (L) side of the valley for most of the journey to Zommug, though the locals follow a more direct route down the south (R) side of this drainage. The vegetation here is considerably more lush than on the Dingri side of the pass, capable of supporting hundreds of yaks and a half-dozen *drogpa* families.

Where the trail from the pass meets the cart track, cross the track and continue descending without a trail toward the valley floor. The hummocks can make walking difficult, though eventually a trail materializes at the base of the south (R) ridge. The cart track winds down into the valley, staying near the base of the north (L) ridge. **One hour** below the pass the valley narrows and the trail swings over to the left near two *drogpa* camps. The road from the pass is also forced near these two camps. Cross the cart track, then cross to the north (L) bank of the main stream.

The trail climbs for **a few minutes** from the stream to the top of a boulder-strewn ridge. The white walls of Zommug village (15,700 ft, 4790 m), the highest permanent settlement in the Everest region, are only **20 minutes** away to the left (northeast). The trail descends from this ridge crest to a wooden bridge, then climbs above a rushing creek to the town. The best sites for camping are a few minutes downstream from the bridge, away from the village.

Zommug is set high above the valley in a moonscape of barren hills with views of Mount Everest and Gyachung Kang. Because crops cannot survive at this elevation, all of the forty families residing here rely upon animal husbandry. Every morning, in a large pasture above the town, dozens of *dri,* the female yaks, are tethered for milking. During the summer the villagers supply yaks to haul gear for Everest expeditions.

If you are trekking with pack animals, Zommug will be the last place where your guide can find shelter before continuing on to Dza Rongphu monastery. As in other towns near Everest, choose your host carefully and watch your belongings.

The drainage north of Zommug is Changku Lung, "Wolf Valley." A **half-hour** walk in this direction above the village provides grand views of Gyachung Kang's massif. **One hour** farther is an unnamed pass (16,500 ft, 5030 m) into the Ding Valley. This is a beautiful alternative route to Dingri, and it is a good idea to hire a guide. This trek takes **2 long days** of walking. Ding La (16,400 ft, 5000 m) must be crossed as well.

Dza Rongphu monastery is only **1 day** south from Zommug. You can choose between an easier, lower route via the valley bottoms, or a very scenic but more demanding trail that climbs a high ridge.

The lower route descends from Zommug to the Dzakaa Chhu, the main river draining the Rongphu area. The trail initially remains high on the ridge side, then drops near the stream to join the cart track. The confluence with the Dzakaa Chhu is at the end of a **1¹/₂-hour** descent from Zommug. The desert environment and gravel wastelands along the river are a dramatic change from the green meadows of the Zommug Valley. Find a suitable ford above the confluence and cross to the south (R) bank of the stream. The route to Dza Rongphu follows a trail on the west (L) bank of the river for **1¹/₂ hours** to a wooden bridge, past the ruins of Chhöphug *gompa*. The caves here are worth investigating, though these days birds are the main inhabitants rather than meditating monks.

When you reach the wooden bridge, cross to the east (R) bank of the Dzakaa Chhu. The road to Dza Rongphu monastery from the highway and Phadhruchi runs along the top of the river embankment. The walk to the monastery is **less than 3**

hours up the valley. This portion of the trek and the walk to the base camp are described earlier in this chapter in the sections "The Trek to Everest Base Camp via Pang La" and "From Rongphu to Everest Base Camp."

———————

The high route to Dza Rongphu crosses the ridge across the valley due south from Zommug. From the summit (16,500 ft, 5030 m), the views of Everest and the upper Rongphu Valley are outstanding. To use this route, descend south from the town, reaching the main stream that drains the valley in **10 minutes.** Cross to the south (R) bank, then cross the cart track from Lamna La, which runs along this side of the stream. Continue heading south, climbing without a trail into the rounded hills. As you ascend, aim for the lone rock cairn that can be seen on the ridge top, keeping to the right of a deep rocky gully. The easiest route up is to follow the crests of the ridge spurs. **One hour** (not including rest breaks) after crossing the stream, reach the cairn and the summit ridge. Gyachung Kang is the huge flat-topped peak straight ahead (southwest). The winding gravel bed of the Rongphu Valley twists below toward the south, disappearing into the gray hills at the foot of Everest. Nuptse (25,849 ft, 7879 m) and the Nuptse–Lhotse ridge, which are in Nepal, are to the right of Everest, but the summit of Lhotse (27,940 ft, 8516 m) is hidden.

Follow the parallel tracks leading south from the cairn over the stony ridge top. The high point of the ridge (16,500 ft, 5030 m) and a *la-dzay* with prayer flags are **5 minutes** past the cairn. There are good views from here into the Dzakaa Chhu Valley. The village of Chhösang is below to the east and a section of the trail leading toward the last bridge crossing over the Dzakaa Chhu is visible through the ridges to the south. Continue south from the *la-dzay* to begin the steep descent into a tributary valley of the Dzakaa Chhu. The trail quickly disintegrates, so choose any convenient route down, staying to the west (R) side of the deep gully draining the ridge. Using the gravelly route beside the Dzakaa Chhu as a bearing, descend in **45 minutes** from the ridge top to a stone goat corral (15,400 ft, 4690 m) above the creek. This drainage coming in from the right (west) is the route from Pang La. A trail to the Chhöphug caves descends to the left (east) around a ridge spur and down the west (L) side of the Dzakaa Chhu. The hermitage is **less than 1 hour** from here.

To continue to Dza Rongphu, descend from the corral and cross to the south (R) bank of the creek. The trail soon turns into the Dzakaa Chhu Canyon, a desert expanse of sand and gravel. The wooden bridge crossing over to the road leading up to Rongphu is **45 minutes** to the south.

PHADHRUCHI TO DINGRI VIA DINGRI LAMA LA

The 1¹/₂-**day** trek from Phadhruchi to Dingri over Dingri Lama La (16,000 ft, 4880 m) is the easiest of the four pass crossings from the Dzakaa Chhu Valley to the Dingri plains. It is also the final leg (the first leg if you are approaching the pass from Dingri) of an **8- to 10-day** loop walk to the base camp that begins in Dingri and crosses Langma La.

The route to Dingri Lama La from Phadhruchi initially heads north on the road leading to the Lhasa–Kathmandu Highway. After **45 minutes** a smaller road into the Gara Valley, marked by a pile of prayer stones, veers off to the left (northwest). Turn here and follow this track across the barren plain, reaching the quiet, whitewashed settlement of Nyumda in **15 minutes.** The desert has been brought to life here with irrigation; shimmering fields of barley and mustard cover the valley floor during the summer.

Ruins lie scattered throughout this region atop high embankments and craggy ridges. **Forty minutes** past Nyumda the ruins of Seyum *gompa* are perched above the rocky mouth of a tributary entering from the right (north). Across the main valley are the remains of an old *dzong.*

The road remains on the north (L) side of the valley for most of the way to the pass. Few vehicles ever come this way, making it seem more like a wide country path than a motor road. Small settlements dot the valley floor and wherever water flows there are barley fields. **Less than 2 hours** from Nyumda the track passes the ruins of a feudal landlord's residence. **Ten minutes** farther is the village of Trongpa. At the base of a cliff above this town is Karay *gompa,* a functioning monastery with five monks in residence.

From Trongpa the valley starts edging around to the left (west). The surrounding ridges become more rocky and begin to close in on the broad valley plain. Across the river along the south (R) bank are an extensive series of ruins that may have been a fortified town. The ruins of Rayjung, a fortress/monastery destroyed during the Cultural Revolution, are on a hillside above the road **30 minutes** beyond Trongpa. The *dhrapa* affiliated with this temple reside in Gara, a village **another 5 minutes** up the road.

Gara (14,800 ft, 4510 m) is the largest settlement in this valley. It is divided into two main groups of houses located **a few minutes** apart. Many of the buildings are beautiful three-storied residences with unusual inward-sloping walls. Their large, high-walled courtyards look like miniature fortresses. The painted stripes on these houses consist of three colors; most other homes in the Dingri and Rongphu areas have just two. The interiors of these buildings are a maze of rooms leading in different directions, all connected by a network of zigzagging staircases.

If you are walking with a guide, this is one of the last places to spend the night before ascending Dingri Lama La; only a few small clusters of houses lie beyond Gara. The pass is still a **4-hour** climb up the valley from this town. If you stay in Gara for the night, it is possible to reach Dingri the next day with an early start and **a long, steady day** of walking. Burros and horses can be hired in Gara.

The terrain in this area is noticeably wilder, with picturesque rock formations bursting from the ridge tops like rows of flatirons. Large tributaries enter from both sides of the main valley, and each of these leads up to a high pass that crosses into one of the adjacent valleys. **One hour** beyond Gara the cart track passes below the ruins of Nyasa *gompa.* A small *lhakhang* here has been rebuilt by the local monks. In **5 minutes** the road climbs onto a rocky outcrop above the river, overlooking the arid pasturelands that have replaced the cultivated fields. The meadows provide numerous potential campsites beside the river, which is now just a stream.

In **1 hour** the road crosses to the south (R) bank of this drainage. Continue up the valley for **another hour** to where an obvious shortcut climbs up the south (R) ridge to bypass several large switchbacks in the road. Dingri Lama La (16,000 ft, 4880 m) is a **40-minute** climb, not including rest stops, from the base of this ridge. The pass is a broad, gentle summit marked with *la-dzay* and prayer flags. Good pasturing grass covers the nearby ridges, but below to the west the

Dingri plains and the surrounding hills are dry and barren.

Descend from the pass into a long, winding valley, reaching another large *ladzay* beside the track in **1 hour. Less than 10 minutes** beyond here the road turns left (west) toward Lungjhang, and follows the stream through a rocky cleft between the ridges. A wide trail leaves the road at this turn and continues straight ahead (northwest) to Naylung, the only village before Dingri. **Fifteen minutes** beyond this junction the trail passes a long *mani* wall, then ascends a low, rocky saddle in the ridge. Descend to Naylung (14,900 ft, 4540 m) in **30 minutes** from the saddle, passing the ruins of Tsariphug *gompa* on the hill to the left (south).

Dingri is **3 hours** of steady walking beyond Naylung. If it is late, consider staying here for the night. The route to Dingri descends from Naylung for **20 minutes,** then fords the main stream of this drainage. The cart track from Dingri Lama La runs along its south (L) embankment. The terrain becomes very arid as the valley turns right to meet the plains. **One hour** after the stream crossing are several ruined houses near the valley mouth. The track eventually extends beyond the last ridges, then swings right (north) onto the Dingri plains. Dingri, which is easily recognized by its large cluster of white buildings at the foot of a large, lone hill, is **about 2 hours** away to the right (northwest).

Beyond Everest Base Camp

Note: Trekking beyond Everest base camp (16,900 ft, 5150 m) should not be attempted unless you are prepared to take the time to acclimatize properly while ascending to the higher camps. Acute Mountain Sickness (AMS) is a serious environment-related illness that can strike anyone, especially at these

Trekking above Everest base camp (photo by Kathy Butler)

extreme elevations. You should be well acquainted with the symptoms of AMS and be capable of monitoring others in your group, as well as yourself, for the adverse affects that can occur on a trek such as this. Headache, nausea, vomiting, and shortness of breath are early AMS symptoms that indicate a person should descend immediately to prevent more serious complications, including death. AMS and other health-related problems are discussed in more detail in the chapter "Staying Healthy."

This adventure, which I call the Highest Trek in the World, is an incredible journey to Camp III (20,800 ft, 6340 m) and to the base of the North Col via the East Rongphu Glacier (also called the Rongphu Shar Glacier). Nowhere else on this planet can you hike on a trail to such a high elevation without the need for crampons, ice axes, or mountaineering skills. This eastern tributary of the main Rongphu Glacier flows through a remarkably flat valley in a great arc around the Changtse massif (24,878 ft, 7583 m), Everest's North Peak. Along the central crest of this glacier a wide corridor of morainal debris, known to climbers as the Serac Highway, winds safely between the towering ice pinnacles all the way up to Camp III.

The East Rongphu Glacier is relatively free of crevasses and other hazards on its surface, though ice conditions and the location of the trail vary from year to year as well as throughout a single summer. Caution should always be used when traveling upon a glacier. Climbing gear may not be necessary, but common sense definitely is. If the weather deteriorates or trail conditions become unsafe, turn back and be satisfied with where you stopped. Or try again in another day or two.

A trek of this caliber is best left for a professional trekking company to organize: the food and equipment requirements are more than most people want to carry at these elevations, and arranging yaks to haul gear beyond base camp is not possible unless you can supply tents and warm clothing for the yak herders.

The best months for good walking conditions on the glacier are June, July, and August, though this is also when monsoon clouds can obscure Everest's summit for days at a time. The route up the East Rongphu Glacier is not particularly difficult to follow, with the exception of the rough terrain between Camp I and the Interim Camp near Camp II. To ensure proper acclimatization, I highly recommend walking up to the Rongphu base camp from Dingri or by the route over Pang La East. After reaching base camp, a total of **9 to 10 additional days,** including rest days, are required to safely complete the round-trip journey to Camp III and back. **At least 1 night** should be spent at Dza Rongphu monastery and **at least 2 nights** should be spent acclimatizing at base camp. Don't just laze around during these rest days: a dayhike to higher elevations is one of the best ways to help your body adjust to the altitude. Allow **a minimum of 5 days** to reach Camp III from the base camp, plus **2 more days** for the return trek.

The daytime temperatures on the glacier during the summer are quite mild despite the elevation, but that doesn't mean it can't get cold. Light snowfalls occur; at times it may rain. What is considered sufficient sun protection for the rest of Tibet can be harmfully inadequate here, especially if the sun is reflecting off fresh snow. Sun block should be applied frequently and dark glacier glasses are absolutely necessary. A broad-brimmed felt hat like ones the Tibetans wear is a good pre-

Ice seracs on the East Rongphu Glacier

trek investment.

The ascent to Camp I from Everest base camp is a steep climb that initially follows the trail along the east (L) side of the main Rongphu Glacier (the beginning of this walk is described in "Rongphu Glacier Dayhike." **One hour** south from the glacial terminus is an elevated flat area between the ridge and the lateral moraine, suitable for pitching several tents. The trail forks here, the smaller track leading up the ridge side to the left (east) toward Camp I and the East Rongphu Glacier. The larger path continues straight (south) from this camp, descending into a ravine carved by the crashing meltwaters of the tributary glacier. This is the route used by climbers attempting either Everest's North Face or Changtse. Due to the difficulty of this crossing, some expeditions erect a single-cable bridge over the creek; even yaks have trouble swimming this torrent during July and August. The advance base camp for these climbs, known as Tilman's Camp or the Lake Camp, is **several hours** farther south in a shallow basin above the main Rongphu Glacier (18,500 ft, 5640 m). Beyond this camp it is sometimes possible to continue across the upper part of the Rongphu Glacier to Lho La ("South Pass"; 19,704 ft, 6006 m), with its breathtaking views overlooking the Khumbu Glacier in Nepal. Use caution, for although the glacier is relatively flat it is prone to forming crevasses.

The trail to the East Rongphu Glacier climbs quickly in a series of steep switchbacks above the turnoff at the small campsite. Although Camp I can be reached in **less than 1 hour** of actual walking time from here, the breaks needed to fill your lungs during the ascent can easily double this figure. Take advantage of these rest stops and enjoy the views of the Himalaya and the Rongphu Glacier's frozen waves of blue ice. The graceful, bullet-shaped summit across the glacier to the southwest is Pumori; behind this peak is Kala Pattar, a popular trekking destination for viewing Mount Everest on the Nepal side. **Thirty minutes** above the campsite the trail passes a tall rock cairn. A camp is located on a hill off to the right overlooking the gorge, but the traditional first camp is still **another 15 minutes** up the ridge.

Camp I (17,900 ft, 5460 m) is set in a barren world of morainal hills under beautifully sculpted, yellow-orange granite cliffs. It is easy to recognize, for dozens of tent sites have been leveled throughout the rocks and boulders. The next camp is too far to reach in a single day, so to help yourself acclimatize spend the remainder of the afternoon exploring the gravelly snout of the East Rongphu Glacier, only **20 minutes** beyond this camp.

The glacial terminus resembles the tailings of a huge gravel quarry, with great mounds of crushed rock and sand filling the valley floor. The outlet creek emerges from the base of these hills, though little ice is visible until farther up the valley. The trail descends to the water's edge along a cairned route, then angles to the south over the gravel hills, reaching the west (L) side of the glacier in **10 minutes.** Depending on the season or whether a climbing expedition has been up this way recently, the trail across these hills can be difficult to follow and laced with dead ends where the ice has melted or collapsed. Look carefully for the small rock cairns that usually mark this route.

The trail descends from the gravel mounds onto a small mud plain beside the glacier. It then climbs from these flats into a large jumble of rocky moraine. The route is generally well marked, though it is easy to be sidetracked onto different dead ends. Keep looking for the rock cairns. The trail climbs and descends over the gravel hills, always staying above the west (L) edge of the ice. There is one particularly unstable section where small rock and gravel slides often obliterate the trail, making progress slow, especially for loaded yaks. **Ninety minutes** above the glacial terminus the trail climbs high onto the hills above the west (L) flank of the glacier. The large tributary ice floe entering from the left (east) is the Far East Rongphu Glacier. Directly across from it and in the middle of the main glacier is the Interim Camp (18,900 ft, 5760 m) between Camps I and II. This is a good place to spend two nights acclimatizing before advancing to Camp II. Nearby, the first ice seracs, or *nieve penitentes,* rise like white sails from the dark debris-laden surface of the glacier. (*Nieve penitentes,* a Spanish term that means "snow nuns," is used in the Andes to describe the peaks of ice rising from the surface of glaciers, for they resemble the white-robed attire of many South American Catholic nuns.)

The Interim Camp is a **15-minute** descent from the trail's highest point along these hills. A smaller path branching off to the right from the main trail was used by the British expeditions in the 1920s and '30s. It stays high on the hills and passes dangerously close to the long wall of crumbling cliffs. Stay on the larger trail, descending along the right side of a yawning crevasse on a safe, well-marked trail. The campsite is located near a depression on the glacier's surface. A long gravel-covered hill rises behind this camp and continues up the center of the glacier. The hill is a good landmark, for the route to camps II and III follows this central spine of ice and talus. The Interim Camp is just to the right (south) of this ridge on a smaller, adjacent hill. If there are no tents visible, look for flattened tent sites with beds of straw laid over the rocks. A creek flows below the camp along the base of the glacier's central ridge, though early in the season it is usually hidden by a thick snow bridge. For trekkers who have climbed 2000 feet (610 m) in two days, this Interim Camp is a well-placed rest stop. Not far from camp are views of Everest emerging above the smooth white wall of Changtse.

When the snow bridge spanning the creek is intact, the climb onto the central ridge behind this camp takes **20 minutes.** By mid- to late August this bridge has often melted, exposing short but slippery inclines of ice that can be a problem to get past, especially for loaded yaks. Hunt around for an alternative access. It may be necessary to cut a few steps in the icy slopes and pile up small rock platforms to help the yaks through.

The scenery from this ridge top is stunning. Huge pinnacles of ice soar as high as 50 feet (15 m) above the glacier's surface along both sides of this rocky spine, resembling dozens of Sydney Opera Houses sailing on a choppy gray sea. The trail remains a safe distance from these icy turrets as it roller-coasters over the great heaps of gravel. At times the path becomes rather faint, though the route used by the expeditions typically follows the ridge crest and is usually marked with rock cairns. Unfortunately, candy wrappers are as good as cairns for identifying the way.

About 2 hours above the Interim Camp the central ridge line leads into a confusion of ice at the confluence with the Changtse Glacier, which enters from the right (west). Camp II (19,600 ft, 5970 m) is only **10 minutes** from here, but the correct route can be difficult to find. This camp is located at the far west (L) side of the glacier, below a large cliff at the southern limit of the Changtse Glacier junction. The abundance of rusty tin cans is a sad tribute to the many expeditions that have camped here. The most historic bit of refuse in this area is an old cloth-and-rubber insulated wire that pops up now and again amongst the rocks and gravel. This is the original telephone line laid between base camp and the North Col in 1924 to keep the British climbers informed about the advance of the monsoon from India. It's not unusual to see the herders using lengths of it to tie down loads on their yaks.

Camp II is set in a beautiful location; glaciers large and small spill into the valley from every direction and the appropriately named Serac Highway continues to extend its unusual gravel arm through the center of the ice formations.

Mount Everest looming over Camp III on the East Rongphu Glacier

Depending on how your party feels, a decision must be made between moving tents up to Camp III or visiting it as a dayhike and spending a second night at Camp II. Camp III is another 1200 feet (370 m) higher. If anyone has a rough time trying to sleep here or wakes up with a headache in the morning, the best decision would be to visit Camp III and spend a second night at Camp II.

The route to Camp III returns to the center of the seracs from the second camp. The glacier now bends to the left (southeast) around the eastern flank of Changtse, and the trail soon ascends the largest series of hills on this part of the trek. This is a hard way to start the morning, though soon the morainal spine mellows into a gentle incline that is sometimes no more than 30 feet (9 m) wide between the icy walls. **Eighty minutes** beyond Camp II is a small camp that can be recognized by its garbage. The seracs here are very close together. The infamous "Unclimbed Ridge," the Northeast Ridge of Mount Everest, can be seen at the end of the valley. (The Northeast Ridge was finally climbed by Russell Brice and Harry Taylor in 1988. No one has yet reached the summit via a complete traverse of this ridge.)

As the glacier turns sharply to the right the seracs quickly lose most of their height. **Less than 30 minutes** beyond the small camp the icy pinnacles disappear. The trail along the moraine now follows a series of low gravel humps on the west (L) edge of the glacier. As if a magic spell has been cast, the rough, broken surface of the glacier transforms into a smooth, vast plain of snowy ice fields lapping onto the ridgesides and spilling over the passes in great white sheets. Nowhere else is there an area so large and flat this high. Follow the cairns (and the candy wrappers) along the gravel slopes to the top of a ridge. There are a few cleared tent sites here and several discarded oxygen bottles. The main camp is still **10 minutes** farther up the valley, depending on how well your lungs are handling this climb.

Camp III (20,800 ft, 6340 m), the advance base camp for the North Col route up Mount Everest, is situated within a group of flattened gravel mounds beside the glacier. The Pinnacles, the frightening group of rock palisades that kept the Northeast Ridge unclimbed for so long, rise nearly 1 mile (1480 m) straight up from this camp. Toward the west is the North Col (23,182 ft, 7066 m), a snow-choked dip in the mountains straddling Everest's Northeast Ridge and Changtse. Most amazing of all is the ridge extending above the Pinnacles to the southwest: the striated rock summit of Everest. The top of this mountain appears phenomenally close, for it is little more than 8000 feet (2400 m) higher than Camp III. This is the closest nonclimbers can get to the top. With a pair of binoculars, you're almost there.

The gravel hills can be followed beside the glacier for **another 40 minutes** beyond Camp III, passing more littered campsites along the way. The elevation is around 21,200 feet (6460 m) where the moraine ends at the snowfields extending from the foot of the North Col. Don't attempt to walk across the glacier unless a safe route has been previously established.

The return journey from Camp III to base camp is a long walk that can be completed in **1 day.** If you have the time (and enough food), spend **2 days** walking out so you can enjoy the scenery and get your eyes off the ends of your boots.

The Kangshung Valley to East Everest Base Camp Trek

The Kangshung Valley/East Everest base camp region is one of the most remote trekking destinations in Central Tibet. The round-trip walk of **9 to 10 days** to this secluded base camp begins at Kharta (12,300 ft, 3750 m), a small administrative post on the Phung Chhu, not far from the Nepal border. Unlike the arid environs found a few ridges over in the Dzakaa Chhu Valley, this region is well watered by India's summer monsoon. Forests of scrub juniper and dwarf rhododendron cover the higher ridges and dense thickets of willows edge the creeks in the lower valleys. Farther to the south, in the Kaama Tsangpo Valley, the monsoon is virtually unimpeded, supporting a lush forest of conifers and deciduous trees.

Kharta is located 55 miles (90 km) to the southeast of Phadhruchi on a road descending the lower stretches of the Dzakaa Chhu. Trucks and tractor carts gather paying passengers in Phadhruchi for this half-day journey, though several days can pass without a vehicle going this way. If time is not a factor, walk to Kharta for **3 or 4 days** through the beautiful gorges and valleys of the Dzakaa Chhu. A burro and a guide can be hired in Phadhruchi and numerous camping sites can be found along the route.

To reach Kharta, follow the road that branches left (east) from the Rongphu road at the bridge crossing in Phadhruchi. The broad, green Dzakaa Chuu Valley narrows into a spectacular rocky gorge dotted with unusually large stands of scrubby trees, then opens out again into a deep desert canyon. About halfway to Kharta the Phung Chhu enters from the left (north), punching through a wild range of rugged peaks to absorb the Dzakaa Chhu. The road climbs above this confluence and remains high on a plateau of silt and rock debris all the way to Kharta, a small gathering of walled compounds that includes a boarding school for Tibetan children, two shops, a small health post, a few residences, and a very basic guest house. The "cadre" for this area arranges yaks and guides for trekkers heading to the Kangshung base camp and resides in the guest house. Few foreigners pass through Kharta, so the daily rates for a pack animal are about half the price commanded in the Dingri–Phadhruchi area. Tents and stoves are necessities due to the remote nature of this walk. All food should be purchased before arriving in Kharta.

The most direct route used by climbing expeditions to reach the Kangshung Valley and the base camp takes **4 to 5 days** via Langma La (17,500 ft, 5330 m). This is a spectacular walk with steep-sided valleys, glacial lakes, and, if weather allows, some of the grandest Himalayan scenery to be found. An alternate route to the East Everest area crosses Shao La (16,300 ft, 4970 m), a lower pass to the south of Langma La that approaches the Kangshung Glacier via the Kaama Tsangpo Valley. This walk is becoming popular with commercial trekking agencies, but requires **5 to 6 days.**

The route to both Langma La and Shao La heads south from Kharta on a trail that runs between the school walls and the compound below the guest house. This willow-lined path winds gently through terraced barley fields for **10 minutes** to an ancient-looking settlement called Chhöthang. Beyond these houses the trail descends a short way to join the road from Kharta. Follow this road to the south for **a few minutes** to where a smaller cart track turns off to the right (southwest) and climbs a hill of glacial moraine. This is the route to the Kangshung Glacier. The main road continues a short way toward the river along the base of this morainal ridge.

The cart track climbs from the road to the top of the ridge in **5 minutes.** Leaving the Phung Chhu behind, cross a desert plateau of scrub and boulders for **15 minutes** to reach the edge of the Kharta Tsangpo Valley. The track descends from here to the north (L) bank of this tributary, milky white with the glacial meltwaters spilling from the slopes of Kharta Changri (23,149 ft, 7056 m) and Khartaphu (23,720 ft, 7230 m) peaks. Fortified by this flowing water, the nearby desert terrain supports thickets of wild roses; brilliant red and black white-capped river chats flash above the water, hunting for insects. As the track winds upstream the valley walls open up, revealing distant views of great forested ridges. Langma La is at the head of a large tributary that enters from the left (south). The route over Shao La also ascends to the south via an adjacent valley.

About 1 hour from Kharta a long *mani* wall stretches beside the cart track. Meadows speckled with wildflowers line this section of the river. The track crosses to the right bank **30 minutes** beyond the *mani* wall. A small bridge has been erected here for foot traffic. About 100 yards (90 m) past this crossing a large trail branches left up to Kharta Yulbaa, the main village in the region. Most of the yaks for expeditions to the East Face come from here. The route to Langma La does not ascend to this settlement, but remains alongside the river. The vegetation is fairly thick here, with small parties of Prince Henri's laughing thrushes stealing through the undergrowth. Not far past the turnoff the cart track shrinks to a narrow trail.

The ridges to the north quickly recede from the river bank, exposing a gently sloping agricultural basin of terraced fields on the north (L) side of the valley. A small fortresslike settlement guards the entrance to this region. The rock walls of these houses are not painted white as in other areas in Central Tibet, enhancing the feeling that they are fortifications. Stacks of firewood are piled neatly atop the flat roofs of each building, creating an orange-brown ring of color above the somber gray walls.

The terrain on the south (L) bank becomes steeper and the trail climbs away from the river. **Less than 1 hour** beyond the turnoff for the village the trail forks before a small creek. The higher trail up to the left ascends beside this creek to Shao La. Well-acclimatized groups can reach this pass on the second day out of Kharta, though most parties would be wise to camp short of the pass and complete the crossing on the third day. There are several good campsites en route. Though it is a bit too far to reach in a day from Kharta, one of the finest places to pitch a tent is just below the pass beside a stunning aqua glacial tarn. If you camp at this lake or beside any body of water, be sure that your kitchen crew washes and rinses the cooking gear a good distance from the water.

Once over Shao La the trail drops steeply toward the Kaama Tsangpo. The route forks at a meadow camp high on the ridge side. The left branch descends through larch-and-pine forest into what has been called one of the most beautiful valleys in the world. **A long day**'s walk down from Shao La along the north (L) side of the valley is Sakyithang, a former salt depot and frontier trading post above the confluence with the Phung Chhu. The area is also a pilgrimage site, with old *chötaen* and Chhökyung Tsura, a protector's shrine. Logging in these forests was supposed to stop with the inauguration of the Chomolangma Nature Preserve, yet reports filter in that the cutting continues unabated. Luckily the trees are being felled with handsaws and hauled out by porters, a slow process that should prevent major deforestation before it is halted.

The junction to the right from the meadow camp ascends the north (L) side of the Kaama Tsangpo Valley across thick, scrubby slopes toward the Kangshung Valley. The base camp is **2¹/₂ days** from Shao La.

To continue to the Kangshung base camp via the Kharta Tsangpo Valley, take the lower right-hand trail at the fork where the routes split for Shao La and Langma La. Cross the creek and descend past a stone house with some of the largest old twisted birch trees to be found in the Himalaya. The trail rises behind this house and soon crosses another creek before climbing up the ridge side. Across the valley and high above the barley fields is a small white building tucked in a stand of stunted junipers. This *lhakhang,* tended by a monk and a nun, is called Tarpaling. Lower on the ridge is the site of Ganden Chhöfel *gompa,* a monastery that was visited when the Everest Reconnaissance team explored this valley in 1921.

Twenty minutes beyond the stone house a large creek spills down the ridge. Rock-hop across it, then descend past several large boulders onto a pleasant tree-lined path. This trail wanders for **15 minutes** through a series of barley fields and over several stone fences to reach the village of Lundrubling. Yaks cannot cross these stone barriers; another trail starts near the large creek, skirting the fields by traversing the slopes above the town. The two trails merge on the high barren ridge of moraine behind Lundrubling. On the far side of this ridge is the valley leading up to Langma La.

Lundrubling is a medieval-looking collection of stone houses and muddy alleyways. It is the last village before the pass, though a few other agricultural settlements are farther up the Kharta Tsangpo Valley. There are no shops here, but families often have milk, yogurt, *chhang, araa,* vegetables, and yak or goat meat for sale. Judging from the mud-encrusted pigs roaming around, there's a good chance a side of pork could be arranged as well.

Several trails continue west up the valley beyond the village. All of these eventually climb high onto the morainal ridge to meet the well-graded yak trail that bypasses the town. The most obvious route leads west through the barley fields, then ascends steeply up the ridge along the north (L) side of a small creek. Following this trail, intersect the wide yak path **25 minutes** from Lundrubling. Continue climbing through a series of switchbacks for **another 10 minutes** to the small cairns at the ridge summit (13,900 ft, 4240 m).

The trail to Langma La now turns left (south), away from the Kharta Tsangpo. Descend from this summit for **a few minutes** and arrive at several sprawling campsites along the stream draining this side valley. Cross to the west (L) bank on a stone walkway and follow the trail onto a low ridge, the top of which is crowned with a prominent campsite (14,000 ft, 4270 m) offering grand views. Deep marmot holes puncture the grassy flats, and tall willows and wild rosebushes nearby act as a sanctuary for redstarts, rose finches, and little warblers. Although this camp is only **4 hours** from Kharta, it is a good place to spend the night to acclimatize before the steep climb to the pass. Firewood is available, but encourage your kitchen staff to cook with their fuel stoves rather than using the local wood.

The obvious trail that leads from this hilltop camp into the bushes near the stream is not the route to Langma La. The correct trail rises steeply up the west (L) ridge from here. The upper section can be seen cutting through the brush-covered slopes farther along the ridge. Ascend steadily on a rocky trail, passing groves of stunted juniper and sprays of wildflowers. The bushes eventually give way to alpine grasses, and **40 minutes** above the campsite the trail reaches the crest of a ridge spur (14,600 ft, 4450 m). This low hill extending across the valley is the terminus of a former glacial advance. When the glacier retreated it also dumped the large boulder sitting in the creek and left the upper portion of the valley considerably broader and flatter than the lower section.

The trail is somewhat obscure from here onward as it climbs along the west (L) ridge side. Ascend from the spur for **1 hour** through more juniper and clusters of dwarf rhododendron to reach the nose of another ridge (15,650 ft, 4770 m). The valley swings right (west) and enters a box canyon enclosed by dark, jagged peaks. The route to Langma La ascends to a well-defined gap in the ridge with a plummeting waterfall. Although this looks like the pass, the true summit crosses a higher ridge farther to the west.

From the last ridge spur, traverse along the slopes for **20 minutes** to a meadow called Lhatse (16,100 ft, 4900 m), where stone shelters have been constructed under the ledges of several large boulders. This last camp before Langma La is a beautifully stark, high mountain setting at the base of a crumbling cliff. Consider stopping here for the night in order to acclimatize for the pass crossing. Strong parties can push on to Langma La, which is a **stiff 2 hours** away, not including rest stops, with **another hour** of descending before the next suitable camp.

The approach to the pass climbs onto the talus cascades immediately behind the Lhatse camp. Zigzag steeply through this rubble to a field of larger, broken rocks. Reach the waterfall summit (16,500 ft, 5030 m) **40 minutes** from the camp. The source of this water is a pale aqua lake surrounded by ramparts of crumbling rock. Cross to the south (R) side of the creek, then climb for **a few minutes** to the crest of a small ridge spur where a *la-dzay* with prayer flags overlooks the lake. Langma La is the notch in the ridge another 1000 feet (300 m) up to the west. The trail descends from the *la-dzay* down to the far end of the lake. Cross to the north (L) side of the inlet to begin the final climb to the pass. Rushing water surges everywhere, racing noisily through the broken cliffs at the base of these mountains. Despite this austere environment, patches of grass and delicately petaled blue poppies manage to find a foothold between the rocks. **About 1 hour** from the lake the trail climbs onto a huge glacial moraine. Continue climbing through more switchbacks, reaching the summit prayer flags (17,500 ft, 5330 m) in **another 30 minutes.**

On clear days the view south from Langma La is outstanding. Makalu (27,805 ft, 8475 m) is the impressive peak to the southwest that dwarfs all of the other summits from this angle, including Everest. Chomolonzo (25,557 ft, 7790 m) is the closer, north peak of Makalu; Pethangtse (22,106 ft, 6738 m) is the lone bullet-shaped summit a little farther to the right (west); and the big trio at the far west end of the Kangshung Valley, from left to right, are Lhotse Shar (27,513 ft, 8386 m), Lhotse (27,890 ft, 8501 m), and Everest (29,028 ft, 8848 m). The valleys and ridges below the snowline are richly covered with grasses and thick vegetation nurtured by the monsoon rains that manage to sneak behind these mountains.

The trail from Langma La descends steadily, passing above two small lakes. After **10 minutes** angle around a rocky ridge spur, then continue descending to the right under smooth granite cliffs. The trail can be easily lost, so look for the small rock cairns that help mark this route. The trail passes to the right of a tall rounded boulder near the base of the cliffs. Perhaps a half dozen lakes of varying sizes can be seen from here, scattered across several shallow basins lower in the valley. Descend southwest from the boulder to a crumbling stone hut beside Shurim Tsho (16,500 ft, 5030 m; my yak man called it Shumori Tsho), a deep lake located

Woodcutter in the east Everest region

1 hour below the pass. The terrain is considerably flatter here and the trail turns right (west) from the hut. Descend in **15 minutes** to a smaller lake. Follow the trail down the north (R) side of this lake's outlet for **5 minutes,** then hop over to the south (L) side. Angle to the left (southwest) across the tundra for **5 minutes,** then swing to the right (south) around the end of a ridge. Beyond here the path becomes a braid of narrow animal trails. Choose one of these tracks and continue the gentle descent.

About 15 minutes beyond the creek crossing are several good areas for camping off to the right (west). This is a spectacular location (16,000 ft, 4880 m) in clear weather, with craggy glaciated peaks rising steeply all around. Makalu is just across the valley and still reigns over its larger cousins to the west. The tundra is lush, considering the elevation, attracting a *drogpa* family each summer. If you camp here, keep an eye on your gear. The children of these nomads know that unwatched backpacks and tents are a treasure trove of food and useful items, all of which would be sorely missed in the middle of a remote trek.

The next suitable campsites are **another 2 hours** away at the bottom of the valley. The descent from the tundra camps into this drainage continues south. The grassy slopes are like the moorlands of Scotland, especially when misty waves of fog pour over the hilltops. Follow the animal tracks over the hump of a low ridge for **30 minutes** to a shallow glacial pond. Cross to the south (L) side of the outlet creek, where a good trail quickly materializes. Descend first to the left (south), then down the scrubby south (L) edge of a low gully. **Twenty minutes** beyond this pond the trail leaves the ridge side, turning left (south) onto a long, narrow plateau of sloping green pasture. This odd piece of land, suspended on the edge of a very steep drop-off, was the gap between the ridge and the lateral moraine of a tremendous glacier that once flowed out of the mountains on the right. The glacier has retreated considerably, but it must have been at least 1000 feet (300 m) thick to deposit a moraine of this height. Several other troughlike depressions located farther up the ridge from this plateau suggest that previous glacial advances were even larger.

The Kangshung Valley is directly across the canyon to the west; near its mouth the Kangdoshung Glacier spills from the west side of Chomolonzo. Past advances of this glacier have left a great wall of debris that swirls onto the valley floor. The great piles of rock and rubble farther up the valley are the terminus of the much larger Kangshung Glacier. The drainage to the left (south) that descends from the mouth of the Kangshung Valley is the head of the heavily forested Kaama Tsangpo Valley.

The trail from Langma La follows a meandering creek bed down the narrow strip of pasture for **30 minutes,** weaving between glacially deposited boulders that geologists refer to as glacial erratics. A campsite (14,900 ft, 4540 m) with several fire rings is **15 minutes** beyond a prominent triangular erratic in the middle of the meadow. Unfortunately, this spot is a long walk from a reliable water source, except during the height of monsoon. The panorama here is stunning. At the far end of the Kangshung Valley Mount Everest finally emerges from hiding, providing the best views of its East Face until the base camp. The trail turns sharply to the right from this camp, plunging off the edge of the elevated pasture. Descend rapidly through scrub juniper and dwarf rhododendron, reaching the valley floor (14,100 ft, 4300 m) in **30 minutes.**

Good campsites straddle both sides of the stream between the meadow edges and the willow groves. The next camp of any size is **more than 2 hours** away, including a rugged 1200-foot (370 m) ascent alongside the Kangshung Glacier. The approach to this glacier from Shao La enters these same meadows by way of a trail that climbs the north (L) side of the Kaama Valley. A wooden bridge spans the stream between two low hills of moraine bordering the lower end of the meadow campsites. At one time these hills were a continuous ridge of deposits, probably left by an advance of the Kangdoshung Glacier. The flow of the stream would have been blocked by the intruding wall, causing a small lake to form. Eventually the water sliced an exit low enough to drain the lake, leaving these flat meadows and willow groves in its place.

The route up the Kangshung Valley crosses the bridge to the west (R) bank of the stream, following the base of the hillside briefly before reentering the dense scrub. Some of the rhododendrons in this area are at least 6 feet high (1.8 m), remarkably tall for this elevation. Beyond here the valley floor is a succession of rolling morainal hills. **Thirty minutes** past the bridge is a creek crossing that can be troublesome during heavy rains. The trail remains easy to follow and eventually turns to the right (west) as the hills smooth out. A deteriorating herder's hut (14,250 ft, 4340 m) is located **30 minutes** beyond the creek crossing, though it is not easy to find unless you are directed there. The hut is **a few minutes** to the right (north) of the trail in a shallow, marshy depression. The roof has several large holes in it, but there is enough room nearby to pitch one or two small tents. My yak man called this part of the valley Pethang. In 1921 George Mallory of the British Reconnaissance used a base camp farther up the valley known by a similar name, Pethang Ringmo.

The Kangshung Valley, which we nicknamed Thunder Valley, absolutely roars with the sound of rushing water, rock falls, and avalanches. During the summer monsoon the snow that accumulates daily on the peaks starts rumbling about noon and continues to fall noisily throughout most nights. Another interesting feature of this area and the Kaama Tsangpo Valley is the giant wild rhubarb, with great leaves several feet long and thick, tasty-looking stalks. Watch out. I stewed a batch one morning to complement our breakfast. The yak man declined his share with apprehension, but we thought it was great. When it came time to load the yaks we were so nauseated we had to unpack our gear and layover an extra day to recover. The wild mint that grows in this region is much safer and makes a nice tea.

Continue ascending along the north (L) side of the valley through the dense scrub. **Less than 1 hour** past the creek crossing, the trail reaches a steep slope where the hills of moraine suddenly fall away to the river. When the 1921 British Reconnaissance came up this valley, the Kangdoshung Glacier reached all the way across to this point, nearly sealing off the valley. The glacier is now considerably smaller, leaving this giant scar. The trail traverses these rocky slopes for **a few minutes** to the base of a large rock slide, which is relatively stable but should be crossed with caution. The trail climbs steeply for about 100 feet (30 m) beside a long talus slope before turning into the field of fallen boulders and loose scree. The route across the slide is cairned and not hard to follow, taking **about 45 minutes** to ascend to the far side. To be safe, walk this section one at a time and give each person a few minutes' lead before anyone else starts to cross.

From the end of the slide the trail traverses high above the rushing river along scrub-covered slopes. Mount Everest and Lhotse come into view, and **30 minutes** beyond the slide the trail descends into a grassy basin of meadows

Chomolonzo peak appearing through the mist above the Kangshung Valley

(15,300 ft, 4660 m). This large grazing area is a fine, protected camp, though Everest is hidden from view. A more spectacular camp is **another hour** up the valley. To reach this site, cross the main stream draining the basin and ascend the hills to the west. A trail follows the south (L) side of a smaller tributary flowing from these hills. After **35 minutes** cross to the north (R) bank of this creek. The trail continues climbing up the main valley (west), though the source of the creek turns away to the right. Wind through a series of small drainages between the morainal hills for **20 minutes,** then emerge onto a large meadow of lush grass (16,150 ft, 4920 m).

This is one of my favorite camps in the Himalaya. During the monsoon this lovely plateau is ablaze with a thick carpet of yellow wildflowers. All around are huge snowy-white ice floes pouring from the peaks into the Kangshung Glacier. Mount Everest, Lhotse, and Lhotse Shar dominate the west end of the valley; the Makalu–Chomolonzo massif provides endless excitement with its booming avalanches. Although this view of Everest cannot rival the grandeur of its North Face, the gentleness of so many flowers in such rugged alpine terrain makes this a memorable camp. The yak man said the name for this particular part of the valley is Opka.

The meadow is graced with three unusual yak dung storage shelters constructed with stones mortared together by yak dung. If you don't have a tent for your guide these small enclosures can be waterproofed with sheets of plastic or a rain fly.

Most expeditions establish their base camp **2 to 3 hours** farther up the valley (16,400 ft, 5000 m) at the site George Mallory referred to as Pethang Ringmo. This is where the Kangshung Glacier bends to the right, spilling off the northern flank of Mount Everest. It is also the last point to which yaks can carry loads up the valley. Beyond here climbers must either use porters or carry the gear themselves across the glacier to begin their assault on the East Face. Because the Opka meadows are so delightful, the higher camp could be saved for a dayhike, but one advantage of sleeping at the base camp is the opportunity to hike onto the high ridge (19,600 ft, 5940 m) to the north of this camp, overlooking both the Kangshung and the upper Kharta Tsangpo valleys. Lieutenant Colonel Charles K. Howard-Bury ascended this spectacular vantage point. Looking to the left of Everest he could see "a huge amphitheater of mighty peaks culminating in a new and unsurveyed peak, 28,100 feet in height, to which we gave the name Lhotse, which in Tibetan means the South Peak." The massive, Matterhorn-like peak looming above the base camp to the left of Lhotse Shar is Pethangtse (22,014 ft, 6710 m). En route to this ridge-top viewpoint are two beautiful glacial lakes nestled between the rocky slopes.

The return to Kharta, which is considerably lower in elevation than base camp, can be completed in just **3 or 4 days** by recrossing Langma La. Returning to Kharta by way of the Kaama Valley and Shao La is slightly longer and requires **4 to 5 days.**

10   The Shishapangma Region

(Map 8, page 231)

Shishapangma (26,397 ft, 8046 m) is probably the least known of the world's fourteen highest peaks, despite being only 50 miles (80 km) northeast of Kathmandu. The mountain is hidden from Nepal, tucked behind the Langtang Himal and the main Himalayan range. It was the last 8000-meter (26,246 ft) peak to be climbed and is the only one entirely within Tibet.

Shishapangma, Xixabangma in Chinese, is known to the Nepalese Hindus as Gosainthan, a sacred abode of the god Shiva. The meaning of Shishapangma is not certain; translations vary from "Range or Crest above the Meadow" to an explanation the locals gave us, "Meadow of Dead Meat." The first group of mountaineers to attempt its summit was a huge Chinese expedition in 1964; they also built a road to what is now the north base camp. The first expedition to attempt the mountain from the south was a British team in 1982 that made its way up Shishapangma via the immense 6500-foot (2000 m) southwest face.

With the opening of Tibet to tourism in the early 1980s, Shishapangma suddenly became one of the most visible and easily visited 8000-meter peaks. It towers impressively over the Lhasa–Kathmandu Highway, and a road goes to the base of it. Groups regularly drive to the north base camp and several expeditions attempt the summit from this side every year.

On the opposite side of the mountain, where yak trails are the only roads, the round-trip journey to the southern Shishapangma base camp takes **4 to 5 days** and is one of Tibet's best-kept trekking secrets. The access for this route is the Tshongde Phu Chhu Valley. The river, marked Phu Chhu or Nyanang Chhu on some maps, is a tributary of the wild Bhö Chhu, the headwaters of Nepal's Sunkosi River.

The trailhead is at Nyelam, also known as Nyanang (km marker 694; 12,400 ft, 3780 m), an old trading post on the Lhasa–Kathmandu caravan route, 23 miles (37 km) from the border town of Khasa. (Nyelam means "the Road to Hell"; its Nepalese name is Kuti.) From Nyelam, the Tshongde Phu Chhu Valley seems an insignificant drainage, but not far upstream it transforms into a spectacular arena of snowy peaks and tumbling glaciers. In addition to hosting the Shishapangma massif, the valley is buttressed along its western flanks by the Jugal Himal, a surprisingly rugged, unbroken chain of peaks along the frontier with Nepal with at least ten summits over 21,000 feet (6500 m).

For groups driving overland from Nepal across Tibet, Nyelam is the logical place to spend most of a day and a night acclimatizing before crossing the first and one of the highest passes en route, Thang La (17,060 ft, 5200 m). Nyelam is only a few hour's drive up the Bhö Chhu Canyon from the border, yet the elevation gain is more than 5000 feet (1500 m); Thang La is almost 5000 feet higher again. The town of Nyelam is of little interest and the hotel facilities are quite basic, but nearby are several fine dayhikes. Even if you have already been to Lhasa and have arrived in Nyelam for a trek, consider spending a day out walking to get in shape for the ascent into the mountains.

Dayhikes near Nyelam

A well-known historical site near Nyelam is Pelgyeling *gompa* (km marker 683), a simple, attractive temple that has been rebuilt over the meditation cave of the eleventh- and twelfth-century poet-*lama* Milarepa. The hike to this cave hermitage takes **2¹/₂ hours** and is a scenic walk above the Bhö Chhu Canyon, following the highway the entire way. Pelgyeling is 7 miles (11 km) north of Nyelam, set below the road on a steep slope overlooking the river. A path clambers down the hillside from several houses, passing a long building of monks' residences to the main temple below it. The monastery was completely destroyed in the 1960s, the buildings dismantled rock by rock. The villagers rebuilt the site with financing from Sera monastery and donations raised by the Pelgyeling *rimpoche,* who is now living in Kathmandu.

The interior of Pelgyeling's small assembly hall is simple but well kept by the handful of monks associated with the monastery. The beautifully executed frescoes are the work of a Nepalese artist. A large figure of Sakyamuni is on the wall behind the altar. On the right-hand wall is a portrait of Milarepa in the classical pose with his hand held to his ear, indicating he is singing one of his lessons. The white cotton dress he wears is the special garb of tantric practitioners who have mastered *tummo,* the art of spiritually generating unusually high body temperatures. The red sash across his shoulder is a strap used to support one's back and knees during extended periods of deep meditation. On the opposite wall is a painting of Marpa the Translator, Milarepa's beloved *guru.* Unlike most ascetics of his time, Marpa did not renounce his family and possessions; he was a married man with children and tilled the fields near his home. Instead of being portrayed in the robes of a monk or a hermit, he is always shown wearing the clothes of a lay person.

To the left of the assembly hall entrance is the black doorway to the Stomach Cave, where Milarepa spent many winters in meditation wearing only his thin cotton robes. The low opening leads into an enchanting rock overhang, the ceiling blackened from fires and speckled with dabs of *tsampa* offerings like stars on a dark sky. A large boulder rests inside the cave, suspended by a rock support in a peculiar manner. Milarepa is said to have lifted this boulder using his powers of concentration during a debate with several scholarly monks from a monastery in Nyelam. The monks were convinced that Milarepa was a heretic, and challenged his knowledge of Buddhist doctrine and logic. While discussing whether space is obstructing or nonobstructing, the yogic master chose the seemingly illogical position that the large rock in the cave was nonobstructing. To prove his point, Milarepa used a special meditational technique to pass his body through the boulder in several different ways. He then lifted up the great rock with his hands, and

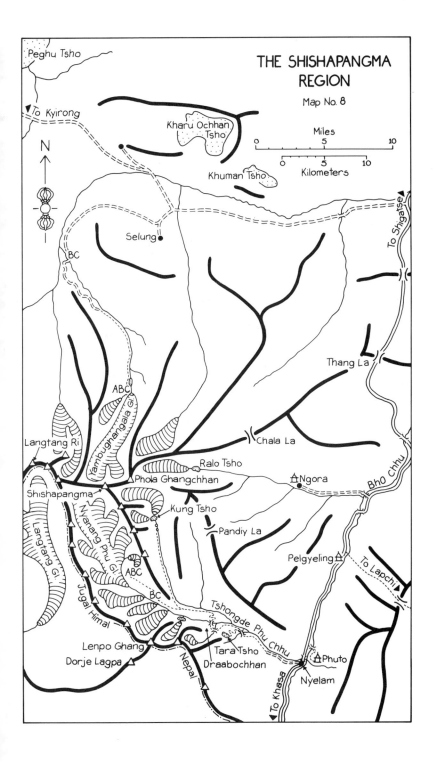

Shishapangma's rarely seen Southwest Face

called to his disciple Rechungpa to place a stone pillar underneath for support. The caretaker of the cave will show you the imprints of Milarepa's fingers where he held the rock. A lone figure of the poet-*lama* has been placed on the spot where he once meditated.

The *drubphuu* of Rechungpa is set into the slopes above the main temple. Rechungpa is considered by many Tibetans to have been the greatest, as well as the most unruly, of Milarepa's disciples. In the Yarlung Valley a large Kargyüpa monastery was built over one of his meditation caves (see "Dayhikes near Tsethang"). A small door in the hillside near the wooden dwelling of a resident monk leads into his low black cave, the ceiling also decorated with pilgrims' *tsampa* offerings. On the altar are huge clay *tsha-tshas* of the *bodhisattva* Chenrezig, as well as several very old wooden statues, probably of Indian origin. Outside the cave near the monk's residence is a shrine for the *gön-po* Mahakala.

In the next valley to the east from Pelgyeling is Lapchi, one of the most sacred pilgrimage sites in Tibet and another important Milarepa meditation cave. Unfortunately the trek from Pelgyeling over Ghang La, which takes **2 days,** enters an area closed to foreigners; the well-preserved monastery at Lapchi and its nearby cave hermitages straddle the Nepal–Tibet border.

A hermitage site close to Nyelam is Phutö *gompa,* a small, dilapidated building above the Bhö Chhu's east (L) bank. If you look across (west) the river from the Nyelam hotel, it's possible to see the prayer flags of this old Nyingmapa retreat, **2 to 3 hours** away, which is hidden in a steep stream gully cutting into the ridge. The trick is to find the crossing to the east (L) side, for the bridge sometimes washes away during monsoon. The two monks who once resided here are gone and the site is unoccupied, but the views looking back toward the Jugal Himal are worth the effort to reach this site. Farther up the drainage from the hermitage is a stunted forest where the Chinese residents from Nyelam come to gather large edible mushrooms during the summer.

If you have an entire day free at Nyelam but not enough time for a several-day trek, the hike up to the Draabochhan *drogpa* camp (13,500 ft, 4110 m) takes **3 hours** and is a beautiful walk along the tumbling Tshongde Phu Chhu. Depending on how early you start, it may be possible to reach the end of the Nyanang Phu Glacier and a large lake, located **about 1¹/₂ hours** beyond the camp. About the only way to glimpse Shishapangma's south side on a dayhike from Nyelam is to tackle the **4-hour** ascent to Tara Tsho (14,200 ft, 4330 m), an unusual holy lake trapped high in a ridge of glacial moraine above the Tshongde Phu Chhu Valley. Both of these walks are detailed below as part of "The South Shishapangma Base Camp Trek."

Dayhikes from the North Shishapangma Base Camp

The north Shishapangma base camp (16,100 ft, 4910 m) is 28 miles (46 km) southwest of the Lhasa–Kathmandu Highway. The access road leaves the highway near kilometer marker 614 to enter a broad, sparsely inhabited desert valley. Some 18 miles (29 km) from the turnoff the road fords a deep creek, then immediately divides on the far west (L) side. The larger, right-hand fork leads to one of Tibet's immense lakes, Peghu Tsho, then continues west to the town of Kyirong and beyond to the Mount Kailas region.

The left-hand turn is the road to the northern base camp. A few kilometers beyond this junction is Selung (15,400 ft, 4690 m), the largest village in this region and the only permanent settlement en route to the base camp. All of the nearly fifty families residing here are herders; this is the place to hire yaks for expeditions climbing Shishapangma. Selung is also the source of some of the finest horses in Tibet. If you need accommodation, a former village elder enjoys having foreign visitors. His house is one of the first buildings on the right as you enter the settlement. Though there are no shops, some supplies can be purchased through him or other families.

The base camp is another 10 miles (15 km) from Selung around a ridge of barren hills. The lone but massive summit looming over the road beyond Selung is not Shishapangma, but Ghangbenchhan (23,658 ft, 7211 m), the tallest of the peaks forming the watershed between the headwaters of the Trisuli and Arun rivers. As the road swings around to the south both Shishapangma (26,397 ft, 8046 m) and its pointy neighbor Phola Ghangchhan, "Big Snow Grandfather" (25,269 ft, 7702 m), finally come into view. (Phola Ghangchhan is known as

Molamenquing in Chinese.) The base camp is an elongated series of meadows wedged between the ridge and the river draining from Shishapangma and the Yambughangala Glacier, the main ice floe on this side of the mountain. The summit route established by the 1964 Chinese expedition ascends the west (L) side of this glacier, then traverses its upper flanks to approach the mountain.

One of the best dayhikes from base camp is to follow the river up toward the advance base camp and explore the snout of this glacier's unusually jumbled surface of frozen ice waves. Another good hike follows the crest of the ridge directly across (south of) the river from the base camp, providing outstanding views of the entire Shishapangma–Peghu Tsho region. The base camp is so far from the glacier that most people cannot walk to the advance camp and return in a single day, but a jeep route has been established that crosses to the river's south (L) side at the base camp and continues 5 miles (8 km) south to a plateau above the river (16,900 ft, 5150 m). Except for the river crossing near base camp the track is generally very good. If you are with a commercial group, try to cajole your driver into taking you the extra distance and have him pick you up later in the day.

The plateau embankment is about 150 feet (45 m) above the river and marked with cairns. The walk from here to advance base camp takes **3 to 4 hours** and follows the west (L) bank for most of the way, though you might need to cross over and back again depending on the course of the river. The advance camps (17,500 ft, 5330 m) are usually established above a small lake near the nose of the Yambughangala Glacier or a little farther up in the trough between the glacier and the west (L) ridge. If you have time, climb up the side of the ridge or up the moraine for views of the ice floe. A spectacular display of icy white pinnacles extends for its entire length, an unusal feature for a Himalayan glacier.

For the best views of Shishapangma, don't follow the river from the end of the jeep track. Instead, climb up the ridge and head south along its crest. Aim for the obvious summit (19,300 ft, 5880 m) of these gently sloping hills, though you need not be on top to enjoy the panoramas. The walk is a deceptively long, breath-consuming journey, so allow **at least 4 to 5 hours** to reach the top from the end of the jeep track. Bring plenty of water, for this is a dry ridge, and carry extra clothing for protection from the afternoon winds. If your time is short but you are well acclimatized, it is possible to combine these two walks by descending from the ridge crest to the glacier and the advance camps, then returning via the river to the end of the jeep track.

The South Shishapangma Base Camp Trek

The round-trip trek from Nyelam to the south Shishapangma base camp takes **4 or 5 days** and is one of Tibet's finest high alpine walks. It is also one of the few treks that does not involve a pass crossing, plus the pace is leisurely enough to allow dayhikes into remote side valleys where blue sheep and even a snow leopard or two are known to live. The best time is generally from mid-May through October, though snowstorms may occur any month of the year. The rain shadow created by the Shishapangma massif blocks most of India's monsoon, bringing only sporadic summer showers to the barren northern slopes. On the southern side the climate is remarkably different. Here the monsoon manages to push over the Jugal Himal, bringing rain most nights (and some days) from June until early September and nourishing lush meadows and outstanding displays of wildflowers high into the mountains. A tent is highly recommended and a fuel stove is necessary.

Nyelam has a number of shops and small department stores where basics such as noodles, milk powder, tea, yak butter, sweets, and canned fruit are available. Rice can usually be purchased through one of the Chinese restaurants, and they may also sell a few fresh vegetables. Kerosene can be found if you ask around, and it should be possible to have a Tibetan family to make you a batch of *bhalay,* wheat flour flat breads.

Hiring pack animals at Nyelam is often a problem in the summer. All of the horses and yak are pastured high in the hills, a half-day walk above the town at a herding camp called Draabochhan. Most commercial trekking companies will send someone to arrange pack animals in advance. Otherwise, your only choices are to send word up to the herders and hope that someone will arrive the following day, or hire porters to carry your gear to the camp. Hiring someone may seem the logical alternative, but the Khasa–Nyelam–Dingri area is notorious for its troublesome porters. They only carry small loads, charge twice as much as a pack animal would cost, and typically complain the entire way. On a winter visit to Tibet in 1987 the road between Khasa and Nyelam was blocked with snow up to 20 feet (6 m) deep in places, forcing us to hire two porters to get our gear to Nyelam. Halfway along the porters sat down and demanded double the price we had negotiated, plus their friend who was walking along with them but not carrying a load was to be paid as well, or they weren't going any farther. We eventually settled on a wage lower than their demand, but we were forced to pay their friend in order to secure a deal. Also, watch your gear in this area: these folks have been known to remove things from unlocked packs and side pockets. Don't let your porters stray behind or get too far ahead on the trail.

The route to Draabochhan and the south Shishapangma base camp starts at Tundya *mani,* a small prayer-wheel temple in the upper part of Nyelam. A path leads around the shrine's left side, then enters a series of terraced potato fields in the hills behind the town. In **less than 10 minutes** the last houses are passed and the trail leaves the terraces. Descend toward the south (R) bank of the Tshongde Phu on a wide track, passing a hydroelectric plant on the opposite shore. It doesn't take long to notice a remarkable transformation in the vegetation as you near the river. Little creeks and springs tumble everywhere from the hills of glacial rubble, nourishing a delightful array of greenery and color: flowering shrubs and wild rosebushes crowd beside the trail, yellow primroses stretch upward on stems almost 2 feet tall, several types of Edelweiss crouch near the ground, and the tallest mountain irises I've ever seen rise majestically between the rocks. As the valley broadens, cultivated fields once again line both sides of the trail. At the head of these terraces, **less than 1 hour** from the temple, is a small stone hut and a much larger but ruined farmhouse (12,800 ft, 3900 m). The first snowy peaks of the Jugal Himal poke over the ridges to the left (west).

The trail now threads through a section of thick brush along the left side of the old farmhouse. The path remains somewhat indistinct for **a few minutes** until it passes a large glacial boulder, then opens out and leads onto rolling morainal hills. **Twenty minutes** above the ruined house cross a wood and stone bridge spanning a creek. The route to base camp continues to the right up the main valley.

The smaller trail to the left heading west up the creek's west (L) ridge is the pilgrimage trail to the holy lake Tara Tsho. Prayer flags flutter from the bushes and a cairn can be seen on the first of two camellike humps along the ridge line. Tara Tsho is a long climb of $2^{1}/_{2}$ **to 3 hours** from here on a steep trail. The lake is quite large, though it remains hidden until you're fairly close. The shoreline (14,200 ft, 4330 m) is speckled with hundreds of small stone offering piles and larger cairns with prayer flags, for each year a pilgrimage occurs here on the Saga Dawa festival. Tara Tsho has neither inlet nor outlet, and is said to be 130 feet (40 m) deep. According to local legends, the lake manifested from a piece of ice brought here by a *lama* returning from Mount Kailas. My guess is that the lake actually did originate from a piece of ice, but from a huge chunk left by the glacier that once filled the valley. The lake sits in a broad plateau of glacial debris that must have been deposited by an enormous ice floe. As the glacier retreated, a section of ice could have been stranded in the huge tailings of moraine. Today the seepage from rain and melted snow, and perhaps an underground stream, helps to maintain the lake's water level. The snowy summits of the Jugal Himal rise impressively beyond the lake, and on the far side (north) of the valley is the Shishapangma massif. The main summit is at the back of this group; Phola Ghangchhan is the tall pointed peak to the right.

The pilgrims make from one to three circumambulations of the lake, then descend to Nyelam the same way they arrived. If you're continuing up the valley to the herders' camp at Draabochhan, you can descend directly from the lake to this camp. There's no trail, but it is possible to pick a route down to the valley floor. From the far right (north) corner of the lake, climb to the ridge top (14,800 ft, 4510 m), then continue north. As you descend, aim for a large boulder with prayer flags in the middle of the Draabochhan meadows.

The main trail to the south base camp bypasses Tara Tsho, continuing up the Tshongde Phu Chhu on the right fork from the wood and stone bridge. The valley begins to open again with views of the distant mountains from large meadows surrounded by thick stands of white and purple rhododendrons, which bloom in June. **About $1^{1}/_{2}$ hours** above the bridge, cross another creek on a simple plank bridge. The giant boulder to the right is Draabochhan, the Big Rock. A small stone herders' hut (13,500 ft, 4110 m) is **a few minutes** farther to the left. Although these meadows are only **3 hours** from Nyelam, consider stopping for the night in this picturesque valley to acclimatize. Potential campsites are everywhere, but ask the herders first before setting up your tents. The next camps en route to the base camp are beyond the top of the huge morainal ridge to the north across the valley, nearly 1500 feet (450 m) higher than here.

If you arrive here early in the afternoon, you can hike farther up the Tshongde Phu Valley for $1^{1}/_{2}$ **hours** to a large milky lake that sits precariously behind a wall of glacial debris.

Dri *(female yak) milking time in the pastures above Nyelam*

Other dayhikes from Draabochhan include the hard **2-hour** ascent to Tara Tsho straight up the south (R) ridge spur to the southeast, and the walk up the sweeping side valley below this same ridge. Following this valley, in **less than 1 hour** you'll reach a sprawling meadow beneath a glacier that pours from a basin of peaks. The locals call the main summit of this group Jhakyung, the "Garuda Peak"; in Nepal it is known as Gyalzen peak. Blue sheep descend from the ridges to graze on the meadow, and when we were at the south base camp a snow leopard attacked a baby yak here. I cannot help but feel an energizing sense of awe knowing that somewhere high among these ridges, one of these magnificent cats might be peering down at me, silently watching my every move.

The route to the south base camp leaves the valley floor at Draabochhan, crossing the river on a wooden bridge near the big rock. Before setting off, look north across the valley for the stone cairns atop the north (L) wall of glacial moraine. The main trail swings far to the left from the bridge before it turns back toward these cairns, but dozens of interlacing yak tracks make it easy to lose the way through the boulders and thick bushes. Reach the cairns on the ridge top in **1 hour** from Draabochhan. From the summit the trail angles left and parallels the ridge crest, sometimes becoming faint but staying above the plateaulike trough that separates the hills of moraine from the true northern (L) ridges. In **30 minutes** pass the mouth of a broad tributary valley entering from the right. A route up this drainage crosses Pandiy La to the village of Ngora, **1 day** away from here. Ngora can also be reached by a jeep road that turns off the Lhasa–Kathmandu Highway at kilometer marker 667. Near this village is Ngora *gompa,* a small Nyingmapa temple. A little farther up the valley is Ralo *drubphuu,* the meditation cave of Ra Lotsawa, a renowned eleventh-century scholar and translator of tantric texts who was born in Nyelam. Also near Ngora is Ralo Tsho, a large lake at the base of another glacier from the Shishapangma massif. An old caravan route heads north from Ngora over Chala La to Selung village and Peghu Tsho, on the north side of Shishapangma.

The route to the south base camp continues straight ahead (northwest) along hills thick with dwarf rhododendrons. Some trails stay on the hillside while others descend to the edges of large meadows that separate the moraine from the north (L) ridge. **One hour** beyond the valley to Ngora is Shingdip (14,950 ft, 4560 m), a beautiful meadow camp with a large boulder near the junction of converging morainal valleys. The south base camp is only **2 hours** beyond here following the main valley west, but it is nearly 1500 feet (450 m) higher in elevation. Consider stopping here for the night, or perhaps two nights.

If you do take a rest day, consider a dayhike of **2¹/₂ to 3 hours** up the valley to the right (north) to Kung Tsho (16,200 ft, 4940 m), a turquoise lake at the base of glaciers flowing from Shishapangma, Phola Ghangchhan (25,269 ft, 7702 m), Pungpa Ri (24,426 ft, 7445 m), and Nyanang Ri (23,199 ft, 7071 m). A trail follows the west (R) side of the stream up to two smaller lakes in a flat basin. Kung Tsho is close to the base of the mountains **30 minutes or more** farther to the left (northwest). The best view of the peaks, including Shishapangma, is from the ridges of moraine along the east (L) side of the valley, **1 hour or more** beyond the two smaller lakes.

From Shingdip, a cross-country route continues west toward the base camp. As you ascend the main valley, angle left toward the hills until you reach the crest of the ridge. The edge of the moraine falls steeply to the Nyanang Phu Glacier, and the Jugal Himal towers across the valley. Stay on the ridge for **1 hour or more** until it ends at a deep circular basin. Drop to a small saddle (15,800 ft, 4820 m), then angle into the hills on the right. As you ascend, look farther up to the right (north) for a craggy, pyramid shaped peak of dark gray rock. Using this summit as a bearing, chose a route a little to its left; the base camp (16,350 ft, 4980 m) is just below it by a glacial lake.

Shishapangma is out of view from base camp, but the Jugal Himal is a worthy stand-in. Directly across the valley is the star in this cast of snowy rock faces, Lenpo Ghang (23,238 ft, 7083 m), the highest peak in the range. To its left is Gur Karop Ri (22,552 ft, 6874 m), and behind them but hidden is Dorje Lagpa (22,938 ft, 6990 m), a prominent double summit visible from Kathmandu. On a higher ledge above the base camp is another glacial lake.

Shishapangma can first be seen from a boulder-studded plateau **1 hour** above the base camp. Walk around the left (south) side of the lake, then ascend the steep ridge behind it, angling up to the left as you go. Dwarf rhododendrons just inches tall cover the hillside here, though not much higher they are replaced by tundra grasses, hearty cushion plants, and stunted but colorful wildflowers. Continue climbing over rolling hills for **30 minutes,** then angle up to the right toward an obvious boulder with cairns stacked on top. Reach the rock in **another 15 minutes.** The Jugal Himal wraps arms of peaks around the valley, trying to gather in the group of summits that make an appearance farther up to the right (north). Sweeping high at the back of these newcomers is the steep southwest face of Shishapangma. The closest mountain was appropriately dubbed the "Ice Tooth" by the 1982 Southwest Face expedition, and what appears to be the tallest summit from this angle is Nyanang Ri. Looking back southeast down the valley is the main Himalaya range, including Gauri Shankar (23,405 ft, 7134 m) and Melungtse (23,559 ft, 7181 m), marching ruggedly across the distant skyline.

The advance camp (17,100 ft, 5210 m) is **about 1 hour or more** farther north up the valley beyond a flat, stony ridge extending from the Ice Tooth. The top of this ridge (17,900 ft, 5460 m) looks directly onto an unusually thick mass of white ice oozing down the face of this peak. The route to the advance camp area crosses a low point at the far left end of the ridge. From this narrow saddle (17,500 ft, 5330 m) descend to an almost paisley-shaped lake in the valley draining the Ice Tooth. The advance camp used by the 1982 British expedition was a "friendly place in a little hollow amongst grass and boulders" a short distance above the top end of the lake. Higher in the valley below Ice Tooth is a deep, cobalt blue glacial lake.

The return to Nyelam from base camp can be completed in **1 long day,** though if you have hired pack animals, the guides will probably want to stop for the night in Draabochhan. With an early start from this herders' camp it is possible to reach Khasa, complete the China–Nepal border crossing formalities, and drive to Kathmandu in a single day.

Mount Kailas from the hills above Darchhan

11 The Mount Kailas Region

(Map 9, page 242)

> *In a hundred ages of the gods I could not tell thee the glories*
> *of [the Himalaya] . . . there is no mountain like [the Himalaya]*
> *for in it are Kailas and Manasarovar.*
>
> from the Hindu epic *Ramayana*

Few mountains in the world can rival the grandeur of Mount Kailas (22,028 ft, 6714 m), the famed holy peak in Western Tibet. Situated to the north of the Himalayan barrier, this legendary snow-shrouded rock dome is revered by four different religions as one of the most sacred pilgrimage destinations in Asia. The sources for four of South Asia's greatest rivers are nearby and at the base of the mountain are two vast lakes, Manasarovar (in Tibetan Mapham Tsho, the "Victorious Lake") and Raksas Tal (in Tibetan Langka or Langak Tsho, the "Demon Lake").

Hindus regard Mount Kailas as the earthly manifestation of Mount Meru, their spiritual center of the universe, described in ancient texts as a fantastic "world pillar," 84,000 miles high, around which all else revolves, its roots in the lowest hell and its summit kissing the heavens. On top is the abode of their god Shiva, Lord of the Mountains, who shares this lofty peak with his consort, Parvati. Sprawling below is the sacred Manasarovar, where a ritual bath will deliver a pilgrim to Brahma's paradise and a drink of its waters relinquishes the sins of a hundred lifetimes. For the Jains, a religious group in India with many Buddhist-like doctrines, Kailas is acclaimed as the site where their first prophet achieved enlightenment. Though they look much like the Hindu pilgrims, Jains can often be identified by the small cloth bag clutched in their right hand that contains their prayer beads.

Mount Kailas is known to the Tibetans as Ghang Rimpoche ("Precious Jewel of Snow") or by its aboriginal name, Ti-se. Tibetan Buddhists, like the Hindus, recognize Kailas as the manifestation of Mount Meru, the "navel of the world," rising "like the handle of a mill-stone" into the heavens. From the slopes of Mount Meru a stream is said to pour into Mapham Tsho, and from this lake flow four rivers in the four cardinal directions toward the oceans: the Seng-ghe Khabab or Khambab ("River from the Lion-Mouth") to the north; the Tamchhog Khabab ("River from the Horse-Mouth") to the east; the Mabjha Khabab ("River from the Peacock-Mouth") to the south; and the Langchhan Khabab ("River from the Elephant-Mouth") to the west. These mythical rivers are now associated with the

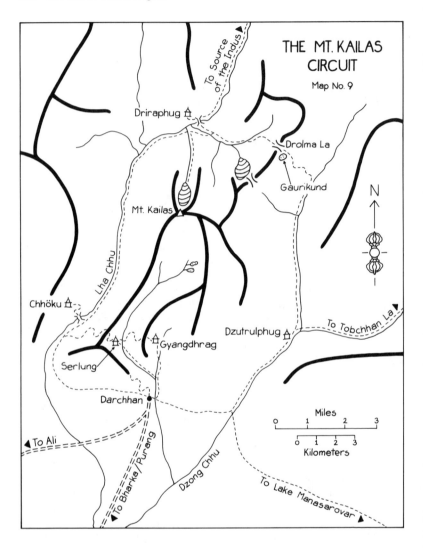

four major rivers originating near Kailas: the Indus, the Yarlung Tsangpo (Brahmaputra), the Karnali, and the Sutlej, respectively. Kailas is also regarded as the residence of Demchog, the fierce-looking deity worshipped in the Chakrasamvara tantric cycle of Tibetan Buddhism, and his consort, Dorje Phagmo. The mountain also has a special association with the poet-saint Milarepa, who spent several years here meditating in a cave.

Mount Kailas is sacred to the Bön religion as well, for it is the site where its founder, Shanrab, is said to have descended from heaven, and formerly it was the spiritual center of Zhang Zhung, the ancient Bön empire that once included all of Western Tibet. The Bön circumambulate the mountain, but in their traditional counterclockwise manner, opposite to the Buddhists and Hindus.

The pilgrimage to Kailas and Manasarovar has always been considered the most difficult in Asia, if not the world. The distances were tremendous, the weather particularly harsh, supplies almost nonexistent and bandit attacks a constant worry. Nevertheless pilgrims came from the far corners of Asia, defying these hardships to walk the 32-mile (52-km) circuit around Kailas.

Even with the convenience of roads and four-wheel-drive vehicles, the standard route north from Lhasa is still an arduous adventure requiring **a minimum of 6 to 7 days** to drive the 1100 miles (1800 km) to Kailas. A shorter southern route from Lhasa along the Yarlung Tsangpo takes **4 to 5 days** in good conditions, but this road is passable only before the monsoon starts in June, then again after the rains stop in September. A third approach from Kashgar, in far western China, has been popular with tour groups since the Karakoram Highway between Pakistan and China was opened to foreigners in 1986.

Mount Kailas is located within the southwest corner of Ngari, the westernmost province of Tibet. Its lone, conical summit rises magnificently above all the neighboring peaks, the highest point at the west end of the Ghangtise–Nyanchhan Thanglha range. Across the broad Bharka plains to the south, beyond the waters of Manasarovar and Raksas Tal, towers another impressive mountain, Gurla Mandhata (in Tibetan Maymo Naa-nyiy; 25,355 ft, 7728 m). The inhabitants of this region are primarily *drogpa,* the sturdy nomadic herders. At this end of the Tibetan plateau the land is so high and barren that fields of barley are a rare sight.

The *kora* around Mount Kailas starts and finishes at Darchhan, a small, windblown settlement at the base of the holy mountain. From Darchhan the pilgrimage circuit enters the Lha Chhu ("Gods' River") Valley, a spectacular canyon below the mountain's western flanks. As the *kora* swings behind Kailas's sheer northern face, the trail climbs to Drolma La (18,200 ft, 5550 m), the highest point en route, then descends quickly into the Lham Chhu Khyer Valley before turning back toward Darchhan.

The best time of year to trek in Western Tibet is between mid-May and mid-October. The weather is generally stable and visibility is at its best during the first and last months of this season, though temperatures are typically cool during the day and below freezing at night. The other months are warmer, but include the period when the monsoon pushes beyond the Himalaya, swelling the creeks and coating the valleys with greenery and wildflowers. Be prepared with sufficient cold-weather gear, for occasional storms will dump snow on the circuit, particularly near the pass. Fuel stoves are necessary unless you plan to cook over a yak dung fire with the pilgrims, and tents are highly recommended.

If you come to Kailas from Lhasa or Kashgar, stock up on supplies in the market town of Ali (also known as Shiquanhe or Seng-ghe Drong—"Lion Village"), 150 miles (250 km) northwest of Darchhan on the northern road from Lhasa, where fresh fruits and vegetables, meat, sugar, and so on are usually available. Or else try the bazaar at Purang (Taklakot in Nepali), the Indian/Nepali border town 70 miles (112 km) south from Darchhan. There are no shops in Darchhan, though standard Tibetan food such as *tsampa,* yak butter, and brick tea are usually available. Entrepreneurs working from canvas tents also sell a few food items such as canned mandarins, noodles, and beer.

Due to the high elevations in the Kailas region, consider spending at least two nights in Darchhan acclimatizing before setting off on the pilgrimage circuit.

Dayhikes near Mount Kailas

The summit of Mount Kailas is visible from Darchhan, though the best views in the area are a climb of **1 hour** not including rest stops up the ridge directly behind (north of) the town. From the guest house, walk above the *gompa* and the pilgrim camps to the base of the ridge. Although the ridge looks difficult from below, a faint trail leads from the camping area to a small rocky draw. Follow this path up through the rocks for **less than 10 minutes** to a scenic overlook with prayer flags and stone cairns (15,500 ft, 4720 m). Continue climbing up to the left (northwest) along the spine of the ridge to a huge prayer wall. The views here are outstanding in all directions, though the panorama from the ridge top is worth the additional **45-minute** climb. Choose your own route along the meandering ridge line, aiming for the pointy hill with a pillar-shaped cairn on the summit (16,500 ft, 5030 m).

The southern "sapphire" face of Kailas is stunning from here, its symmetrical white slopes and brownish red base halved by a vertical slash known to the Hindus as the "Stairway to Heaven." According to Buddhist legend, this large cleft in the mountain occurred during a contest between Milarepa and Naro Bön Chung, a resident Bönpo priest who challenged the presence of Buddhists at Kailas. To decide which was the deserving religion of the area, the two men engaged in a test of magical strength. The last of several competitions was a race to the summit of the holy peak. Naro Bön Chung set off first early in the morning, riding upon his magical drum. Milarepa remained in bed until the Bön priest was nearly at the summit, then "snapped his fingers, donned a cloak for wings," and in a second arrived on top before his rival. Naro Bön Chung fell down in defeat, and his drum sliced a deep groove as it tumbled down the southern face. Naro Bön Chung then begged permission to continue circumambulating the mountain in the counter-clockwise Bön manner, and asked for a place to stay where he could see the mountain. The victorious Milarepa agreed. Tossing a handful of Kailas's snow onto a nearby peak to the east, he offered it as a dwelling place to the priest. This summit is now called Bönri, the Bön mountain, and below it is Bönri *gompa*.

The two valleys below Kailas's south face are the Serlung Chhu and Gyang-dhrag Chhu drainages, and across the Bharka plains to the south are the shores of Raksas Tal. A small portion of Manasarovar can be seen farther to the east, in front of Gurla Mandhata's snowy massif.

An interesting **half-day** outing from Darchhan climbs into the foothills to Gyangdhrag (also spelled Gengta on maps) *gompa,* a pilgrimage site not on the main *kora* route. Starting from the guest house, walk along the Darchhan Chhu, the stream flowing from the foothills, for **a few minutes** to the wooden bridge. Cross to the east (L) side where traders, usually Khampas from Eastern Tibet, sell goods to pilgrims. From the top of the embankment, head east across the stony plain for **a few minutes** toward the base of the hills. A wide, obvious track leads steeply up the east (L) ridge, a route that locals claim can be negotiated by four-wheel-drive vehicles. **Less than 30 minutes** from the guest house the trail levels out,

Pilgrim circumambulating Mount Kailas, Lha Chhu Valley

staying high above the stream. The valley soon divides, with the left branch leading to Serlung *gompa* and the base of the mountain's south face. The trail continues traversing above the right branch into a high, dry amphitheater hugged by the hills of Kailas. The square-sided Gyangdhrag temple is elevated on a lone, conical hill rising in the center. Cross the Gyangdhrag Chhu, then ascend past hundreds of small devotional cairns to a group of *chötaen*. Where the trail divides, follow the left fork around the base of the hill, reaching the monks' residences in **2 hours** from the guest house. The entrance stairway to the monastery (16,400 ft, 5000 m) climbs up from here.

Fifteen monks are now associated with Gyangdhrag, the first of the Buddhist temples that were founded around Kailas in the thirteenth century. Like all religious structures around Kailas, Gyangdhrag was destroyed during the Cultural Revolution; it was rebuilt in 1983. The first floor comprises the assembly hall and *lhakhang*. The three figures upstairs in the *gön-khang* are the fierce, horse-riding Gauri Lapchi; blue, four-armed Gönpo; and Apchhi, the protectress of Drigung monks. Also at Gyangdhrag is a *zhabjay* of Buddha, one of four located around Kailas. According to Swami Pranavanada, an Indian holyman who spent many years in this area and wrote the informative pilgrim's guide *Kailas Manasarovar*, the stone footprint was moved here in the 1940s from Shapje (Zhabjay) La, a pass located **1 hour** east of the *gompa*.

Serlung (also spelled Silung) *gompa*, the only other temple at Kailas that is not on the main pilgrimage *kora*, is **1¹/₂ hours** west of Gyangdhrag. The trail starts near the *chötaen* behind the monks' residences, climbs the far west (R) ridge, then descends to the Serlung Chhu. The *gompa* is on the east (R) bank. Farther upstream from Serlung the valley divides into two tributaries. The west branch leads to the site of Serdung Chug-sum ("Thirteen Reliquary *Chötaen*"), at the base of Kailas's south face. The east branch is the route to Tsho Kapala, neighboring glacial lakes said to have black water in one, white in the other. According to tradition, only those who have completed thirteen circuits around the holy mountain are worthy of visiting these sacred lakes.

Some pilgrims continue west from Serlung *gompa*, crossing a pass on the west (R) ridge to enter the Lha Chhu ("Gods' River") Valley near Chhöku *gompa*, the first monastery on the Kailas *kora*. To return to Darchhan from Serlung, follow the trail downstream along the Serlung Chhu to intersect the track between Gyangdhrag and Darchhan.

The Mount Kailas Circuit Trek

Perched on the upper edge of the Bharka plain, Darchhan ("Big Prayer Flag"; 15,150 ft, 4620 m) is the pilgrim's gateway to Mount Kailas. It is 3 miles (5 km) north of the main Ali–Purang Highway, about 15 miles (24 km) west of the Bharka village junction. Although Darchhan has fewer than a dozen permanent buildings, during summer it swells into a tent city from the influx of pilgrims. The largest structure is the decaying Darchhan *gompa*. This two-story stone building formerly housed a monk-officer from Bhutan's Drugpa Kargyüpa sect; now it is a little-used Drugpa monastery that is often locked. Nearby is a group of herders' dwellings and down the hill is a compound where the local public security officers are quartered. A modest but welcome guest house is in an adjacent section. The camping area designated for foreign pilgrims and tourists is a few hundred yards east of the guest house on the east (L) side of the Darchhan Chhu.

Indian pilgrims and commercial trekking groups typically spend **3 days** completing the Kailas *kora*, camping one night near Driraphug *gompa* and a second night at Dzutrulphug *gompa*. The hearty Tibetans often walk the circuit in one long day, starting hours before dawn and finishing in the evening; they believe that walking three or thirteen circuits is particularly auspicious. Some pilgrims complete the *kora* doing full body prostrations along the ground, a slow journey that can take two weeks. For Tibetans, walking around this holy mountain is more than an act of merit: one circuit is said to purify all the sins of a lifetime; 108 circuits will bring enlightenment during this lifetime. In *da lo,* the Year of the Horse in the twelve-year Tibetan calendar (1990 was a "Horse" year; 2002 will be the next), walking the *kora* is equal to thirteen circuits completed during other years.

If you have the time, spend **4 days** on the Kailas circuit. A leisurely pace gives you time to visit all three of the monasteries plus time to explore the Ghangjam Glacier below Kailas's sheer north face. Hiring pack animals at Darchhan is usually not a problem, although it can take a day or more for the animals to arrive. Yaks and horses are commonly used. The guest house manager can help with the arrangements.

The pilgrimage circuit around Mount Kailas is a wide, obvious trail **a few minutes** uphill from the Darchhan guest house. Lined with rocks and small devotional cairns, the *kora* heads west from the pilgrims' tents along the base of the foothills. Kailas quickly slips out of view as the trail undulates over a desert terrain of scrub and sandy soil. Most pilgrims start out in the predawn hours, bundled in thick overclothes made from reversed sheepskins.

The trail climbs in and out of small gullies, following the seam where the Bharka plain laps against the foothills. Gurla Mandhata rises unchallenged, a massive block of rock and ice tilted to one side, dwarfing the distant spires of India's Garwal Himal. **Fifty minutes** from Darchhan the trail ascends a low ridge of moraine topped with prayer flags and Kailas's north face reemerges above the hills. Heaped beside the trail are stone cairns and offerings of clothing, an act considered auspicious at the most holy of pilgrimage sites. On this ridge is the first of four *chha-tsal ghang,* or prostration sites, found around the *kora.* Pilgrims perform body prostrations at these stations, first touching their joined hands to the head, the mouth, and the heart, in quick succession before reclining on the ground, face down with arms extended over the head in an act of complete devotion.

Beyond the ridge opens the magnificent desert valley of the Lha Chhu, where immense eroded walls of purple sandstone and conglomerate rock sweep into craggy pinnacles, and the towers of mythical castles loom above the river plain. Descend into the valley for **30 minutes** to Serzhong ("Golden Trough," or "Grazing Area"). This is the site of a religious festival on Saga Dawa. Each year the Darbochhe, the tall flagpole standing here, is taken down, redecorated with prayer flags, then raised on this day to celebrate the enlightenment of Buddha. A route crossing over from Serlung *gompa* enters the valley here, and nearby is the first of the Buddha footprints on the Kailas *kora.*

A few minutes down from Serzhong the main trail comes to a long *mani* wall and Chötaen Kangnyi ("Two-legged *Chötaen*"), where pilgrims receive blessings by walking through this entrance gate to the Lha Chhu. Continue descending from here to the river's gravel flood plain. The main trail stays near the hills, though other paths traverse the plain. The bridge crossing (15,450 ft, 4710 m) to Chhöku *gompa,* the first temple on the Kailas circuit, is **40 minutes** below Serzhong. Several large meadows isolated in the gravel expanse are fine campsites.

Chhöku *gompa* (15,800 ft, 4820 m) clings to the side of an immense cliff face. It is a steep **15-minute** climb from the bridge along a trail strewn with boulders and pieces from the cliffs. Chhöku ("Religious Figure"; also called Nyanri *gompa* and Nyanpo *ri dzong*) was first established in the thirteenth century as a shrine. The present building was rebuilt after the Cultural Revolution. The central figure in the main *lhakhang* is original: a squat, pudgy statue of Opaame, the Buddha of Boundless Light, made from a beautiful white stone, perhaps marble. Two other objects of interest to pilgrims are a silver-lined conch shell that Milarepa is said to have recovered from the depths of Manasarovar, and a large copper cauldron brought here by a renowned Indian ascetic. Along shelves on the back wall are the 108 volumes of the *Kangyur.* The separate, smaller building overlooking the cliff is a *gön-khang* dedicated to Ghangri Lhatsen, the protecting deity residing in Nyanri, the high ridge rising behind Chhöku. Several meditation caves are located near the *gompa,* including Langchhanphug, the "Elephant Cave," where Guru Rimpoche is said to have stayed.

Although a trail continues on the Lha Chhu's west (R) bank, cross back over the bridge to rejoin the main pilgrimage circuit. The trail now waltzes under the walls of the Lha Chhu Canyon, its huge ramparts of weathered rock towering thousands of feet high. The valley's unusual natural formations have been interwoven with myths of the area, particularly with Gesar of Ling, the hero of Tibet's great epic story. A long, trailing waterfall spilling off the west (R) side of the canyon is known as the tail of Gesar's horse; a huge square boulder on a ledge above the trail is one of the dice rolled by Gesar to help him make military decisions; a great hole in the rock with water pouring through is where Gesar's wife, Dugmo, made *chhang;* and three boulders nearby were used to mash up the yeast cakes when she was fermenting her brews.

The *kora* stays along the valley floor, sometimes climbing over alluvial ridges spilling from the cliffs. **About 1 hour** beyond the Chhöku bridge crossing the trail passes a chairlike granite rock. It is the saddle of Kyang Go, Gesar's horse, where pilgrims sit to receive a blessing. A little farther is a boulder surrounded by *mani* stones and covered with dabs of yak butter and coins. The large imprint in this rock is the first footprint, or *zhabjay,* of Buddha located on the main *kora.*

The Lha Chhu now swings right (east) as two large tributaries enter from the north. The second of these valleys, the Dronglung ("Wild Yak") Valley, is one of several routes that lead to the Seng-ghe Khabab, the source of the Indus River. The meadows along this stretch of the Lha Chhu are popular picnic spots for pilgrims. Golden-backed marmots race between burrows screaming at these intruders, the smell of yak chip fires permeates the air, and the first view of Kailas's "golden" north face appears above the hills. On the right bank **less than 10 minutes** up-

Interior of Gyangdhrag gompa, *the first monastery founded at Mount Kailas*

stream from here is a campsite established for Indian pilgrims. These lucky folks are among several hundred each year selected by means of a lottery system to enter Tibet and perform *parikrama,* the circumambulation around Kailas. Commercial trekking groups walking the *kora* in 3 days usually camp at the meadows, though less crowded sites can be found upstream.

The main pilgrimage trail stays above the Lha Chhu's south (L) bank, crossing the Ghangjam Chhu, then leading to a stone hut **30 minutes** beyond the meadows. Driraphug *gompa,* the second temple on the *kora,* is directly across the river on the north (R) ridge. The sheer icy north face of Mount Kailas is now unveiled, framed perfectly by rounded, symmetrical hills "like a huge silver dome placed on a pedestal with two guards on either side" according to Swami Pranavananda. To Buddhists these hills are the thrones of the Riysum Gompo *bodhisattvas* Chana Dorje and Chenrezig, while a third hill farther east is the residence of Jambayan.

If time permits, the **half-day** hike up this valley provides excellent views of the Kailas massif and the Ghangjam Glacier. From the hut, head up the ridge toward a row of stone *chötaens.* **A few minutes** above here and to the left is a large hole where pilgrims dig for a medicinal white clay called Ghang Rimpoche *ku-sha,* the "flesh" of Kailas. Valued for its ability to ease the pain of childbirth, it is also used to cure headaches and colds, and is applied topically for wounds, skin diseases, and leprosy. The best route up to the glacier is in the center of the valley, along the east (R) side of the creek, where a faint trail winds through the rocks. Reach the base of the glacier (17,300 ft, 5270 m) after **1 hour** of steady climbing, not including rest stops.

The main pilgrim trail to Drolma La continues straight ahead (east) from the stone hut up the Drolma Chhu, a tributary of the Lha Chhu. To visit Driraphug, don't follow the main trail. Instead, descend to the river's edge in **less than 10 minutes.** During the drier part of the season it is possible to rock-hop across; otherwise use the footbridge **a few minutes** upstream. The *gompa* is up on the ridge **a few minutes** downstream from the bridge, and just below it is a "sleeping house" with six empty dirt-floored rooms for hire. A short distance up the hill is Driraphug (16,450 ft, 5010 m), the "Female Yak Horn Cave." This was the meditation cave of Gyalwa Gotsangpa, a Drigungpa monk credited with discovering the route around Mount Kailas. As the story goes (it has numerous versions), Gotsangpa had followed a *dri,* or female yak, up the Lha Chhu Valley. The yak led him into this cave, where he realized that the yak was really an emanation of Khadro Sengdong, the "Lion-faced *Dakini,*" the female guardian spirit of these upper valleys. The site is now enclosed by a shrine and the only resident is a caretaker. Ask him to point out the horn marks and indentations from the monk's hat on the cave ceiling, above a small image of Gotsangpa. Driraphug is still affiliated with the Drigung Kargyüpa sect.

Beyond Driraphug the Lha Chhu turns toward the north. The route used by Swami Pranavananda to reach Seng-ghe Khabab, the source of the Indus, follows this valley up to its headwaters and crosses Lhe La. The Swedish explorer Sven

Hedin also ascended the Lha Chhu, though his route was over two adjacent passes, Tsethi La (18,465 ft, 5628 m) and Tsethi Lachhan La (17,933 ft, 5466 m). Hedin was the first Westerner to venture around the Kailas *kora*. Seng-ghe Khabab is **2 to 3 days** away from Driraphug.

The pilgrimage route to Drolma La leaves the Lha Chhu and climbs into the Drolma Chhu Valley toward the pass. From Driraphug, follow the river upstream for **a few minutes** to the bridge. Cross to the east (L) side, then begin a steep ascent on a moraine of white granite rocks. Reach the second of two high points in **40 minutes.** The meadow below the trail is the last good campsite (17,050 ft, 5200 m) before the pass. Directly across the valley from here is Pölung ("Incense Valley"), a large basin cradled by Kailas's rocky eastern arm. This entire region is a geology lesson on glaciation: all of the valleys are broad and U-shaped, scoured by ancient ice floes; the granite they scraped away was cast aside in tremendous moraine piles. The trail climbs less ferociously above the meadows for **20 minutes** to Shiwa-chal cemetery. The site is littered with piles of clothing and surrounded by small stone cairns. Pilgrims make offerings here to ensure the smooth passage of their spirit into the Bardo, the interim period that follows death. Just above the trail is a rock where pilgrims sometimes leave one of their teeth or draw blood from their gums or a small cut to appease Shinje, the Lord of Death. Dying here is considered a very meritorious act. **A few minutes** above is the reddened footprint of Milarepa imbedded in a rock, and just beyond is an area pockmarked with deep holes where pilgrims dig into the soil, hoping to find the hairs of Yeshe Tshogyal, the Tibetan consort of Guru Rimpoche.

Across the valley (south) another tributary opens to reveal the snow-choked approach to Khadro Sanglam ("Road of the Lion-Faced *Dakini*) pass. This alternative route around Kailas bypasses Drolma La, which tradition says can be crossed only if you have completed twelve previous circuits around the mountain. With binoculars, a cairn can be seen on the snowy summit.

The trail now levels out, weaving between the chunks of granite that cover the valley floor. After **20 minutes** the rocky path swings to the right up a ridge of glacial rubble. This is the final 600-foot (180 m) climb to the pass; the top is **less than 1 hour** away. Kailas's North Face peers over neighboring ridges for the last time. A small lake is tucked into the base of the pass. The incessant mumblings of prayers by the Tibetan pilgrims turns to hushed pants as they labor up the steep switchbacks. About halfway up is a small glacial creek that crosses the trail; pilgrims wash their hands in it to cleanse away their sins, then rub their hands across a smoothed rock. The trail is lined with mounds of rock, devotional cairns, and stones etched with prayers. Nature also plays at decorating the trail, spraying the rocks with brilliant orange patches of lichen. Near the summit is a large boulder covered with coin offerings and blessing strings; the prominent white crack on its face represents the correct path to Enlightenment.

Even without the glimmering, white cap of Mount Kailas in view, Drolma La (18,200 ft, 5490 m) is a stunning spectacle. Stretching 150 feet across the summit are thick garlands of colorful prayer flags dancing in the wind. The large boulder among all this festivity is Drolma Do, Drolma's Rock. When the monk Gotsangpa was first trying to find his way around Kailas he wandered into the valley of the

Lion-Faced *Dakini,* where a pack of twenty-one wolves led him to this boulder. The wolves were actually the twenty-one emanations of Drolma, the goddess of mercy, the protectress who resides here. Once on the summit, the wolves magically merged into one wolf, which merged into the boulder and disappeared. Pilgrims prostrate themselves before this revered throne of Drolma, some climb on top to attach more prayer flags, and others struggle through the tangle of flags to complete the traditional three circuits around the rock. On the far side of Drolma Do the atmosphere is festive, for this is both the physical and the spiritual pinnacle of the Kailas pilgrimage. Groups and families settle down among the rocks, huddling around yak dung fires as they prepare a kettle of tea. Leather bags of *tsampa* are opened, small wooden bowls are produced from their sheepskin coats, tea is poured, and the feast begins.

The pilgrim trail continues east from the summit. Gaurikund Lake (in Tibetan Tuuje Chempo Tsho, the "Lake of the Great Compassionate Bodhisattva") quickly comes into view, a milky green glacial tarn about 200 feet (60 m) below the main trail. Hindu pilgrims are meant to take a ritual bath here, though the surface ice is often too thick to actually do so. Buddhist pilgrims receive their blessing by slurping from a handful of water, then running the remainder through their hair. Beyond the lake the *kora* descends steeply through an eerie world of shattered granite. The trail levels out briefly in a basin where tundra grasses manage to grow between the rocks and water, hidden under the stony paving, flows noisily. Gurla Mandhata can be seen to the south, and below is the welcome greenery of the Lham Chhu Khyer Valley. The bottom is a knee-cracking **45-minute** descent, 1300 feet (400 m) below Drolma La. The Tibetan picnics that started on the pass continue here on the grassy meadows, where both water and warmth are in abundance. To the right of the trail near a stone hut is the third of Buddha's footprints, the Zhabjay Dragdog, imbedded in a large boulder. The pilgrimage route now divides on the valley floor. The main trail stays on the stream's west (R) bank, but the ground can be very wet in places. A drier path follows the east (L) bank and offers the best views of Kailas's east face. If you choose the alternative path you will have to recross the stream later, though it can be rock hopped during the drier months.

Except for a few marshy patches, the walking is easy along the broad meadows of the Lham Chhu Khyer Valley. The hills here are more rounded and not as tall as the Lha Chhu Canyon. Several times I heard a sudden rush of air swooshing above my head: lammergeiers! The area seemed to be a haven for these graceful bearded vultures; I found myself referring to this region as Lammergeier Valley.

Twenty minutes after reaching the valley floor a tributary enters from the west. Kailas, like an ever-changing chameleon, now presents the only view of its "crystal" east face. The route over Khadro Sanglam La descends this drainage to rejoin the main *kora.* The third of the prostration stations is at the valley mouth.

Continue descending along the valley floor for **1 hour or more,** then climb the shoulder of a rocky moraine. Dzutrulphug *gompa* is **40 minutes** from the top. The large drainage entering from the east is the Tobchhan Chhu ("Great Strength River"). The river assumes a new name, Dzong Chhu ("Fortress River"), below its confluence with the Lham Chhu Khyer. The main valley now slices to the

Family of pilgrims brewing tea while on pilgrimage around Mount Kailas

right, passing three *chötaen*-like peaks on its east (L) bank. Many rows of *mani* walls appear beside the trail near the *gompa*. Like the other temples around the circuit, Dzutrulphug ("Miraculous Cave"; 15,800 ft, 4820 m), the cave shrine of Milarepa, is an earth-colored structure built into the mountain above the trail. The cave's name comes from the legendary contest between Milarepa and Naro Bön Chung. At one point during the competition it started to rain, so they stopped to build themselves a rock shelter. Milarepa used his powers to set a great roof stone in place, but once inside they discovered the ceiling was too low. The poet-saint pushed the stone upward, but the shelter became too drafty, causing him to go outside to push the stone back down with his foot. The caretaker will point out Milarepa's handprints and finger marks on the black ceiling, but the footprint on top of the stone is now covered by the shrine's roof. The present caretaker is not a monk, but through his efforts the sacred objects that now grace this temple were buried during the Cultural Revolution, earning him the privilege of residing here. The Milarepa figure on the altar has a golden base said to be *rangjön,* or self-manifested. The rectangular piece of stone beside the cave entrance is the remaining half of a 7-foot (2 m) column said to be Milarepa's walking stick. Pilgrims used to try to lift this pillar as a test of strength, but it was damaged during the Cultural

Revolution. After the building had been destroyed the rock overhang was dynamited five times, but the Miraculous Cave remained intact. This *gompa* dates back to the 1220s, though the present building was rebuilt in 1983.

The meadows below Dzutrulphug are used as the second campsite for Indian pilgrims. Commercial trekking groups also establish their final camp on these grassy flats before heading onto Darchhan. Immediately below the *gompa* is another sleeping house with six rooms.

Darchhan is only **2 hours** from Dzutrulphug. Initially the trail is a wide, delightful stroll under weathered, mesalike hills reminiscent of the southwestern United States. Several small tributaries enter from the right (west), one spanned by a bridge. According to the Swami's guide, a shortcut leads over the hills in this region leads to Gyangdhrag *gompa,* via Shapje La.

The Dzong Chhu narrows into a gorge and the surrounding hills swirl into a kaleidoscope of colors. Shrubs reappear near the trail and Raksas Tal comes into view. Pass a group of three *zhabjay* rocks, then come to the final *chha-tsal ghang* cairn at the end of the gorge. The Bharka plain is straight ahead, edged by the white teeth of the Indian Himalaya.

The trail now leaves the Dzong Chhu and returns to the desert. The route for the pilgrimage around Lake Manasarovar leads off to the left (southeast) near a group of prayer walls. The Kailas *kora* turns right (west), following the base of the foothills. The pilgrimage circuit ends with the return to Darchhan, **1 hour** past these *mani* walls. *Om mani padme hum.*

Other trekking possibilities in the Kailas region include the **4-day** pilgrimage circuit around Lake Manasarovar, or more difficult outings such as reaching the source of the Indus River or the Yarlung Tsangpo. According to Swami Pranavananda, the headwaters of the Indus lie 34 miles (55 km) to the northeast of Driraphug *gompa* on the Kailas *kora,* via Lhe La. To reach the Yarlung Tsangpo's source, it is necessary to start from Seralung *gompa* on the east shore of Lake Manasarovar, then continue another 63 miles (102 km) east up the Tag Tsangpo Valley and over Tag La (17,400 ft, 5300 m) to find the glacial origin.

Bicycling in the Ra Chhu Valley near Dingri (photo by Tim Young)

12   Bicycling In Tibet

by Tim Young

Riding a bicycle is a challenging way to see Tibet. It is slow enough to intimately visit the countryside, yet fast enough to actually cover some distance. Only thirty years ago there were no roads in Tibet. All travel was by foot or by animal on trails following the trade routes. Today the region has an adequate dirt road system designed by the Chinese to accommodate their low-geared six-wheeled trucks. By coincidence, these roads are engineered at a perfect grade for cyclists: long gradual climbs with 6 percent to 8 percent grades.

Since Tibet produces few manufactured goods, everything modern in Lhasa is brought in by truck caravans. The main supply roads enter Tibet from Golmud, in the northern province of Qinghai, and from Chengdu, to the east in Szechuan province. The other major roads enter Lhasa from Kathmandu and from Western Tibet. The northern road from Golmud was recently sealed, distinguishing it as the highest paved road in the world.

Tibet requires more planning than most other cycling destinations in Asia. A big concern is receiving permission to get a person and a bicycle into the country. You will probably require some assistance from a travel agency in the United States, China, or Nepal in order to obtain permits and conquer support logistics. In the early days of Tibet travel, no special permission was required for bicycles; you simply carried or rode them into Lhasa. During a recent bike trip in Tibet, I led a group of four American cyclists on a month-long journey along the Lhasa–Kathmandu Highway. For this trip we carried our bikes as luggage on the flight from Kathmandu to Lhasa. Our Lhasa-based travel agent met us at the airport and smoothed our way through customs. I still had to spend more than a week, however, working with my host organization to secure an elaborate collection of stamps and permissions from various official agencies in Lhasa; hopefully this procedure will be easier for future cycling groups.

If you go to Tibet with a tour group, the travel company and the group leader will be responsible for handling the permit issue. If you make your own arrangements, be sure to secure a permit before bringing your bike into Tibet; an official paper or note in your visa, obtained from the Chinese embassy issuing your visa, will give you permission and save you from a refusal by the Chinese customs officials.

Another concern regarding bicycling in Tibet is your fitness for a journey of this caliber. This is the highest mountain biking in the world. Although the road engineers may brag about conquering nature, the roads cross such radical geography that they can be closed for days or even months due to snowstorms or landslides. The demands of big climbs, rough roads, remote surroundings, and extremely high elevations must all be taken into consideration.

In addition, be prepared for a reception by as curious a group of people as anywhere in the world. People in some of the more remote areas have never seen a bicycle, and everyone, even in cosmopolitan Lhasa, seems to be fascinated by multispeed, go-anywhere bicycles. In September 1988 I was cycling in the backcountry of the Everest region. A yak herder who was going my way gave me directions to Dingri. He laughed at the sight of me starting up a steep pass that reduced my progress to walking. He was hours ahead of me in climbing the pass, but he failed to understand the advantages of a mountain bike on the downhill. When I beat him and his yak into Dingri the next day, all he could do was grin and ask to try my bike.

Preparations

Tibet is worth the difficulties that traveling by bicycle entails. I have listed a few topics for you to consider before you set off.

BICYCLE EQUIPMENT

A mountain bike is best, but at this time there are no mountain bikes available in Tibet; all of your equipment must be brought with you. Your bike should be of good quality, dependable, and in first-class mechanical shape. Riders must be capable of handling a multitude of repairs on their own, carrying the necessary tools and spare parts in case of breakdowns.

On my last trip in Tibet we had the tools for a complete overhaul on any of the bicycles. Each cyclist carried one spare tube (we also had one spare tire for every two bikes); extra cables; an extra rear derailleur, chain, and freewheel; extra spokes; and a sewing kit. In addition each of us had a basic repair kit. This was a vehicle-supported trip, so we also had tools for other repairs. If you choose to travel self-contained in Tibet, you will need to carry a complete repair kit and the necessary spare parts. If this is the case, one way around excessive weight is to have the group use the same bike components so that several people can share the tools and spares.

OTHER SUPPLIES

Whether you travel with a support truck or self-contained, you will need a sturdy waterproof tent, a sleeping bag, a first-aid kit, and sufficient quantities of food and water. Resupplying on the road can be quite difficult at times; the smaller villages may have only *tsampa,* yak butter, meat, and Tibetan brick tea. Some truck stops sell only instant noodles or simple rice dishes. Many villages do not even have a store. One alternative is to ask the locals if they have any vegetables, noodles, or meat for sale; they are generally very helpful.

Maps are important and so is the ability to ask questions, such as "Is there a market in the next town?" and "How far is the next village?" Most maps have some inaccuracies, which are not such a big deal if you're in a vehicle. However, a 20-mile correction at the end of a long day on a bicycle could be impossible. Carry an emergency supply of food just in case you don't quite make your destination.

WEATHER AND CLOTHING

Summers mean cool nights and warm days. It can rain for days at a time in July and August, and frost in September is common. Strong winds and sand storms are not unusual, nor is snow on the passes. At higher elevations, freezing temperatures can occur any time of the year. During September at 17,000 feet (5180 m), the nights are usually in the low teens to single figures. In January nighttime temperatures can drop to -33° F. (-27° C.) and daytime temperatures often hover just below freezing.

Bring enough clothing to meet the coldest expected temperatures. Because it is not possible to buy or rent quality gear in Tibet, plan on bringing all your equipment with you. For spring, summer, or autumn cycling, light cycling pants and a short-sleeve shirt usually will be sufficient. If you add a pair of warm-up pants, a long-sleeve jersey, a wind shell, and gloves, you can handle most conditions in good weather. For poor weather, you should also have a fleece or down jacket, an extra layer of synthetic long underwear, a rain jacket, wind or rain pants, warm shoes, and a hat. If you are camping, remember that sitting still in the cold night air will require extra clothing to stay comfortable.

PHYSICAL PREPARATION

It is wise to arrive in Tibet in good physical condition. Cyclists should train to build up their cardiovascular system, for nowhere will it be put to a test like Tibet. Hill training that gets the heart rate up and keeps it up for an hour at a time is highly recommended. The higher the elevation the better, even though Tibet will be higher yet. A well-designed strength training program two or three times a week to build overall power and condition the upper body is an excellent supplement. While physical fitness does not prevent altitude sickness, it does help the body deal with all the other physical demands of rough, remote travel.

Standard cycle touring advice applies: arrive at a good weight; be healthy and rested. Eat well (always a challenge in Tibet) and consider taking a vitamin and mineral supplement. Drink plenty of water to remain properly hydrated. Be sure to acclimatize properly before your cycling tour begins. You might need up to a week or more to get used to the change in elevation. Once you're in Tibet, relax. Don't push it. Go on some walks around town, then after several days of taking it easy try a few short rides around Lhasa. Work in some hills; the rides to the nearby monasteries of Sera and Drepung are a great way to combine sightseeing with cycle training.

Classic Bicycle Routes

LHASA TO KATHMANDU

This is the most popular bicycling choice in Tibet, and with good reason. In just under 600 miles (1000 km) and **13 to 16 days** this route crosses six major passes, traverses the backbone of the Himalaya, offers a look at the North Face of Mount Everest, and visits two of Asia's most interesting cities. The reverse of this route, from Kathmandu to Lhasa, can also be done.

Plan on **at least 3 weeks** to do the trip justice and not hurt yourself. A month

is even better, since you should spend about a week in Lhasa acclimatizing. It takes
5 days to reach Gyantse (km marker 251); consider taking a day off in this interesting town.

Shigatse (km marker 0/4904) is **a long day**'s ride from Gyantse. A worthwhile
side trip en route is to Shalu monastery, which is 3 miles (5 km) south of the main
road from the town of Tsunde (km marker 19). Once in Shigatse, you could enjoy
a week in the busy market, but at the least you should spend a day there stocking
up on supplies, for this is the last market of any consequence before Nepal.

Three or four days of cycling are required to reach the town of Shegar (turnoff at km marker 482/3) from Shigatse, during which you must cross Lagpa La
(17,126 ft, 5220 m), the highest pass on the route. The trip to Dingri (km marker
544) from Shegar takes **1 day,** then it's **another day** of riding to Thang La (km
marker 637; 17,060 ft, 5200 m), the second highest pass on this route. From
there the road makes the greatest downhill plummet in the world, a 15,000-foot
(4600 m) vertical drop from the plateau towards the Sunkosi River in Nepal.
Plan on **1 day** to reach the border and at least **a half day** for customs formalities before crossing into Nepal. Kathmandu is 67 miles (116 km) from the
border, though frequent landslides in the steep-walled canyon can change a 1-day
trip into several. If you are on your own, it is important to ask questions regarding
the roads ahead so you can plan properly.

Suggested Itinerary from Lhasa to Kathmandu

Route	Passes	Time
Lhasa to Gyantse	Kampa La	5 days
Gyantse to Shigatse 56 mi (90 km)	None	1 day
Shigatse to Shegar 144 mi (232 km)	Tsuo La	3–4 days
	Lagpa La	
Shegar to Nepal border 151 mi (244 km)	Thang La	3–4 days
Border to Kathmandu 72 mi (116 km)	Banepa Pass	1–2 days
Totals: 587 mi (946 km)		13–16 days

MOUNT EVEREST BASE CAMP

For an extra 105 miles (170 km) and several giant climbs, the adventure
cyclist can actually ride a mountain bike all the way to the Rongphu/Mount
Everest base camp. It is a beauty of a ride, but only for those willing to take on
the challenge of rough roads and few supplies. It starts from the Lhasa–Kathmandu
Highway at kilometer marker 494, then shoots up a dizzying set of forty-six
switchbacks to Pang La (16,900 ft, 5150 m), with its stunning views of Mount
Everest, the Himalaya, and the Dzakaa Chhu Valley. It is a push to reach Dza
Rongphu monastery in **2 days** from the highway; count on **3 days** if you're carrying full panniers of gear. The road was built by the Chinese for their 1960 climb
of Mount Everest, though in many places it is little more than tracks over river
rocks and glacial moraine. There are several small villages on the way, but only
Phadhruchi and Passum have shops or a guest house. The smaller settlements
have little food available, although a resourceful cyclist can round up some eggs,
a few vegetables, *tsampa,* and yak butter.

From Dza Rongphu monastery, Mount Everest looms at the valley's head as if there were not another mountain in the world. The monastery is a great place to spend a night on the way up. You must bring all of your food with you, though sometimes the monks have a few packets of leftover expedition food for sale. Beyond the monastery it is **less than a half day** up to the base camp (16,900 ft, 5150 m), near the base of the Rongphu Glacier.

There are two ways to exit from the Rongphu region, both taking **2 to 3 days** for the return to the highway. You can either retrace your steps along the road, or cross one of the trekking passes into the Dingri Valley (see "The Dingri to Dza Rongphu Loop"). These passes are considerably more remote and difficult, and should be attempted only by skilled and well-equipped riders.

THE LHASA VALLEY

Mountain bikes are the perfect means of getting around the sprawling environs of Lhasa, and an excellent way to meet people. You can use your bike to shop for yogurt at the Barkor or cruise the streets with the locals on their Chinese-built one-speeds. In the immediate vicinity of Lhasa, try the rides to Drepung and Sera monasteries. The historical sites of Samye monastery and the Yarlung Valley, near Tsethang, are just **a few days** to the south. This route follows the river valley at elevations below 12,000 feet, so a relatively easy round trip could be completed in **7 days or so**. Another possibility from Lhasa is a visit to Ganden monastery, which is a pleasant 28-mile (45 km) ride to the east up the Kyi Chhu, followed by a steep 1500-foot (460 m) climb above the valley. The round trip could be done in **2 days** of riding, though it's worth allowing an extra day for visiting the monastery.

OTHER OPTIONS

Tibet offers an almost endless choice of bicycling opportunities. The only constraints are time, supplies, and permission. Eastern Tibet is traversed by reasonable road networks supported by thousands of miles of yak trails. Because the river valleys are low with the mountains rising to tremendous heights, hill climbing by bicycle in this region can be fierce. There are beautiful stands of 500-year-old primary growth forest, a sight that may not last. Adventurous cyclists should set out for the "wild west" of Tibet. The few roads that do exist on maps of this area may vanish altogether due to the winds and sandstorms that hit the high plateau. The farther west you go, the fewer permanent towns (and supplies) there are, for most people here make their living by nomadic herding.

No matter where you decide to cycle in Tibet, adequate advance planning is essential for the success of your journey. Good luck!

Tim Young spent six and a half years on the "Too Tyred Tour," an around-the-world bicycle expedition, and has traveled by bicycle in over fifty countries. While on tour he crossed from Kathmandu to Lhasa during winter and rode through Eastern Tibet into Yunnan province in China. He returned to Tibet in the autumn of 1988 to lead the first commercial bicycle tour to Everest base camp. Currently living in Jackson Hole, Wyoming, Tim works as a bicycling equipment designer and leads custom biking tours.

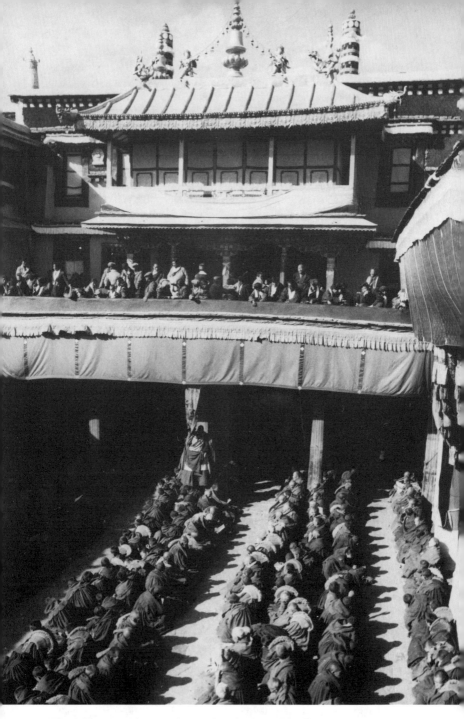

The Jokhang in Lhasa is the site for Monlam Chenmo, the greatest religious festival of the year

SECTION III

THE COUNTRY
AND ITS PEOPLE

Tsamda hot springs near Dingri

13 The Natural History of Tibet

Physical Geography

Tibet can be subdivided into three natural regions according to its primary watersheds: the Northern Plateau, the Outer Plateau, and the Southeastern Plateau. The largest of these regions is the Northern Plateau, a vast 400,000-square-mile (1.04 million sq km) tract of high basins, huge lakes, and extensive ridge systems. It is bounded to the north by the Astin Tagh and the Altin Tagh mountains, and along its southern edge by the 1500-mile-long (2500 km) Ghangtise–Nyanchhan Thanglha range, which includes the sacred Mount Kailas (22,028 ft, 6714 m) in the west and the main Nyanchhan Thanglha summit (23,330 ft, 7111 m) near Lhasa.

The principal feature of the Northern Plateau is the Jhang Thang, a mostly uninhabited expanse of bleak alpine plains and large lake basins. It is the world's largest and highest plateau, averaging 16,400 feet (5000 m) in elevation. The entire region is intersected by heavily eroded ridges and mountains, the largest being the Kun Lun ranges. Due to an annual precipitation of only 4 to 10 inches (100 to 250 mm), the vegetation here is very sparse, consisting primarily of coarse tundra grasses and herbaceous plants well adjusted to the high salt content of the soil. The only woody plants are a few species of thorny shrubs.

Until the 1950s no road entered the Jhang Thang, though several caravan routes traversed its fringes. The uninhabited far western corner, the highest and most barren part of the Jhang Thang, provides a totally unspoiled environment for Tibet's unique wildlife, particularly the Tibetan antelopes, wild yak, and wild asses. Chinese and Western conservationists are currently working on a plan to set aside what would eventually become the world's largest wildlife preserve in the north-ern Jhang Thang. The proposed area encompasses 100,000 square miles (385,000 sq km), which is roughly the size of Colorado.

The two other regions of the Northern Plateau are the Zaidam Basin (in Tibetan Tshadam, or "salt marsh") and the Kokonor/Qinghai Lake basin, the largest lake in Tibet. If you are traveling to Lhasa from mainland China via Golmud, the train you take to Golmud across Qinghai province passes along the lake's northern shore.

The Outer Plateau is a relatively thin but lengthy strip of land to the south of the Ghangtise–Nyanchhan Thanglha mountain belt. It parallels the northern side of the Himalaya and follows the watersheds of two major South Asian rivers, the Indus and the Yarlung Tsangpo (Brahmaputra). The western end of this plateau is the narrowest and has a cold, arid climate. It also provides the sources for the Karnali and the Sutlej rivers, two other major drainages descending through South

Asia. Correctly identifying the sources of these four rivers proved to be one of the last great geographical mysteries of the earth, for they all originate in this remote corner of Tibet near Mount Kailas.

The central part of the Outer Plateau is bisected by the broad, fertile river valleys of Ü and Tsang provinces. The largest population centers of modern Tibet (Lhasa, Shigatse, and Tsethang) as well as many of the greatest religious institutions are located here, for this is the country's agricultural heartland. The climate is considerably more temperate than in other parts of the plateau and the summer monsoon is not entirely blocked by the Himalaya. The Lhasa Valley (12,000 ft, 3660 m) is at about the same latitude as New Orleans and annually receives 10 to 20 inches (250 to 500 mm) of precipitation. The hills and high valleys are covered with grassy steppe vegetation that supports nomadic families and their herds, and along the southern frontier with Nepal and India are forests of fir, larch, birch, and pine. Farther east the Outer Plateau broadens considerably. The large tracts of grasslands and alpine steppe in this region are the source of some of the largest rivers in Southeast Asia and China: the Salween, the Mekong, the Yangtze, and the Yellow rivers.

Tibet's Southeastern Plateau is a rugged, heavily forested area intersected by mountain ridges and deep river gorges. It is the smallest of the three main plateau regions and has the lowest elevations in Tibet. This plateau's southern boundary dips below the main Himalaya chain and includes the great 180-degree bend in the Yarlung Tsangpo around Namche Barwa (25,446 ft, 7756 m), the end of the Himalaya. The eastern limits are formed by the Hengduan Mountains and the deep, parallel valleys of the Salween, Mekong, and Yangtze rivers. The population centers of Chamdo and Jyekundo are in this region.

The unusually deep gorge cut by the Yarlung Tsangpo funnels the monsoon much farther north than in other regions of Tibet. Tributary valleys near Namche Barwa, particularly the drainages of the Po Tsangpo and the Yigrong Chhu, are lush with plants such as oaks, rhododendrons, laurels, and magnolias. On the higher slopes the forest is a mix of pine, fir, and deciduous trees. Unfortunately, these tall stands of virgin growth are currently under heavy logging pressure—they are the primary timber source for Szechuan, China's most heavily populated province.

Geology

According to Tibetan Buddhist tradition, Tibet lay under a great ocean of water after the Universe had been created. Then, by the blessing of Chenrezig, Tibet's God of Compassion, the waters slowly receded and from the depths rose a land surrounded by vast chains of mountains.

The geologic history of the Tibetan plateau and the Himalaya presently being pieced together by geologists has fascinating similarities to this account. The area now known as Tibet is actually an accretion of separate continental fragments that collided with the Asian continent over a period of some 200 million years. A succession of large and small seas, collectively known as the Tethys Sea, was created, uplifted, and eventually drained as each fragment merged with the mainland. The most recent of these bodies of water existed until about 50 million years ago and extended from Asia across to Greece. In the hills to the south of Dingri near Mount Everest it is sometimes possible to find shell fossils from this ancient ocean alongside the trails. Even the rock on the summit of Mount Everest was once under water, though long before these Tethys Seas were formed; climbers have found fossils of small marine animals called crinoids imbedded in the layers of limestone near the top.

How is it that some of the highest landmasses on earth were once submerged under oceans? Using fossil evidence, the dating of rocks, and clues from the magnetic alignment of rock crystals, most Western geologists now believe that this fantastic upheaval of the earth's surface resulted from the forces of plate tectonics. According to this theory, the continents and the ocean floors are not a continuous, static surface enveloping the earth like an eggshell, but are instead a giant mosaic of rigid yet movable sections, or tectonic plates, that overlie the planet's hotter, softer interior.

At present the continents and ocean floors consist of seven major plates and twelve or more smaller plates. Geologists believe there was a time, however, when the earth's landmasses were all bunched together into one huge "super continent," called Pangaea. About 250 million to 200 million years ago (the Triassic period, when the first reptiles and the earliest dinosaurs appeared) this great continent started to break apart, initially creating two distinct land areas. To the north was Laurasia, a landmass from which present-day North America, most of Asia, and all of Europe originated. From the great southern continent of Gondwanaland came Australia, Antarctica, Africa, South America, and India.

Over the next 100 million years Laurasia and Gondwanaland continued to break up, their various pieces drifting across the globe toward their present locations. It was during this period that numerous smaller fragments of Gondwanaland, including segments of Southern Tibet and the Indian subcontinent, broke away and started an amazing northward journey toward the Asian mainland. The rocks that are now part of India and the Himalaya may have originally been 5000 miles (8000 km) farther to the south, near present-day Antarctica.

The collision of the Indian subcontinent with the Asian plate is one of the most dramatic geological events of the last 150 million years. India's persistent northward movement has caused massive changes in both landmasses, uplifting the Tibetan plateau and the Himalayan range to their extraordinary heights. Tibet is the largest and highest plateau in the world, averaging over 15,000 feet (4500 m) in elevation. Even more spectacular was this collision's role in the creation of the 1900-mile-long chain of Himalayan peaks that span south and central Asia, boasting ten of the world's fourteen highest summits, and the emergence of a dozen or more related mountain ranges. When this great uplift of the Himalaya and the Tibetan plateau occurred is still subject to much debate. The inaccessibility of these areas and the complex nature of their rock structures have prevented geologists from accurately detailing the sequence of events. Some regions of the Himalaya seem to have been uplifted at different times, but there is no conclusive evidence indicating whether portions of Southern Tibet were elevated before the collision with India, whether the two regions were elevated at the same time, or whether the uplift of the Himalaya and Tibet was rapid and relatively recent.

Geologists believe that the Indian subcontinent is still pushing into Asia. Nevertheless, the upward growth of the Tibetan plateau may have reached its limit and there is evidence that it has begun to collapse on itself, with the surface of the plateau spreading apart. The thick crust of the Tibetan plateau is rather weak, so as it spreads the plateau could lose the ability to hold itself up. A manifestation of this collapse is the Mustang Valley, a broad north–south trending valley along the upper reaches of the Kali Gandaki River north of the Himalaya. Photos of this area taken from the *Challenger* space shuttle indicate that a large block of the plateau's crust has dropped here along a fault system as the surrounding crust has spread apart.

The great upheaval of the Himalaya, however, seems far from over. Evidence of this is the frequency of large slips along major faults underneath the mountains, which have caused several big earthquakes over the last 100 years. One particularly severe earthquake, in 1934, was estimated at 8.4 on the Richter scale (the 1906 San Francisco earthquake was probably 8.3); it knocked down buildings in Calcutta and Kathmandu, and destroyed Tengboche monastery near Mount Everest. In 1988 a less severe earthquake of more than 6 on the Richter scale left 25,000 people homeless around its epicenter near the Nepal–India border. Buildings collapsed in Kathmandu, windows cracked in Lhasa, and the *chötaen* at Dza Rongphu monastery near Mount Everest was reduced to rubble. More welcome indications that the Himalaya is still geologically active are the many hot springs and large thermal sites found near the mountains. Nepal claims more than 600 hot springs, while Tibet has a significant geothermal area in the Yangpachan Valley where steam-driven generators provide the majority of Lhasa's electricity.

Mammals

Less than a hundred years ago explorers and mountaineers marveled at the abundance of wildlife in Tibet. "As far as the eye could see, the whole country seemed covered with [Tibetan antelope] does and their young [with] 15,000 to 20,000 visible at one time." So wrote Captain C. G. Rawling in his 1905 publication *The Great Plateau,* after exploring trade-route possibilities for Britain along the upper Yarlung Tsangpo and Western Tibet. Sadly, one must go to the remote northwest corner of the Jhang Thang Plateau to observe wildlife in numbers similar to those of a century ago. Despite this bleak situation, a variety of wildlife can still be observed in Central Tibet once the roads are left behind for the trails. It is also not unusual to see signs of nocturnal mammals, whose movements can be detected only by footprints, scat (droppings), or active burrows.

The number of mammal species within Tibet is considerable if the more temperate forested regions along the border with Nepal, India (Assam and Sikkim), and Bhutan are included. Most trekkers won't be visiting those areas, however, so the following field guide identifies the wildlife found primarily in the valleys, plateaus, and mountains of Central and Western Tibet, and a few species that sometimes enter Tibet from Nepal. (In addition to this list are several other species which may enter Tibet from the Nepal side of the border.) In the Khasa–Nyelam area, gray langur monkeys and Assamese macaques can be found in the coniferous forests up to 12,000 feet (3660 m) elevation. Himalayan tahr, takin, serow, goral, and a few other animals may drift in as well. Mammals found in the southern forests or Eastern Tibet are not included. The common English name for each mammal is listed first, followed by the scientific name in parentheses, and then one or more italicized common Tibetan names. (Local names can vary with each region.) Each outline includes a brief discussion of the animal's habitat and a physical description to aid identification. Animal names marked by an asterisk are fully protected species in Tibet and the rest of China, and the sale of any product from these animals is illegal. If you see any shop or vendor selling skins, horns, or other products from these animals, you can do your part by informing local government officials, especially the Forestry Bureau office (Ministry of Agriculture) in Lhasa or Shigatse.

CARNIVORES

Wolf (*Canis lupus*), *changku*. A large nomadic hunter resembling the Alaskan wolf, with a long coat and thick bushy tail often tipped with white. Footprints can measure 5 inches (13 cm) from heel to toe. Color of coat ranges from black to silver gray, though brownish gray is most common. Usually avoids rugged mountain terrain, choosing caves, holes, and overhanging rocks for shelter and den sites.

Red fox and **Tibetan sand fox** (*Vulpes vulpes* and *Vulpes ferrilata*), *wa* or *wamo*. The larger red fox is nearly $3^1/2$ feet (1 m) from head to tail. Coat is usually red and luxurious with a very full, bushy tail often tipped with white. Tibetans use the pelts as wraparound hats. Found in mountainous areas with forest and shrub, and in nearby grasslands. The sand fox has a short, grayish coat with a shorter tail and smaller ears. More common on upland plateaus and open plains, though the habitats of both foxes overlap. Look for black hair behind the red fox's ears to help identify in the field.

Tibetan brown bear (*Ursus arctos*), *dom*. The most endangered species on the Tibet plateau, yet omitted from the list of endangered animals in China. Habitat is now mostly reduced to the Jhang Thang. A large bear standing almost 6 feet (1.8 m) tall, with a heavy neck ruff and hairy ears. Has a broader build and lighter brown coat than the Himalayan (Asiatic) black bear (*Ursus thibetanus*) found in Tibet's southern forests.

Stone marten or **beech marten** (*Martes foina*). A brown minklike animal with a large white patch under the chin and throat that extends to the forelegs. Body can be more than 2 feet (60 cm) long, with a tail at least half that length. Sometimes seen scavenging near human settlements, even near Lhasa. The larger yellow-throated or forest marten (*Martes flavigula*) lives in Southern and Eastern Tibet.

Weasel (*Mustella altaica* Pallas and *Mustella sibirica* Pallas), *tremong*. Typically seen bounding between rocks above the tree line, but can also be found living in the walls and roofs of homes. Much smaller than martens, but similarly built and with a light throat patch. *Mustella sibirica* can be upwards of 2 feet (60 cm) long, with a tail half that length. Coat varies, though often it is a golden fawn shade. *Mustella altaica,* the pale weasel, is about 5 inches (13 cm) smaller, with a more grayish brown coat, white paws, and a more creamy white throat patch.

Ferret or **Eversman's polecat** (*Mustella eversmanni*). A large weasel nearly 2 feet (60cm) long, with a relatively short tail. Closely resembles the critically endangered black-footed ferret of North America, with a dark brown coat, black feet, and a distinctive raccoonlike black mask.

Eurasian badger (*Meles meles*). Very rare member of the weasel family, similar to the North American badger. Probably burrows in the grassy plains near pika colonies.

Pallas or **Manul cat** (*Felis manul* Pallas). This unusually beautiful feline is the only small cat on the plains of Tibet. Similar in size to a small domestic cat, has distinctive black marks on the face, stripes on its lower back, and a long, thick, striped tail that ends in a black tip.

Lynx (*Lynx lynx*), *yi, amu,* or *de-zay*. Similar to the North American lynx, with long tufts on the ears and a short stubby tail. Coat is plain sandy gray. Found primarily in open spaces on hills and rocky areas.

*Snow leopard (*Panthera uncia*), *saa* or *sha*. This magnificent high-altitude cat of Asia's mountain ranges can still be found in low numbers where blue sheep are common. Mostly a nocturnal hunter, covering large territories while stalking prey. Only the forest leopard (*Panthera pandus*) in Tibet's southern forests rivals its size, which is comparable to a good-sized dog, with a wide bushy tail nearly 3 feet (90 cm) long. The coat is a soft, pale gray, with distinctive markings like broad, pale rosettas.

Yeti or **Abominable snowman,** *migö*. Periodic sightings in Tibet by local inhabitants and mountaineers continue to fuel the controversy of whether this ape-like creature of the high Himalaya exists or not.

HOOFED ANIMALS

*Tibetan wild ass (*Equus hemionus kiang*), *kyang*. The largest of the Asiatic wild asses, standing 4 feet (1.2 m) at the shoulder. Once found in abundance on the plains and hills across Tibet, its domain is now mostly limited to the northern plains. The upper half of its body is a fawn/rust color; the throat, chest, and abdomen are white. A distinctive line of black hairs extends from the head along the back and down the back legs.

Musk deer (*Moschus sifanicus*), *laa* or *lawa*. A small, stocky deer with no antlers, standing less than 2½ feet (75 cm) tall at the shoulder. Often seen alone or in small groups on steep terrain and near cliffs, preferring thickets of brush. Found primarily near Lhasa and in the hills to the south and east. Coat is gray brown with some white markings. Hind legs are heavy and elongated, causing it to bound like a large rabbit. Has unusual 2-inch-long (5 cm) tusklike upper canine teeth, which are most prominent in the males. Musk obtained from a gland in the male's belly is highly prized in Asia for its medicinal qualities. Another species (*Moschus chrysogaster*) lives in the forests near Tibet's southern borders.

*White-lipped deer (*Cervus albirostris*), *sawa*. The only big, elklike deer with large, branched antlers in Central Tibet. Now mostly found east of Lhasa in limited numbers. Has a brown coat, a cream-colored belly, and a characteristic white chin and muzzle. The red deer or Sikkim stag (*Cervus elaphus*) is grayish red, also has a rack, and lives in Tibet's southern forests.

*Wild yak (*Bos grunniens*), *dhrong* or *yaa*. A large, black shaggy-haired species of wild cattle once found in abundance on the Tibetan plains. Now considered rare, though still found in local concentrations. Prefers rolling and

*Tibetan antelope (*Pantholops hodgsoni*) (photo by George B. Schaller)*

steep hills but will venture into open terrain. Most yaks seen in Tibet are either domestic or hybrid yak-cattle crosses. If a yak has any white markings, it is domestic or a crossbreed.

Tibetan gazelle (*Procapra picticaudata*), *gowa.* The most widespread ungulate in Tibet, with populations across the Jhang Thang and into the mountain valleys. Similar to Thomson's gazelle of East Africa, having a tan or fawn coat, a conspicuous white heart-shaped rump patch, and a small black tail. Male has closely ringed 12- to 14-inch (30 to 35 cm) thin black horns that curve back and out. The female has no horns. At a distance can be difficult to distinguish from a blue sheep.

*Tibetan antelope or **chiru** (*Pantholops hodgsoni*), *tsod* and *tsö.* The most abundant of the hooved animals on the Tibetan plateau, found primarily in the north and northwestern Jhang Thang. A medium-size antelope with long, light-gray/fawn hair. The male is readily identified by its 2-foot-long (60 cm), ridged, lyre-shaped horns that rise almost vertically from the head. The female has no horns.

Blue sheep or **bharal** (*Pseudois nayaur*), *na, nawa,* or *naya.* Widely distributed throughout the Tibetan plateau east of 80 degrees east longitude. A rather stocky, gray brown animal with white hindquarters, black tail, and black markings on the front of each leg. Both sexes have thick horns that sweep out and back; the male's are larger. Prefers remote and rugged cliffs between the upper limits of forest and the vegetation limits (10,000 to 16,000 ft, 3050 to 4880 m). Has certain behavioral patterns more typical of wild goats. Wildlife biologist George B. Schaller has suggested that a more appropriate common name would be the blue goat. Commonly seen near Dza Rongphu monastery and Everest base camp.

Tibetan argali sheep (*Ovis ammon hodgsoni*), *nyan.* This cousin of the Marco Polo sheep is Tibet's largest wild sheep and the most endangered ungulate on the Tibet plateau. Has been omitted from the list of fully protected species in China. Males are enormous, standing nearly 4 feet (1.2 m) at the shoulder, with massive horns spiraling over 4 feet in length. The female has smaller horns. Coat is buffy brown with a prominent short, white ruff on the chest in winter and white stomach, belly, and rump.

HARES AND RABBITS

Pika or **Himalayan mouse-hare** or **rock hare** (*Ochotona curzoniae* and *Ochotona macrotis*), *abra, dzabra,* or *pu-se*. This small, playfully cute, tailless relative of the rabbit is the most frequently seen mammal in Tibet. Has light brown fur and resembles a guinea pig. The black-lipped pika (*Ochotona curzoniae*) is the most common of several species in Tibet, living in large colonies on the plains and in valleys. A large-eared species (*Ochotona macrotis*) more similar to the North American pika lives among rocks and talus.

Tibetan woolly hare or **gray-rumped hare** (*Lepus oiostolus*), *righong*. Endemic to the Tibet plateau. A brownish hare about the size of a North American jack rabbit, with a large patch of gray fur over the rump. Prefers rocky and shrub-covered plains or hillsides that can provide cover.

RODENTS

Himalayan marmot (*Marmota himalayana*), *jhiba* or *jhibi*. A large burrowing member of the squirrel family and the largest rodent in Tibet. Found throughout Tibet in colonies on the plains and in grassy mountain valleys. A close cousin of the North America marmot, with beautiful golden brown fur and a short tail.

House mouse (*Mus musculus*), *tsi-tsi*. Typically found in houses and monasteries. Varies in color from light to dark brown, with a body 2 to 3 inches (5 to 8 cm) long and a tail equally as long.

Hamster (*Cricetulus longicaudatus*). A sandy-colored ratlike animal found on grassy or vegetated plains. Usually smaller than a pika and with a short tail. Lives in communal burrows with openings smaller than a pika's burrow.

Vole (*Alticola stoliczkanus* and *Pitymys leucurus*). Lives higher in elevation (18,000+ ft, 5490 m) than any other mammal. Related to the lemming, the mountain vole (*Alticola stoliczkanus*) is a pleasant-looking rodent 3 to 4 inches (8 to 10 cm) long with gray fur, a white belly, small ears, and a short, hairy tail. *Pitymys leucurus* is similar in size, resembles the North American pine vole, and looks more like a mouse. Fur is brown to dark brown and the tail is very short with little hair. Both types of vole live in burrows and do not hibernate.

Fish

The two main types of fish in Tibet are carp and scaleless loaches. Tibetan carp are schizothoracines, a subfamily of Cyprinidae, the carp family. They are the predominant freshwater fish in Tibet, growing to 2 feet (60 cm) or more in length and having a mottled greenish brown color. Carp that live at lower elevations typically have scales and two pairs of fleshy "whiskers" called barbels protruding near the mouth; these are used as an aid for finding algae or vegetable matter along river and lake bottoms. At higher elevations these fish become more omnivorous and have less need for barbels. Between 9000 to 12,300 feet in elevation (2750 to 3750 m), the carp in this niche have only one set of barbels. From 12,300 to 15,600 feet (3750 to 4750 m), the diet is so specialized that the carp no longer have barbels nor do they have scales.

Scaleless loaches (subfamily Nemachilinae, family Cobitidae) are carplike fish that resemble a whiskered trout with a carp's mouth. They are more slender and elongated than the Tibetan carp, and are most easily recognized by three pairs of barbels near the mouth. As the name implies, they have no scales. Scaleless loaches live only in open-valley rivers and can be found at elevations up to 17,000 feet (5200 m), the highest of Tibetan fish. Dozens of different species are found on the Qinghai–Tibet plateau and adjacent areas, measuring from 4 to 21 inches (10 to 55 cm) long.

Birds

Despite extreme elevations and relatively low rainfall, a remarkable variety of resident and migratory birds can be found in the fertile river valleys as well as in the hills and higher alpine regions of Central Tibet. According to Vaurie's *Tibet and its Birds,* 504 species of birds have been recorded across geographical Tibet. In just the Central Tibet area nearly 200 species of birds have been recorded. Surely others will be found as more information is collected on the avifauna of this area. The best season for bird-watching is generally from March until October. The spring migration starts around late February/March with the arrival of ducks and graylag geese, and finishes about May with the arrival of wading birds. Tibet's summer residents leave about late September/October. The autumn migration occurs between October and mid-November. Cranes pass through during the first two weeks of October and the eagles from about mid-October to mid-November. If you want to see waterfowl, head for Central Tibet's large lakes such as Yamdrog Tsho and Nam Tsho, where large mixed flocks commonly congregate along the shores until the waters freeze in winter. The towering black-necked crane (*Grus nigricollis*) is endemic to Tibet and has received much attention since being placed on the Endangered Species list. Standing 5 feet (1.5 m) high, it is the tallest of Tibet's birds. It can sometimes be seen in the marshes to the north of Lhasa near Damzhung (km marker 1773/4), along the shores of Nam Tsho, along the Phung Chhu near Dingri, and in the Yarlung Tsangpo Valley near Samye monastery.

The following is a checklist of species that can be encountered in Central Tibet. It does not include birds that are primarily found in the southern or eastern forested regions of Tibet, nor birds in the far north or far west. The list is arranged according to family groupings. The common name for each bird is listed first, followed by its scientific Latin name in italics. The notation LV after the Latin name indicates that this species is found in the Lhasa Valley.

Although no one publication adequately covers all of the birds in Tibet, *The Birds of Nepal* by Robert Fleming Sr., Robert Fleming Jr., and Lain Singh Bangdel (1984, third edition) is certainly the most applicable of the various books and field guides on Himalayan birds. Many of Central Tibet's species can be found in this volume, which contains useful descriptions and numerous color plates. For other titles concerning birds found in Tibet, consult "Suggested Reading" in Appendix B.

BIRD CHECKLIST

Ducks and Geese (*Anatidae*)

☐ Brahminy or ruddy shelduck (*Tadorna ferruginea*, LV)
☐ Mallard (*Anas platyrhynchos*, LV)
☐ Pintail (*Anas acuta*, LV)
☐ Merganser (*Mergus merganser*, LV)
☐ Green-winged teal (*Anas crecca*, LV)
☐ Gadwell (*Anas strepera*, LV)
☐ Wigeon (*Anas penelope*)
☐ Shoveler (*Anas clypeata*, LV)
☐ Common pochard (*Aythya ferina*)
☐ White-eyed pochard (*Aythya nyroca*)
☐ Tufted pochard (*Aythya fuligula*, LV)
☐ Bar-headed goose (*Anser indicus*, LV)
☐ Graylag goose (*Anser anser*)

Grebes (*Podicipedidae*)

☐ Great crested grebe (*Podiceps cristatus*, LV)
☐ Black-necked grebe (*Podiceps caspicus*)

Cormorants (*Phala-crocoracidae*)

☐ Great cormorant (*Phalacrocorax carbo*, LV)

Cranes (*Gruidae*)

☐ Black-necked crane (*Grus nigricollis*)
☐ Demoiselle crane (*Anthropoides virgo*)
☐ Common crane (*Grus grus*)

Storks (*Ciconiidae*)

☐ Black stork (*Ciconia nigra*)

Hawks, Eagles, and Vultures (*Accipitridae*)

☐ Dark or black kite (*Milvus migrans*, LV)
☐ Upland buteo (*Buteo hemilasius*)
☐ Common buteo (*Buteo buteo*)
☐ Long-legged buteo (*Buteo rufinus*)
☐ White-eyed buzzard (*Butastur teesa*)
☐ Golden eagle (*Aquila chrysaetos*)
☐ Steppe eagle (*Aquila nipalensis*)
☐ Lammergeier or bearded vulture (*Gypaetus barbatus*, LV)
☐ Himalayan griffin (*Gyps himalayensis*, LV)
☐ Marsh harrier (*Circus aeruginosus*)
☐ Pale harrier (*Circus macrourus*, LV)
☐ Northern or hen harrier (*Circus cyaneus*)
☐ Goshawk (*Accipter gentilis*)
☐ Northern sparrow hawk (*Accipter nisus*, LV)
☐ Pallas's fishing eagle (*Haliaeetus leucoryphus*, LV)

Falcons (*Falconidae*) and Allies

☐ Eurasian kestrel (*Falco tinnunculus*, LV)
☐ Eurasian hobby (*Falco subbuteo*, LV)
☐ Saker falcon (*Falco cherrug*, LV)
☐ Merlin (*Falco columbarius*)
☐ Osprey (*Pandion haliaetus*, LV)

Pheasants and Partridges (*Phasianinae*)

☐ Elwes's or Harman's eared pheasant (*Crossoptilon harmani*)
☐ Himalayan snow cock (*Tetraogallus himalayensis*)
☐ Tibetan snow cock (*Tetraogallus tibetanus*, LV)
☐ Tibetan partridge (*Perdix hodgsoniae*, LV)

Rails and Coots (*Rallidae*)

☐ Common moorhen or Indian gallinule (*Gallinula chloro-pus*, LV)
☐ Coot (*Fulica atra*, LV)

Plovers, Sandpipers, and Snipes (*Charadriidae*)

☐ Eastern plover (*Pluvialis dominica*, LV)
☐ Mongolian plover (*Charadrius mongolus*)
☐ Redshank (*Tringa totanus*, LV)
☐ Green sandpiper (*Tringa ochropus*, LV)
☐ Wood sandpiper (*Tringa glareola*)
☐ Common sandpiper (*Tringa hypoleucos*, LV)
☐ Ruff and reeve (*Philomachus pugnax*)
☐ Solitary snipe (*Gallinago solitaria*, LV)
☐ Common or fantail snipe (*Capella gallinago*, LV)
☐ Pintail snipe (*Capella stenura*, LV)

Ibisbill (*Recurvirostridae*)

☐ Ibisbill (*Ibidorhyncha struthersii*, LV)

Gulls and Terns (*Laridae*)

☐ Great black-headed gull (*Larus ichthyaetus*, LV)
☐ Brown-headed gull (*Larus brunnicephalus*, LV)
☐ Common black-headed gull (*Larus ribibundus*)
☐ Common (Tibetan) tern (*Sterna hirundo*, LV)

Sand Grouse (*Pteroclidae*)

☐ Sand grouse (*Syrrhaptes tibetanus*)

Pigeons and Doves (*Columbidae*)

☐ Blue rock or "city" pigeon (*Columba livia*, LV)
☐ Blue hill pigeon (*Columba rupestris*)
☐ Snow pigeon (*Columba leuconota*)
☐ Rufous turtledove (*Streptopelia orientalis*, LV)

Cuckoos (*Cuculidae*)

☐ Common or Eurasian cuckoo (*Cuculus canorus*, LV)

Owls (*Strigidae*)

☐ Great horned or eagle owl (*Bubo bubo*, LV)
☐ Little owl (*Athene noctua*, LV)
☐ Short-eared owl (*Asio flammeus*)

Hoopoes (*Upupidae*)

☐ Hoopoe (*Upupa epops*, LV)

Woodpeckers (*Picidae*)

☐ Wryneck (*Jynx torquilla*, LV)

Swifts (*Apodidae*)

☐ Black or Eurasian swift (*Apus apus*, LV)
☐ White-rumped swift (*Apus pacificus*, LV)

Swallows and Martins (*Hirundinidae*)

☐ Collared sand martin (*Riparia riparia*, LV)
☐ Plain martin (*Riparia paludicola*)
☐ Mountain crag martin (*Hirundo rupestris*, LV)
☐ House martin (*Delichon urbica*)
☐ Asian house martin (*Delichon dasypus*, LV)
☐ Barn swallow (*Hirundo rustica*)
☐ Striated or red-rumped swallow (*Hirundo daurica*, LV)

Larks (*Alaudidae*)

☐ Horned lark (*Eremophila alpestris*, LV)
☐ Little or Oriental skylark (*Alauda gulgula*, LV)
☐ Long-billed calandra lark (*Melanocorypha maxima*)
☐ Short-toed lark (*Calandrella* spp., LV)

Pipits and Wagtails (*Motacillidae*)

☐ Blyth's pipit (*Anthus godlewskii*)
☐ Hodgson's tree or olive-backed pipit (*Anthus hodgsoni*)
☐ Richard's pipit (*Anthus novaeseelandiae*)
☐ Rose-breasted pipit (*Anthus roseatus*)
☐ Yellow wagtail (*Motacilla flava*, LV)
☐ Yellow-headed wagtail (*Motacilla citreola*, LV)
☐ Gray wagtail (*Motacilla cinerea*)
☐ Pied or white wagtail (*Motacilla alba* spp., LV)

Shrikes (*Laniidae*)

☐ Gray-backed shrike (*Lanius tephronotus*, LV)

Magpies, Jays, Crows, and Allies (*Corvidae*)

- ☐ Magpie (*Pica pica*, LV)
- ☐ Hume's ground pecker (*Pseudopodoces humilis*, LV)
- ☐ Red-billed chough (*Pyrrhocorax pyrrhocorax*, LV)
- ☐ Yellow-billed chough (*Pyrrhocorax graculus*, LV)
- ☐ Raven (*Corvus corax*, LV)

Minivets (*Campephagidae*)

- ☐ Long-tailed minivet (*Pericrocotus ethologus*, LV)

Wrens (*Troglodytidae*)

- ☐ Wren (*Troglodytes troglodytes*, LV)

Dippers (*Cinclidae*)

- ☐ Brown dipper (*Cinclus pallasii*, LV)
- ☐ White-breasted dipper (*Cinclus cinclus*)

Accentors (*Prunellidae*)

- ☐ Robin accentor (*Prunella rubeculoides*, LV)
- ☐ Brown accentor (*Prunella fulvescens*, LV)
- ☐ Alpine accentor (*Prunella collaris*, LV)
- ☐ Himalayan or Altai accentor (*Prunella himalayana*)

Warblers (*Sylviidae*)

- ☐ Tickell's leaf warbler (*Phylloscopus affinis*, LV)
- ☐ Pallas's or yellow-rumped warbler (*Phylloscopus proregulus*)
- ☐ Greenish warbler (*Phylloscopus trochiloides*, LV)
- ☐ Severtzov's or Stoliczka's tit warbler (*Leptopoecile sophiae*)

Thrushes, Chats, Redstarts, and Allies (*Turdidae*)

- ☐ White-capped river chat (*Chaimarrornis leucocephalus*, LV)
- ☐ Guldenstadt's or white-winged redstart (*Phoenicurus erythrogaster*, LV)
- ☐ Plumbeous redstart (*Rhyacornis fuliginosus*, LV)
- ☐ Black redstart (*Phoenicurus ochruros*, LV)
- ☐ Blue-fronted redstart (*Phoenicurus frontalis*, LV)
- ☐ Hodgson's redstart (*Phoenicurus hodgsoni*, LV)
- ☐ White-throated redstart (*Phoenicurus schisticeps*, LV)
- ☐ Bluethroat (*Erithacus svecicus*, LV)
- ☐ Siberian or Eurasian rubythroat (*Erithacus calliope*)
- ☐ Himalayan or white-tailed rubythroat (*Luscinia pectoralis*)
- ☐ Desert wheatear (*Oenanthe deserti*, LV)
- ☐ Collared bush or stone chat (*Saxicola torquata*)
- ☐ Blue rock thrush (*Monticola solitarius*)
- ☐ Common or Eurasian blackbird (*Turdus merula*, LV)

Laughing Thrushes (*Timaliidae*)

☐ Prince Henri's laughing thrush (*Garrulax henrici*, LV)
☐ Streaked laughing thrush (*Garrulax lineatus*)
☐ Variegated laughing thrush (*Garrulax variegatus*)
☐ Giant babax (*Babax waddelli*, LV)

Titmice (*Paridae*)

☐ Gray or great tit (*Parus major*, LV)

Wallcreepers (*Sittidae*)

☐ Wallcreeper (*Trichodroma muraria*, LV)

Sparrows and Snow Finches (*Ploceidae*)

☐ Tree sparrow (*Passer montanus*, LV)
☐ Cinnamon sparrow (*Passer rutilans*, LV)
☐ Mandelli's or white-rumped snow finch (*Montifringilla taczanowskii*)
☐ Adam's or Tibetan snow finch (*Montifringilla adamsi*, LV)
☐ Eurasian snow finch (*Montifringilla nivalis*)
☐ Red-necked snow finch (*Montifringilla ruficollis*)
☐ Blanford's snow finch (*Montifringilla blanfordi*)

Finches (*Fringillidae*)

☐ Tibetan twite (*Acanthis flavirostris*, LV)
☐ Hodgson's or plain mountain finch (*Leucosticte nemoricola*)
☐ Brandt's mountain finch (*Leucosticte brandti*)
☐ Mongolian desert finch (*Rhodopechys mongolica*)
☐ Nepal or dark rose finch (*Carpodacus nipalensis*)
☐ Common rose finch (*Carpodacus erythrinus*, LV)
☐ Beautiful rose finch (*Carpodacus pulcherrimus*, LV)
☐ Pink-browed rose finch (*Carpodacus rhodochrous*)
☐ White-browed rose finch (*Carpodacus thura*)
☐ Eastern great rose finch (*Carpodacus rubicil-loides*, LV)
☐ Great rose finch (*Carpodacus rubicilla*, LV)
☐ Red-breasted rose finch (*Carpo-dacus puniceus*)

Buntings (*Emberizidae*)

☐ Rock bunting (*Emberiza cia*, LV)

14 The People and Their Culture

by Charles Ramble

The People of Tibet

Tibetans are the descendants of a number of nomadic peoples who apparently migrated southward and westward from the Central Asian steppes and the Chinese borderlands before settling down to cultivate the fertile Tsangpo Valley. The development of a fixed, agriculture-based civilization provided a nucleus for the new Tibetan empire when, in the sixth and seventh centuries, one noble family in Yarlung managed to unite the warring chiefs around it; but it was surely their nomadic heritage, the hardiness it engendered, and a willingness to live in the saddle that enabled these warriors to push the frontiers of their empire to the west of Mount Kailas, north of the Kun Lun Mountains, and even as far as the gates of Xian, the capital of T'ang China.

Settled agriculture permitted the development of the extraordinarily rich Buddhist civilization, channeling much of the Tibetans' martial ferocity into religious zeal. About a quarter of Tibet's population continues to pursue a nomadic life-style, while the farming majority still exhibits remarkable mobility for an agrarian society. Tibetans think nothing of trading expeditions and pilgrimages lasting many months, or even years. The nomadic life was always considered more prestigious than that of the farmer. The chief reason for this attitude is that those working the land were not usually free to move around since tax obligations compelled them to remain and farm their hereditary plot. Revenue on land and livestock was not the only form of tax that farmers were required to pay. These varied from one region to another but might include supplying pack animals for visiting officials, free labor, the provision of a soldier to the army, and even a "monk tax," which required that one son be sent to the regionally dominant monastery. While agriculture might not have provided much scope for profit, even the peasantry could amass considerable wealth through trade as long as they could ensure that there was someone to take care of their land and meet the necessary tax obligations.

Parallel to the economic hierarchy in Tibet was a system of social stratification based principally on descent through the male line. The political relevance of this situation has been largely replaced by the new order of the Communist meritocracy, but it is clear that certain aspects survive into the present. There were four main ranks in the hierarchy, the two highest being the nobles and the priests.

Unlike the Indian caste model, in which the priests (the Brahmans) always occupy the first position, the relative status of priests and nobles in Tibet was never so clearly defined. As a general rule the nobility was probably higher. In the Dingri area the priests came first, but this may have been because the local aristocracy belonged to a lower category: the Tibetan nobility was itself subdivided into four grades. We should be careful not to confuse these priests with the monastic community, who could be recruited from all but the lowest strata of society. The idea that priestly qualities are transmitted from father to son is probably a Buddhist adoption of an ancient Tibetan tradition. The priests in question must necessarily marry and consequently belong to the older lamaist sects, the Nyingmapa and the Bön, for whom celibacy is not always obligatory. The great majority of Tibetans belonged to the commoner rank, which formed the bulk of the taxpaying farmers and nomads. Last came the outcastes. These people were usually landless, and included artisans such as blacksmiths who survived on the patronage of the farming communities in which they lived, or vagrants who earned a living in exchange for their labor or for slaughtering livestock.

Marriage between members of different ranks was unusual and generally prohibited. In a few regions it was customary for priests and nobles, or for priests and commoners, to intermarry, but intermarriage with outcastes was far more unusual and this seems to be the case up to the present day. Commoners claim that outcastes "do not have the same mouth" as themselves, and will not share a cup with them. A number of priestly lineages survive, and reverence for their hereditary sanctity has again become overt. Noble families are also represented, but of course no longer form part of the Tibetan political machinery. Those who remained in Tibet after 1959 predictably did not thrive in the new climate, and most were astute enough to leave. Many of the large ruins one sees in villages in Central Tibet are the shells of abandoned noble houses, stripped of their timbers and other usable building materials and left to decay.

The nobility formed an integral part of the Tibetan administrative system. The ruling classes of Tibet fell into two principal divisions: the monastic hierarchy and the various ranks of the laity, almost all of noble status. In all parts of Tibet, land was considered to belong to the ruler, and in Tibet the absolute ruler was the Dalai Lama. The taxpaying peasantry merely leased land from the government. In addition, some land was under the direct control of the Dalai Lama or his district commissioners (the *dzongpon*), and the entire produce of this went to the state. This land, having no tenants, was worked by conscripted labor provided by the peasants as part of their tax requirements. Only three entities in Tibet could hold revenue-yielding estates: the church (who held about 42 percent), the government (37 percent), and the nobility (21 percent).

DOMESTIC LIFE

With the exception of a disastrous experiment in the 1960s to introduce winter wheat, barley has always been the principal crop of the Tibetan plateau. In lower areas it is just possible to follow a spring crop of barley with one of buckwheat, but in most places a single annual harvest in August/September is generally the limit. In this case subsidiary crops such as buckwheat, mustard (grown for its oil), peas, turnips, and potatoes are relegated to a few minor plots.

Family portrait

The staple food throughout Tibet is *tsampa*, which is made by roasting barley in heated sand, separating it out again by means of a sieve, and grinding the grain to flour in a water mill or a household quern. *Tsampa* made from dried peas is sometimes added to the roasted barley flour to produce an especially nutritious mixture. *Tsampa* is mixed in a cup or a little goatskin bag with tea or the whey from yogurt and eaten as a dough called *pag*. Fresh vegetables do not figure prominently in Tibetan cuisine, and night blindness, resulting from a deficiency of vitamin A, is common in many areas.

Tibetans also use barley to produce beer, known as *chhang,* which is made by adding yeast to boiled and cooled grain and storing the mixture in earthenware fermenting jars. A potent form of beer, called *nyingkhu,* is made by allowing the barley to ferment in a large volume of water, which is drawn off after a couple of weeks and drunk. A milder, thicker drink is produced by pouring water through a sieve containing fermented grain and squeezing the alcoholic content out of it. The residue is dried for animal feed. The fermented mash can also be used as the basis of a distilled alcohol called *araa.*

Agricultural produce is supplemented by pastoralism. Most households keep sheep and goats, plus at least a few cattle, yaks, or *dzo,* the crossbreeds of these animals. Most of the large yak herds in Tibet are under the care of the nomadic and seminomadic population. The herds move with the seasons, ascending to the high pastures in spring and summer, then returning to the lower settlements with the onset of colder weather. Nomads, of course, cover a considerably larger area than farmers do; they also embark on long trading expeditions from the lakes and plains regions of the high northern plateau, loading bags of salt and animal products onto yaks and sheep alike, then heading for the areas of settled cultivation in the south, even as far as Nepal, to trade their goods for grain.

Milk and its derivatives are the chief product from livestock. Butter is used principally in salted Tibetan tea, as an oil for the hair and face, and for a range of ceremonial purposes such as fueling ritual lamps. A dried cheese called *churpi* is made from buttermilk; it will keep indefinitely.

Yaks are the source of many important materials, and little of the animal goes to waste. The meat is eaten raw and fresh while the animal is being butchered and for a few days thereafter, or raw and dried in the following months. The blood, which in some areas is drunk fresh and warm by young men as an aphrodisiac and general tonic, is the major ingredient in sausages, as are the lungs, spleen, and stomach. The stomach is also used as a receptacle for fat and butter. Horned animal skulls often adorn rooftops and lintels as a deterrent to potentially harmful spirits, while the horns themselves have a number of other, chiefly magical, functions. Yak hides are sometimes dried as floor coverings or, with the hair removed, cut into a long spiral for use as rope. Wood is scarce on most of the plateau, making dried yak dung an important source of fuel. The ash from the burned dung is spread on the fields as a meager fertilizer. The long, coarse hair that grows as a skirt on the flanks and legs of the yak is woven into ropes, sacks, blankets, and, most important for the nomads, warm and durable tents. The finer wool beneath is spun into yarn for clothing or compressed into felt to make large-brimmed hats and the soft, rope-soled boots worn by both sexes. Both men and women spin the wool, though only women weave, using either backstrap looms or more sophisticated devices with treadles. Sewing is considered to be men's work, and leather-sheathed needle cases are among the numerous objects that might hang from a man's belt beside his flint and striker and his silver knife sheath.

The division of labor between the sexes is generally not as clearly defined in Tibet as in many other Asian societies. Both men and women fetch water, for example, and men will often perform tasks such as milking animals, cooking, and taking care of children. Women generally have nothing to do with butchering animals or handling and cooking fresh meat (although dried meat is acceptable), and nowhere do women plow the fields. Other agricultural chores such as weeding, irrigating, harvesting, and threshing are usually performed by both sexes.

The usual form of marriage in Tibet once was fraternal polyandry, accord-ing to which a woman would marry all the brothers in a household—except, of course, the family monk, traditionally the second brother. The brothers' status in the house and their sexual rights to their wife were normally determined by seniority, and the youngest of several brothers might opt out of the marriage, forfeiting his rights to the inheritance and finding a wife of his own. The chief rea-son for the prevalence of polyandry seems to have lain precisely in this matter of inheritance: with only one childbearing woman in each generation of a household there could be only one line of succession (all the brothers were addressed indiscriminately as "Father" by the children) and the landholding, which in many cases could barely support a family, did not need to be subdivided among heirs. Polyandrous marriages are still widespread in Tibet, but monogamy is increas-ingly common, with young couples building new houses for themselves away from the rest of the family.

As for the houses themselves, architectural styles vary from one place to another, with climate being a major design factor. In the monsoon-washed south-eastern region, for example, all houses have pitched roofs, and the abundance of forests makes it possible to use large quantities of wood in the construction. The ground floor often serves as an animal shelter, with the family living on the first floor, while the attic, generally open-sided to allow air to circulate, is used for drying fodder. Flat roofs are the rule in Central Tibet, and only wealthy houses have two stories. Walls are made of sun-dried mud bricks covered in mud plaster and painted with a wash of white lime. Livestock is kept in a courtyard, which may sometimes contain a roofed stable to protect weaker animals in the winter months.

FROM COLLECTIVIZATION TO THE PRESENT

The collectivization of agriculture and pastoralism during the 1960s was not popular with most Tibetans, and the reintroduction two decades later of the private sector in the form of the "responsibility system" has been a welcome move. Ani-mals and fields were redistributed equally to individuals, entirely irrespective of age and sex. This was clearly the fairest way to go about the division, but since it was the household that had been, and had again become, the basic economic unit, larger families obviously did better. Predictably enough, the economic parity with which the responsibility system began has not lasted: some people flourished in the new environment of commercial freedom while others failed disastrously. Interestingly, it seems that among both farmers and nomads there is a trend for families to return to the economic niche they occupied before collectivization. The Tibetans' business acumen is apparently as hard to kill as their religious faith.

Religious freedoms have reappeared in the past ten years and, with them, religious practice has come into the open. The government is providing limited funding for the restoration of certain monasteries and the public is supplement-ing this with voluntary donations. Restoration, of course, can never be synony-mous with replacement.

The resurgence of popular religion is evident from a glance at the appearance of villages. Hilltop cairns devoted to territorial divinities and shrines to household gods that stand at rooftop corners have a cared-for look about them, and are often

Over half the population of Tibet consists of nomadic herders living in woven yak-hair tents

decorated with red clay and surmounted by little flags of many colors. The tradition of prayer-flags probably has its origin in the ancient custom (which still survives) of hanging black and white wool in trees; flags printed with appropriate prayers are the more respectable Buddhist version of the practice. The bamboo stems that support the flags on the shrines do not grow on the dry plateau but are brought from the cloud forests of the Nepalese borderland. The white swastikas painted over doorways are an ancient symbol of good fortune that found their way into Tibet from India. Traditionally, the feet of Buddhist swastikas point clockwise, while the direction is reversed among the Bönpos. The abundance of counterclockwise swastikas in Central Tibet does not indicate a large Bönpo population; they are slips of the artists' brushes occasioned by decades of unfamiliarity with the convention.

Another favorite doorway design is a round sun sitting in the shallow cup of the moon, often with a squiggle appearing from the top of the sun. As far as most villagers are concerned the emblem is some sort of protective sign, but it originates from a fundamental tantric idea. The moon is the masculine principle and represents Means, while the sun represents Wisdom, the passive feminine principle (the gender attributed to the sun and moon actually varies in certain contexts). The squiggle at the top is the "drop," the "thought of enlightenment," which arises from the union of Wisdom and Means.

Theocratic societies are rarely characterized by good government, and in Tibet the introspective conservatism of the former monastic establishment left the country without any effective foreign policy, and consequently with no diplomatic defense against the disastrous events of the 1950s. But Tibetans, to their credit, never seem to have confused church politics for religious matters. Buddhism flourished in Tibet long before there was a theocracy. It has survived it by three decades, and may well outlive another regime.

Charles Ramble is an anthropologist who has carried out research in Tibetan communities in both Nepal and Tibet. He has lived in Nepal and India for fifteen years and is currently the senior naturalist of Machan Wildlife Resort in Nepal's Royal Chitwan National Park.

History and Religion

It is difficult to differentiate Tibet's history from the growth of its religions, for the religious aspirations of the great monastic orders were often intertwined with politics and intrigue; as the wealth and landholdings of the monasteries increased, so did their ability to exert temporal power over Tibet. Modern Tibetan history dates back to the seventh century A.D., when a standard written language was introduced. The traditional accounts of history before this time are based on both fact and legend. A mythical king is said to have descended from heaven onto Lhabab Ri, a mountain in the Yarlung Valley near Tsethang, and established his palace at Yumbu Lagang, a structure believed to be the oldest in Tibet. His descendants are the line of kings that included King Songtsen Gampo, the skillful seventh-century administrator and commander who led his armies from their small kingdom in the Yarlung Valley, conquering a huge area that sprawled across Central Asia to China and included almost all of the Himalaya. The great Tibetan empire lasted about 250 years, until the royal dynasty collapsed in the ninth century, not from external pressures but from internal strife centered around religion. From that time onward Tibet's political and religious history are almost inseparable.

BUDDHISM IN TIBET

Tibetan Buddhism is by far the predominant religion in Tibet and the entire Himalayan region. Although its roots can be traced back to the teachings of Sakyamuni, the historical Buddha, the highly ritualized tantric form practiced in Tibet bears little resemblance to Theravada Buddhism as practiced in Sri Lanka, Thailand, and Burma. Buddhism was slow to find Tibet relative to its appearance throughout the rest of Asia. The first Tibetan Buddhist temples, including the well-known Jokhang in Lhasa, were built in the seventh century during the reign of King Songtsen Gampo, some 1300 years after the death of Sakyamuni. Although this king is traditionally acknowledged as one of the great Buddhist kings in Tibet, he apparently followed the pre-Buddhist practices of his ancestors, known as the Bön religion. King Thrisong Detsen was even more sympathetic to the new religion, helping to found Samye monastery, Tibet's first Buddhist institution, in the eighth century. He also invited several Indian Buddhist scholars to teach in Tibet including Guru Rimpoche (his Sanskrit name is Padmasambhava, the "Lotus Born"), a tantric master/sorcerer who is now revered as the founder of the Nyingmapa Buddhist tradition in Tibet.

Adherents of the Bön religion, however, resisted this growth of Buddhism. The clash between these two groups over political influence ultimately caused the royal dynasty to collapse following the murder of King Langdarma in the ninth century, who is infamously remembered in Tibet as the great persecutor of Buddhism. Although organized religion languished due to a lack of wealthy patrons, both the Buddhists and the Bön priests continued their teachings on a smaller grassroots level without temples or shrines.

Some 100 years after Langdarma's death monastic Buddhism started reestablishing itself. Religious scholars returned, temples were built, and the Indian tantric texts were translated and brought to Tibet. In the eleventh century the Indian Buddhist master Atisa was invited to Western Tibet by descendants of the old royal dynasty. His teachings emphasized monastic discipline and the tradition of direct instruction from teacher to student, laying the foundation for Tibet's first great school of Buddhism, the Kadampa sect. Later that century disciples of Atisa founded two important monasteries in Central Tibet, Reteng and Narthang.

This second diffusion of Buddhism spread quickly in Tibet, encouraging more Buddhist scholars and ascetics to venture north of the Himalaya. The form of Buddhism that particularly interested the Tibetans was tantricism, a school of thought that emphasizes highly ritualized worship of deities and the use of specialized meditational and yogic techniques to achieve spiritual enlightenment, even in one lifetime. This tradition is called Vajrayana Buddhism, the "Diamond Path."

Some Tibetans traveled to India to study Sanskrit tantric texts. Most notable of these translators were Drogmi, the founder of the spiritual tradition embraced by Sakya monastery and the Sakyapa sect, and Marpa, whose teachings formed the basis of the Kargyüpa Buddhist sect, the "Oral Tradition," which emphasizes direct instruction of a student by his master, as well as strict self-denial and intense meditational techniques. Through the disciples of Marpa's renowned student Milarepa, Tibet's poet-saint, six major monasteries and Kargyüpa subsects were founded in Central Tibet during the twelfth century, including Tshurphu, Taglung, Drigung, and Daensathil monasteries.

Large monastic centers continued to flourish through the thirteenth and fourteenth centuries despite the constant political turmoil among them over the control of Tibet. In the mid-thirteenth century the Sakya *lamas* became administrators of the country with the help of the Mongol armies residing on the northern borders, the descendants of Genghis Khan. Eventually the Mongols became religious patrons of the Sakyapa sect under Kublai Khan, emperor of the Yuan dynasty in China, who handed over control of Tibet to these *lamas*. The other great monasteries also sought patrons among different Mongol chiefs, leading to sporadic armed conflicts between the various factions. When the Yuan dynasty began to weaken, a powerful lord from the Yarlung Valley, Changchub Gyaatsen, successfully led his armies against Sakya in the mid-fourteenth century and became the new ruler of Tibet. His descendants, the Phagmodhru family, ruled Tibet until the late fifteenth century, when their ministers, the Rimpung princes of Tsang province, usurped control of the country.

During this time a respected Kadampa scholar and teacher named Tsong Khapa founded Ganden monastery. A firm believer in scholarship and strict monastic discipline, his uncompromising religious views quickly attracted many followers and patrons from the Lhasa area. Tsong Khapa's school of reformed teachings became known as the Gelugpa sect, the "Model of Virtue." Two of his main disciples founded Drepung and Sera monasteries near Lhasa. Regardless of their virtues, the Gelugpas didn't take long to become involved in worldly affairs, particularly politics.

The Rimpung princes were ousted by their own ministers, the governors of Tsang province, in the 1560s. The new rulers were patrons of Tshurphu and Naynang monasteries, to the northwest of Lhasa. An intense rivalry between these Kargyüpa strongholds and the Gelugpa monasteries around Lhasa prompted the abbot of Drepung, Sonam Gyatsho, to seek foreign assistance. Late in the sixteenth century he met with Altan Khan, chief of the Mongol tribes who were still based north of Tibet. The Khan and Sonam Gyatsho exchanged gifts and bestowed honorific titles upon each other; the abbot was given the title Ta-le (a Mongolian word meaning "ocean," now better known as Dalai, or Dalai Lama). As a result, the first two abbots of Drepung were retroactively named the first and second Dalai Lama, and Sonam Gyatsho is revered as the third in this lineage. Following his death, a young boy was recognized as the spiritual incarnation of Sonam Gyatsho, establishing the tradition for choosing the Dalai Lama that exists to this day.

In the early seventeenth century a dispute between the kings of Tsang and the Gelugpas led to the sacking of Drepung and Sera monasteries. The Gelugpas retaliated, assisted by their Mongol patrons. The conflict reached its peak in the 1640s when the Mongols captured and killed the king of Tsang, and Tshurphu monastery was sacked. The head of the Gelugpa hierarchy at that time, the fifth Dalai Lama, went on to become one of the most powerful and influential figures in Tibetan history; the Gelugpas were to maintain a religious domination over Tibet until the twentieth century.

The political role of the Gelugpas was more tenuous, especially following the death of the fifth Dalai Lama. A Mongol army invaded in the early eighteenth century and established their general as the governor of Tibet. The sixth Dalai Lama died mysteriously in the company of this general; a dispute over the boy chosen to be the next Dalai Lama encouraged the Chinese Manchu emperor to have his armies march on Lhasa. The Chinese delivered a boy who was grandly accepted by the Tibetan people as the seventh Dalai Lama, but the Chinese remained as overlords of Tibet's political affairs until the collapse of the Manchu dynasty. In 1911 the thirteenth Dalai Lama expelled the Chinese from Tibet and reestablished the Gelugpa theocracy. The Gelugpas remained in control of Tibet until 1950 when Communist Chinese armies entered Lhasa. The fourteenth Dalai Lama fled to India in 1959, establishing a Tibetan government-in-exile based in Dharamsala, to the north of Delhi. Monasteries that were destroyed during the Cultural Revolution are now slowly reestablishing themselves, sometimes with financial aid from the Chinese government, but the educational system that was so crucial to Tibetan Buddhism has been mostly dismantled. Some of the religious traditions have managed to survive, though, and are now being taught by *lamas* living in exile in India.

OTHER RELIGIONS

What many people don't realize about Tibetan Buddhism is that it existed on two major, but very different, planes: the religion as it was practiced by the monks and the daily rituals of the lay people. Tibetan Buddhism is an amalgam of religious ideas, both indigenous and of foreign origin (mostly Indian), that matured and developed into a unique monastic culture. Tibetan Buddhism is also called Lamaism due to the importance of great monasteries and the vast numbers of monks. But when you see pilgrims burning incense at holy sites, pouring offerings of *tsampa* and *chhang* onto the hearths, and walking around prayer walls, these are not purely Buddhist rituals but carryovers from the old folk religions that have persisted for millennia in Tibet. The Tibetans' lives are greatly influenced by their concern for appeasing the local deities residing in the ground, in springs, atop mountains, and within their homes. To anger these spirits could be disastrous; to propitiate them with the pleasant smells of incense bush and other offerings can bring harmony to their lives and family, good harvests, and safe crossings over the mountains. If you have the opportunity to drink *chhang* in someone's home, watch what is done before the first sip: the ring finger is inserted into the *chhang* and offering drops are flicked into the air. When the butter tea is being made, a dab of butter will be smudged onto the churn as an offering before it is served. Other ancient rituals are performed before a house can be built, before a new wife moves into her husband's home, and before the fields can be plowed, all folk traditions that are now an integral part of the Tibetan Buddhist religion.

The other main religion in Tibet is Bön. Many Westerners assume it is the pre-Buddhist religion of Tibet, but this is only partially true. The Bön religion as it is known today traces its origins to a Buddha-like historical figure named Shanrab, who is said to have lived in a land to the west of Tibet, perhaps near present-day Iran. The religion has a bigger following in Northern and Eastern Tibet, though two important Bön monasteries, Maenri and Yungdrungling, were established near Shigatse.

The pre-Buddhist Bön religion was not an organized monastic order, but rather a class of priests who specialized in funeral rites and sacrifices. Each of the Tibetan royal kings, even those who are said to have championed Buddhism, were buried at Chonggye Valley with funerals conducted by Bön priests. After the death of King Langdarma these priests seem to have disappeared; in about the eleventh century a new religion appeared that also called itself Bön, its followers the Bönpo. It differed from the religion of the older Bön priests, having many doctrinal similarities to the new tantric schools of Buddhism that were being established in Tibet. Like the Guru Rimpoche cult of the Nyingmapa sect, the Bönpo developed a mythology and religious cult around Shanrab.

Initially the Bön religion remained small, with individual lamas relying on the patronage of a few families. With the rapid growth of Buddhist monastic centers in Central Tibet, Bönpo decided they too needed a major religious center and founded Maenri *gompa* in the early fifteenth century. A canon of Bönpo texts, much like the Buddhist Kangyur and Tangyur, was compiled, and they also adopted pilgrimage circuits, prayer wheels, and *mani* walls. The Bönpo practitioners, however, spin the wheels and walk around sacred sites in a counterclockwise manner, opposite to the Buddhists; even the swastika they use is the reverse of the Buddhist symbol. In the Bön monasteries, the similarities to Buddhism are uncanny. The maroon-robed monks are nearly indistinguishable from their Buddhist counterparts and the statue of Shanrab on the main altar is almost identical to the Buddha, down to the blue head-covering with the rounded protuberance on top. If you are interested in seeing a Bön monastery, see the description of an

Left: Fresco of Milarepa, Tibet's beloved poet-saint; he is typically shown with his hand held to his ear, for he would sing his teachings to his disciples, Pelgyeling monastery. Right: Nun on pilgrimage

outing to Yungdrungling, near Shigatse, in the section "Shigatse."

Not to be forgotten are the Tibetan Muslims. Though Islam has never been a major religious force in Tibet, Arab and Kashmiri traders have long lived in Tibet, selling goods in the bazaars alongside the Nepalis and Tibetans. Mostly through intermarriage, a population of Tibetan Muslims now reside in the larger cities, particularly in Lhasa. The mosque is tucked into the maze of buildings to the east of the Barkor.

Festivals

The Tibetan year is based upon a lunar calendar of twelve months, with the New Year usually occurring sometime in February. Each month consists of thirty days, with the full moon on the fifteenth day and the new moon on the thirtieth day. The majority of Tibetan festivals are religious in nature. On the tenth day of every month the Nyingmapa sect celebrates special Guru Rimpoche days, the most important of these being in the sixth month to commemorate his birth. An informative Tibetan/Western pocket calendar with dates of the Tibetan festivals is printed annually by the Rigpa Fellowship, 44 St. Paul's Crescent, London, England NW1 9TN.

First month, first to third days: Losar, the Tibetan New Year. The largest and most popular nonreligious festival of the year, Losar is primarily a family-oriented festival, celebrated in homes and with friends by eating special pastries and drinking plenty of *chhang*. On New Year's Day in Lhasa pilgrims throng the Jokhang temple to make offerings of butter in the burning lamps. The great incense burners around the Barkor billow scented smoke continuously as queues of worshipers wait to add their offerings of juniper boughs. Everyone dresses in their finest clothes and many people parade around the Barkor. Early in the morning of the third day pilgrims climb the hills around Lhasa to light fires of incense bush. In town, new colored prayer flags are hung out above each home and small incense fires burn everywhere.

First month, eighth to sixteenth days: Monlam Chenmo, the Great Prayer Festival. Founded in 1409 by Tsong Khapa to celebrate the miracles performed by Buddha in India, at Sravasti, Monlam Chenmo is the greatest ritual event of the year. In former times up to 20,000 monks would crowd into Lhasa from the great Gelugpa monasteries for this festival. More recently more than 1000 monks have come for the public and private prayer celebrations held in the Jokhang temple. The festival ends with an early-morning procession of the Future Buddha (Dawa Jhampa) around the Barkor on the sixteenth day.

First month, fifteenth day: Butter Sculpture Festival. On the eve of the full moon thousands of pilgrims come to see great sculptures made with colored yak butter that have been erected around the Barkor. As part of the ceremony, a grand orchestra of monks perform below the largest sculptures at the entrance to the Jokhang. The sculptures remain all night, then are removed before sunrise the following morning. Traditionally, wealthy noble families of Lhasa would finance a sculpture to be placed along the Barkor; now they are made by the monks at the Jokhang.

Fourth month, tenth day: *Lama* mask dances at Tshurphu monastery.

Fourth month, fifteenth day: Saga Dawa, Buddha's Enlightenment and Ascent to Heaven. Saga Dawa is the biggest religious festival after Monlam Chenmo, and celebrates the enlightenment of Buddha and his entry into nirvana upon his death. Thousands of pilgrims crowd into the Jokhang, and the Lingkor circumambulation route around Lhasa has a steady flow of worshipers for the entire day.

Fourth month, fifteenth to eighteenth days: Tamang, the Gyantse Horse Racing Festival. The largest annual festival in Gyantse, with horse racing, yak racing, and *lama* mask dancing. Also, a fourteenth-century giant *thangka* is hung one morning before sunrise from the monastery's display wall. This festival also marks the anniversary of the 1904 battle at Gyantse between Tibetans and Colonel Younghusband's invading British troops.

Fifth month, fourteenth to sixteenth days: Tashilhumpo Giant *Thangka* Festival. Immense silk applique hangings of the Buddhas of the Three Times (Opaame, Sakya Tupa, and Dawa Jhampa) are displayed on three consecutive days

Conch-shell horns are sounded before the start of prayer ceremonies

at Tashilhumpo. Get to the monastery early each morning to file past these works of art before the gates are closed. *Lama* mask dancing may be held in the lower courtyard of the monastery.

Sixth month, fourth day: Chhökor Düchhan, the Wheel of Dharma Festival. This celebration of Buddha teaching his first sermon after achieving enlightenment at Bodhgaya is also a special day for paying homage to the holy mountains. Pilgrims climb Gepel Ri, the holy mountain behind Drepung, to make offerings of incense and prayer flags on the summit. A giant silk applique *thangka* may be displayed at Ganden monastery.

Sixth month, thirtieth day: Drepung Monastery Giant *Thangka* Festival. The large *thangka* is displayed for only a few hours early in the morning on a hill beside Drepung. This marks the start of the Yogurt Festival (see below); after the *thangka* comes down the first opera dances are performed in the main courtyard.

Seventh month, first to seventh days: Zhodü, the Yogurt (or Opera) Festival. Norbulingka is the scene of a week-long picnic of eating and drinking, with

Tibetan Opera performances in the gardens and at other venues around town. Opera troupes from around Tibet perform the entire week.

End of seventh month to mid eighth month: The Bathing Festival. Tibetans perform ritual bathing in rivers and lakes for purity and longevity in this thanksgiving festival. People erect tents and come to the rivers for picnics and plenty of splashing, especially on Thieves Island in Lhasa. The festival starts when a certain star, considered the abode of a god who converts water into a life-giving ambrosia, rises at dawn above the highest peak in Lhasa.

Eighth month, ninth to eleventh days: Zaymo Chempo, mask dances at Tashilhumpo.

Ninth month, twenty-second day: Lhabab Düchhan, the Gods Descending Festival. One of the four major religious festivals of the year, Lhabab Düchhan celebrates Buddha's return to earth after spending three months in heaven teaching the law of Buddhism to his mother and the gods. Throngs of worshipers vie to visit the Jokhang and pilgrims circumambulate the Barkor and the Lingkor.

Tenth month, fifteenth day: Pelden Lhamo Feast, or the Fairy Maiden Festival. Celebration of the protectress Pelden Lhamo, with special prayer ceremonies at the Jokhang. One of the highlights is the procession around the Barkor with a Pelden Lhamo statue, which otherwise remains covered during the rest of the year.

Tenth month, twenty-fifth day: Ganden Angchhu, the Lantern Festival. Lamps and candles are lit on the rooftops of monasteries and homes to celebrate the death and entry into nirvana of Tsong Khapa. Traditionally Tsong Khapa's image was carried in a great procession accompanied by monks carrying torches and lamps.

Twelfth month, thirtieth day: Banishing the Evil Spirits Festival. A day for exorcising the evils from the old year so the New Year will begin on a good note. Tibetans busily clean their homes, chasing away the bad spirits to let the benevolent ones come in. *Lama* mask dances were traditionally held throughout the country on the twenty-ninth day, though now they seem to be confined to Tashilhumpo monastery on the thirtieth day. The mask dance is a symbolic performance of good triumphing over evil.

APPENDICES

Mount Cho Oyu (26,748 ft, 8153 m), one of the world's fourteen highest peaks, is situated on the Tibet–Nepal border

Appendix A

Trekking and Mountaineering Agencies

China Tibet International Sports Travel (TIST)
Jigme Wangchuk, Manager, Sales and Marketing
Himalaya Hotel
Lhasa, Tibet
People's Republic of China
Phone: 23775, 22293
Telex: 68019 TIST CN

Chinese International Travel Service (CITS), Lhasa Branch
Chang Chan, Manager
168 West Beijing Road
Lhasa, Tibet
People's Republic of China
Phone: 24277, 24417
Telex: 68009 ZMLAS CN

Chinese Mountaineering Association (CMA)
9 Tiyuguan Road
Beijing, People's Republic of China
Telex: 20089 CMA BJ CN

Chinese Workers Travel Service (CWTS)
G.T. Sonam, Deputy General Manger
Lhasa Holiday Inn, Room 1110
Lhasa, Tibet
People's Republic of China Phone:
24285
Telex: 68025 WTBC CN

Chinese Youth Travel Service (CYTS)
Wang Song Ping, President
Lhasa Holiday Inn, Room 1103
Lhasa, Tibet
People's Republic of China
Phone: 24173
Telex: 68017 CYTS CN

Lhasa Travel Company
Tsewang Sida, Deputy Director
Sunlight Hotel
Lhasa, Tibet
People's Republic of China
Phone: 23196
Telex: 68016 TRCLS CN

Tibet Mountaineering Association (TMA)
Gao Mouxing, Director
No. 7 East Lingkor Road, near Himalaya Hotel
Lhasa, Tibet
People's Republic of China
Phone: 22981
Telex: 68029 TMA CN

Appendix B

Suggested Reading

CULTURE AND RELIGION

Anderson, Walt. *Open Secrets: A Western Guide to Buddhism.* New York: Viking Press, 1979.

Avedon, John. *In Exile from the Land of Snows.* London: Wisdom, 1985.

Aziz, Barbara Nimri. *Tibetan Frontier Families.* New Delhi: Vikas, 1978.

Bell, Charles. *The People of Tibet.* London: Oxford, 1928.

Dalai Lama. *My Land and My People.* New York: Potala, 1983.

———. *My Tibet.* Berkeley: University of California Press, 1990.

Evans-Wentz, W.Y., ed. *Tibet's Great Yogi Milarepa: A Biography from the Tibetan.* London: Oxford University Press, 1969.

Govinda, Lama Anagarika. *The Way of the White Clouds.* Boston: Prajna, 1985.

Stein, R.A. *Tibetan Civilization.* Palo Alto, CA: Stanford University Press, 1972.

Tucci, Giuseppe. *The Religions of Tibet.* Translated by Geoffrey Samuel. London: Routledge and Kegan Paul, 1970.

———. *Tibet: Land of Snows.* London, 1967.

Waddell, L. Austine. *Tibetan Buddhism.* New York: Dover, 1972.

Yeshe, Lama. *Introduction to Tantra: A Vision of Totality.* London: Wisdom, 1987.

GUIDEBOOKS

Batchelor, Stephan. *The Tibet Guide.* London: Wisdom, 1987.

Buckley, Michael. *Tibet: A Travel Survivial Kit.* South Yarra, Australia: Lonely Planet, 1986.

Dowman, Keith. *The Power Places of Central Tibet: The Pilgrim's Guide.* London: Routledge and Kegan Paul, 1988.

Pranavananda, Swami. *Kailas Manasarovar.* New Delhi, India, 1949.

Swift, Hugh. *Trekking in Nepal, West Tibet and Bhutan.* San Francisco: Sierra Club Books, 1989.

HEALTH AND MEDICAL INFORMATION

Bezruchka, Steven. *The Pocket Doctor.* Seattle: The Mountaineers, 1988.

"First Aid: Quick Information for Mountaineering and Backcountry Use." Seattle: The Mountaineers, 1982.

Hackett, Peter. *Mountain Sickness: Prevention, Recognition and Treatment.* New York: American Alpine Club, 1980.

Wilkerson, James A., ed. *Medicine for Mountaineering*. Seattle: The Mountaineers, 1985.

HISTORY AND EXPLORATION

Allen, Charles. *A Mountain in Tibet*. London: Futura Macdonald & Co., 1983.

Bruce, Charles G. *The Assault on Mount Everest, 1922*. London, 1923.

David-Neel, Alexandra. *My Journey to Lhasa*. London: Virago, 1983.

Flemming, Peter. *Bayonets to Lhasa*. Hong Kong: Oxford University Press, 1984.

Harrer, Heinrich. *Seven Years in Tibet*. London: Pan Books, 1956.

Holdich, Thomas. *Tibet the Mysterious*. London, 1908.

Hopkirk, Peter. *Trespassers on the Roof of the World*. London: Oxford University Press, 1982.

Keay, John. *When Men and Mountains Meet*. London, 1977.

MacGregor, John. *Tibet: A Chronicle of Exploration*. London, 1925.

Norton, Edward F. *The Fight for Everest: 1924*. London, 1925.

Richardson, Hugh. *Tibet and its History*. Boston: Shambala, 1984.

Rowell, Galen. *Mountains of the Middle Kingdom*. San Francisco: Sierra Club Books, 1983.

Sandberg, Graham. *The Exploration of Tibet*. Delhi, 1973.

Shakabpa, Tsepon, W.D. Ti*bet: A Political History*. New Haven, CT: Yale University Press, 1967.

Snellgrove, David, and Hugh Richardson. *A Cultural History of Tibet*. Boulder, CO: Prajna Press, 1968.

Snelling, John. *The Sacred Mountain*. London and The Hague, East West Publications, 1983.

Thomas, Lowell. *Out of this World: Across the Himalayas to Forbidden Tibet*. New York: Greystone Press, 1950.

Tucci, Giuseppe. *To Lhasa and Beyond*. New Delhi: Oxford and IBH Publishing Co., 1983.

LANGUAGE BOOKS

Bell, Charles A. *English-Tibetan Colloquial Dictionary*. Calcutta: Firma KLM Pvt. Ltd., 1977.

Bloomfield, Andrew, and Tshering Yangki. *Tibetan Phrasebook*. Ithaca, NY: Snow Lion Publications, 1987. (Includes language cassettes.)

Lay, Dr. Nancy Duke. *Say It in Chinese (Mandarin)*. New York: Dover Publications, 1980.

Thonden, Losang. *Modern Tibetan Language* (2 volumes). Dharamsala, India: Library of Tibetan Works and Archives, 1984. (Separate language tapes available.)

MOUNTAINEERING

Baume, Louis C. *Sivalaya: Explorations of the 8000-metre Peaks of the Himalaya.* Seattle: The Mountaineers, 1978.

Hall, Lincoln. *White Limbo.* Macmahon's Point, Australia: Weldons, 1985.

Howard-Bury, C.K. *Mount Everest: The Reconnaissance, 1921.* London, 1922.

Scott, Doug, and Alex MacIntyre. *The Shishapangma Expedition.* Seattle: The Mountaineers, 1984.

Venables, Steven. *Everest: The Kangshung Face.* Bangalore, India: Arnold Publishers, 1989.

NATURAL HISTORY

De Schaunesee, Rudolphe Meyer. *The Birds of China.* Washington, D.C.: Smithsonian Institution Press, 1984.

Dick, John Henry; Salim Ali, and S. Dillon Ripley. *A Pictorial Guide to Birds of the Indian Subcontinent.* Bombay: Oxford University Press, 1983.

Fleming, Robert Sr., Robert Fleming Jr., and Lain Singh Bangdel. *Birds of Nepal.* Kathmandu, 1984.

Mierow, Dorothy, and Tirtha Bahadur Shrestha. *Himalayan Flowers and Trees.* Kathmandu: Sahayogi Press, 1987.

Molnar, Peter. "The Geologic Evolution of the Tibetan Plateau." *American Scientist* 77, (July–August 1989) 350–60.

———. "The Geologic History and Structure of the Himalaya." *American Scientist* 74, (March–April 1986) 144–54.

Polunin, Oleg and Adam Stainton. *Concise Flowers of the Himalaya.* Delhi: Oxford University Press, 1987.

Schaller, George. *Mountain Monarchs: Wild Sheep and Goats of the Himalaya.* Chicago: University of Chicago Press, 1977.

Vaurie, Charles. *Tibet and its Birds.* London: H.F. and G. Witherby, 1972.

Appendix C

Glossary of Tibetan and Foreign Words

ani	Buddhist nun
ani gompa	Buddhist nunnery
araa	distilled alcohol usually made from barley
ba	nomadic herder tent made from woven yak hair
bhalay	flat Tibetan wheat bread
bodhisattva	(in Tibetan, *changchub sempa*) an enlightened being who has devoted himself to freeing all other beings from suffering. Chenrezig, the patron saint of Tibet, is a *bodhisattva*
chhang	Tibetan beer, usually brewed from barley
chha-tsal ghang	special site where pilgrims prostrate
chhu	water, river, or stream
chötaen	(also spelled *chorten*) traditionally a domelike or conical monument, set on a square base and topped by a thick spire; it may contain sacred objects, funeral remains, or clay offering tablets
dhrapa	novice monk
drubphuu	meditation cave
dukhang	assembly hall in a monastery for recitation of prayers; usually where the books and sacred objects of a monastery are kept
dzong	fortress
gompa	monastery
gom-chhaen	religious hermit (ascetic)
gön-khang	special place or protector's temple in a monastery where the *gönpo* is worshipped
gönpo	protecting deity of a particular monastery, Buddhist sect, or region
khang	house
khangtsaen	monks' residence hall
kora	pilgrimage ritual of encircling a sacred place, such as a shrine, a monastery, or a mountain; used loosely in this text to refer to a route used by pilgrims
la	mountain pass
la-dzay	a votive pile of stones, like a large cairn, found at the top of mountain passes as an offering to the gods
lama	a high, learned monk
lha	god or deity
lhakhang	"house of the god"; a temple
"Lha Sö!"	verbal offering to the gods, often shouted to express thanks when one safely reaches the summit of a mountain pass
lingka	park or garden, e.g., Norbulingka, the Dalai Lama's Summer Palace in the Lhasa Valley

lu	serpent demon/protectors which reside in rivers, springs, rocks, and the earth
lungdaa	prayer flag
mandala	magic circle; an elaborate, geometrically arranged diagram often painted on the ceilings and walls of monasteries, used for the worship of deities or as an aid for meditational practices
mani	prayer, or related to prayers; also used as a term for a prayer wheel or a wall with carved prayer stones
mantra	a special type of sound, syllable, or oral prayer, usually associated with a specific tantric ritual or deity worship
momo	steamed or boiled dumpling containing meat
Om mani padme hum	"Hail to the jewel in the lotus"; the prayer, or *mantra* of Chenrezig, the God of Compassion and the patron saint of Tibet
phuu	cave (also spelled *phug*)
rangjön	self-manifested; especially religious statues and words or characters etched in rock
ri	mountain, ridge, or hill
rimpoche	"precious teacher"; a special title used for high, learned, often incarnate monks
rithrö	hermitage or religious retreat
tantra	(in Tibetan *gyü*) "thread" or "continuity"; a highly specialized form of yogic meditation and ritual divided into four classes or teachings (also called Tantras), which emphasize a "quick path" to enlightenment, as opposed to other types of Buddhism that teach a more gradual means of attaining the highest spiritual level
thangka	Tibetan scroll painting
truku	an incarnate *lama* who is the human manifestation of a Buddhist deity or *bodhisattva,* i.e., the Dalai Lama; often the spiritual head of a monastery
tsampa	toasted barley flour, the staple food for most Tibetans
tsha-tsha	a small, clay offering tablet imprinted with religious figures or shaped like a miniature *chötaen,* deposited by pilgrims at holy sites
yab-say-sum	"father and his two sons"; Tsong Khapa, the founder of the Gelugpa sect, and his two main disciples, Gyaltshab and Khaydhrub
yuan	Chinese dollar
zhabjay	footprint; a religiously significant, often oversized footprint embedded in rock at many monasteries and pilgrimage sites

Appendix D

Mountaineering Peaks in Tibet

The Mount Everest–Shishapangma Region

Mount Everest (Qomolangma): 29,028 ft, 8848 m
Cho Oyu (Chowuyo): 26,748 ft, 8153 m
Shishapangma (Shixiapangma): 26,397 ft, 8046 m
Gyachung Ghang (Gyelchongkang): 25,990 ft, 7922 m
Phola Ghangchhan (Molamenchen): 25,134 ft, 7661 m
Changtse (Zhangzi or Jangzi): 24,770 ft, 7550 m
Lapchi Ghang (Labchikang): 24,170 ft, 7367 m
Cho Oye (also Cho Aui or Nangpai Gosum 2; in Chinese, Chowuyi): 24,120 ft,
   7352 m
Shifeng (also Nubzi; possibly also known as Porong Ri): 23,924 ft, 7292 m
Ghangbenchhan (Kangbochen): 23,658 ft, 7211 m
Melungtse (Meilongze): 23,559 ft, 7181 m
Kelakangri (Telakangri): 21,870 ft, 6666 m
Tsangla (Zangia): 21,309 ft, 6495 m
Pulerri: 21,010 ft, 6404 m

Southern Tibet/Bhutan Border Region

Kulakangri: 24,780 ft, 7553 m
Kangkeduo (Kanggado; Kang To): 23,162 ft, 7060 m

North of Lhasa

Nyanchhan Thanglha (Nychenthangla): 23,330 ft, 7111 m

Central Tibet

Nechinghangsang (Nychenkangsa): 23,641 ft, 7206 m
Jiang Sanglamo (Jangsanglamo): 20,748 ft, 6324 m
Jei Tongsusong (Jeidhongsusong): 20,485 ft, 6244 m

Western Tibet

Gurla Mandhata (Namonani): 25,355 ft, 7728 m

INDEX

acclimatization, 45-46
accommodations, 53-54
Advance base camp, 206
airlines, 26, 54
Ali, 99, 243
Alien's Travel Permit (ATP), 19, 26
Altan Khan, 285
altimeter, 94
Altin Tagh, 263
altitude sickness, 44-48
Amdo, 17
Andrade, Father, 18
Angker Ri, 120
Arun River, 192
Arun River Valley, 190
Astin Tagh, 263
Atisa, 161

Barkor, 54
Berutsana, 131
Bharka, 99, 246
Bharka plains, 243
Bhö Chhu, 229
Bhö Chhu Canyon, 230
Bhutan, 17
bicycling, 255-59
birds, 271-76
bites, animal, 51
Bön, 242, 286
Bönpo, 133
Brahmaputra River, 242
Brice, Russell, 219
bronchitis, 48
Buddhism: Theravada, 283; Tibetan, 283-85; Vajrayana, 284
Bumpa Ri, 117-18
buses, 54
Buton Rimpoche, 179

Camp I, 214
Camp II, 214
Capuchin monks, 18
Chag La, 161, 168
Chagpo Ri, 103-4
Chakrasamvara tantricism, 107
Chala La, 238
Chambaling ani gompa, 179
Chamdo, 264
Changchub Gyaatsen, 284
Char La, 182
Chay, 193
Chengdu, 20
Chhöding drubphuu, 104, 110

Chhöku gompa, 246, 247
Chhölung, 207
Chhölung gompa, 207
Chhöphug gompa, 197
Chhösang, 197
Chimphu caves, 134
Chinese Mountaineering Association (CMA), 34
Chitu La, 120
Cho Oyu, 187, 195
Cho Oyu base camp, 206
Chokyi Gyaatsan, 174
Chomolangma, 187
Chomolangma Nature Preserve, 191, 221
Chubsang ani gompa, 105-8
clothing, 30-31
cold, common, 48
conditioning, physical, 25
coughs, 48
cultural considerations, 55-58

d'Orville, Albert, 18
Daadan drubphuu, 107-8
Daensathil monastery, 284
Dalai Lama: fifth, 103; first, 174; fourteenth, 122; photographs, 56; sixth, 103; third, 174; thirteenth, 19
Damzhung, 98, 159
Darchhan, 99
Dawa Dzong, 99
Dechen Dzong, 98, 118, 135
dentists, 52
Dharamsala, 285
Dhraglha Lu-phuu, 103
diarrhea, 40-43
Ding La, 197
Ding Valley, 197
Dingri, 24, 206, 211
Dingri Lama La, 195, 204, 207
Dingri plains, 187
dogs, 60
Dorje Drag monastery, 98
Dorjeling ani gompa, 148
Dorjeling monastery, 97
Doya La, 197
Draabochhan, 233
Dragmar, 132, 135
Drepung monastery, 109, 112-15
Drigung Kargyüpa, 249
Driraphug gompa, 246
Drog Ri, 124
Drogmi, 284

Drolma Ri, 174
Drugpa Kargyüpa, 246
Dusum Kyenpa, 149
dysentery, 40, 42
Dza Rongphu, 97
Dza Rongphu monastery, 19, 187,
  197, 199
Dza Rongphu *rimpoche,* 197
Dzakaa Chhu Valley, 187
Dzong Chhu, 251
Dzong Lugari, 184
Dzutrulphug *gompa,* 246

East Rongphu Glacier, 214
Emmaling, 131
environmental awareness, 60
equipment, 29-32
Everest base camp, 19, 97, 192,
  213, 258
Everest base camp, East, 196, 219
Everest, Mount, 17, 187
Everest, Sir George, 187

festivals, 287-90
first-aid kit, 38-40
fish, 270-71
food, 60-62
Foreign Exchange Certificates
  (FEC), 55
Franciscans, 18
frostbite, 49-50

Gabet, Joseph, 18
Gambay Utse, 113
Gampa La, 128, 136
Ganden, 54, 118, 125
Ganden monastery, 98
Ganggar, 205
Ganggar Ri, 205
Gansu, 17
Gara, 212
Gara Valley, 195
Garwal Himal, 247
Gaurikund Lake, 251
Geden Drub, 174
Gelugpa sect, 104, 284
Genghis Khan, 284
geography, physical, 263
geology, 264-66
Gephel Ri, 109, 113
Gephel *rithrö,* 113
Gesar of Ling, 248
Ghangjam Glacier, 246
Ghangtise–Nyanchhan Thanglha
  range, 263
Gokar La, 118, 125
Gondephug, 206

Gruber, Johann, 18
Guge, 18
Guring La, 168
Guru Rimpoche, 131
Gutsuo, 205
Gyachung Kang, 195, 198
Gyalpo Khang, 137
Gyaltshab, 122
Gyalwa Gotsangpa, 249
Gyama Valley, 120, 136
Gyangdhrag *gompa,* 244

Haypo Ri, 132
health, 37-52
Hebu, 125
Hedin, Sven, 249-50
helicopters, 37
Hengduan Mountains, 264
Hengduan Shan, 17
Himalaya, 17
homes, visiting, 57-58
Hong Kong, 20
hospitals, 51-52
hotels, 53-54
Huc, E. R., 18
hypothermia, 48-49

immunizations, 37-38
Indus River, 241
inoculations, 37-38
Interim Camp, 214
Islam, 287

Jains, 241
Jesuits, 18
Jhang Thang, 17
Jhanra *gompa,* 162
Jogsumba, 137
Jokhang, 101
Jugal Himal, 229
Jyekundo, 264

Kaagön Samdayling *ani gompa,* 108
Kaama Tsangpo Valley, 220
Kadampa sect, 122, 137, 284
Kailas, Mount, 233, 241, 246
Kali Gandaki River, 266
Kangshung base camp, 221
Kangshung Face base camp, 187
Kangshung Glacier, 220
Kangshung Valley, 24, 219
Kangyur, 286
Karakoram, 17
Kargyüpa sect, 284
Karma Kargyüpa, 149
Karma Pakshi, 151
Karmapa, 148

Karmapa, sixteenth, 150
Karnali River, 242
Kashgar, 243
Kathmandu, 18, 257
Kawaguchi, Ekai, 19
Khadro Sanglam, 250
Kham, 17
Kharta, 192, 219
Kharta Yulbaa, 221
Khaydhrub, 122
Khumbu La, 199
Khumbu Valley, 199
kilometer markers, 95-99
King Langdarma, 107, 283
Kong La, 159
Kongpo, 17
Kublai Khan, 18, 284
Kung Tsho, 238
Kyetrag, 206
Kyetrag Glacier, 206
Kyi Chhu, 103
Kyirong, 98, 233

Ladakh, 17
Lagaen La, 159
Lagpa La, 95, 97
Lahaul, 17
Lamna La, 190, 198
Langkor, 205
Langkor monastery, 98
Langma La, 220
Langtang National Park, 192
language, Tibetan, 63-89
Lapchi, 232
Lasaa La, 148
Leten, 153
Lha Chhu Valley, 246
lhakhang, 102-3
Lhamo Lhatsho, 136
Lhasa, 17, 101, 257
Lhatse, 97, 174
Lhe La, 249
Lho La, 199
Lhodrag, 17
Lingkor, the, 101
Lonchen Gurgartse, 134
Losar, 117, 287-88
Lundrubling, 222
Lungjhang, 205

Madhrogongkar, 54, 98
Maendrub Tsari, 188
Maenri monastery, 286
Makalu, 187
Makalu–Barun Conservation
    Project, 192
mammals, 266

Manasarovar, 241
Manchu dynasty, 19
Manning, Thomas, 18
maps, 28-29; key to, 95
Marpa, 230
Marques, Father, 18
Milarepa, 98
Mindroling monastery , 98
monasteries, visiting, 57
money, 54-55
Mongolia, 18
Mongols, 18
Monlam Chenmo, 288
monsoon, 24
Muslims, Tibetan, 287
Mustang Valley, 266

Nagchhu, 54, 161
Nam Tsho, 24, 123, 159
Nam Tsho Qu, 161
Namche Barwa, 35, 264
Nangpa La, 199, 206
Naro Bön Chung, 244
Narthang, 184
Narthang monastery, 97, 177, 184
Naychhung monastery, 113
Naylung, 207
Naynang gompa, 149
Nepal, 18
New Year, Tibetan, 117, 287-88
Ngan-tsang, 161
Ngari, 17, 243
Ngor, 177
Ngor monastery, 181, 183
Ngora, 98, 238
Ngora gompa, 238
Ngorchhan Kunga Zangpo, 183
Nonda, 137
Norbulingka, 103
North Col, 214
Nyanang, 229
Nyanang Phu Glacier, 233
Nyanchhan Thanglha range, 24, 123,
    148, 159
Nyang Chhu, 173
Nyango, 131
Nyelam, 45, 229, 230
Nyingmapa sect, 131

Opera Festival, 115

Padampa Sangye, 108-9, 205
Panchhan Lamas, 173
Pandiy La, 238
Pang La, 192, 204
Pang La East, 194
Passum, 197

Peghu Tsho, 192, 233
Pehar, 112
Pelden Lhamo, 112
Pelgyeling *gompa*, 230
Pelgyeling monastery, 98
Pelron, 184
Pembogo La, 116, 161
people of Tibet, 277-81
Phabhongkha temple, 105, 107
Phadhruchi, 190, 211
pharmacies, 52
Phenyul Valley, 118
photography, 32-34
Phung Chhu, 192
Phurbu Chog, 104
Phutö *gompa*, 233
Plateau, Northern, 263
Plateau, Outer, 263
Plateau, Southeastern, 263
pneumonia, 48
Polo, Marco, 18
Potangtse *dzong*, 181
protector Demchog, 109
protectress Dorje Phagmo, 109
Purang, 99, 243
Puse La, 206

Qinghai, 17

Ra Chhu Valley, 206
Raksas Tal, 241
Ralo Tsho, 238
Rawling, C. G., 266-70
Rechungpa, 230
religions, 283-87; folk, 285-87
renminbi, 54
Reteng *gompa*, 161
Riphuu hermitage, 179
Riysum Gompo, 107
Rongphu base camp, 187
Rongphu Shar Glacier, 214
Rongshar Valley, 206
Rowell, Galen, 19
Royal Dynasty, 133
Rubruquis, William de, 18
Rumtek monastery, 150

Saga Dawa, 102, 288
Sagarmatha National Park, 192
Sakya monastery, 97, 179
Sakya Pandita, 179
Sakyapa sect, 133, 284
Sakyithang, 221
Samding monastery, 96, 109
Samye, 118, 125, 133, 135, 136
Sangye Gyatsho, 103
Selung, 233

Seng-ghe Drong, 243
Sera monastery, 104-7
Sera Tse, 110
Serlung *gompa*, 245
Shalu, 177, 181
Shalu monastery, 97. 177, 178, 179
Shanrab, 242, 286
Shao La, 190, 220
Shapje La, 245
Shegar, 97
Shigatse *dzong*, 176
Shigatse, 17, 173, 178
Shiquanhe, 99, 243
Shishapangma, 24, 192, 229
Shishapangma base camp: north, 233; south, 234
Showa La, 181
Shuga La, 120, 125
Sikkim, 17
sinusitis, 48
sky burials, 124
snowblindness, 50-51
Sonam Gyatsho, 174
Songtsen Gampo, 63
Spiti, 17
State Oracle, 112
sunburn, 40
Sutlej River, 242
Szechuan, 17, 20

Tagdhrukha, 97
Taglung *gompa*, 161
Tangyur, 286
Tara Tsho, 233
Tashilhumpo, 173
Tashilhumpo monastery, 97, 174
Tashiy Chhökorling monastery, 107
Tashiy Do hermitage, 159
Taylor, Harry, 219
Thang La, 98, 229
Thieves Island, 103
Thrisong Detsen, 132
Thubten Chhöling *gompa*, 197
Tibet Autonomous Region (TAR), 17
Tibet Mountaineering Association (TMA), 34
Tibet, Central, 24; Western, 17
Tigu La, 155
Tingri plains, 187
Tobing River, 148
Toling, 99
Tölung, 148
Tonmi Sambhota, 63, 108
transportation, 54
Trisuli River, 192
Tsabarung, 157
Tsamda, 97

Tsamda hot springs, 98, 206
Tsang, 17
Tsang kings, 174
Tsaparang, 18, 99
Tseb La, 136
Tsethi La, 250
Tsethi Lachhan La, 250
Tshongde Phu Chhu Valley, 229
Tshurphu, 148, 151-52
Tshurphu La, 154
Tshurphu monastery, 148, 149
Tsong Khapa, 104
Tsunde, 178

Ü province, 17

vaccinations, 37-38
Vairocana, 131
visas, 26

water, purification of, 43-44
weather, 24
women trekkers, hints for, 22-23

Xinjiang, 17

Yamalung Valley, 129
Yambughangala Glacier, 234
Yamdrog Tsho, 109
Yangpachan, 97, 148
Yangpachan monastery, 159
Yangpachan Valley, 123, 148
Yarlung Tsangpo River, 241
Yeshe Tshogyal, 250
Yon Valley, 138
Yuan dynasty, 284
Yumbu Lagang, 98
Yungdrungling monastery, 286, 287
Yunnan, 17

Zhamaapa *truku,* 149
Zhanagpa, 149
Zhang Zhung, 242
Zommug, 198, 202
Zurkar, 134

The End